HISTORY
OF
LOUISIANA.

Charles Gayarré

HISTORY
OF
LOUISIANA.

THE FRENCH DOMINATION.

BY

CHARLES GAYARRÉ.

WITH CITY AND TOPOGRAPHICAL MAPS OF THE STATE, ANCIENT AND MODERN,

WITH

A BIOGRAPHY OF THE AUTHOR,

BY

GRACE KING.

BIBLIOGRAPHY

BY

WM. BEER,

LIBRARIAN NEW ORLEANS PUBLIC LIBRARY,

TOGETHER WITH AN EXHAUSTIVE INDEX.

FIFTH EDITION.

IN FOUR VOLUMES.

VOL. I.

A FIREBIRD PRESS BOOK

PELICAN PUBLISHING COMPANY
Gretna 1998

Entered according to Act of Congress in the year 1882
By Charles Gayarre

In the clerks office of the District Court of the United States for the Southern District of New York.

Copyright 1903
by F. F. Hansell & Bro., Ltd

Reprinted 1965
by Pelican Publishing Company

Second printing—1974
ISBN 1-56554-535-4

Manufactured in the United States of America
Published by Pelican Publishing Company, Inc.
1000 Burmaster Street, Gretna, Louisiana 70053

PUBLISHER'S NOTE TO THE 5TH EDITION

Gayarré's *History of Louisiana* was last published in 1903. The history consists of four volumes: the French Domination in volumes I and II; the Spanish Domination in volume III; and the American Domination in volume IV.

The first three volumes were copyrighted in 1854 and the 4th volume, the American Domination, in 1866. The second edition of four volumes was printed by James A. Gresham of New Orleans; the third edition by *Hawkins* of New Orleans; and the fourth edition by F. F. Hansell & Brother of New Orleans. The fourth edition contains a life of Gayarré by Grace King.

In this fifth edition we have added an introduction by Prof. E. M. Socola of the Department of English of the Louisiana State University in New Orleans. Otherwise this reprint is an exact reproduction of the fourth edition of Gayarré done by the offset method. This fourth edition issued by F. F. Hansell & Brother is the best edition as it contains an index which the others did not have.

 PELICAN PUBLISHING COMPANY
New Orleans, U. S. A.

GAYARRE'S HISTORY OF LOUISIANA

Introduction by E. M. Socola

The republication of Gayarré's *History of Louisiana* will be welcomed by both the historical scholar and the general reader. Though they earned considerable notice as they appeared, the volumes did not sell very widely or very well during Gayarré's own lifetime, and half a century has now elapsed since the posthumous edition of 1903. As a result the *History* has become a scarce item, expensive and difficult to obtain, in a period when renewed and more mature interest in local and regional history has increased the demand for it.

The faults of the *History* are many, of course, and they are well known. The first volume begins with a tissue of romantic inaccuracies that embarrassed even Gayarré in his later years, and the fourth volume deteriorates into a mere chronicle of legislative sessions. But the body of the work—notably that portion of the narrative contained in the second and third volumes—constitutes a solid and durable achievement that in many respects has never been superseded. No one concerned with the history of the lower Mississippi Valley or with the colonial ventures of France and Spain in North America can afford to overlook this minor monument of nineteenth century historical writing.

It is somewhat ironic that Charles Gayarré should be remembered today primarily—perhaps almost entirely—as the author of the *History of Louisiana*. Until his sixtieth birthday, politics and public life were his principal concerns and absorbed his best energies. The collection of historical materials and the writing of history were dignified pursuits for leisure hours. It was only in the bitter Reconstruction years that he came to think of himself as a professional writer, and by then all of his best work, including the four volumes of the *History of Louisiana*, was already done.

Gayarré's interest in the gentlemanly hobby of history developed early. Certainly one ingredient in his historical interest was the family pride which is unmistakable in his passages on Estevan and Juan Antonio Gayarré, Pierre Bou-

Introduction by E. M. Socola

cher, and (most notably) Etienne de Boré. Perhaps a more important influence, though, was his association with William Rawle. For two years, at a formative and impressionable age, he studied law with Rawle in Philadelphia and had the opportunity of observing a distinguished lawyer and public servant whose interests extended far beyond the limits of his profession. Significantly enough, one of Rawle's continuing interests was history. He helped to found the Historical Society of Pennsylvania and served as its first president, and he could become very eloquent and persuasive when he spoke on the importance of "historical inquiries" and on the necessity of contributing what one could to what he called "the treasury of literature."[1] On the pleasures of scholarly activity he wrote to young Gayarré (who had lately returned to New Orleans): "Very little of what is worth having can be acquired without considerable pains—but this word, in its proper signification, ought not to be applied to sedulous study. There is more pleasure in habitual industry than in idleness . . . We have among us, in this city, a few instances of men entirely unhappy from the possession of considerable fortunes without occupations & without the possession of literary propensities. Time is to them a burthen. The day begins with uncertainty how to spend it—proceeds with listlessness — & ends in lassitude."[2]

There was little danger that Gayarré's days would proceed with listlessness or end in lassitude. In the fall of 1830, a few months after having been elected to the Louisiana Legislature, he published the first volume of his *Essai historique sur la Louisiane*. And in the following fall, shortly before being appointed Presiding Judge of the City Court of New Orleans, he published the second volume of that work.

The *Essai historique* was largely an exercise in translation and literary composition. Gayarré had read François Xavier Martin's *History of Louisiana* "with pleasure and much profit," but at the same time he had found its style "as lifeless as the minutes and records of proceedings in a court of justice."[3] It had then occurred to him that a comparable work in the French language was needed and might, when

---

[1]. Thomas I. Wharton, "A Memoir of William Rawle," *Memoirs of the Historical Society of Pennsylvania*, IV, part I (1840), 64.

[2]. Rawle to Gayarré, 12 June 1829, Gayarré Papers (Archives LSU).

[3]. Charles Gayarré, *Fernando de Lemos* (New York, 1872), p. 246.

Introduction by E. M. Socola

completed, "excite some interest among that part of our population for whom French is still the mother tongue."[4] And so he had set to work to render Martin's *History* into French.

So far, at least, as prose style was concerned, the *Essai historique* was a distinct improvement on Martin's *History*. In his desire to include everything that seemed important, Martin had interrupted his narrative at many points to insert data on the founding and progress of other American colonies —including those planted by the English, Swedes, and Dutch; on relevant "transactions on the opposite side of the Atlantic;" and on "the mutations of the crown" in the kingdoms of France, England, and Spain. In addition, he had yielded to the temptation to give lengthy summaries of those documents which semed to him to be significant. And finally, there was much truth in the New Orleans *Bee's* charge that the whole work was "very inelegantly written."[5] What Gayarré did was to strip documentary passages and extraneous details from the *History* and concentrate on the main thread of narrative, thereby achieving a simpler account that was easier and more pleasant to follow. He did not confine himself, however, to improving the flow of the narrative and substituting his own more vivid language for Martin's "inelegant" prose. In many of the passages that he translated from Martin he sought to improve the dramatic quality (at the expense of historical authenticity) by the use of such devices as directly quoted speeches or conversations in place of the third person accounts given by Martin.[6]

The *Essai historique* was hardly the work on which to build a lasting reputation; but writers were not numerous in Louisiana in the 1930's, and though it was recognized that his work was "chiefly an abstract" of Martin's *History*,[7] Gayarré enjoyed a certain measure of local renown as a result of its publication.[8]

[4.] *Essai historique sur la Louisiane* (2 vols., New Orleans, 1830-31), I, iii.
[5.] N. O. *Bee*, 13 November 1835.
[6.] An excellent example of this process is to be found in Gayarré's treatment of the death of Joseph Villeré (*Essai historique*, I, 152-153). The "improvements" can be detected by comparing his account with Martin, *History of Louisiana*, II, 4-5—the passage on which it is based. For Grace King's rather far-etched attempt to explain and justify the liberties that Gayarré took in such passages, see p. xv of this volume.
[7.] N. O. *Bee*, 13 November 1835.
[8.] See, for example, the long annd enthusiastic review in the N. O. *Bee*, 10 September 1831.

Introduction by E. M. Socola

Gayarré's next venture in historical writing, the *Histoire de la Louisiane*, did not appear until fifteen years later, and it was a very different kind of work from the *Essai historique*. In its composition, Gayarré relied upon two important collections of documents copied from the French archives. One of these collections had been copied by Pierre Margry and had been presented to the state by John Perkins, who had commissioned the work. The other body of documents had been selected and copied from the Archives of the Ministry of Marine at Paris by Felix Magne of New Orleans, one of the publishers of *L'Abeille*. Gayarré had been very much impressed by Magne's documents and had persuaded Governor Mouton to purchase them for the archives of the state.[9] Unfortunately the very richness of these sources led Gayarré into stylistic faults that he had condemned in Martin.

In his preface to the first volume of the *Histoire* (1846), Gayarré explained that he had first planned to write this new work in English, thus giving it a chance of more extended circulation. But the method that he had evolved had made it necessary to modify that initial resolution. He had decided, he said, to let the early colonists "tell the history themselves," as far as possible. "If it is true to say that the style is the man, I will have done well to have reproduced verbatim the dispatches of all those who played leading roles in the history of Louisiana. Thus, ten lines from the hand of Bienville will teach the reader more about this personage, than any appreciation written by the author himself . . . I feel that in English my work would be destitute of the charm which I have given it, in my eyes at least, by borrowing the leanguage of the first colonists."[10]

The program outlined in this preface, had it been skilfully executed, might have produced an entertaining and illuminating work. Such, unfortunately, was not the case. The earlier portions of the first volume were drawn, with a few modifications and deletions, from the *Essai historique;* page after page was simply copied word for word from that earlier work. But whatever virtues the *Essai* had had as a lively

---

[9.] Gayarré to Francis Parkman, 14 June 1857, Parkman Papers (Massachusetts Historical Society); *House Misc. Documents, 46th Congress, 2nd Session,* Vol. II, Misc. Doc. No. 22; *Histoire de la Louisiane* (2 vols., New Orleans, 1846-47), I, ii-iii.

[10.] *Histoire de la Louisiane*, I, iii-vi.

Introduction by E. M. Socola

narrative were now lost, for along the way long transcripts of documents were inserted; and as the work progressed, the narrative became slimmer and the documents lengthier and more abundant. The second volume, which appeared in 1847 and brought the history up to 1769, looked more like a sourcebook of documentary material than a history in any accepted sense. The resultant failure was effectively, if unkindly, summed up in the *North American Review*:

> The letters of Bienville, D'Artaguette, Vaudreuil, and others, who had an active share in the early administration of Louisiana, are interesting and valuable when combined with other materials of history; but they contain many repetitions, criminations, and profitless disputes, and, when taken alone, they furnish but a meagre record of the progress of affairs. M. Gayarré seems to have published them almost entire, with no principle of selection or abridgement . . . The volumes now before us are of oppressive dimensions, and might with more propriety be considered as a collection of state papers and other historical materials, than as a finished history . . . The author is now Secretary of State of Louisiana, and he appears to have drawn the materials of his book almost at random from the shelves of his office.[11]

By 1847, then, Gayarré had published two histories of Louisiana in French, but neither of them could be considered a work of enduring importance. The first was a translation and revision of another historian's work. The second was essentially a collection of documents with narrative passages borrowed from the earlier "translation." It was at this point that a history of considerably more significance began to take shape—and it had its origins in a chance invitation.

Each winter for several years, a series of free lectures had been offered in New Orleans under the auspices of the People's Lyceum. The topics were, as a rule, of a rather general nature and were calculated to entertain as well as to instruct. Among the twelve topics announced for the 1847 series were "An Inquiry into the Influence of Forms of Gov-

---

[11]. *North American Review*, LXV, 3-4 (July, 1847). Gayarré was also sharply criticized for writing the *Histoire* in French: see *De Bow's Review*, I, 389 (May, 1846). For favorable reviews see *La. Courier*, 25 February 1846; *N. O. Bee*, 26 February 1846; and *Southern Quarterly Review*, IX, 362-363 (April, 1846).

Introduction by E. M. Socola

ernment on Human Destiny," "History: the Record of Men's Duty to their Age," "The Elements of General Literature," and "The Brief History and Influence of Cities."[12] Gayarré was invited to address the Lyceum during this 1847 season at what he later said had been "a most inopportune moment." The Legislature was in session and his duties as Secretary of State permitted him little leisure just at that time. "I could not decline, however, the honor conferred upon me; and with a mind engrossed by other subjects, and with a hurried pen, I wrote the . . . Lecture."[13] In this casual fashion were written the opening pages of what was to grow into the *History of Louisiana*.

Gayarré delivered his Lyceum lecture on the evening of Friday, March 26, 1847, in the old Methodist Church on the corner of Poydras and Carondelet streets.[14] He began by reminding his audience that he had lately completed a history of Louisiana. Hence it was only natural, he said, that he should choose that subject for his lecture:

> But in reverting now to the History of Louisiana, my intention is not to review its diversified features with the scrutinizing, unimpassioned, and austere judgment of the historian. Imposing upon myself a more grateful task, because more congenial to my taste, I shall take for the object of this Lecture, THE POETRY, OR THE ROMANCE OF THE HISTORY OF LOUISIANA.[15]

Defining poetry as "that which is most pleasing to the eye or to the mind, and ennobling to the soul," he declared that Louisiana's history was "full of poetry of the highest order and of the most varied nature." He then proceeded to examine the earliest portions of Louisiana history for illustrations, enlarging, as he proceeded, on the romantic possibilities of his subject. Inviting the imagination to "riot" in the mysterious migrations of "powerful Choctaws," "undaunted Chicasaws," and "unconquerable Mobilians," he was moved to exclaim: "What heroic poems might not a future Ossian devise on the red monarchs of old Louisiana!" Hernando De

---

[12.] *La. Courier*, 26 February, 5 and 12 March, and 2 April 1847.
[13.] *Romance of the History of Louisiana* (New York, 1848), p. 10.
[14.] *La. Courier*, 25 and 26 March 1847.
[15.] *History of La.*, I, 9. (The lecture was later used as the first chapter in the first volume of the *History of La.*, and it may be read there in its entirety.)

Introduction by E. M. Socola

Soto's expedition became a glorious spectacle: "What materials for romance! Here is chivalry, with all its glittering pomp, its soul-stirring aspirations, in full march, with its iron heels and gilded spurs, toward the unknown and hitherto unexplored soil of Louisiana." And so it went.

With some wisdom, Gayarré at first attached "little importance to this trifling production."[16] But the enthusiastic reception accorded the lecture by those who heard it and by those who read it in the June issuee of *De Bow's Review*[17] convinced him that he should "resume the subject." Thus, a few months after his appearance on the Lyceum platform, he began a continuation which ran to three additional "lectures." These, together with the original lecture, he published in the spring of 1848 under the title *Romance of the History of Louisiana*. In his preface to the *Histoire*, Gayarré had indicated his intention of rewriting his history in English at some future date, for the benefit of his "Anglo-American compatriots."[18] It does not appear, however, that at the time he published the *Romance* volume he looked upon it as the beginning of a new history in English. In fact, he was very careful to announce at the outset that this latest production was not really history, in the strict sense of thee word:

> To write history, is to narrate events, and to show their philosophy, when they are susceptible of any such demonstration . . . To relate events, and, instead of elucidating and analyzing their philosophy, like the historian, to point out the hidden sources of romance which spring from them — to show what materials they contain for the dramatist, the novelist, the poet, the painter and for all the varied conceptions of the fine arts — is perhaps an humbler task, but not without its utility. When history is not disfigured by inappropriate inventions, but merely embellished and made attractive by being set in a glittering frame, this artful preparation honies the cup of useful knowledge, and makes it acceptable to the lips of the multitude. Through the immortal writings of Walter Scott, many have been induced to study more serious works, who, without that tempting bait, would have turned away from what appeared to them to be but a dry and barren field, too unpromising to invite examination . . .
> It was in pursuing such a train of reasoning that I came to the conclusion that the publication of these Lec-

---

[16]. *Romance of the History of Louisiana*, pp. 11-12.
[17]. "Romance of Louisiana History," *De Bow's Review*, III, 449-462 (June, 1847).
[18]. *Histoire de la Louisiane*, I, vi.

Introduction by E. M. Socola

tures might show what romantic interest there is in the history of Louisiana; that it might invite some to an investigation which, so far, they perhaps thought would not repay them for the trouble; and to study with fondness what hitherto had been to them an object of disdainful neglect. I have attempted to accumulate and to heap up together materials for the use of more skilful architects than I am, and have contented myself with drawing the faint outlines of literary compositions, which, if filled up by the hand of genius, would do for Louisiana, what has been done for Scotland . . ."[19]

Gayarré's three new lectures did indeed set the history of Louisiana from 1699 to 1717 "in a glittering frame." His method is nowhere better illustrated than in the passages dealing with Anthony Crozat, the proprietor of the colony. In order to enliven his account, Gayarré chose to give credence to the romantic legend that Crozat had obtained his charter with the idea of amassing a fortune sufficiently large to enable his daughter to marry a young duke with whom she was in love. Then after describing the failure of Crozat's scheme, a matter of historical fact, he went on to the melodramatic and wholly fanciful account of the deaths of the disappointed daughter and her grief-stricken father. Gayarré even changed the name of the daughter from Marie Anne to Andrea, explaining in a note which he subsequently appended (and which never fails to startle readers of the *History*): "Perhaps it was owing to some capricious whim — perhaps there is to me some spell in the name of Andrea" (I, 186).

Another excellent example of Gayarré's "embellishment" of history is the colorful passage on Lamothe Cadillac's appearance. Gayarré had never seen a portrait of Cadillac, and, as he later admitted, he knew "nothing *historical* about his looks."[20] This did not deter him, however, from writing a detailed and amusing description of the governor's physical appearance, with the most careful attention to Cadillac's "ponderous wig, the curls of which spread like a peacock's tail," to his "stout, cocked up, snub nose," and to his "mocking smile" (I, 119). How had he arrived at these details? "I somewhat fancifully sketched his personal appearance," he explained to Silas Farmer, "so as to make it agree with his

---

[19]. *Romance of the History of Louisiana*, pp. 16-18.

[20]. Gayarré to Silas Farmer, 23 January 1884, Silas Farmer Papers, Burton Historical Collection (Detroit Public Library).

[21]. *Ibid.*

Introduction by E. M. Socola

character as it presented itself to me historically and traditionally."[21]

The literary influences on *Romance of the History of Louisiana* are not difficult to discern. Like so many of his fellow Southerners, Gayarré was under the spell of Walter Scott, but there were others to whom he was also significantly indebted. In his treatment of explorers and Indians, he was guided to some extent by the Leather-Stocking novels of Cooper, as he himself indicates in more than one place (I, 26, 61). The exaggerations and distortions in the account of Cadillac's administration show the unmistakable influence of Knickerbocker's *History of New York;* and this debt to Irving, like the debt to Cooper, is acknowledged, at least by implication, in the course of the narrative (I, 128). And, of course, there are the quotations from Byron. Moved by these influences to an awareness of the literary possibilities of his materials, Gayarré had chosen to write a book that was not a history of Louisiana but a disquisition on the "Romance of the History of Louisiana." And few criticisms could have been leveled against him if he had let the matter rest there.

But in 1851 Gayarré published *Louisiana; Its Colonial History and Romance* (ultimately to become Volume I of the *History of Louisiana*) and used as the first section of the new work the four lectures of *Romance of the History of Louisiana*. Even at the time Gayarré seems to have entertained some doubts as to the wisdom of his course.[22] The "second series" had its own title page, which read "Louisiana: Its History as a French Colony . . . Second Series of Lectures," to distinguish it clearly from the "Romance" section that preceded it. And in the separate preface that he wrote for the new lectures, Gayarré went out of his way to point out that he had been "more sparing of embellishments" than in the first series: "I can safely declare that the *substance* of this work, embracing the period from 1717 to 1743, . . . rests on such evidence as would be received in a court of justice."

The substance of the second series of lectures was, indeed, historical narrative of a far sounder sort than that found in the *Romance* series. The period from 1717 to 1743 included the rise and fall of the Mississippi Company, the foundation of New Orleans, a war against the Natchez In-

---

[22]. Gayarré's later comment on the *Romance* lectures is interesting: "It is wise for the historian to confine himself to his line of composition, and never divest himself of his magisterial robes [for] the fanciful dress of the romance writer."—N. O. *Times-Democrat*, 24 June 1883.

Introduction by E. M. Socola

dians, and a good many changes in the colonial administration. Gayarré's account of these matters was based on reliable documentary evidence, much of it already published in the *Histoire*. For his chapter on John Law's life, he seems have gone to the best available biographical sources; and for his detailed description of the Natchez Indians, he relied heavily upon Le Page du Pratz, whose account of his own experiences among the Natchez was then considered authoritative. Although he made no attempt to cite his sources systematically, he could have "footnoted" almost everything of importance in his narrative if he had wished to do so.

Not only had Gayarré been much more "sparing of embellishments," but almost without exception he had labeled the embellishments as such in one way or another. These efforts to separate fact from fiction are immediately apparent to the modern reader who may be on his guard against Gayarré's love of the "poetry" of history. Before describing John Law at the dinner table, he carefully notes: "With no very great stretch of the imagination, we may easily conceive the occurrence of such a scene as the following;" and after describing a dream in which Law sees the former master of his castle, he remarks: "These are the scenes in which the imagination of the historian may be permitted to indulge, to give more graphic force to the truths of his narrative." After repeating the romantic legend of the Chevalier d'Aubant and his wife, the Princess Charlotte, he observes: "The particulars of this adventure are found in many memoirs of the epoch, and in the notes and papers of Duclos: but Levesque, in his history of Russia, Grimm, in his correspondence, and the sceptic Voltaire, in a letter which he published on the 19th February, 1781, deny the truth of the story as being too improbable." And after telling the story of the mysterious Turk on whose grave in New Orleans a date tree is supposed to have grown, he comments: "Whether this story be true or not is now a matter of so little consequence, that it would not repay the trouble of strict historical investigation." Through this policy of labeling his embellishments, Gayarré sought to prevent anyone from judging his latest work as merely "the abundance of an idle brain."

In matters of historical judgment, too, the new lectures marked a change for the better. Instead of contenting himself with pointing out the "poetic" aspects of his subject, as

Introduction by E. M. Socola

he had done in the *Romance* series, Gayarré now adopted a rather critical attitude towards the historical events which he chronicled. He sought to show, for example, that France's commercial policy had been very unwise and had actually retarded the development of the colony. He was openly skeptical of the information in some of the dispatches that he cited. And in describing the colonists' war with the Natchez Indians, he was careful to point out that the trouble had begun only when a French officer had made unreasonable demands on the Natchez chief and had treated that native dignitary in a high-handed and insulting manner.

The new series was not without its failings, however. Gayarré's prose still tended to be excessively ornate, and his love of romantic legends led him into frequent digressions. Unable to restrain his enthusiasm for some of the colonial figures, most notably Bienville, he occasionally inserted extravagant panegyrics. As we read through the volume today, a more basic defect emerges. In the second "lecture" of the new series, Gayarré pauses to tell the story of Manon Lescaut and then, in returning to his account of "the administration of affairs in Louisiana," makes a statement that reveals the underlying weakness of this volume. "Let us turn," he writes, "from the field of sentiment to a dryer one, where the facts to be collected by the historian, although no doubt more deserving, are of a less captivating nature." Why, one may ask, should this historian who professed to have a great love of his subject find the historical record "less captivating" than the Abbé Prévost's sentimental tale? As we read through the succeeding lectures of the series, the answer becomes apparent. What we have is a chronicle of Indian wars and commercial edicts and changes in colonial personnel, rather than a history in the fuller meaning of the word. Nowhere is there the sense of a critical intellect intent upon finding a broad understanding of Louisiana's colonial history or seeking to trace the continuous development of attitudes or institutions. And it is this inability to synthesize, this failure to see the woods for the trees, that leads Gayarré inevitably to give disproportionate attention to the more entertaining episodes, regardless of their ultimate historical significance. There is no attempt at the end of the volume—or anywhere else, for that matter—to sum up the achievements and failures of the colonial administration during the decades under

Introduction by E. M. Socola

consideration; and the narrative is so arranged that the reader has some difficulty in arriving at any general conclusions for himself.

In 1852 Gayarré published *Louisiana; Its History as a French Romance. Third Series of Lectures* (which was to become Volume II of the *History of Louisiana*). Once again he found it necessary to explain the relation of the *Romance* lectures to those that followed and to insist that with the beginning of the second series of lectures he had checked the "freaks" of his imagination. The new volume was meant to be "a detailed and accurate" history of Louisiana from 1743 to 1769, and he invited his readers to note "a change of tone and manner, corresponding with the authenticity and growing importance of the events which [he] had to record." Not content to let the matter rest there, he went on to list the sources that he had used: "Bossu, Perrin du Lac, Charlevoix, Pittman, Dumont, Le Page du Pratz, Hennepin, Lahontan, Baudry des Lozières, Laharpe, and Laval: and I also refer to voluminous manuscripts copied from the archives of France and Spain, which have become the property of the State. These are my vouchers . . ." (II, 13-15).

In the first two lectures of this second volume, Gayarré rather hastily disposes of the administrations of the Marquis de Vaudreuil, Kerlerec, and D'Abbadie, covering the period from 1743 to 1765. The remaining five lectures deal with the years 1765-1769; and it is in these that we find him exercising powers of analysis and interpretation that had hitherto lain dormant. In describing the exciting events of those years—the arrival and expulsion of Ulloa, the resistance of the colonists to the cession of Louisiana to Spain, the arrival of O'Reilly, and the subsequent punishment of those responsible for the revolt—Gayarré had to take into account the emotional response to those events that still existed. Louisianians were accustomed to speak of the Irish-born Spanish governor as "Bloody" O'Reilly and to look upon the execution of Lafrénière and his associates as the most outrageous incident in the whole of their colonial history.[23] Judge Martin, in dis-

---

[23]. William O. Scroggs, whose volume *The Story of Louisiana* (Indianapolis, 1924) was used for years as a textbook in the public schools of Louisiana, was only following this tradition when he entitled his chapter on O'Reilly's punishment of Lafrénière and his associates "Martyrs for Liberty" (pp. 111-115).

Introduction by E. M. Socola

cussing the episode, had said: "Posterity . . . will doom this act to public execration. No necessity demanded, no policy justified it."[24] And Gayarré himself, in the *Essai historique*, had spoken of O'Reilly's "frightful crime," describing it as "an act of vengeance, not of justice."[25]

Now Gayarré sought to show that this conventional interpretation of O'Reilly's acts, to which he himself had once subscribed, was too extreme. Lafrénière, the would-be "Cromwell" of the colony, had "assumed false and untenable grounds" in arguing for the expulsion of Ulloa and had, at best, acted very unwisely. And though it might have been better if O'Reilly had contented himself with expelling the leaders of the revolt from the colony, it was nevertheless true that he had congratulated himself on "the extreme lenity of the course he pursued." Aubry, the French governor, emerged as one who had to bear a large part of the responsibility for the executions because of his denunciation of Lafrénière and the others to the Spanish. Finally, on the supposed murder of Joseph Villeré, which he had so luridly described in the *Essai historique,* Gayarré was disposed to examine traditional accounts with a more skeptical eye: "This atrocity of the bloody shirt is not probable. It is not mentioned in the official French dispatches which I have seen, and rests on popular tradition, which delights in tales of similar exaggeration." The concluding remarks on these events of 1768-69 (II, 348-351) are impressive for their historical insight and maturity; in them we find Gayarré at his best.

One critic of the *History of Louisiana* has maintained that "Gayarré's Spanish heritage prejudiced him toward other nations in Louisiana's history."[26] Another has suggested that since "Gayarré was of Spanish origin on the paternal side, and his forefather was one of the men who made history in Louisiana under that flag," he was unable to "go beneath the surface to seek the causes that stirred Lafrénière and his associates to the revolt that ended in their own destruction."[27] This charge of pro-Spanish bias simply does not stand up under examination. Certainly Gayarré was

---

[24]. Martin, *History of Louisiana*, II, 7.
[25]. *Essai historique*, I, 156-157.
[26]. Wilford B. Yearns, Charles Gayarré, Louisiana's Literary Historian," *La. Historical Quarterly*, XXXIII, 265 (April, 1950).
[27]. Henry P. Dart, "Remy's Lost History of Louisiana," *La. Historical Quarterly*, V, 13 (January, 1922).

Introduction by E. M. Socola

proud of the great-grandfather who had served in Louisiana under Ulloa and O'Reilly, as well as of the grandfather who had served under Galvez before being transferred to Mexico. But those who argue that this pride in his Spanish ancestors produced a slanted history ignore the fact that Gayarré's ancestry was really predominantly French and that he had many family ties with the French colonists of the 1760's. (As a matter of fact, his mother's sister had married a grandson of Lafrénière.[28]) They forget his lifelong reverence for the memory of Etienne de Boré, whose "extreme attachment to the French interest" had in 1796 — at the time of General Collot's visit to Louisiana — caused Governor Carondelet to consider having him arrested and transported to Havana (III, 385). And finally, they fail to take into account the striking changes which Gayarré's thinking underwent in the years between the publication of the *Essai historique* and that of *Louisiana; Its History as a French Colony*. These changes may most reasonably be attributed to his study of the documentary materials from the French and Spanish archives[29] to which he had gained access during the 1840's and which had rendered his old anti-Spanish interpretation of O'Reilly's administration no longer tenable. The truth of the matter seems to be that no matter how much he may have come to prefer Charles III to Louis XV, or the Spanish "domination" in Louisiana to the French, in his treatment of the events of 1768-69 Gayarré was attempting to piece together the truth as impartially as possible from all the evidence available to him.

For the modern reader this second volume of the *History of Louisiana* is especially attractive. By 1852 Gayarré had found the middle ground between the dry overdocumentation of the *Histoire*, on the one hand, and the romantic inventions and "embellishments" of the *Romance* series, on the other; and in passage after passage, we find a sureness of grasp and an acuteness of insight that go far toward redeeming the failures of his earlier work. The final pages of the volume, tinged though they are with the romantic nationalism of the early 1850's, show Gayarré moving towards a broader understanding of the events that he had already recorded and

---

[28]. See Gayarré's "A Sugar Plantation of the Old Regime," *Harper's Magazine*, LXXIV, 606 (March,188q).

[29]. See footnote 31 below.

Introduction by E. M. Socola

contain the promise of increased perspective in succeeding volumes—a promise that, unfortunately, was not to be fully realized.

In 1854 Gayarré republished *Louisiana; Its Colonial History and Romance* and *Louisiana; Its History as a French Colony* under the title *History of Louisiana: The French Domination*. At the same time, he added a third volume entitled *History of Louisiana: The Spanish Domination*.[30]

The first two volumes of the *History* had been based, in large part, on materials already available in the *Histoire de la Louisiane*. Now, in *The Spanish Domination*, Gayarré was dealing with a period about which he had written nothing since he had completed the *Essai historique* in 1831. For the framework of this new volume he still leaned fairly heavily on Martin's history, as may be seen in the numerous citations of and quotations from that work. But the real substance of *The Spanish Domination* was drawn from the documents which Pascual de Gayangos had unearthed and copied for him in the archives of Spain.[31] The pride that Gayarré felt in the possession of these extensive materials is apparent time and again. (See, for example, the note early in the first chapter referring the reader to "the deliberations of the Council of the Indies on O'Reilly's acts in Louisiana, which are in manuscript in the office of the Secretary of State at Baton Rouge.") Conscious that he was using documentary sources to which no other American historian had even had access,[32] Gayarré seems to have been determined to make the most of

---

[30]. Gayarré's dedication of this third volume to George Bancroft reflects the pride and pleasure that he felt in the famous historian's praise of the earlier volumes: Bancroft to Gayarré, 16 November 1852, quoted in N. O. *Times-Democrat*, 24 June 1883; Bancroft to Gayarré, undated [probably August or September, 1854], Gayarré (Archives LSU).

[31]. In 1847, on the recommendation of William Hickling Prescott, Gayarré engaged Gayangos to examine the Spanish archives and to copy documents relating to the Spanish colonial administration in Louisiana. He was able to obtain an appropriation of $2000 from the Louisiana Legislature to finance the work, and the copies were delivered to him in the fall of 1849. Gayangos' difficulties with suspicious Spanish officials and chaotic archives are described in detail in the correspondence that Gayarré published in his *Report of the Secretary of State on the State Library* (Baton Rouge, 1850).

[32]. In 1882, during a visit to Oliver Wendell Holmes, Gayarré met Henry Adams, who expressed wonder at Gayarré's having been able to obtain so much documentary material from the Spanish archives. — Gayarré to G. W. Cable, 6 August 1882, Cable Papers (Howard-Tilton Library, Tulane University).

Introduction by E. M. Socola

his opportunity. Unhappily, this determination led to two major faults that most modern readers will find in the volume. First of all, a disproportionate amount of space is given to a few topics on which Gayarré had found a great deal of new information. Secondly—and we are reminded of the *Histoire*—large portions of the volume are directly quoted from one source or another. Both of these faults are apparent in Gayarre's account of the extended quarrel between the French Capuchins and the Spanish Capuchins. Though the relevant correspondence between New Orleans and Havana and New Orleans and Madrid is interesting and frequently quite amusing, the fact remains that the quarrel itself proved to be a tempest in a teapot so far as having any real effect on the religious or civil life of Louisiana. Nevertheless, the quotations from this correspondence occupy almost fifty pages in *The Spanish Domination* (III, 49-97).

A second instance in which we find Gayarré giving way to the temptation to go into minute detail occurs in his treatment of General James Wilkinson's activities. In the adchives at Seville, Gayangos had found a good many copies of letters which Wilkinson had allegedly written to Governor Miro with regard to the projected separation of Kentucky. Gayarré was certain that Miro had sent true copies of these letters to his government and that he had the evidence to show that Wilkinson had actively conspired with the Spanish to bring the Western territories under the domination of Spain.[33] Hence he felt justified in quoting at great length from these letters and from other documents having to do with similar intrigues directed to the same end—meanwhile relegating all of the other events of Miro's administration to a decidedly minor place.

The same kind of overriding concern with one event—this time unquestionably a major one—led Gayarré to devote the whole last third of his volume to the negotiations leading to the Louisiana purchase and to the actual transfer of Louisi-

---

[33]. For a different view of the authenticity and significance of these letters, see the defense of his great-grandfather that James Wilkinson, of New Orleans, read to the Louisiana Historical Society in 1917. Wilkinson argued that "Gayarré's secret bitterness against Wilkinson arose ... from a belief that the latter had tricked and deceived the Spaniards, Gayarré's grandfather having been one of the intendants of Spain."—*La. Historical Quarterly*, I, 93-94 (September, 1917). This thesis is further developed in Wilkinson's biography of the General, *Wilkinson, Soldier and Pioneer* (New Orleans, 1935).

Introduction by E. M. Socola

ana from Spain to France and then from France to the United States. The result is that one reaches the end of *The Spanish Domination* with a somewhat limited understanding of ordinary domestic affairs in Louisiana between 1770 and 1803.[34]

The Spanish Domination has received more praise than any of Gayarré's other volumes. "It was," wrote John Spencer Bassett, "the best part of his history; for having discarded the tendency to romance and confined himself to sober facts, he now wrote better than before; and having more interest in this than in the American regime, he wrote better than he was to write again. The Spanish period was filled with political intrigue and clashing personal ambition. The designs of evil men followed one another with tragic steps until at last the whole fabric of violence fell before the advent of the strong and rather prosaic government of American democracy. This scene of strife was a fine field for the graphic powers of such a narrator as Gayarré, and he made the most of it."[35] Such an evaluation necessarily calls for qualification; and without attempting to minimize Gayarré's achievement in *The Spanish Domination,* one *can* wish that he had been able to construct a better proportioned narrative and that he had not given over so much of the volume to quotation of sources.

The American Domination (which did not appear until 1866), is like *The Spanish Domination,* a work of uneven merit. Perhaps its chief strength is to be found in the portraits of its central figures, Claiborne and Jackson, both of whom are presented to us with a good deal of wisdom and insight. Claiborne emerges as a patient and conscientious administrator, occasionally handicapped by a tendency to vacillation and a disposition to believe rumors—and one has only to compare the treatment of this nineteenth century governor with the earlier caricature of Cadillac to be reminded of the vast difference between this last volume of the *History* and the first. Even more effective are the passages on Jackson, whose personal magnetism and force of character had so

---

[34]. Gayarré's own later awareness of this deficiency in his history is hinted at in a sketch that he published in the N. O. *Times-Democrat,* 12 August 1883.
[35]. *The Middle Group of American Historians* (New York, 1917), pp. 53-54. *The Spanish Domination* was favorably reviewed in a number of periodicals at the time of its publication. Gayarré was particularly pleased with the review that William Gilmore Simms wrote for the Charleston *Mercury.* — Gayarré to George Bancroft, 24 December 1854, Bancrof Papers (Massachusetts Historical Society).

Introduction by E. M. Socola

impressed Louisianians at the time of the Battle of New Orleans.[36] But the admiration for Jackson's heroic quality that we find recorded in these passages did not blind Gayarré to the General's shortcomings, and in the account of the arrest of Louaillier and Hall and of the expulsion of the French from New Orleans, Jackson's stubbornness and his explosive temper receive due attention.

Gayarré did considerably less research for this final volume of the *History* than he had done for the two preceding volumes, and the reader quickly becomes aware that the sources are extremely limited. In the first half of the volume, covering everything from the transfer to the British invasion of 1814, Gayarré seldom goes beyond the letters and public papers of Governor Claiborne, which ordinarily are simply quoted driectly.[37] For his account of the British campaign against New Orleans and Jackson's victory, he relies almost completely on the *Historical Memoir* of Lacarriere Latour. On occasion these sources are supplemente with extracts from debates in Congress, notices of the proceedings of the state legislature, or quotations from the proclamations of Jackson and others; and, of course, Gayarré still depended upon F. X. Martin when other materials were lacking. In Gayarré's favor, it should be noted that these sources are skilfully and judiciously used and that some events that might otherwise be puzzling are explained in the light of social and political divisions of the time.

For the attentive reader, *The American Domination* also provides some illuminating glimpses of Gayarré's personal responses to the Civil War. Gayarré had begun the volume in 1859, had written the central portions in 1861, and had not finished the final chapters until somtime towards the end of

---

[36]. See especially IV, 379-381.

[37]. Once again, as in the preface to the *Histoire*, we find Gayarré defending this practice by insisting that the best way to convey "a correct idea" of the "moral tone and the manners of society at any particular epoch" is "to borrow the very language of those who have described them as witnesses, and frequently as participators in what they recorded."—IV, 369.

Introduction by E. M. Socola

1864 or the beginning of 1865;[38] and along the way he had not been able to resist including a few observations on contemporary events. [39] The final paragraph, with its description of Louisiana as "the seat of desolation—the footstool of subjugation" (IV, 693), is a moving comment on the collapse of the Confederacy and of Gayarré's own hopes of 1861[40]

One can only regret that Gayarré chose to end his history with Jackson's departure from New Orleans in 1815 and to give the years between 1815 and 1861 that one brief (and totally inadequate) "Supplemental Chapter." A fuller history of those years, though it might have been sharply partisan, would be invaluable today — for Gayarré had a first-hand

---

[38]. Since some altogether inaccurate statements on the subject have appeared in print, it may be appropriatee here to review the evidence for dating the various portions of the volume. In the first chapter, Gayarré uses the words "at this time, in 1859" and warns of the misfortunes that would result if the "adversaries of slavery" should ever gain a majority in Coniress (IV, 37, 57). But only the first five chapters, at most, could have been written before 1861, for in the course of Chapter VI we find reference to the "sentiments entertained and expressed by Louisiana, in 1861" (IV, 271). Early in January of 1862, Gayarré wrote to James De Bow: "I am ready for the Press, to the 2d of December 1814." — Gayarré to De Bow, 2 January 1862 (De Bow Papers, Duke University). The first eight chapters must have been completed by this time, since Chapter IX begins with Jackson's arrival in New Orleans at the beginning of December, 1814. Then, near the end of the "Supplemental Chapter," there is a reference to the Southern states being "in arms," that indicates that the whole work, except for the last paragraph, was probably completed before the fall of the Confederacy. Hence Gayarré's remark to Evert Duyckinck: "Whilst the country was burning, and my fortune melting, I was not fiddling, but finishing my 4th and last volume of the History of Louisiana." — Gayarré to Duyckinck, 31 May 1865 (Duyckinck Collection, New York Public Library). The final paragraph, with its lament over the fall of the Confederacy, was probably added somewhat later.

[39]. IV, 308, 390, 531.

[40]. For those hopes see Gayarré's speech in support of secession, N. O. Daily Crescent, 25 December 1860.

[41]. One caution to users of the History may be in order: Professor Wilford B. Yearns checked many of Gayarré's quotations against available printed sources and found "no completely accurate quotation until Volume III, page 582." Professor Yearns found that Gayarré's concern was with improving the literary quality of "poorly styled texts" and consisted for the most part of "changing word order, rephrasing, substituting words, and improving punctuation." In summing up his findings, Yearns observes: "Stylists like Barbé Marbois and John W. Monette suffered little alteration, while the formalized phrasing of treaties and laws was left almost intact. [Gayarré] never distorted a meaning by his revisions and usually made stylistic improvements. He apparently was never criticized for these liberties and in comparison with other local historians was quite accurate at quoting." — La. Historical Quarterly, XXXIII, 268 (April, 1950).

Introduction by E. M. Socola

knowledge of personalities and events in nineteenth century Louisiana that few men could have matched.

In his later years Gayarré wrote a number of historical sketches, and two or three of them are of considerable interest. But it was the *History of Louisiana*, rather than the earlier volumes in French or those later sketches, that constituted his real achievement as an historian. And in spite of the shortcomings that have been discussed in the preceding pages, that achievement was far from trivial. Though he lacked both the discipline and the perspective that are the necessary equipment of the first-rate historian, and though he certainly lacked the sustained literary powers of a Prescott or a Parkman, Gayarré did nevertheless bring to his task an inquiring mind, a persistent interest in finding fresh historical evidence, a thorough knowledge of his subject, and a feeling for the drama of history. His contribution to what William Rawle had called the "treasury of literature" was a readable, authoritative,[41] reasonably comprehensive, and occasionally eloquent history of his native state that is of very real intrinsic value even today.

E. M. SOCOLA

New Orleans
July, 1965

CHARLES GAYARRE.

Charles Gayarré, the Historian of Louisiana—name and title came together seventy-three years ago, and so closely has the slow process of time welded them together that it would take as many years again to divorce them or for our ears and tongues to unlearn their habit of coupling one with the other; and Louisianians, prone, perhaps, to over rather than under sensibility in regard to their prophets, throw into the pronunciation of name and title a warmth of sentiment that indeed distinguishes both in an original manner from other historians and other states of the Union. To Louisianians, indeed, it seems that Gayarré was not only the historian of Louisiana but the history of it as well; and when upon the morning of February 11th, 1895, it became known that Charles Gayarré had passed away, when the little black-bordered notices of his death were affixed to the posts on the street corners of New Orleans, according to the old local custom, the feeling aroused was, not simply that a great and a good and a useful life had ceased to exist in the community, but also that a great, good and useful volume had been closed—the volume of the past of City and State—which had stood so long open and ready for all who wished to profit by it that, like old folios and precious classics in public libraries, it seemed chained to our eternal service.

He was born in the month of January, 1805, and baptised in the parish Church of the Cathedral of New Orleans, receiving the name of Charles Etienne Arthur, or, as it stands in the Spanish register, Carlos Estevan Arturo. The ceremony was performed, registered and signed by Fr. Antonio de Sedilla, the Père Antoine whose name is connected with the church of Louisiana in the same indissoluble manner as the name of the infant he baptised, with its history.

The Cession of Louisiana to the United States was still a recent event in the city. The official act and pageant of transfer had taken place only the winter before. The American flag, waving over the Place d'Armes was a new and strange sight as yet in the eyes of the community, and English an outlandish speech to its tongues. In the Cabildo, the old Domination still reigned if it did not govern; in the Cathedral it reigned and governed, the new one that succeeded it, displacing it no more than the echo of the Te Deum that celebrated its advent had displaced the Te Deums chanted in its walls to celebrate other temporal changes.

Of the large group at the baptismal font the infant was the only American, the others were all colonists, French or Spanish.

Ninety years later, Charles Etienne Arthur Gayarré was again borne into the church of St. Louis, to receive its last, as he had received its first blessing on his life. His life had been a long one, overspanning the average, not by years, but by generations. He had seen the new things of his parents' day become old and the old linger along in the heart, now, themselves, like the echo of a cathedral chant; he had seen the transplanted flag, language and government become home-bred to the soil, and the people, who had stood around his baptismal font, disappear in the dim distance of tradition. In his childless old age, when time was bearing him ever farther and farther away from his native time, he used to sigh over his isolation and the dreariness of that land of exile in which octogenarians live. Of all the friends that he started with in youth, a goodly circle of them, but one, a schoolmate, survived to accompany him to the end. A few months later, he too was carried to the old St. Louis cemetery, within whose walls is buried the old city they knew and loved so well, an old city itself now, where the tombs are slowly sinking out of sight—burying themselves in the soil.

Fr. Antonio's certificate of baptism, with other certificates antedating it, signed by him or his no less celebrated predecessor Pére Dagobert, the baptism, marriage, death of father, mother, grandparents, great grandparents, uncles, grand-uncles, with testaments, titles of property, and preciously guarded letters, remain in the archives of the Gayarré family. They must have been laid aside in some miraculous casket, it would seem, to have been preserved entire, through the fierce tempest, of war, ruin and devastation, that scattered and made flotsam and jetsam of all that the lives they certified to held as tangible possessions. The old documents, now, are fast perishing too; they seem held together only by the firm, strong handwriting upon them. As we look at them, we realize that birth was not the beginning of Gayarré's connection with the history of Louisiana. Through them we can trace back that beginning to the hereditary sources that, in their turn, spring from yet other sources, or, as we may say, other far running lives.

Like poets, historians are born, not made. We know them, as we know the natural fruits and flowers from the artificial, not by the careful precision of their perfection, but by the inevitable marks and blemishes of their seed and growth. These are their vital certificates. Therefore, it is to be always remembered, when Louisianians speak of their historian with the affection which, as we have said, is part of their nature, they do so, not in spite of, but in virtue of the blemishes that spoil his perfection, indeed, but make him inimitable.

As a child Gayarré lived in intimate touch with the chronicles of a century earlier than his own. By merely listening to his home gossip, the tales of maternal and paternal reminiscence, and talk of nurse, teacher and playmate, he could see and feel in imagination, not only the very beginning of the colony, but the conception of its beginning in Canada and in Normandy. What followed thenceforth—French and Spanish Domination, the Cession to France, and the Cession to the United States—he knew as the child seventy-five years later knew the events of the Civil War and of the Reconstruction. What historians of to-day study painfully from documents (now that Gayarré is no more), he knew as he knew his family ties. Our historical questions were to him questions of memory; and his memories have become to us historical documents.

He tells us, in some of the most charming and most valuable pages he ever wrote, "A Louisiana Plantation under the Old Régime," how he passed his childhood on the plantation of his grandfather, Etienne de Boré. It was situated six miles above the City, measuring from the Cathedral, and was reached by the public road winding along the river bank. In front it presented an imposing appearance. The avenue of pecan trees that led from the high road, was arrested by a deep moat, edged on its farther side, by an impenetrable hedge of Yucca, or "Spanish Bayonet." Behind this, was a great grass-covered rampart, bearing a massive brick wall. But nature then as now in Louisiana, proved a mocker of the imposing. The waters of the jealous moat had become in time thick with dainty fish. The Yucca hedge, with its sharp-pointed dagger leaves, sent up such luxuriant staffs of its beautiful, waxen, bell-shaped flowers, that it made the Spring glorious to the child, and the sturdy rampart and surrounding brick wall, so protected an inner hedge of wild orange, that its golden fruit made the winter as resplendent. The drive to the house described a circle and was bordered with sweet orange that its golden fruit made the winter as resplendent. The it glorious.

De Boré's family, as may be learned from the pages of the present volume, belonged to the old Norman nobility. He was born in the Illinois district in 1740, was educated in France, and as soon as age permitted, entered the "Mousquetaires du Roi," or Mousquetaires Noirs, the household troops of the King, a corps that none but a noble could enter, and whose privates held the rank of captains, and captains the rank of lieutenant generals in the regular army. After ten years' service at court, he was transferred to the command of a company of cavalry; but, having married the daughter of DesTrehans des Tours, a representative of an old French family, who for many years had been the royal treasurer in the colony of Louisiana, he resigned, in 1772, his position in the army and came to Louisiana, where his wife possessed much property.

The colony having by this time become quieted in the rule of the Spanish government, he bought the plantation of the patriot Masan, who had been sentenced to imprisonment in Moro Castle by O'Reilly, and made of it the home described by his grandson. There, as history relates, after successive failures of the indigo crop threatened him with complete ruin, he embarked all that remained of his wife's fortune and his own, in the hazardous attempt of making sugar and succeeded, for the first time in the colony, in securing the granulation of the juice. This meant not only his own financial salvation and that of all the colonists who like himself had suffered from the indigo failure, but their assured prosperity in the future and eventual acquisition of great wealth.

The plantation above de Boré's, the Foucher plantation (the site of Audubon Park), belonged to de Boré's son-in-law, Pierre Foucher, who was known in revolutionary days as a red republican, notwithstanding that one of his sons-in-law was a Marquis, and another, a Bourbon soldier. Adjoining lay the plantation of the patriot Lafrénière, the impassioned leader of the revolt against the cession of Louisiana to Spain, which resulted in the expulsion of Ulloa. When Lafrénière and his son-in-law, Noyan (Bienville's nephew), were put to death by O'Reilly, the plantation became the property of Lafrénière's second son-in-law, LeBreton, whose son married the daughter of de Boré. In the days of the historian's childhood, the LeBreton plantation had passed into the possession of the de Macartys, and Lafrénière's great grandson, Deschappelles LeBreton, lived with his grandfather de Boré, serving on the managerial staff of the plantation. The other two managers had also their historical significance to the child. One was the nephew of General Klein, of Napoleon's army, afterwards Peer of France; the other was the son of General Duphot of the French embassy, whose killing by the Pope's partisans in Rome, brought about the abolition of the Roman republic.

As the ex-mousquetaire gave his plantation a military appearance, so he ruled it with military discipline. His staff made their report to him every night, and received their orders for the next day's work. Every morning at dawn, a great bell assembled the whole force of labourers in front of the master's house, where they knelt and said a prayer before being detailed to work, a member of the family always presiding during the prayer, with head uncovered. "I vividly remember," writes the historian seventy years after, "how I felt when, about eight years old, I was called upon for the first time to preside over the prayers of the dark assemblage." When the day's work was done, the same ceremony dismissed the negroes to their rest. Before retiring at night and on meeting in the morning, the members of the family respectfully saluted M. de Boré. "For a kiss on my forehead, I returned one upon his hand, as if he were a monarch, and the same feeling of reverence was shown by all who approached him," writes the historian.

From his service at court, de Boré derived the authority, to cite in manners, customs and pronunciation, "la cour de Versailles," the standard that reigned tyrannously supreme on his plantation. One of the anecdotes that the historian loved to quote (which is quoted here merely to preserve a personal memory) was, that when a very small child riding a stick horse on the gallery of his home, he dropped or lost his whip, and so began to cry out " J' ai perdu mon fouet," pronouncing it " foi." Some young ladies and gentlemen sitting on the gallery gaily took up his cry to tease him, adding "he called ' fouet,' ' foi.' " M. de Boré, overhearing the teasing, came out upon the gallery in defence of his little favourite, and turning to the gay group said, " The child is right, and you are wrong. Sachez mesdames et messieurs qu' à la cour de Versailles, on dit ' foi,' et non ' fouet.' (Know ladies and gentlemen, that at the court of Versailles, they say ' foi ' and not ' fouet.')"

The portrait of the ex-mousquetaire and planter bears out the character given him by his grandson. It represents a man of sixty, of quiet dignity and simple manners, looking at one with piercing, shrewd, yet kindly eyes, and with pleasant paternal smile, in short, a man of business ability, a good disciplinarian, and of benevolent disposition. He died at the age of seventy-eight. In his last moments, he summoned his grandson Charles, then a boy of thirteen, to his bedside, and giving him his last admonitions, blessed him with true patriarchal solemnity. According to his directions, his funeral and tomb were of the plainest kind, and the thousand dollars which might have been spent upon them were given to the Charity Hospital.

Madame de Boré died when her grandson was so young that he retained in his mind, he says, " but a dim vision of her, as a lady seated near a small round table, with a white marble top, encircled by a diminutive copper railing. On the table were her workbasket and a beautiful Louis XV. snuff box. She was educated in France at St. Cyr, and became a model of its training, such as Madame de Maintenon herself might have praised. Her friends, old gentlemen of the young historian's day, used to describe her to her grandson as a wonder of fascination, one of them, in a fit of enthusiasm interrupted by an octogenarian cough, exclaiming, " Celà eut valu la peine de faire cinquante lieues seulement pour voir Madame de Boré prendre une prise de tabac." ("It would have been worth a journey of fifty leagues just to see Madame de Boré take a pinch of snuff.") With the ladies, she was an unfaltering maintainer of the manners and etiquette of the days of her youth and school, but her tact in correcting tactlessness or administering a reproof for breach of etiquette was as celebrated as her own faultlessness.

The house was furnished in the style of plain simplicity that prevailed among the wealthiest planters of the old régime; but the table and the wines went to the other extreme. In the memory of the historian they were as he wrote, "superb;" and the hostipality they graced was worthy of them. Every Sunday there came regularly to dinner a score or two of guests from New Orleans. Among them some Knights of St. Louis, wearing their decorations, struck the imagination of the future historian. There was something, he writes, in them or in their appearance, dress, physiognomy, in their manners, peculiarities of conversation, and language, in their bows and greetings, in their accent and modulation of voice, that produced on him the most vivid impression. They were historical souvenirs in flesh and blood; "but," he adds, "waifs of fortune though they were, they were characterized by a certain loftiness of manner and a loyal esteem and regard for one another. They were not prodigal of their demonstrations, but what they expressed could be relied upon as sincere, for they never hesitated to manifest antipathy, reprobation, or opposition when necessary." As he grew in years, the writer confessed that the faith of these men of the Old Régime in one another struck him more and more in contrast with the universal distrust of man's honour and integrity which he had observed spreading in later times over the community, like a stain of oil over a carpet.

It was before the day of these reminiscences that occurred that stirring event on the de Boré plantation that almost caused the indignant removal of the family to France and the loss of her historian to Louisiana. The French General Collot, on his travels from the Western States to New Orleans, stopped to visit M. de Boré. As soon as this was known in the City, the Governor of the colony, Baron de Carondelet, who had received confidential information that General Collot was intrusted by the French government with a secret mission against which the Spanish authorities had been warned to be on their guard, sent an armed boat by river and fifty dragoons by land to arrest him, and had him taken to New Orleans and imprisoned in Fort Charles. As de Boré expressed his feelings without restraint at this insult put upon his guest, and as he was known for his intense devotion to France, Carondelet, it is said, thought seriously of having him arrested also, and transported to Havana, but was deterred by the consideration of de Boré's distinguished position in the community, his character, family connections, and the great boon he had conferred upon the Colony, by his successful experiment of sugar making. What an imaginative child hears, he sees; and the historian in after days could relate this event as if his heart and not his memory merely had been tinged with it; and it was in the same way that he could relate that truly royal moment in the hospitality of his old home when the three illustrious visitors, the Duc d'Orleans, the Comte de Beaujolais, and the Duc de Montpensier, visited it. As the old Mousquetaire repeated it to his grandson, "Little did I think, when in the household troops of Louis XV., that the day would come when three princes of the blood would be my guests on the banks of the Mississippi."

When the colony was transferred from Spain to France, M. de Boré was appointed mayor of the City of New Orleans for reasons that Laussat explains in his confidential dispatch:

"I thought also of securing, without loss of time, an imposing support in the civil department of the government, and I selected for Mayor of the city, M. Etienne Boré, a native of Louisiana, of a distinguished family, formerly Mousquetaire in France, one of the largest and most skilful planters of the province, and a gentleman renowned for his patriotism and for a character of undeviating independence. I made a powerful appeal to him in the name of his country, whose interests required his services, and I had the satisfaction to win him over. After M. de Boré, and through his influence, I secured the services of some of the most distinguished among the colonists."

The name of Gayarré comes into the history of Louisiana with the Spanish Domination. Don Estevan Gayarré, the Contador Real, and one of the commissioners who accompanied Ulloa to take possession of the colony in the name of the King of Spain, seems to have excited none of the animosity that Ulloa provoked, and even fomented to a state of frenzy. When Ulloa was expelled, Don Estevan remained in Louisiana with his young son, Don Juan Antonio Gayarré, and exercised his office during the administration of O'Reilly. After O'Reilly's departure from the colony, Don Estevan sought and obtained leave to return also to his native country and be put on the list of retired pensioners. He died in Spain at the close of his century. Don Juan Antonio Gayarré, although a youth of eighteen, was appointed by O'Reilly Commissary of War, an office he retained under Unzaga and Galvez. He was one of the brilliant list of young Spanish officers who effected practically the pacification of Louisianians with Spain, by uniting themselves with the families of the French officials of the province. Don Juan Antonio Gayarré married Constance de Granpré, the daughter of the most distinguished of these, the Chevalier de Granpré, who had come into Louisiana in the time of Bienville, and received the Cross of St. Louis for his long and faithful service. It is of particular interest to note that this Chevalier de Grandpré was a descendant of Sieur Pierre Boucher, who was not only the governor of Trois Rivieres, in Canada, and the first Canadian ennobled by Louis XIV., but was also, and this is the point of most importance in the present relation, the author of a " Histoire véritable et naturelle des Moeurs et Productions du Pays de la Nouvelle France, vulgairement dite, le Canada. Paris, 1664," the first published account of that country.

Don Juan Antonio Gayarré distinguished himself, second only to his brilliant commander in chief, Galvez, in the glorious little campaign against the English, in 1779, which resulted in the conquest of Manchac, Baton Rouge, Natchez, Mobile, and Pensacola, or the whole English province of West Florida In the distribution of honours and rewards that followed the successful termination of the war, Don Juan Antonio Gayarré was appointed Contador Real of the rich post of Acapulco. He died there, and his wife returned to her birth place, New Orleans, bringing three sons with her. Of these, Carlos, married the youngest daughter of de Boré, and became the father of the historian. He also lived on the plantation of his father-in-law.

"M. de Boré," the historian relates, "although of the Old Régime, became an enthusiastic admirer of Napoleon; and he had in his parlor a fine engraving of the Battle of Austerlitz at the moment when General Rapp, on horseback and bare-headed, rushes into the presence of the Emperor, shouting, 'Victory! Victory!' To which Napoleon replies, 'I never saw thee, Rapp, looking so handsome.' Carlos Gayarré, on the contrary, although born in Louisiana, remained fixedly loyal to Spain and to his Spanish ancestors. Always at the head of his bed, there hung his coat of arms, with its three mountains, spanned by a bridge surmounted by the turbaned head of Abderahman, the testimonial of the proud day for the Gayarrés when they defeated the Sultan in their native valley of Ronceil, about the year 800." When Napoleon invaded Spain, Don Carlos Gayarré, in the presence of his father-in-law, respectfully suppressed his feelings. But, when came the announcement of French triumphs in Spain, he would retire to his bed chamber, in which his little son would hear the sound of passionate playing of a guitar and the passionate singing of Spanish patriotic songs. He held an office under the Commissary of War, when the colony was transferred to France, and was one of the Spanish officers who consented to receive a commission under the French Republic. The Colonial Prefect, Laussat, appointed him first lieutenant of the third company of Louisiana militia in 1803. In 1807, he was appointed captain of the fourth company by Governor Claiborne. His name is enrolled in the first Masonic Lodge founded in Louisiana, the Polar Star. One of the relics remaining of him is a little packet which contains his regalia and the certificate of the degrees that he took in the order. His portraits represent him in the prime of his youth and manly beauty; he did not live beyond it, dying in 1813.

Gayarré tells us that he learned his alphabet from one Lefort, who lived in a house on the upper limit of the Foucher plantation, and kept a school which was well attended by the children of the planters on both sides of the river. Lefort was a man of culture, but rough and given to whipping his pupils unmercifully. When past eighty, the historian related that he had not yet forgotten the blows given him, when a child of six, for imperfect pronunciation of the English word "the." At nine years of age, Gayarré was promoted from this teacher, and sent as a boarder to the College of Orleans. In the opening pages of Fernando de Lemos, he describes this historic institution of learning, with its courtly president, Jules D'Avezac, whom the students affectionately nicknamed "Titus," and its corps of professors, composed of original types of scholars and gentlemen. The rules of life and study there were Spartan in their austere simplicity, and they were enforced with Spartan sternness. No puerilities, except in age, were permitted the scholars. Even the afternoon walks and the weekly visits to the theatres were administered with rigid regard to duty rather than amusement.

Gayarré was at this college in the memorable year of the British invasion. He relates that on the afternoon of the 23rd of December, about three o'clock, there was a great commotion in the learned precincts. The news had arrived in New Orleans that the British had landed in Louisiana, and that they had been seen on a plantation below the City. Studies were suspended, class rooms closed, alarmed pupils hurried to and fro, parents poured in to take their children away. Gayarré and his cousin, Frederic Foucher, were left so long that they began to fear that they had been forgotten and were to shift for themselves in face of the British invasion. At the last moment, however, an aunt sent for them. She lived in a house on Dumaine and Royal streets, and the two boys stood on the gallery, with her and other ladies of the household, and looked at the troops marching by hastening to meet the enemy below. At seven o'clock the battle began, "and the roar of artillery and discharge of musketry was almost as distinctly heard as if the battle were in the immediate neighborhood. There was not the slightest noise in the City; it held its breath in awful suspense." The two boys and the ladies, petrified into absolute silence by their apprehensions, stood on the balcony until half past nine o'clock, when the firing gradually ceased; and then they passed a never to be forgotten hour of anxiety. "Were their defenders retreating pressed by the enemy? What was happening?" About eleven o'clock, the City's awful silence was broken, the furious gallop of a horse was heard and the cry of the horseman, shouting as loud as he could, "Victory! Victory!"

Early the next morning the children were sent to their homes. On the 8th of January, when the decisive battle on the field of Chalmette was fought, the child stood on the gallery of his grandfather's house, with the ladies of the family, who were pale and trembling with fear. No man was visible; the only one, de Boré, who had remained at home on account of age, had, when the battle began, gone up to the top of the balcony for observation. When the firing ended, he came down from his post and announced to his daughter that the Americans were victorious. His soldier's ear had distinguished that the American guns had silenced the English.

The Tennesseeans, when the war was over, camped on the lower line of the de Boré plantation, and their gallant generals Coffee and Carrol, were entertained during their stay in New Orleans in the de Boré house, where General Jackson was also a frequent visitor, and more than once the great hero of the hour in New Orleans stopped to pat the little ten year old Charles on the head and propose to take him to Tennessee.

In contrast with the glaring light of publicity which pours upon the personality of writers to-day from the many and the various illuminating mediums of the journalistic world, the writers of 1828 seem to live in a dim twilight indeed. We grope after them, as it were, with a rush light. All that is known of Gayarré's youth is what can be gathered from his descriptions of other people. He stayed at the College of Orleans until he completed his education, and in 1825, when twenty years old, made his first publication, a pamphlet on the subject of the Livingston Criminal Code, opposing some of Livingston's views and particularly his recommendation of the abolition of capital punishment, which the young creole combated as an innovation of dangerous application in the State of Louisiana. The pamphlet, whether it aided popular opinion on the subject or not, certainly reflected it; for Livingston's system of penal law for the State of Louisiana, though it was admired and commended by the most celebrated philosophers, statesmen and philanthropists of that day, was never adopted by the State for which it was framed. In

1826 Gayarré went to Philadelphia, and remained there for three years for the double purpose of studying law and perfecting himself in the English language, which was still taught and spoken as an alien tongue in New Orleans. He studied in the office of William Rawle, the distinguished jurist and legal author. He was admitted to the Pennsylvania Bar in 1828; a year later, upon his return to New Orleans, he was admitted to the practice of law in Louisiana.

This period is looked upon by Louisiana lawyers of to-day as the classical era of the legal profession in the State. Indeed, they feel that it is no partial judgment that cites it, both for intellect and character, as pre-eminent in the history of the judiciary of the whole country. It was a time in New Orleans, as elsewhere in the United States, of strongly marked individualities, when every man of prominence was, in the old parlance, a character as well as, in the modern sense of the word, a force in the community. The young creole felt the exciting and inciting stimulus of his associates. In his "New Orleans Bench and Bar of 1823," written sixty years after his admission to it, he gives an account of the impression made upon him; and of all the men of his own generation, and we may say of the two generations since, he is the only one who has left a description of the men of that time that possesses the living quality of true history, the quality of transmitting the enthusiasm felt in one century to another; and, the reflection obtrudes itself here again, it would seem there is no test whose application so easily distinguishes the born from the self-made historian, as this one of the quality and vitality of the impressions he receives through life and the power of such impressions to evoke the enthusiasm of later and successive generations.

The man of that era whose character, to us of to-day, was most strongly marked, whose individuality was most clearly cut against the background of the time, was Francois Xavier Martin, Associate Justice of the Supreme Court of Louisiana, and author of a then recently published history of Louisiana. As no one, to judge by the accounts that have come down to us, received so keen, so just, and so true an impression of Martin's greatness of intellect as Gayarré, so none so fully showed the effect of it.

Martin was the determining force in Gayarré's life. He was, in effect, Gayarré's literary progenitor.

The two old volumes, so rare nowadays and so dear to Louisiana book lovers—Martin's first edition of 1827, and Gayarré's "Essai Historique sur la Louisiane," 1830—stand to one another in a nearer and more sentimental relationship than that of mere literary succession, as the preface of each shows. In addressing himself as an old man to "Louisiana's Youthful Citizens" and in enumerating the steps by which Louisiana advanced from Indian barbarism through Colonial dependence to the liberty of territorial government and at last to State sovereignty in the Federal Union, Martin not only presents the theme which he asserts must be the most interesting to a young Louisianan but also, at the same time, traces for the young historian a plan of future work which Gayarré faithfully carried out in after years.

Gayarré's preface in his first essay at writing history is an ingenuous response to Martin's appeal. "A Louisianian by birth and blood," he describes himself, "who has read with emotions of filial piety the History of Louisiana which Judge Martin has published in English." He acknowledges that he owes most of his material to the venerable magistrate and makes a timid apology for his feeble essay as an attempt to bring the history of Louisiana within reach of those whose tongue is French.

Had Gayarré never written any other history, this first work of his would assuredly have maintained in our local literature the position in excellence that it occupies in point of time, as second only after Martin. Possessing the charm as well as the faults of youth, it would have proved perhaps a necessary intermediary between the ponderous tone of the magisterial historian and those readers who prefer their facts hot rather than cold and are not averse to a history that yields them profit of pleasure as well as of knowledge.

In this particular case, as in all other lines of intellectual heredity, one is always curious to know how much or how little, the historian who comes after is indebted to him who went before. Although Martin evidently inspired Gayarré to write history, his own inspiration, as we know, came practically from the need of satisfying his insatiable love of work, which was one of his ways of living. He was no sooner settled in Louisiana than he began in a methodical way to collect materials for a history, which was suggested to him, as his history of North Carolina had been, as a farther utilization of his legal researches. Every publication that had any relation to the subject, all the important documents found in the archives of the State, local traditions and personal reminiscences and testimony, he patiently sifted and weighed as he did the evidence in his court, but issuing it after full deliberation upon it in what is in spirit and form—a decision—rather than a history. Gayarré translated Martin into French, almost literally, making no original research for material. Where he differed from his predecessor, and a pretty point of difference it is, to historical students, is in regard to tradition and oral testimony. As an intimate friend of the de Boré family and a frequent visitor at their plantation, Martin was enabled to know and pass upon whatever material that household in particular, among many others, possessed years before Gayarré was in the position to use the same sources of information. In the "Essai Historique," therefore, we note that the young historian is apt to add to his narrative what the elder one judicially rejected, such as, to cite briefly a particular instance, the last words of Lafrénière, and the dramatic dialogue between Villeré and his Spanish guards that precedes his killing. Martin gives an impartial account of it; Gayarré repeats evidently the words of those who related it to him with his own passions added. And so it is in all the variations of the local traditions. Gayarré writes, as the young in fact should do, from the standpoint of feeling and popular opinion. In his later histories, written when he was of mature age, there is a noticeable change in standpoint. The youthful and fiery denunciator of the Spaniards becomes their apologist and defender.

But it was hardly the day in New Orleans (if such a day has ever existed in the calendar of the City) for literary advancement. The political field offered the only career for ambition, and its brilliant rewards, then as now, dazzled and blinded the eye to their ephemeral nature. Gayarré, a representative of the most distinguished families of the old population, and as ardent an American and Democrat as could be found among the new, speaking with equal fluency the language of both, having given proof of superior intellectual ability, and possessing an independent fortune, might be said to have been born and bred to the political qualifications of his time, and as such he stood in the estimation of his constituents without a rival. He rose quickly to the summit of the expectations of his friends and of his own ambition. At once upon his return from Philadelphia, and before he published his "Essai Historique" he was elected, by a unanimous vote, a representative of the City of New Orleans in the Legislature. There he received the compliment of being chosen by the Legislature to write an address complimenting the French Chamber on the Revolution of 1830. In 1831 he was appointed Assistant Attorney General. In 1832 he became presiding judge of the City Court of New Orleans. In 1835, when he had barely reached the constitutional age, he was elected to the Senate of the United States.

The calamity of his life, as he always felt it, overtook him here. A distressing form of malady had fastened upon him, seriously impairing his capacity for work. Obtaining no alleviation of his trouble from his home physicians and filled with gloomy apprehensions of chronic invalidism for the future, he resolved to go to France and seek medical assistance before entering upon his new duties in Washington. Three eminent physicians of Paris, called in consultation, gave in writing their opinions that his disease was of such a nature and had reached so advanced a stage that he could not safely return to America. He, therefore, resigned his seat in the Senate and remained in Europe for medical treatment until 1843. Readers of "Fernando de Lemos" can follow him, as, under the thin disguise of a pseudonym (a favourite literary device of the period), he travels hither and thither in France, now to some springs to drink the waters, now to some city or town in search of historical information, conversing on the road with his fellow travellers of all conditions, and storing their expressions and opinions in his wonderful memory. The prestige of his name, family, and official title, enhanced by his rare intellectual gifts, gained him a welcome into the literary and political salons of Paris in its brilliant period before the revolution of 1848. The book is but a dull substitute for the personal recital, which, with its infinite charm of manner and language, remained to the last moment of the author's life—a delight to his friends. The balls at the Tuileries, the salon of Madame

Ancelot, the fancy ball at the Spanish Ambassador's, Louis Phillippe, the old lady of houor of Josephine, de Tocqueville, Balzac, Lamartine, Casimir Perier, the famous physician Koref, the hangman of Paris, Mademoiselle Lenormant, and all the long list of historic Louisiana families then living in Paris, with *their* anecdotes and *their* experiences—many a dreary hour in his own life and in the lives of others he beguiled into a pleasant one by these reminiscences.

He learned to know Paris as he knew New Orleans; and he loved it second only to his native city. Of the cure he sought there and did not find, for he was a chronic sufferer throughout his long life, he says: " One thing I know, that in the stimulating hot-houses of that great city, which claims to be the capital of the world, and in which the accumulated civilization of centuries strengthens, fertilizes, and heats the intellect into its highest artificial development, a resolute will, feverishly excited by so many causes, and braced up by the magnetic influence and congeniality of mind acting on mind, can triumph over the weakness of the diseased body and conquer physical pain with more ease than elsewhere. One can rise from the couch where hours of agony had been endured, one can put on the elegant dress prepared by the most fashionable tailor, and, although debilitated by a long fast, turn night into day whilst toying with the frivolous, or gathering wisdom and learning from the sage." This absence, which apparently cost the loss of his services to the State for eight years, proved, on the contrary, a period of unexpected usefulness to her. As soon as his health permitted, he threw himself ardently again into the study of the history of Louisiana, working now, not from the material furnished by Martin and local traditions, but from the vast collections of historical documents lying stored in the archives of the ministry of the Marine and Colonies in Paris, a field hitherto unexplored by American historians. His researches in it were so thorough that little of moment has been added to them by after gleaners.

Profiting, also, by his family and social relations in Paris, he secured access to private archives and obtained the copies of documents, that but for him would, perhaps, never have been exhumed. When he returned to Louisiana, he brought with him, therefore, a new history of the State, practically complete. He wrote it in French, in order to preserve the text of the official documents copied from the French archives which form the bulk of the volume, and published it in New Orleans, the first volume in 1846, the second in 1847. The work has been so long out of print that it is rarer, now, than the " Essai Historique;" but covering as it does, the official history of Louisiana from its colonization by Iberville, to its cession by France to Spain, it is a treasure of reference to the student fortunate enough to possess a copy. The only rival that it has in Louisiana bibliography, is Gayarré's later and last history. A good appraisement of its value can be made by comparing it with other histories of the same scope published in the United States at that date, or for a score of years afterwards. Had it been written in the language of the country and brought thus within the reach of the commonalty of writers and teachers, it is but truth to say, it would have elevated the standard of historical research at the time and advanced by a generation the method of the study of original documents that is the rule to-day.

As it was written in the intimate language of the people of Louisiana, and studded with the names of families distinguished then in the service of the State, as they had been for a century in that of the Colony, and repeating as it did from authentic sources old stories of heroism in the pioneer days, that had fallen into the mythical status of folklore and nursery tradition the history could not fail to awaken local enthusiasm and a revival of interest in the past of the State whose future greatness was becoming the political creed of the hour.

But the work has the defect of its quality: the rigidity of a continuous series of copied documents. Even while composing it, Gayarré conceived the plan of a larger, freer, more comprehensive use of the same material and the addition to it of a new volume to be collected from the study of American archives, to be written in the language of his country, not of a portion of his State—the plan, in short, of the present work. Circumstances, the shaping force in life, made the usual modifications in carrying this idea into effect.

The Committee of a "People's Lyceum," (the old city having progressed thus far in its Americanization) invited Gayarré to deliver one of their twelve annual lectures. As a bird from a cage his heart seems to have bounded from the hard and fast confines of the official documents that encompassed him into the open air and flowery pastures of "The Poetry or Romance of the History of Louisiana." He culled from it, not one lecture, but the series that form the contents of the first volume of this publication. In his preface, he confesses to an humble imitation of Sir Walter Scott, in this use of imagination as a bait to lure readers into knowledge of history.

Time abounds with such attempts, and the knowledge of history has lost, rather than gained from the concession of gilded facts to readers, these proving generally the most annoying errors to get rid of afterwards. In this case, however, the damage caused may well be overlooked, in comparison with the good achieved. The "Poetry and Romance of Louisiana" is the portal through which most readers enter the history of Louisiana. If thereafter one never feels quite sure of the true reality of the realm one enters, if there happens to the reader what the author confesses happened to him, that in it the things of the heart become confused with the things of the mind, the gain has been, that in Louisiana, the popular sentiment for the history of the State, is vivid and picturesque, and that there is not only a popular but a true poetic sentiment for it that has made itself felt most notably in the educational systems of the day. As a source of inspiration to the dramatist, poet, and novelist, which the preface hopes the book might become, it has been in truth too generously prolific. To withdraw its contributions, if such an experiment could be made, from the fiction and drama of the country since its publication, would produce indeed something like a collapse in our native pseudo-historical literature.

The second volume of the "French Domination" is also formed of a series of lectures, but the author says it is, so far as he could make it, detailed and accurate history; in other words, there are in it no adventitious charms. While, however, it holds fast to the chronological documents of the French version, it is not shackled (painfully shackled we might say) by them. It rises out of them and above them, expanding with freedom and ease into a narrative that, in truth, gives such full satisfaction of charm and interest as makes a Louisianian well nigh afraid to express any other opinion upon it than this, the difficulty being to know, not how to praise it, but how not to over praise it. In it, Gayarré exhibits for the first time his magnificent store of local traditions and personal reminiscence and his matchless charm in using them. Here again, as in the case of the French history, one has but to compare this volume with any volume of its kind, published up to that time or since, to arrive at the proper estimate of value that should be accorded it in the historical literature of the country.

Meanwhile, by what in the experience of after time, seems a political anomaly, he was twice chosen by the city of New Orleans as her representative in the Legislature, purely in recognition of his pre-eminence in the State as a man of letters (for he never pretended to political influence); and he was also appointed by two succeeding governors to the office of Secretary of State, a position which he filled for seven years. This period represents the proudest and pleasantest years in his life and also in that of the State, which was then in the full glow of her maturity as an American commonwealth. The friction between the old and new population had duly changed rough into polished surfaces; the irritating chafing under the yoke of strange conditions had ceased, yoke and neck having become habituated to one another; and the "life of the commonwealth," to quote the contended words of our historian, "was but a quiet ever swelling stream of prosperity." The banks of such a stream have ever proved fertile soil for intellectual culture, and they seemed to prove so then in Louisiana. But the stream of prosperity, alas! has found so many impediments in its course, in the life time of the present generation (whose whole strength, indeed, has at times been devoted to keep a current alive in it) that it seems only a part of the usual vain and feeble boasting over an age gone by, to say that great institutions, handsome buildings, schools, colleges, charities, noble private benefactions, and public libraries, flourished, then, with every promise of continuous developments, where to-day the seeds of them are being so laboriously resown. There was, however, no consummation of that old and passed prosperity that commends itself so much to the student of to-day as the manifest appreciation, public and private, of the importance of the knowledge of the history of the State as an element in the wise development of the State. This is an idea that we are familiar with at present, one that has become a part of the educational outfit of every State in the Union. At that time, Gayarré was, we may say, the evangelist of it—and, rare as the exception sounds, he did not preach in a Louisiana desert.

Appropriations for a statue of Washington by Powers to be placed in the Rotunda of the State House, for an equestrian statue of General Jackson to be placed in Jackson Square, for a monument on the battlefield of Chalmette, for swords and gold medals to Mexican War generals, and for various commemorative bronze medals, adorn the legislative records of that period. They all of them bear the signature of Gayarré. The Secretary of State, furthermore, had the expenditure then of an annual appropriation of one thousand dollars for the purchase of books for the State Library, Gayarré's scholarly use of this money during the seven years of his office changed a mere accumulation of volumes into a library worthy of the name, whose historical section, even in what may be called an infirm and invalided condition, commands to-day the respect and admiration of scholars. Each rare and valuable book in it bears the date of Gayarre's incumbency.

Shortly after his return from France, by his personal influence upon Governor Mouton, he had secured the purchase, by the State, of the historical documents, copied by M. Felix Magne from the archives of the Marine and Colonies in Paris, that had served him in his French history, and which were an indispensable source of authority for future use. The two bulky volumes for which one thousand dollars were paid, are the precious heirlooms of the Louisiana Historical Society to-day. The Historical Society was resurrected, in truth, to receive them and to carry on further work under the new historical impulse. Established in 1836, it had languished and become inert from lack of the special direction of effort, necessary in such societies for healthful activity. When Gayarré became Secretary of State, he, with a group of friends, revived the Society, reorganized it, adopted a constitution for it, and elected Martin, the venerable historian, president, with John Perkins and J. D. B. DeBow, secretaries. If to the above names be added those of B. F. French and Edmond Forstall, the list of the century's eminent servitors of the history of Louisiana and, as such, of Gayarré's disinterested collaborators, will be complete. It is a list, the like of which will hardly be seen again in the annals of the Society. French was the publisher of the "Historical Collections of Louisiana;" DeBow, the editor of "DeBow's Review;" Forstall was the author of "An Analytical Index of the whole of the Public Documents, relative to Louisiana, deposited in the Department de la Marine et des Colonies, et Bibliothèque du Roi," at Paris. Perkins, delegated by the Society to make researches in Europe for interesting historical matter relative to Louisiana, secured the services of M. Pierre Margry, to make a transcript, chronologically arranged, of all the papers in the different archives of the French government, referring to Louisiana, from the date of Iberville's landing to the time of its cession to the United States. This undertaking, vast as it proved to be, was superbly carried out by Margry; and the pride of the remark may be excused here, it was to this commission of the Louisiana Historical Society, that the historical students of the United States are indebted for what was a consequence of it, the compilation and publication of Margry's great and momentous work "Découvertes et Etablissements des Français, dans l' Ouest et dans le Sud de l'Amérique Septentrionale."

Pushing his influence farther, Gayarré obtained from the Legislature of 1847, an appropriation of two thousand dollars to be expended under the auspices of the Historical Society in procuring copies of original documents relating to the history of Louisiana from Spain. In his report, as Secretary of State, for 1850, he gives the account of the disbursement of this money, and his correspondence with the United States Minister to Spain and with Sen. Pascal de Gayangos on the subject. Several packages of documents, dealing with the transactions of the Spanish Domination were received by the Society, an addition of great value to those already possessed in Louisiana. The investigations, however, were far from complete; another appropriation was needed. "I can not but hope," writes the Secretary, in his report to the Legislature on the State Library for 1850, "that you will come to the conclusion that any money employed in the elucidation of our history would be a useful application of the public treasure." The Governor's message for 1853, recommended a still more liberal assistance by the State in favor of another effort, unfortunately an ineffectual one, and incidentally furnishes a rare example of executive appreciation: " Judge Gayarré, the Secretary of State, will present a report showing the condition of the State Library, with suitable recommendations and suggestions in reference thereto. I agree with him, especially in his recommendation that the French and Spanish historical documents belonging to the State should be published. Those documents now existing in manuscript should be published, not only for their preservation, but as a source of interest and information to the public. The industry and enterprise of the Secretary of State has enabled him already to use them in producing his able and reliable history of Louisiana, a work not only highly creditable to the State, but which has placed his name in the catalogue of our most distinguished historical writers."

The adoption of a new constitution in 1853 occasioned the retirement of the historian from his office, and also, it may be said, of the State from its patronage of men of letters. Since that time, there has been, as it were, an estrangement between the two.

Gayarré's political career was virtually cut short by his refusing in the ensuing election to be controlled by party organization and running as an independent candidate for Congress. He was defeated, fraudulently, as he charged, and proved to the satisfaction of his friends. Then, as now, this charge was a political offense which a party does not forget or forgive.

When, at the inauguration of President Pierce, Gayarré's name and that of Pierre Soulé were laid before the Cabinet for the mission to Spain, the political leader, not the historian, received the appointment. A mis-choice it turned out, politically, and a misfortune for history. Had Gayarré been sent to Spain, it is a foregone conclusion that, backed as he was by his Spanish name, antecedents, high family and social connections in Europe and this country and by his reputation as a historian, he would have carried to a successful conclusion the attempt he meditated making—that of continuing the Gayangos researches among the archives of Spain, for documents relating to the history of Louisiana, the lack of which still leaves a woful gap in our collections of this period. The Secretary of the United States offered him, in extenuation, as it were, the position of Under Secretary of State. He declined it. The publication of the third volume of his history, "The Spanish Domination," just at this time in 1854, seems an opportune comment upon the transaction.

In the "Spanish Domination," which carries Louisiana to the end of her colonial period, the author reaches the culminating point of his story and of his fine qualities as a narrator.

The canon of good taste, which allows praise of the better, but commands silence in the presence of the best, is invoked here in exoneration of a reticence that it seems, in truth, presumptuous to infringe. The volume that contains the administration of O'Reilly, and the account of the famous religious quarrel, between the French and Spanish priests and the description of the contestants, Dagobert, Génoveau, and Cirilo; that gives the account of Galvez and of his famous little war; Miro and the episode of the Inquisition; the Wilkinson intrigue; Carondelet and his administration; and the fine dramatic conclusion of the transfer to France, and cession to the United States—this volume, it would seem, must ever remain what it is at present, the chief standard by which emulative writers of Louisiana history measure their failure or success. The closing words of it may be fitly added here as a sample of that tenderness for Louisiana which Gayarré not only felt himself, but has inspired succeeding historians to feel. "Thus ends the colonial History of Louisiana. I have attempted to write it faithfully, accurately, and impartially, with an unabating love for truth, and with an unselfish desire of serving in this way if not in any other, the country to which I am bound by so many ties—not only of birth, education and habit, but also by so many endearing recollections of the past, and even so many family associations and traditions, which for me, clothe with the charm almost of private interest the relation of public events in Louisiana."

The "American Domination" was at once begun. Although finished before the Civil War, it was not published until after its close, in 1866. Extending from the time of the Cession of Louisiana to the United States until the close of the administration of the first American governor in 1816, it offers a field less brilliant to the eye than the Spanish period and far less picturesque, but one whose interest is more intense and critically important. The grafting of American institutions upon European Louisiana is its theme, an operation for which the American statesmen of the time had but bungling hands and the Louisianians very imperfect endurance. Only an author born and bred in such a reconstruction could write the true history of it, and for this reason alone, if not for many others of more worth, this volume would seem assured for all time of its present position of unquestioned primacy in our local history. A rival to it could only have come out of the same period and the blood whence Gayarré came. With marvelous art, if it be art and not the instinctive dramatic skill of the true historian, he has made the first American governor the protagonist of the episode. Now repellant, now attractive, always earnestly eloquent for the principles which he represented, steadfast, dignified, conscientious, grave, Claiborne stands as the typical character of the new, and, to Louisianians, the strange *régime*. Around him and sometimes against him, break the excitable elements of the old *régime*, in revolt against an unpalatable though inevitable destiny. Chapter by chapter the theme develops, and the new government, like the plot of a good novel, creeps surely on bringing ever remoter circumstances, ever new personages into its scheme of progress—Spanish and French intrigues, debates in Congress, the establishment of a bank, the formation of a colonial council, the judicial organization, religious quarrels, smuggling, education, the right of suffrage, slavery, Jefferson, Monroe, Kemper, Cascalvo, Morales, Father Antoine, Julien Poydras, Daniel Clarke, Wilkinson, Aaron Burr, the Lafittes and Baratarians, Livingston, General Jackson. With masterly skill, each and all, the men and their political, religious, and humanitarian questions and guesses, are brought upon the little Louisiana stage to play their part, and a great part it sometimes was in the constructive history of the country. The question of the opening chapter (for to this, as the author says, could be narrowed the length and breadth of debate in Congress), " are Louisianians capable of self-government? " reaches its splendid finale and answer in the Battle of New Orleans and the volume ends, as it began, with the American governor, who, now in the full maturity of his experience and of his tried and proven wisdom, firmly vindicates the honor and dignity of the sovereign State of Louisiana, and maintains the authority of her courts against the military usurpation of power attempted by a general of the United States army, even though that general was no less a personage than her great deliverer, Andrew Jackson. An extract from his last annual message gives as it were the closing moral of the story:

"I shall not hesitate to say, that if, at any time, I listened to "the doctrine of *doing evil that good might come out of it,* "and that *the end justifies the means,* I am now convinced that "the admission of this principle into affairs of state must prove "invasive of the rights and destructive to the happiness of a "free people. Yes, gentlemen, my experience in Louisiana "has taught me how to reverence the sage advice of the great "Washington when he urges his countrymen to respect the "authority of the laws and cautions them *to resist the spirit of* "*innovation, however specious the pretext, and to permit no* "*change by usurpation; for although this,* says this illustrious "patriot, *may in one instance be the instrument of good, it is* "*the customary weapon by which free governments are destroyed.* "*The precedent must always greatly counterbalance in per-* "*manent evil any partial or transient benefit which the use can* "*at any time yield."*

This, the most carefully prepared and patiently written of Gayarré's works, was not finished until 1860; and the author was looking forward to publishing it and then carrying into effect his long cherished purpose of a prolonged sojourn in Europe and a complete research among the Spanish archives for the missing documents relating to the history of Louisiana, when the portents of the civil war became unmistakable. He determined to remain and share the fate of his State and country. In the excitement of debate over the Secession of the State in 1861, he, as the most competent authority on the subject in the State, was invited to express his views on the right that was claimed for the States of the Union under the Federal Constitution to secede. At an immense meeting of anxious citizens in New Orleans, he advocated with great effect the affirmative on that question, maintaining the doctrine which in Philadelphia he had been taught by William Rawle, the great constitutional lawyer, and which he averred he had never known to be contested at that epoch by any one of the luminaries of the bar in the city where the former colonies of Great Britain had solemnly proclaimed their secession from the mother country.

On the meeting of the convention that was to decide on the secession of Louisiana, a member of that convention, mentioning to Gayarré that the contemplated secession of Louisiana from the Union was looked upon as fraught with peculiar difficulty, from the fact of its having been purchased by the United States, and that this difficulty would probably be brought to the consideration of the State Convention, asked the expression of the historian's views on the question. This elicited the open letter that was laid before the Convention, demonstrating that the orginial States of the Union had no rights that Louisiana did not possess.

He passed the years of the civil war in retirement at his country place, Roncal, serving the cause of the Confederacy in the only way he could, with his pen, his counsel, and his money. As an ease to his mind in the long crisis, he composed a life of Philip II. of Spain, using the authorities he had at hand in his rare French, Spanish and English library. The only originality, therefore, that circumstances permitted, was in his handling of the material of others. This weak point in the work, however, is more than offset by the author's brilliant use of his Latin inheritance, the power of vivid presentment which is displayed to the full in the delineation of the Spanish King, the weak point in other more comprehensive histories.

In 1863, impelled by the prescience, or the apprehension of a non-combatant, he in default of other means of publication, read to an assembly of neighboring farmers, the plan of an address to the Confederate Congress, in which he urged the arming of the slaves and the making of a treaty with France and England, based upon the recognition of the Confederacy in stipulation of a gradual emancipation of the slaves. The address, which is mentioned more for its biographical, than its political interest, was eventually published a year later in the *Mobile Advertiser.*

In 1865, after passing through a war and a revolution such such as many historians have described but few are called upon to suffer, Gayarré penned the last records in the supplemental chapter of this last volume. When he comes to the adoption in

1861 of the ordinance of secession by the State, he can not restrain this cry from his heart:

"Louisiana was then in as high a state of prosperity as any land was blessed with, but with sublime imprudence she did not hesitate to stake the whole of it on the cast of a die, at what she conceived to be the call of honor and duty. Four years have now elapsed; she is now the seat of desolation. Another pen than mine will relate her sufferings, her sacrifices, her heroism in battle, her fortitude and resignation in defeat and humiliation, after prodigies of resistance against overwhelming numbers on land and water. Farewell, O sainted and martyred mother. My task as historian is done, but my love, as thy son, shall cling to thee in poverty and sorrow, and nestle in thy scarred bosom with more rapturous constancy than when thy face was beaming with joy and hope, when wealth was thy handmaid, and the eye of God not averted in anger from that noble brow where once rested the pride of sovereignty."

Although he survived this moment of despair thirty years, he never passed beyond the shadow of its doom. He belonged in truth to that class of the conquered who were to meet the keenest edge of the consequences of the war of secession, those who were confronted with financial ruin past the middle of their age. The courage with which he, and others like him, set about to meet these consequences, and their confidence in the ultimate reward of a living from their hard work, is even more pathetic, in the eyes of another generation, than the sight of the failures and disappointments that awaited them, when, baffled at every turn by the ruthless competition of new conditions, faith, industry, honor and integrity became to them as the rosy illusions of youth.

Returning, however, at once to New Orleans, upon the proclamation of peace, resolute to assume the penalty incurred by the ordeal of arms, he, with countless others, was met by the insuperable barrier of the test oath, in the way of their making a living. "If no oath, no daily bread," he says, was the motto of the National Government. In obedience to a general request, he delivered in 1866 before an assembly, anxious and large, like the one which listened to him four years before on the right of secession, a lecture on "Oaths, Rebellion, and Amnesties." In its printed form, a small pamphlet, it can be read to-day; and by the best of all light—sure knowledge—the historical, the religious, the humanitarian argument or rather pleading that he put forth to the conquering power, can be pronounced, at least now, irrefutable. His convictions, or perhaps illusions, in regard to the great ideal of honest reconciliation that should prevail at such a momentous moment in history, as well as his literary reputation at the North, led to his selection by the Union Democratic party of Louisiana as one of the delegates to the National Philadelphia Convention, held in 1866 to harmonize conflicting views and interests and bring about the reorganization of the Democratic party. The holding of the convention and its failure of purpose have, like the arguments on Oaths, Rebellion and Amnesties, gained historical importance in the lapse of time.

To be mentioned in the same connection, is an interview which he obtained, during the same year, from Secretary Seward, committed at once to writing, and published several years later. It is important as an historical document, and it is not the least curious one relating to the period of the Reconstruction.

The "American Domination" and "Philip II." were published simultaneously in 1866. The latter contains an introductory open letter from Bancroft, an intimate friend of Gayarré's, to the publishers, with so evident a propitiatory intention couched in such deprecatory terms that one can hardly forbear pointing to it as an ominous sign of the times. It is hardly a surprise that the volumes that appeared so inopportunely, did not receive the public recognition they deserved.

"Fernando de Lemos" was published in 1872. Had the author never written anything else, this book alone would have placed Louisianians under inestimable obligations to him, for to the souvenirs of his life in Paris already mentioned he added the far more precious ones of his childhood, youth and manhood in New Orleans, giving, as has been said, the only gallery of the men of that time that we have.

In 1875, he was appointed by the Judges of the Supreme Court, Reporter of their decisions. This seemed at the time a blessed intervention, an opportunity for him. Looking back upon it, through the corrective lens of years, the opportunity is seen aright as all in favor of the State; and futile resentment must ever be felt by the chronicler who is called upon to transmit the record, that when, by some political exigency of the hour, the Supreme Court was superseded, the historian whose reports were a model of their kind was also superseded by one who was considered a more valuable political asset of the party in power; and the record may as well be inserted here, for the sake of history, that whatever services Gayarré might have rendered his State, in exchange for what Goldsmith calls the best encouragement for genius, subsistence and respect, there was, henceforth, always a man younger and of more practical use in politics, preferred before him. And history demands also that the fact be not omitted, that, twice an applicant for an insignificant position, in the gift of the President of the United States, by two different Presidents, negroes were preferred to him.

It is hardly necessary to add more at the present time, which is as yet but the morrow of a painful yesterday. The memory of it is still fresh and sensitive. Some day perhaps the suffering in it will be forgotten in the spiritual gain that comes to one generation from the example of ill fortune nobly borne in another.

The pen, at best of times a frail support, became perforce Gayarré's staff of life in the worst of all times for such work as he was qualified to give. He had inherited, however, from his past days of fortune at least a well known name and reputation. These stood him in good stead with the publishing world. In 1877, he was requested by the editor of the *North American Review* to write upon "The Southern Question," then in its most acute stage in National affairs, as one who could and would treat it, not from a sectional or partisan, but broadly historical point of view. He accomplished his difficult task with remarkable dignity and skill. Whatever may have been its enlightening influence at the time, his exposition of the situation must serve to assist the judgment of the historian of the future.

The Historical Society was again revived by Gayarré at this time. But beyond securing incorporation at the hands of the Legislature, it, to his bitter disappointment, showed little signs of life and none of active usefulness.

"Aubert Dubayet, or the Two Sister Republics," was published in 1882. As name and sub-title imply, it is an historical romance connecting the American and French Revolutions by means of one of Louisiana's favorite heroes, General Aubert Dubayet, of the French Republican army, and Minister of War under the Directory. Like "Fernando de Lemos," it is a landmark of the past of Louisiana, and its value, therefore, one that time increases.

This last book was followed by a period of stringent necessity, and therefore, of the most incessant activity of the author's life, although he was now entering its eighth decade. The ever ready market of the newspaper and magazine was a continual incentive to his energy, and for several years he was a steady contributor to it of such wares as he could furnish, mainly historical articles concerning the early history of New Orleans and Louisiana. The most noted of these are:

"A historical Sketch of the Two Lafittes."

"Historical Sketch of Washington's Surrender at Fort Necessity to Francois Coulon, a French knight of St. Louis, whose descendants are numerous in Louisiana."

"Seward on Reconstruction of the Southern States."
"A Louisiana Sugar Plantation of the old Régime."
"The New Orleans Bench and Bar."
"An Old Street in New Orleans."
"The Normans on the Banks of the Mississippi."
"Don Carlos and Isabelle de Valois."
"The Creoles of History and the Creoles of Romance."

And many long and valuable series of articles in the *Times-Democrat* of New Orleans and other local jounrnals.

As there was no public instruction at that time in City or State upon Louisiana history, and as the ignorance of the youth of the State in its history was becoming of serious import, in face of the misconceptions of a partisan public press and certain malevolences of fiction, Gayarré was solicited by a circle of patriotic ladies and gentlemen to give lectures upon Louisiana history. This he did for three consecutive winters; and once again, as he had done nearly forty years before, he revived not only the study of the history of Louisiana, but the actual love of it.

His record of work, which had lasted sixty-four years, drew to a close only a year before his life ended. But his activity never ceased. Demands upon his time and his courtesy were still met as of old, generously. Information was given, as it had always been, freely to all without discrimination, in spite of great abuses of such kindness in the past. A large correspondence was faithfully attended to, visiting strangers were received with unfailing cordiality. Books, letters, manuscript, were placed at the disposition of any student that needed them. His memory never grew dim, for it was kept polished by incessant use. He was to the end, always the last resource and authority of dispute over questions of Louisiana history. His circle of friends grew smaller, as he lived on, outliving them. But the devotion of those that remained increased only the more. He passed away quietly, painlessly, his hand clasping the hand of his wife, to whom he had been united in a long and happy marriage.

GRACE KING.

February, 1903.

CONTRIBUTIONS TO THE BIBLIOGRAPHY OF GAYARRE'S HISTORY OF LOUISIANA.

BY WM. BEER.

1. Essai Historique sur la Louisiane, 2 v., 12 mo., N. O., B. Levy, 1830. (1) pp., iv. 210; (2) 231 vi. Covers period 1513-1815.
2. Historie de la Louisiane, 2 v., 8 vo., N. O., Magne & Weisse, 1846-7. (1) XI., 376; (2) vii. 247, 2d vol. has for appendix O'Reilly's ordinances. (Publishers price, $5.00.)
3. The Poetry or the Romance of the History of Louisiana, 12 mo., N. Y., Appleton, 1848, pp. 265; publisher's price $0.75, later $1.00.
4. Louisiana, its Colonial History and Romance, 8 vo., pp. 546, N. Y., Harper 1851, copyright Harper Bros. 1850, consists of two series of lectures, some or all of which were delivered at the People's Lyceum of New Orleans.
   The five lectures of the first series are the same as in No. 3, the second series has a separate title; Louisiana, Its History as a French Colony, and consists of 7 lectures, ending at 1743. Original price $2.00.
5. Louisiana, Its History as a French Colony, third series of lectures, 8 vo., pp. 380. New York, Wiley 1852, copyright, C. Gayarré, 1852, with Pitman's plan of New Orleans and appendix of documents; covers 1745-1769.
6. History of Louisiana, 3 v., The French Domination, 2 v. in 1, pp, 540, 380, 8 vo., N. Y., Redfield, 1854, copyright 1854, C. Gayarré, contains 3, 4, 5, same plates with changed pagination.
   History of Louisiana, The Spanish Domination, 8 vo., pp. 649, N. Y., Redfield 1854, copyright 1854, C. Gayarré.
   History of Louisiana, The American Domination, 8 vo., pp. 693, N. Y., copyright 1866, C. Gayarré.

7. Another imprint, N. Y., Widdleton, 1866 in 4 vols. from same plates. Original price, $4.00 per volume.
8. History of Louisiana, second edition, 4 v. 8 vo., N. O., Gresham, 1879, (1) 540, (2) 383, (3) 649, xii, 649, (4) 693. Same plates, smaller paper.
9. History of Louisiana, third edition, 4 v., 8 o., N. O. Hawkins 1855. The only difference between this and Nos. 6-7-8, is the addition of the map of Bonne, 1717 to vol. I, the maps of the Delta of the Mississippi from Thomassy to vol. II, the maps of Louisiana, prepared by Lockett to vol. III, and in vol. IV.

Appendices: Vol. I, The Black Code; Vol. II. Vaudreuil's Police Ordinances; Decree of Superior Council, 29 October, 1768; Vol. III. Morales Regulations of Land Grants, Treaty and conventions of Cession of Louisiana to United States.

10. History of Louisiana, fourth edition, 4 v., 8 vo., N. O., 1903, F. F. Hansell & Bro. From same plates, with same pagination as 6-7-8, with addition of life of Gayarre, by Miss Grace King, bibliography by W. Beer, and maps of Louisiana by Kitchen & Lopez.

CONTENTS.

FIRST SERIES.

FIRST LECTURE.

Primitive State of the Country—Expedition of De Soto in 1539—His Death—Discovery of the Mississippi in 1673, by Father Marquette and Joliet—They are followed in 1682 by La Salle and the Chevalier de Tonti—Assassination of La Salle, ... 9

SECOND LECTURE.

Arrival of Iberville and Bienville—Settlement of a French Colony in Louisiana—Sauvolle, first Governor—Events and Characters in Louisiana, or connected with that Colony, from La Salle's Death, in 1687, to 1701, ... 30

THIRD LECTURE.

Situation of the Colony from 1701 to 1712—The Petticoat Insurrection—History and Death of Iberville—Bienville, the second Governor of Louisiana—History of Anthony Crozat, the great Banker—Concession of Louisiana to him, ... 79

FOURTH LECTURE.

Lamothe Cadillac, Governor of Louisiana—Situation of the Colony in 1713—Feud between Cadillac and Bienville—Character of Richebourg—First Expedition against the Natchez—De l'Epinay succeeds Cadillac—The Curate de la Vente—Expedition of St. Denis to Mexico—His Adventures—Jallot, the Surgeon—In 1717 Crozat gives up his Charter—His Death, ... 115

SECOND SERIES.

FIRST LECTURE.

Creation of a Royal Bank and of the Mississippi Company—Effects produced in France by those Institutions—Wild Hopes entertained from the Colonization of Louisiana—Its twofold and opposite Description—History of Law from his Birth to his Death, ... 191

SECOND LECTURE.

Bienville appointed Governor of Louisiana for the second time, in the place of L'Epinay—Foundation of New Orleans—Expedition of St. Denis, Beaulieu, and others to Mexico—Adventures of St. Denis—Land Concessions—Slave-trade—Taking of Pensacola by the French—The Spaniards retake it, and besiege Dauphine Island—Pensacola again taken by the French—Situation of the Country as described by Bienville—The Chevalier des Grieux and Manon Lescaut—Changes in the Organization of the Judiciary—Edict in Relation to Commerce—Adventures of the Princess Charlotte of Brunswick, of Belleisle, and others—Seat of Government transferred to New Orleans—Other Facts and Events from 1718 to 1722; 233

THIRD LECTURE.

Origin, Customs, Manners, Traditions, and Laws of the Natchez—Decline of that Tribe—Number and Power of the Choctaws and Chickasaws, ... 286

FOURTH LECTURE.

Transfer of the Seat of Government to New Orleans—Its Population and Appearance in 1724—Boisbriant, Governor ad interim—Black Code—Expulsion of the Jews—Catholic Religion to be the sole Religion of the Land—Périer appointed Governor—League of all the Officers of Government against De la Chaise, the King's Commis-

CONTENTS.

Page

sary—He triumphs over them all—Republicanism of the Colonies—The Ursuline Nuns and the Jesuits—Public Improvements made or contemplated by Governor Périer—Census in 1727—Expenses of the Colonial Administration—Edict of Henry the Second against Unmarried Women—Other Facts and Events from 1723 to 1727—Traditions on the Music heard at the mouth of Pascagoula River, and on the Date-tree at the corner of Dauphine and Orleans Streets, 353

FIFTH LECTURE.

Arrival of the Casket Girls—Royal Ordinance relative to the Concessions of Lands—Manner of settling the Succession of Frenchmen married to Indian Women—French Husbands—Indian Wives—History of Madame Dubois, an Indian Squaw—Conspiracy of the Natchez against the French—Massacre of the French at Natchez in 1729—Massacre of the French at the Yazoo Settlement in 1730—Attack of the Natchez against the French Settlement at Natchitoches—They are beaten by St. Denis—The French and Choctaws attack the Natchez—Daring and Death of Navarre and of some of his companions—Siege of the Natchez Forts—Flight of the Natchez—Cruel Treatment of Natchez Prisoners by Governor Périer—Desperation of the Natchez—The Chickasaws grant an Asylum to the Natchez—Conspiracy of the Banbara Negroes—List of the Principal Officers in the Colony in 1730, ... 390

SIXTH LECTURE.

Expedition of Périer against the Natchez—He goes up Red River and Black River in pursuit of them—Siege of their Fort—Most of them are taken Prisoners and sold as Slaves—Continuation of the Natchez War—The India Company surrenders its Charter—Ordinances on the Currency of the Country—Bienville reappointed Governor—Situation of the Colony at that time—The Natchez take Refuge among the Chickasaws—Great Rise of the Mississippi and General Inundation—Extraordinary Number of Mad Dogs—Expedition of Bienville against the Chickasaws—He attacks their Villages—Battle of Ackia—Daring Exploit of the black man, Simon—Bienville is beaten and forced to retreat—Expedition of D'Artaguette against the Chickasaws—His Defeat and Death—History of John Philip Grondel—Other Events and Facts from 1729 to 1736, ... 442

SEVENTH LECTURE.

State of Agriculture in 1736—Exemption from Duties on certain Articles of Importation and Exportation—War between the Choctaws and Chickasaws—Singular Judicial Proceeding in 1738—Bienville's Dispatch on the Sand-bars at the Mouth of the Mississippi—De Noailles is sent to Louisiana to command an Expedition against the Chickasaws—Bienville's Jealousy—Intrigues of the Indian, Red Shoe—General Rendezvous of the French at the Mouth of River Margot—Failure of that Expedition—Its probable Causes—Bienville's Apology—Effects of a Hurricane—Situation of the Colony in 1741—Heroism of a French Girl in a Battle against the Indians—Bienville incurs the Displeasure of his Government—He demands the Establishment of a College—That Demand is refused—Bienville is recalled to France—He departs never to return—He is succeeded by the Marquis of Vaudreuil—Other Facts and Events from 1736 to 1743, ... 497

PREFACE.

To write history, is to narrate events, and to show their philosophy, when they are susceptible of any such demonstration. When the subject is worthy of it, this is a kind of composition of the highest order, and which affords to genius an ample scope for the display of all its powers. But the information so conveyed is limited to the few, because not suited to the intelligence of the many. The number of those who have read Tacitus, Hume, Gibbon, or Clarendon, is comparatively small, when opposed to those who have pored with delight over the fascinating pages of Walter Scott. To relate events, and, instead of elucidating and analyzing their philosophy, like the historian, to point out the hidden sources of romance which spring from them—to show what materials they contain for the dramatist, the novelist, the poet, the painter, and for all the varied conceptions of the fine arts—is perhaps an humbler task, but not without its utility. When history is not disfigured by inappropriate invention, but merely embellished and made attractive by being set in a glittering frame, this artful preparation honies the cup of useful knowledge, and makes it acceptable to the lips of the multitude. Through the immortal writings of Walter Scott, many have become familiar with historical events, and have been induced to study more serious works, who, without that tempting bait, would have turned away from what appeared to them to be but a dry and barren field, too unpromising to invite examination, much less cultivation. To the bewitching pen of the wonderful magician of her romantic hills, Scotland owes more for the popular extension of her fame, than to the doings of the united host of all her other writers, warriors, and statesmen.

It was in pursuing such a train of reasoning, that I came to the conclusion that the republication of my "Lectures on the Romance or Poetry of the History of Louisiana" might be a suitable introduction to the history of that colony, which I have subsequently presented to the public in two other series of Lectures, closing with the French domination in Louisiana, when the Spaniards took final possession of that province in 1769. I have attempted to vary my style in accordance with the events I had to narrate, and to adapt it to the legendary, the romantic, the traditional, and the strictly historical elements I had to weave together, and which, I believe, I have kept sufficiently distinct. But when the sobriety or the importance of the subject required it, I have in no instance permitted my imagination to dally with what it was bound to respect. I have not forgotten that the historian is an impartial witness, who voluntarily appears before the tribunal of the world, to testify as to facts which he has investigated and studied for the instruction and benefit of present and future generations, and that he is under the most sacred obligation " to tell the truth, the whole truth, and nothing but the truth." Feeling as I did the high responsibility I had assumed, I must confess that I experienced the greatest gratification when the most competent of judges,* after a careful examination of my labors, relieved my anxiety by writing to me : " You give at once to your State an authentic history such as scarce any other in the Union possesses. I have for many years been making manuscript and other collections, and all the best that I have found appears in your volumes." If this sentiment, which is, I am afraid, the kindly biased appreciation of friendly partiality, be confirmed by the more austere judgment of the public, I need not say, I presume, that my reward has exceeded my expectations.

* Mr. Bancroft.

INTRODUCTION.

THE POETRY,

OR THE

ROMANCE OF THE HISTORY OF LOUISIANA.

FIRST SERIES OF LECTURES.

FIRST LECTURE.

Primitive State of the Country—Expedition of De Soto in 1539—His Death—Discovery of the Mississippi in 1673, by Father Marquette and Joliet—They are followed in 1682 by La Salle and the Chevalier de Tonti—Assassination of La Salle.

Having been invited by a Committee, on behalf of the People's Lyceum, to deliver one of their twelve annual Lectures, I was not long in selecting the subject of my labors. My mind had been lately engaged in the composition of the History of Louisiana, and it was natural that it should again revert to its favorite object of thought, on the same principle which impels the mightiest river to obey the laws of declivity, or which recalls and confines to its channel its gigantic volume of waters, when occasionally deviating from its course.

But in reverting now to the History of Louisiana, my intention is not to review its diversified features with the scrutinizing, unimpassioned, and austere judgment of the historian. Imposing upon myself a more grateful task, because more congenial to my taste, I shall take for the object of this Lecture, The Poetry, or the Romance of the History of Louisiana.

Poetry is the daughter of Imagination, and imagination is, perhaps, one of the highest gifts of Heaven, the most refined ethereal part of the mind, because, when carried to perfection, it is the combined essence of all the finest faculties of the human intellect. There may be sound judgment, acute perceptions, depth of thought, great powers of conception, of discrimination, of research, of assimilation, of combination of ideas, without imagination, or at least without that part of it which elaborates and exalts itself into poetry; but how can we conceive the existence of a poetical imagination in its highest excellence, without all the other faculties? Without them, what imagination would not be imperfect or diseased? It is true that without imagination there may be a world within the mind, but it is a world without light. Cold it remains, and suffering from the effects of partial organization, unless by some mighty fiat imagination is breathed into the dormant mass, and the sun of poetry, emerging in the heaven of the mind, illumines and warms the several elements of which it is composed, and completes the creation of the intellect.

Hence the idea of all that is beautiful and great is concentrated in the word poetry. There is no grand conception of the mind in which that intellectual faculty which constitutes poetry is not to be detected. What is great and noble, is and must be poetical, and what is poetical must partake, in some degree or other, of what is great and noble. It is hardly possible to conceive an Alexander, a Cæsar, a Napoleon, a Newton, a Lycurgus, a Mahomet, a Michael Angelo, a Canova, or any other of those wonderful men who have carried as far as they could go, the powers of the human mind in the several departments in which they were used, without supposing them gifted with some of those faculties of the imagination which enter into the composition of a poetical organization. Thus every art and almost every science has its poetry, and it is from the unanimous consent of mankind on this subject that it has become so common to say "the poetry" of music, of sculpture, of architecture, of dancing, of painting of history, and even the poetry of religion, meaning that which is most pleasing to the eye or to the mind, and ennobling to the soul. We may therefore infer from the general feeling to which I have alluded, that where the spirit of poetry does not exist, there can not be true greatness; and it can, I believe, be safely averred, that to try the gold of all human actions and events, of all things and matters, the touchstone of poetry is one of the surest.

I am willing to apply that criterion to Louisiana, considered both physically and historically; I am willing that my native State, which is but a fragment of what Louisiana formerly was, should stand or fall by that test, and I do not fear to approach with her the seat of judgment. I am prepared to show that her history is full of poetry of the highest order and of the most varied nature. I have studied the subject *con amore*, and with such reverential enthusiasm, and I may say with such filial piety, that it has grown upon my heart as well as upon my mind. May I be able to do justice to its merits, and to raise within you a corresponding interest to that which I feel! To support the assertion that the history of Louisiana is eminently poetical, it will be sufficient to give you short graphical descriptions of those interesting events which constitute her annals. Bright gems they are, encircling her brows, diadem-like, and worthy of that star which has sprung from her forehead to enrich the American constellation in the firmament of liberty.

Three centuries have hardly elapsed, since that immense territory which extends from the Gulf of Mexico to the Lakes of Canada, and which was subsequently known under the name of Louisiana, was slumbering in its cradle of wilderness, unknown to any of the white race to which we belong. Man was there, however, but man in his primitive state, claiming as it were, in appearance at least, a different origin from ours, or being at best a variety of our species. There, was the hereditary domain of the red man, living in scattered tribes over that magnificent country. Those tribes earned their precarious subsistence chiefly by pursuing the inhabitants of the earth and of the water; they sheltered themselves in miserable huts, spoke different languages, observed contradictory customs, and waged fierce war upon each other. Whence they came none knew; none knows, with absolute certainty, to the present day; and the faint glimmerings of vague traditions have afforded little or no light to penetrate into the darkness of their mysterious origin. Thus a wide field is left open to those dreamy speculations of which the imagination is so fond.

Whence came the Natchez, those worshipers of the sun with eastern rites? How is it that Grecian figures and letters are represented on the earthen wares of some of those Indian nations? Is there any truth in the supposition that some of those savages whose complexion approximates most to ours, draw their blood from that Welsh colony which is said to have found a home in America, many centuries since? Is it possible that Phœnician adventurers were the pilgrim fathers of some of the aborigines of Louisiana? What copper-colored swarm first issued from Asia, the revered womb of mankind, to wend its untraced way to the untenanted continent of America? What fanciful tales could be weaved on the powerful Choctaws, or the undaunted

Chickasaws, or the unconquerable Mobilians? There the imagination may riot in the poetry of mysterious migrations, of human transformations; in the poetry of the forests, of the valleys, of the mountains, of the lakes and rivers, as they came fresh and glorious from the hand of the Creator, in the poetry of barbaric manners, laws, and wars. What heroic poems might not a future Ossian devise on the red monarchs of old Louisiana! Would not their strange history, in the hands of a Tacitus, be as interesting as that of the ancient barbarian tribes of Germany, described by his immortal pen? Is there in that period of their existence which precedes their acquaintance with the sons of Europe, nothing which, when placed in contrast with their future fate, appeals to the imagination of the moralist, of the philosopher, and of the divine? Who, without feeling his whole soul glowing with poetical emotions, could sit under yonder gigantic oak, the growth of a thousand years, on the top of that hill of shells, the sepulcher of man, piled up by his hands, and overlooking that placid lake where all would be repose, if it were not for that solitary canoe, a moving speck, hardly visible in the distance, did it not happen to be set in bold relief, by being on that very line where the lake meets the horizon, blazing with the last glories of the departing sun? Is not this the very poetry of landscape, of Louisianian landscape?

When diving into the mysteries of the creation of that part of the south-western world which was once comprehended in the limits of Louisiana, will not the geologist himself pause, absorbed in astonishment at the number of centuries which must have been necessary to form the delta of the Mississippi? When he discovers successive strata of forests lying many fathoms deep on the top of each other; when he witnesses the exhumation of the fossil bones of mammoths, elephants, or huge animals of the antediluvian race; when he reads the hieroglyphic records of Nature's wonderful doings, left by herself on the very rocks, or other granite and calcareous tablets of this country, will he not clasp his hands in ecstasy, and exclaim, "Oh! the dryness of my study has fled; there is poetry in the very foundation of this extraordinary land!"

Thus I think that I have shown that the spirit of poetry was moving over the face of Louisiana, even in her primitive state, and still pervades her natural history. But I have dwelt enough on Louisiana in the dark ages of her existence, of which we can know nothing, save by vague traditions of the Indians. Let us approach those times where her historical records begin to assume some distinct shape.

On the 31st of May, 1539, the bay of Santo Spiritu, in Florida, presented a curious spectacle. Eleven vessels of quaint shape, bearing the broad banner of Spain, were moored close to the shore; one thousand men of infantry, and three hundred and fifty men of cavalry, fully equipped, were landing in proud array under the command of Hernando De Soto, one of the most illustrious companions of Pizarro in the conquest of Peru, and reputed one of the best lances of Spain! "When he led in the van of battle, so powerful was his charge," says the old chronicler of his exploits, "so broad was the bloody passage which he carved out in the ranks of the enemy, that ten of his men-at-arms could with ease follow him abreast." He had acquired enormous wealth in Peru, and might have rested satisfied, a knight of renown, in the government of St. Jago de Cuba, in the sweet enjoyment of youth and of power, basking in the smiles of his beautiful wife, Isabella de Bobadilla. But his adventurous mind scorns such inglorious repose, and now he stands erect and full of visions bright, on the sandy shore of Florida, whither he comes, with feudal pride, by leave of the king, to establish nothing less than a marquisate, ninety miles long by forty-five miles wide, and there to rule supreme, a governor for life, of all the territory that he can subjugate. Not unmindful he, the Christian knight, the hater and conqueror of Moorish infidelity, of the souls of his future vassals; for, twenty-two ecclesiastics accompany him to preach the word of God. Among his followers are gentlemen of the best blood of Spain and of Portugal: Don Juan de Guzman; Pedro Calderon, who, by his combined skill and bravery, had won the praises of Gonzalvo de Cordova, yclept "the great captain;" Vasconcellos de Silva, of Portugal, who for birth and courage knew no superior; Nuno Tobar, a knight above fear and reproach; and Muscoso de Alvarado, whom that small host of heroes ranked in their estimation next to De Soto himself. But I stop an enumeration which, if I did justice to all, would be too long.

What materials for romance! Here is chivalry, with all its glittering pomp, its soul-stirring aspirations, in full march, with its iron heels and gilded spurs, toward the unknown and hitherto unexplored soil of Louisiana. In sooth, it must have been a splendid sight! Let us look at the glorious pageantry as it sweeps by, through the long vistas of those pine woods! How nobly they bear themselves, those bronzed sons of Spain, clad in refulgent armor! How brave that music sounds! How fleet they move, those Andalusian chargers, with arched necks and dilated nostrils! But the whole train suddenly halts in that verdant valley, by that bubbling stream, shaded by those venerable oaks with gray moss hanging from their branches in imitation of the whitening beard of age. Does not the whole encampment rise distinct upon your minds?

The tents with gay pennons, with armorial bearings; the proud steed whose impatient foot spurns the ground; those men stretched on the velvet grass and recruiting their wearied strength by sleep; some singing old Castilian or Moorish roundelays; others musing on the sweet rulers of their souls, left in their distant home; a few kneeling before the officiating priest, at the altar which a moment sufficed for their pious ardor to erect, under yonder secluded bower; some burnishing their arms, others engaged in mimic warfare and trials of skill or strength; De Soto sitting apart with his peers in rank if not in command, and intent upon developing to them his plans of conquest, while the dusky faces of some Indian boys and women in the background express wild astonishment. None of the warriors of that race are to be seen; they are reported to be absent on a distant hunting excursion. But, methinks that at times I spy through the neighboring thickets the fierce glance of more than one eye, sparkling with the suppressed fury of anticipated revenge. What a scene! and would it not afford delight to the poet's imagination or to the painter's eye?

In two ponderous volumes, the historian Garcillasso relates the thousand incidents of that romantic expedition. What more interesting than the reception of Soto at the court of the Princess Cofachiqui, the Dido of the wilderness! What battles, what victories over men, over the elements themselves, and over the endless obstacles thrown out by rebellious nature! What incredible physical difficulties overcome by the advancing host! How heroic is the resistance of the Mobilians and of the Alabamas! With what headlong fury those denizens of the forest rush upon the iron-clad warriors, and dare the thunders of those whom they take to be the children of the sun! How splendidly described is the siege of Mobile, where women fought like men, and wrapped themselves up in the flames of their destroyed city rather than surrender to their invaders!

But let the conquering hero beware! Now he is encamped on the territory of the Chickasaws, the most ferocious of the Indian tribes. And lucky was it that Soto was as prudent as he was brave, and slept equally prepared for the defence and for the attack. Hark! in the dead of a winter's night, when the cold wind of the north, in the month of January, 1541, was howling through the leafless trees, a simultaneous howl was heard, more hideous far than the voice of the tempest. The Indians rush impetuous, with firebrands, and the thatched roofs which sheltered the Spaniards are soon on fire, threatening them with immediate destruction. The horses rearing and plunging in wild affright, and breaking loose from their ligaments; the undaunted Spaniards, half naked, struggling against the devouring element and the unsparing foe; the desperate deeds of valor executed by Soto and his companions; the deep-toned shouts of St. Jago and Spain to the rescue; the demon-like shrieks of the red warriors; the final overthrow of the Indians; the hot pursuit by the light of the flaming village;—form a picture highly exciting to the imagination, and cold indeed must he be who does not take delight in the strange contrast of the heroic warfare of chivalry on one side, and of the untutored courage of man in his savage state, on the other.

It would be too long to follow Soto in his peregrinations during two years, through part of Alabama, Mississippi, and Tennessee. At last he stands on the banks of the Mississippi, near the spot where now flourishes the Egyptian-named city of Memphis. He crosses the mighty river, and onward he goes, up to the White River, while roaming over the territory of the Arkansas. Meeting with alternate hospitality and hostility on the part of the Indians, he arrives at the mouth of the Red River, within the present limits of the State of Louisiana. There he was fated to close his adventurous career.

Three years of intense bodily fatigue and mental excitement had undermined the hero's constitution. Alas! well might the spirit droop within him! He had landed on the shore of the North American continent with high hopes, dreaming of conquest over wealthy nations and magnificent cities. What had he met? Interminable forests, endless lagoons, inextricable marshes, sharp and continual conflicts with men little superior, in his estimation, to the brutish creation. He who in Spain was cheered by beauty's glance, by the songs of the minstrel, when he sped to the contest with adversaries worthy of his prowess, with the noble and chivalric Moors; he who had reveled in the halls of the imperial Incas of Peru, and who there had amassed princely wealth; he, the flower of knightly courts, had been roaming like a vagrant over an immense territory, where he had discovered none but half-naked savages, dwelling in miserable huts, ignobly repulsive when compared with Castile's stately domes, with Granada's fantastic palaces, and with Peru's imperial dwellings, massive with gold! His wealth was gone, two thirds of his brave companions were dead. What account of them would he render to their noble families! He, the bankrupt in fame and in fortune, how would he withstand the gibes of envy! Thought, that scourge of life, that inward consumer of man, racks his brain, his heart is seared with deep anguish; a slow fever wastes his powerful frame, and he sinks at last on the couch of sickness, never to rise again. The Spaniards cluster round him, and alternately look with despair at their dying chieftain, and at the ominous hue of the bloody river, known at this day under the name of the Red River. But not he the man to allow the wild havoc within the soul to betray itself in the outward mien; not he, in common with the vulgar herd, the man to utter one word of wail! With smiling lips and serene brow he cheers his companions and summons them, one by one, to swear allegiance in his hands to Muscoso de Alvarado, whom he designates as his successor. "Union and perseverance, my friends," he says; "so long as the breath of life animates your bodies, do not falter in the enterprise you have undertaken. Spain expects a richer harvest of glory and more ample domains from her children." These are his last words, and then he dies. Blest be the soul of the noble knight and of the true Christian! Rest his mortal remains in peace within that oaken trunk scooped by his companions, and by them sunk many fathoms deep in the bed of the Mississippi!

The Spaniards, at first, had tried to conceal the death of Soto from the Indians, because they felt that there was protection in the belief of his existence. What mockery it was to their grief, to simulate joy on the very tomb of their beloved chief, whom they had buried in their camp before seeking for him a safer place of repose! But when, the slaves of hard necessity, they were, with heavy hearts but smiling faces, coursing in tournament over the burial-ground, and profaning the consecrated spot, the more effectually to mislead the conjectures of the Indians, they saw that their subterfuge was vain, and that the red men, with significant glances, were pointing to each other the precise spot where the great white warrior slept. How dolorously does Garcillasso describe the exhumation and the plunging of the body into the turbid stream of the Great Father of Rivers!

Then comes an Odyssey of woes. The attempt of the Spaniards to go by land to Mexico; their wandering as far as the Rio Grande and the mountainous region which lies between Mexico and Texas, and which was destined, in after years, to be so famous in American history; their return to the mouth of Red River; their building of vessels capable of navigating at sea; the tender compassion and affectionate assistance of the good Cazique Anilco; the league of the other Indian princes, far and wide, under the auspices of the great king, Quigualtanqui, the Agamemnon of the confederacy; the discovery of the plot; the retreat of all the Indian chiefs save the indomitable Quigualtanqui; the fleet of one thousand canoes, mounted by twenty thousand men, with which he pursued the weary and despairing Spaniards for seventeen long days, assailing them with incessant fury; the giving up of the chase only when the sea was nearly in sight; the fierce parting words of the Indians to the Spaniards: "Tell your countrymen that you have been pursued by Quigualtanqui alone; if he had been better assisted by his peers, none of you would have survived to tell the tale;" the solemn rites with which, in their thousand canoes riveted on the water, they, on the day they ceased their pursuit, adored the rising sun and saluted him with their thanksgivings for the expulsion of the invaders; the hair-breadth escapes of the three hundred Spaniards who alone out of the bright host of their former companions had succeeded in fleeing from the hostile shore of Louisiana; their toils during a navigation of ninety days to the port of Panuco, where they at last arrived in a state of utter destitution, are all thrilling incidents connected with the history of Louisiana, and replete with the very essence of poetry.

When Alvarado, the Ulysses of that expedition, related his adventures in the halls of Montezuma, Don Francisco de Mendoza, the son of the viceroy, broke out with passionate admiration of the conduct of Quigualtanqui: "A noble barbarian," exclaimed he, "an honest man and a true patriot." This remark, worthy of the high lineage and of the ancestral fame of him who spoke it, is a just tribute to the Louisianian chief, and is an apt epilogue to the recital of those romantic achievements, the nature of which is such, that the poet's pen would be more at ease with it than that of the historian.

One hundred and thirty years had passed away since the apparition of Soto on the soil of Louisiana, without any further attempt of the white race to penetrate into that fair region, when on the 7th of July, 1673, a small band of Europeans and Canadians reached the Mississippi, which they had come to seek from the distant city of Quebec. That band had two leaders, Father Marquette, a monk, and Joliet, a merchant, the prototypes of two great sources of power, religion and commerce, which, in the course of time, were destined to exercise such influence on the civilization of the western territory, traversed by the mighty river which they had discovered. They could not be ordinary men those adventurers, who in those days undertook to expose themselves to the fatigues and perils of a journey through unknown solitudes, from the St Lawrence to the Mississippi! That humble monkish gown of Father Marquette concealed a hero's heart, and in the merchant's breast there dwelt a soul that would have disgraced no belted knight.

Whether it was owing to the peaceful garb in which they had presented themselves, or to some other cause, the Indians hardly showed any of that hostility which they had exhibited toward the armed invasion of Spain. Joliet and Father Marquette floated down the river without much impediment, as far as the Arkansas. There, having received sufficient evidence that the Mississippi discharged itself into the Gulf of Mexico, they retraced their way back and returned to Canada. But in that frail bark drifting down the current of the Mississippi, and in which sat the hard plodding merchant, with the deep wrinkles of thought and forecast on his brow, planning schemes of trade with unknown nations, and surveying with curious eye that boundless territory which seemed, as he went along, to stretch in commensurate proportion with the infiniteness of space; in that frail bark, I say, where mused over his breviary that gray-headed monk, leaning on that long staff, surmounted with the silver cross of Christ, and computing the souls that he had saved and still hoped to save from idolatry, is there not as much poetry as in the famed vessel of Argos, sailing in quest of the golden fleece? Were not their hearts as brave as those of the Greek adventurers? were not their dangers as great? and was not the object which they had in view much superior?

The grandeur of their enterprise was, even at that time, fully appreciated. On their return to Quebec, and on their giving information that they had discovered that mighty river of which the Europeans had but a vague knowledge conveyed to them by the Indians, and which, from the accounts given of its width and length, was considered to be one of the greatest wonders of the world, universal admiration was expressed; the bells of the Cathedral tolled merrily for a whole day, and the bishop, followed by his clergy and the whole population, sang a solemn Te Deum at the foot of the altar. Thus, on the first acquaintance of our European fathers with the great valley of the Mississippi, of which our present State of Louisiana is the heart, there was an instinct that told them it was *there* that the seeds of empire and greatness were sown. Were they not right in those divinations which pushed them onward to that favored spot through so many obstacles? Greatness and empire were *there*, and therefore all the future elements of poetry.

Joliet and Marquette were dead, and nothing yet had been done to take possession of the newly discovered regions of the West; but the impetus was given; the march of civilization once begun could not retrograde; that mighty traveler, with religion for his guide, was pushed onward by the hand of God; and the same spirit which had driven the crusaders to Asia, now turned the attention of Europe to the continent of America. The spell which had concealed the Mississippi amid hitherto impenetrable forests, and, as it were, an ocean of trees, was broken; and the Indians, who claimed its banks as their hereditary domain, were now fated to witness the rapid succession of irresistible intruders.

Seven years since the expedition of Marquette and Joliet had rolled by, when Robert Cavalier de La Salle, in the month of January, 1682, feasted his eyes with the sight of the far-famed Mississippi. For his companions he had forty soldiers, three monks, and the Chevalier de Tonti. He had received the education of a Jesuit, and had been destined to the cloister, and to become a tutor of children in a seminary of that celebrated order of which he was to become a member. But he had that will, and those passions, and that intellect which can not be forced into a contracted channel of action. Born poor and a plebeian, he wished to be both noble and rich; obscure, he longed to be famous. Why not? Man shapes his own destinies when the fortitude of the soul corresponds with the vigorous organization of the mind. When the heart dares prompt the execution of what genius conceives, nothing remains but to choose the field of success. That choice was soon made by La Salle. America was then exercising magnetic attraction upon all bold spirits, and did not fail to have the same influence on his own. Obeying the impulse of his ambition, he crossed the Atlantic without hesitation, and landed in Canada in 1673.

When on the continent of America, that fond object of his dreams, La Salle felt that he was in a congenial atmosphere with his temperament. His mind seemed to expand, his conceptions to become more vivid, his natural eloquence to be gifted with more persuasion, and he was acknowledged at once by all who saw and heard him, to be a superior being. Brought into contact with Count Frontenac, who was the governor of Canada, he communicated to him his views and projects for the aggrandizement of France, and suggested to him the gigantic plan of connecting the St. Lawrence with the Mississippi by an uninterrupted chain of forts. "From the information which I have been able to collect," said he to the Count, "I think I may affirm that the Mississippi draws its source somewhere in the vicinity of the Celestial Empire, and that France will be not only the mistress of all the territory between the St. Lawrence and the Mississippi, but will command the trade of China, flowing down the new and mighty channel which I shall open to the Gulf of Mexico." Count Frontenac was seduced by the magnificence of the prospect sketched by the enthusiast, but not daring to incur the expenses which such an undertaking would have required, referred him to the court of France.

To France, then, the adventurer returns with increased confidence; for he had secured one thing, he had gained one point; introduction to the noble and to the wealthy under the auspices of Count Frontenac. The spirit of Columbus was in him, and nothing abashed he would have forced his way to the foot of the throne and appealed to Majesty itself, with that assurance which genius imparts. But sufficient was it for him to gain the good graces of one of the royal blood of France, the Prince de Conti. He fired the prince's mind with his own contagious enthusiasm, and through him obtained from the king not only an immense concession of land, but was clothed with all the powers and privileges which he required for trading with the Indians, and for carrying on his meditated plans of discovery. Nay, more, he was ennobled by letters-patent, and thus one of the most ardent wishes of his heart was gratified. At last, he was no longer a plebeian, and with Macbeth he could exclaim, "Now, thane of Cawdor, the greatest is behind."

La Salle re-crossed the Atlantic with one worthy of being his *fidus Achates*, and capable of understanding the workings of his mind and of his heart. That man was the Chevalier De Tonti, who, as an officer, had served with distinction in many a war, and who afterward became famous among the Indians for the iron hand with which he had artificially supplied the one which he had lost.

On the 15th of September, 1678, proud and erect with the consciousness of success, La Salle stood again in the walls of Quebec; and stimulated by the cheers of the whole population, he immediately entered into the execution of his projects. Four years after, in

1682, he was at the mouth of the Mississippi, and in the name (as appears by a notarial act still extant) of the *most puissant, most high, most invincible and victorious Prince*, Louis the Great, King of France, took possession of all the country which he had discovered. How his heart must have swelled with exultation, when he stood at the mouth of the great river on which all his hopes had centered; when he unfurled the white banner and erected the stately column to which he appended the royal escutcheon of France, amid the shouts of his companions and the discharge of fire-arms! With what devotion he must have joined in the solemn *Te Deum* sung on that memorable occasion!

To relate all the heart-thrilling adventures which occurred to La Salle during the four years which elapsed between the opening and the conclusion of that expedition, would be to go beyond the limits which are allotted to me. Suffice it to say, that at this day to overcome the one-hundredth part of the difficulties which he had to encounter, would immortalize a man. If it be true that man is never greater than when engaged in a generous and unyielding struggle against dangers and adversity, then must it be admitted that during those four years of trials La Salle was pre-eminently great. Was he not worthy of admiration, when to the camp of the Iroquois, who at first had received him like friends, but had been converted into foes, he dared to go alone, to meet the charges brought against him by the subtle Mansolia, whose words were so persuasive, and whose wisdom appeared so wonderful, that it was attributed to his holding intercourse with spirits of another world? How interesting the spectacle! How vividly it pictures itself to my mind! How it would grace the pages of a Fenimore Cooper, or of one having the magic pen of a Walter Scott! Methinks I see that areopagus of stern old Indian warriors listening with knit brows and compressed lips to the passionate accusation so skillfully urged against La Salle, and to the prediction that amity to the white race was the sure forerunner of destruction to all the Indian tribes. La Salle rose in his turn; how eloquent, how pathetic he was when appealing to the better feelings of the Indians, and how deserving of the verdict rendered in his favor!

The enmity, the ambushes of Indians were not to him the only sources of danger. *These* he could have stood unmoved! But what must have been his feelings when he became conscious of the poison which had been administered to him by some of his companions, who thought that, by destroying him, they would spare to themselves the anticipated horrors of an expedition which they no longer had the courage to prosecute! What his despair was, is attested by the name of "*Crève Cœur*," which he gave to a fort he built a short time after—the fort of the "Broken Heart!" But let us turn from his miseries to the more grateful spectacle of his ovation.

In 1684 he returned to France, and found himself famous. He, the poor boy, the ignoble by birth, for whom paternal tenderness had dreamed nothing higher than the honor of being a teacher in a seminary of Jesuits, was presented to Louis XIV. amid all the splendors of his court! That Jupiter among the kings of the earth had a smile to bestow upon the humble subject who came to deposit at the foot of the throne the title-deeds of such broad domains. But that smile of royalty was destined to be the last smile of fortune. The favors which he then obtained bred nothing but reverses. Every thing, however, wore a bright aspect, and the star of his destiny appeared to be culminating in the heavens.

Thus a fleet, composed of four vessels, was put at his disposal, with all the materials necessary to establish a colony, and once more he left the shores of his native country, but this time invested with high command, and hoping perhaps to be the founder of an empire. This, indeed, was something worth having struggled for! But alas! he had struggled in vain; the meshes of adverse fate were drawing close around him. *Here* is not the place to relate his misunderstandings, degenerating into bitter quarrels with the proud Beaujeu, who had the subordinate command of the fleet, and who thought himself dishonored—he, the old captain of thirty years' standing, he, the nobleman—by being placed under the control of the unprofessional, of the plebeian, of him whom he called a pedagogue, fit only to rule over children. The result of that conflict was, that La Salle found himself abandoned on the shores of the Bay of St. Bernard, in 1685, and was reduced to shift for himself, with very limited resources. Here follows a period of three other years of great sufferings and of bold and incessant wanderings through the territory of the present State of Texas, where, after a long series of adventures, he was basely murdered by his French companions, and revenged by his body-servant, an Englishman by birth. He died somewhere about the spot where now stands the town of Washington, which owes its foundation to some of that race to which belonged his avenger, and the star-spangled banner now proudly waves where the first pioneer of civilization consecrated with his blood the future land of liberty.

The rapid sketch which I have given shows, that so much of La Salle's life as belongs to history occupies a space of fifteen years, and is so full of incidents as to afford materials enough for the production of a voluminous and interesting book. But I think I may safely close my observations with the remark, that he who will write the life of that extraordinary man, however austere his turn of mind may be, will hardly be able to prevent the golden hues of poetry from overspreading the pages which he may pen, where history is so much like romance that, in many respects, it is likely to be classed as such by posterity.

Here I must close this historical sketch; here I must stop, on the threshold of the edifice through which I should like to wander with you, in order to call your attention not only to the general splendor, but to the minute perfection of its architecture. Perhaps, at a future period, if your desire should keep pace with my inclination, I may resume the subject; and I believe it will then be easy for me to complete the demonstration that our annals constitute a rich mine, where lies in profusion the purest ore of poetry, not to be found in broken and scattered fragments, but forming an uninterrupted vein through the whole history of Louisiana, in all its varied phases, from the primitive settlement made at Biloxi to the present time, when she wears the diadem of sovereignty, and when, with her blood and treasure, and with a spirit of chivalry worthy of her Spanish and French descent, and of her Anglo-Saxon adoption, she was the first to engage in the support of that war which, so glorious in its beginning at Palo Alto, Resaca de la Palma, Monterey, and Buena Vista, will undoubtedly have an equally glorious, and I think I may add, a poetical termination in the walls of Mexico!

SECOND LECTURE.

Arrival of Iberville and Bienville—Settlement of a French Colony in Louisiana—Sauvolle, first Governor—Events and Characters in Louisiana, or connected with that Colony, from La Salle's Death, in 1687, to 1701.

I closed my last Lecture with La Salle's death, in 1687. A few years after, in the latter part of the same century, a French ship of 42 guns, on one of those beautiful days which are the peculiar offspring of the autumnal climate of America, happened to be coasting the hostile shore of New England. At that time England and France were at war, and the bays and harbors of the British possessions were swarming with the floating battlements of the mistress of the sea. Nevertheless, from the careless manner in which that ship, which bore the white flag of France, hugged the coast, one would have thought that no danger was to be apprehended from such close proximity to captivity or death. Suddenly, three vessels hove in sight; it was not long before their broad canvas wings seemed to spread wider, and their velocity to increase. To the most unpracticed eye it would have been evident that they were in pursuit of an object which they longed to reach. Yet, *they of the white flag* appeared to be unconscious of the intention of their fellow-travelers on the boundless desert of the ocean. Although the French ship, with her long masts, towering like steeples, could have borne much more canvas; although the breeze blew fresh, and the circumstance might have invited to rapidity of motion, yet not one additional inch of sail did she show, but she continued to move with a speed, neither relaxed nor increased, and as if enjoying a holyday excursion on Old Neptune's domains.

High on the quarter-deck stood the captain, with the spy-glass in his hands, and surrounded by his officers. After a minute survey of the unknown vessels, as they appeared, with outlines faint and hardly visible from the distance, and with the tip of their masts gradually emerging, as it were, from the waves, he had dropped his glass, and said to the bystanders: "Gentlemen, they are vessels of war, and British." Then he instinctively cast a rapid glance upward at the rigging of his ship, as if to satisfy himself that nothing had happened *there*, to mar that symmetrical neatness and scientific arrangement which have ever been held to be a criterion of nautical knowledge, and therefore a proper source of professional pride. But the look which he flung at the deck was long and steady. That thoughtful, lingering look embraced every object, animate or inanimate, which there stood. Ay! that abstracted look and those compressed lips must have conveyed meaning, as distinct as if words had been spoken; for they produced instantaneous action, such action as when man prepares to meet man in deadly encounter. It was plain that between that chief and his crew there was that sympathetic congeniality which imparts thought and feeling without the use of language. It was plain that on all occasions when the soul was summoned into moral volition and stirred into the assumption of high and uncommon resolves, the same electric fluid, gushing from the heart, pervaded at once the whole of that human mass. But, if a change had come over the outward appearance of that ship's deck, none had taken place in her upper trimming. The wind continued to fill the same number of sails, and the ship, naiad-like, to sport herself leisurely in her favorite element.

In the mean time, the vessels which had been descried at the farthest point of the horizon, had been rapidly gaining ground upon the intervening distance, and were dilating in size as they approached. It could be seen that they had separated from each other, and they appeared to be sweeping round the Pelican (for such was the name of the French ship), as if to cut her off from retreat. Already could be plainly discovered St. George's cross, flaunting in the wind. The white cloud of canvas that hung over them seemed to swell with every flying minute, and the wooden structures themselves, as they plunged madly over the furrowed plains of the Atlantic, looked not unlike Titanic race-horses pressing for the goal. Their very masts with their long flags streaming, like Gorgon's disheveled locks, seemed, as they bent under the wind, to be quivering with the anxiety of the chase. But, ye sons of Britain, why this hot haste? Why urge ye into such desperate exertions the watery steeds which ye spur on so fiercely? *They of the white flag* never thought of flight. See! they shorten sail as if to invite you to the approach. Beware ye do not repent of your efforts to cull the Lily of France, so temptingly floating in your sight! If ye be falcons of pure breed, yonder bird, that is resting his folded pinions and sharpening his beak, is no carrion crow. Who, but an eagle, would have looked with such imperturbable composure at your rapid gyrations, betokening the thunderbolt-like swoop which is to descend upon his devoted head?

Now, forsooth, the excitement of the looker-on must

be tenfold increased: now the four vessels are within gun-shot, and the fearful struggle is to begin. One is a British ship of the line, showing a row of 52 guns, and her companions are frigates armed with 42 guns each. To court such unequal contest, must not that French commander be the very impersonation of madness? There he stands on the quarter-deck, a man apparently thirty years of age, attired as if for a courtly ball, in the gorgeous dress of the time of Louis the Fourteenth. The profuse curls of his perfumed hair seem to be bursting from the large, slouched gray hat, which he wears on one side inclined, and decorated with a red plume horizontally stuck to the broad brim, according to the fashion of the day. What a noble face! If I were to sculpture a hero, verily, I would put such a head on his shoulders—nay, I would take the whole man for my model! I feel that I could shout with enthusiasm, when I see the peculiar expression which has settled in that man's eye, in front of such dangers thickening upon him! Ha! what is it? What signify that convulsive start which shook his frame, and that death-like paleness which has flitted across his face? What woman-like softness has suddenly crept into those eyes? By heaven! a tear! I saw it, although it passed as rapidly as if a whirlwind had swept it off, and although every feature has now resumed its former expression of more than human firmness.

I understand it all! That boy, so young, so effeminate, so delicate, but who, in an under-officer's dress, stands with such manly courage by one of the guns,— he is your brother, is he not? Perhaps he is doomed to death! and you think of his aged mother! Well may the loss of two such sons crush her at once! When I see such exquisite feelings tumultuously at work in a heart as soft as ever throbbed in a woman's breast·

C

when I see you, Iberville, resolved to sacrifice so much, rather than to fly from your country's enemies, even when it could be done without dishonor, stranger as you are to me, I wish I could stand by you on that deck and hug you to my bosom!

What awful silence on board of those ships! Were it not for the roar of the waves, as they are cleft by the gigantic bulks under which they groan, the chirping of a cricket might be distinctly heard. How near they are to each other! A musket shot would tell. Now, the crash is coming! The tempest of fire, havoc, and destruction is to be let loose! What a spectacle! I would not look twice at such a scene—it is too painful for an unconcerned spectator! My breast heaves with emotion—I am struggling in vain to breathe! Ha! there it goes—one simultaneous blaze! The eruption of Mount Vesuvius—a strange whizzing sound—the hissing of ten thousand serpents, bursting from hell and drunk with its venom—the fall of timber, as if a host of sturdy axes had been at work in the forest—a thick overspreading smoke concealing the demon's work within its dusky folds! With the occasional clearing of the smoke, the French ship may be seen, as if animated with a charmed life, gliding swiftly by her foes, and pouring in her broadsides with unabated rapidity. It looks like the condensation of all the lightnings of heaven. Her commander, as if gifted with supernatural powers and with the privilege of ubiquity, seems to be present at the same time in every part of the ship, animating and directing all with untiring ardor.

That storm of human warfare has lasted about two hours; but the French ship, salamander-like, seems to live safely in that atmosphere of fire. Two hours! I can stand this excitement no longer; and yet every minute is adding fresh fuel to its intensity. But now comes the crisis. The Pelican has almost silenced the guns of the English 52, and is bearing down upon her evidently with the intention to board. But, strange! she veers round. Oh! I see. God of mercy! I feel faint at heart! The 52 is sinking—slowly she settles in the surging sea—there—there—there—down! What a yell of defiance! But it is the last. What a rushing of the waters over the ingulfed mass! Now all is over, and the yawning abyss has closed its lips.—What remains to be seen on that bloody theater? One of the English 42s, in a dismantled state, is dropping slowly at a distance under the wind, and the other has already struck its flag, and is lying motionless on the ocean, a floating ruin!

The French ship is hardly in a better plight, and the last rays of the setting sun show her deck strewed with the dead and the dying. But the glorious image of victory flits before the dimmed vision of the dying, and they expire with the smile of triumph on their lips, and with the exulting shout of "*France forever!*"

But where is the conqueror? Where is the gallant commander, whose success sounds like a fable? My heart longs to see him safe, and in the enjoyment of his well-earned glory. Ah! there he is, kneeling and crouching over the prostrate body of that stripling whom I have depicted: he addresses the most tender and passionate appeals to that senseless form; he covers with kisses that bloody head; he weeps and sobs aloud, unmindful of those that look on. In faith! I weep myself, to see the agony of that noble heart: and why should that hero blush to moan like a mother—he who showed more than human courage, when the occasion required fortitude? Weep on, Iberville, weep on! Well may such tears be gathered by an angel's wings, like dew-drops worthy of heaven, and, if carried by supplicating mercy to the foot of the Almighty's throne, they may yet redeem thy brother's life!

Happily, that brother did not die. He was destined to be known in history under the name of Bienville, and to be the founder of one of America's proudest cities. To him New Orleans owes its existence, and his name, in the course of centuries, will grow in the esteem of posterity, proportionately with the aggrandizement of the future emporium of so many countless millions of human beings.

The wonderful achievement which I have related is a matter of historical record, and throws a halo of glory and romance around those two men, who have since figured so conspicuously in the annals of Louisiana, and who, in the beginning of March, 1699, entered the Mississippi, accompanied by Father Anastase, the former companion of La Salle in his expedition down the river in 1682.

Since the occurrence of that battle, of which I have given but an imperfect description, Iberville and Bienville had been through several campaigns at sea, and had encountered the dangers of many a fight. What a remarkable family! The father, a Canadian by birth, had died on the field of battle, in serving his country, and out of eleven sons, the worthy scions of such a stock, five had perished in the same cause. Out of the six that remained, five were to consecrate themselves to the establishment of a colony in Louisiana.

Before visiting the Mississippi, Iberville had left his fleet anchored at the Chandeleur Islands. This name proceeds from the circumstance of their having been discovered on the day when the Catholic Church celebrates the feast of the presentation of Christ in the temple, and of the purification of the Virgin. They are flat, sandy islands, which look as if they wish to sink back into the sea, from shame of having come into the world prematurely, and before having been shaped and licked by nature into proper objects of existence. No doubt, they did not prepossess the first colonists in favor of what they were to expect. The French visited also *Ship Island*, so called from its appearing to be a safe roadstead for ships, but it offered to the visitors no greater attraction than the precedent. The next island they made had not a more inviting physiognomy. When they landed on that forbidding and ill-looking piece of land, they found it to be a small, squatting island, covered with indifferent wood, and intersected with lagoons. It literally swarmed with a curious kind of animal, which seemed to occupy the medium between the fox and the cat. It was difficult to say whether it belonged to one species in preference to the other. But one of the French having exclaimed, "*This is the kingdom of cats!*" decided the question, and the name of Cat Island was given to the new discovery. Here that peculiar animal, which was subsequently to be known in the United States under the popular name of racoon, formed a numerous and a contented tribe; here they lived like philosophers, separated from the rest of the world, and enjoying their nuts—their loaves and fishes. I invite fabulists, or those who have a turn for fairy tales, to inquire into the origin of that grimalkin colony, and to endear Cat Island to the juvenility of our State, by reciting the marvelous doings of which it was the theater.

It was fraught, however, with so little interest in the estimation of the French, that they hastened to leave it for the land they had in sight. It formed a bay, the shores of which they found inhabited by a tribe of Indians, called Biloxi, who proved as hospitable as their name was euphonic.

On the 27th of February, 1699, Iberville and Bienville departed from Biloxi in search of the Mississippi. When they approached its mouth, they were struck with the gloomy magnificence of the sight. As far as the eye could reach, nothing was to be seen but reeds which rose five or six feet above the waters in which they bathed their roots. They waved mournfully under the blast of the sharp wind of the north, shivering in its icy grasp, as it tumbled, rolled, and gamboled on the pliant surface. Multitudes of birds of strange appearance, with their elongated shapes, so lean that they looked like metamorphosed ghosts, clothed in plumage, screamed in the air, as if they were scared at each other. There was something agonizing in their shrieks, that was in harmony with the desolation of the place. On every side of the vessel, monsters of the deep and huge alligators heaved themselves up heavily from their native or favorite element, and, floating lazily on the turbid waters, seemed to gaze at the intruders. Down the river, and rumbling over its bed, there came a sort of low, distant thunder. Was it the voice of the hoary sire of rivers, raised in anger at the prospect of his gigantic volume of waters being suddenly absorbed by one mightier than he?—In their progress, it was with great difficulty that the travelers could keep their bark free from those enormous rafts of trees which the Mississippi seemed to toss about in mad frolic. A poet would have thought that the great river, when departing from the altitude of his birthplace, and as he rushed down to the sea through three thousand miles, had, in anticipation of a contest which threatened the continuation of his existence, flung his broad arms right and left across the continent, and uprooting all its forests, had hoarded them in his bed as missiles to hurl at the head of his mighty rival, when they should meet and struggle for supremacy.

When night began to cast a darker hue on a landscape on which the imagination of Dante would have gloated, there issued from that chaos of reeds such uncouth and unnatural sounds, as would have saddened the gayest and appalled the most intrepid. Could this be the far-famed Mississippi? or was it not rather old Avernus? It was hideous indeed—but hideousness refined into sublimity, filling the soul with a sentiment of grandeur. Nothing daunted, the adventurers kept steadily on their course: they knew that, through those dismal portals, they were to arrive at the most magnificent country in the world; they knew that awful screen concealed loveliness itself. It was a coquettish freak of nature, when dealing with European curiosity, as it came eagerly bounding on the Atlantic wave, to herald it through an avenue so somber, as to cause the wonders of the great valley of the Mississippi to burst with tenfold more force upon the bewildered gaze of those who, by the endurance of so many perils and fatigues, were to merit admittance into its Eden.

It was a relief for the adventurers when, after having toiled up the river for ten days, they at last arrived at the village of the Bayagoulas. There they found a letter of Tonti to La Salle, dated in 1685. That letter, or rather that *speaking bark*, as the Indians called it, had been preserved with great reverence. Tonti having been informed that La Salle was coming with a fleet from France, to settle a colony on the banks of the Mississippi, had not hesitated to set off from the Northern Lakes, with twenty Canadians and thirty Indians, and to come down to the Balize to meet his friend, who, as we know, had failed to make out the mouth of the Mississippi, and had been landed by Beaujeu on the shores of Texas. After having waited for some time, and ignorant of what had happened, Tonti, with the same indifference to fatigues and dangers of an appalling nature, retraced his way back, leaving a letter to La Salle to inform him of his disappointment. Is there not something extremely romantic in the characters of the men of that epoch? Here is Tonti undertaking, with the most heroic unconcern, a journey of nearly three thousand miles, through such difficulties as it is easy for us to imagine, and leaving a letter to La Salle, as a proof of his visit, in the same way that one would, in these degenerate days of effeminacy, leave a card at a neighbor's house.

The French extended their explorations up to the mouth of the Red River. As they proceeded through that virgin country, with what interest they must have examined every object that met their eyes, and listened to the traditions concerning Soto, and the more recent stories of the Indians on La Salle and the iron-handed Tonti![*] A coat of mail which was presented as having belonged to the Spaniards, and vestiges of their encampment on the Red River, confirmed the French in the belief that there was much of truth in the recitals of the Indians.

On their return from the mouth of the Red River, the two brothers separated when they arrived at Bayou Manchac. Bienville was ordered to go down the river to the French fleet, to give information of what they had seen and heard. Iberville went through Bayou Manchac to those lakes which are now known under the names of Pontchartrain and Maurepas. Louisiana had been named from a king: was it not in keeping that those lakes should be called after ministers?

---

[*] He had lost one of his hands, which he had supplied by an artificial one made of iron.

It has been said that there is something in a name If it be true, why should not I tell you who were those from whom the names of those lakes were borrowed? Is it not something even for inanimate objects to have historical names? It throws round them the spell of romance, and sets the imagination to work.

Louis Phelyppeaux, Count Pontchartrain, a minister and chancellor of France, was the grandson of a minister. He was a man remarkable for his talents and erudition. His integrity was proverbial, and his enlightened and inflexible administration of justice is found recorded in all the annals of the time. When he was appointed to the exalted office of Chancellor of France, Louis the XIVth, on administering to him the required oath, said, "Sir, I regret that it is not in my power to bestow upon you a higher office, as a proof of my esteem for your talents, and of my gratitude for your services."

Pontchartrain patronized letters with great zeal, and during his long career, was the avowed friend of Boileau and of J. B. Rousseau, the poet. He was of a very diminutive size, but very well shaped, and had that lean and hungry look which Cæsar did not like in Cassius. His face was one of the most expressive, and his eyes were lighted up with incessant scintillations, denoting the ebullitions of wit within. If his features promised a great deal, his mind did more than redeem the physical pledge. There is no question, however abstruse, which he did not understand as if by intuition, and his capacity for labor appeared to stretch as far as the limits allotted to human nature. He was constitutionally indefatigable in all his pursuits; and his knowledge of men, which was perhaps superior to all his other qualifications, remarkable as they were, greatly helped his iron will in the successful execution of its conceptions. But, although he knew mankind thoroughly, he did not assume the garb of misanthropy. On the contrary, his manners spoke of a heart overflowing with the milk of human benevolence; and his conversation, which was alternately replete with deep learning, or sparkling with vivacity and repartee, was eagerly sought after. If, on matters of mere business, he astonished, by the clearness of his judgment and his rapidity of conception, those he had to deal with, he no less delighted those with whom he associated in his lighter hours, by his mild cheerfulness and by his colloquial powers, even on the veriest trifles. No man knew better than he, how to temper the high dignity of his station by the utmost suavity and simplicity of address. Yet in that man who, conscious of the misery he might inflict, was so guarded in his expressions that he never was betrayed into an unkind one—in that man, in whom so much blandness was allied to so much majesty of deportment—there was something more dreaded far than the keenest powers of sarcasm in others. It was a *smile*, peculiar to himself, which made people inquire with anxiety, not what Pontchartrain had said, but how Pontchartrain had smiled. That smile of his blasted like lightning what it was aimed at; it operated as a sentence of death, and did such execution that the Pontchartrain smile became, at the court of Louis the Fourteenth, as famous as the *Mortemart wit*.[*] In 1714, resisting the entreaties of the king, he resigned his chancellorship, and retiring into the house of a religious congregation (Les prêtres de l'Oratoire) he devoted the remainder of his life to prayer, reading, and meditation.

[*] The hereditary wit of all the members of that family, male or female, was marked with such peculiar pungency, that it became proverbial, and was called the Mortemart wit.

Jean Frederic Phelyppeaux, Count Maurepas, was the son of Jerome Phelyppeaux, a minister and secretary of state, and the grandson of Pontchartrain, the chancellor. At the age of fourteen, he was appointed secretary of state, and in 1725, in his twenty-fourth year, became minister. This remarkable family thus presented an uninterrupted succession of ministers for one hundred and seventy-one years. The obstinacy with which prosperity clung to her favorites appeared so strange that it worked upon the imagination of the superstitious, or of the ignorant, and was attributed at the time to some unholy compact and to the protection of supernatural beings. Cradled in the lap of power, Maurepas exhibited in his long career all the defects which are usually observed to grow with the growth of every spoiled child of fortune. He was as capricious as the wind, and as light as the feather with which it delights to gambol. The frivolity of his character was such that it could not be modified even by extreme old age. Superficial in every thing, he was incapable of giving any serious attention to such matters as would, from their very nature, command the deep consideration of most men. Perhaps he relied too much on his prodigious facility of perception, and on a mind so gifted, that it could, in an instant, unravel the knots of the most complicated affair. In the king's council, his profound knowledge of men and of the court, a sort of hereditary ministerial training to business, imperfect as it was, enabled him to conceal to a certain degree his lamentable deficiency of study and of meditation. As it were by instinct, if not by the diviner's rod, he could stamp on the ground and point out where the fruits of the earth lay concealed; but instead of using the spade and mattock in search of the treasure, he would run after the first butterfly that caught his eye. To reconcile men to his imperfections, nature had given him a bewitching sweetness of temper, which was never found wanting. Urbane, supple, and insinuating in his manners, he was as pliant as a reed: fertile in courtly stratagems, expert in laying out traps, pitfalls, and ambuscades for his enemies, he was equally skillful in the art of attack and defense, and no Proteus could assume more varied shapes to elude the grasp of his adversaries. There was no wall to which he could be driven, where he could not find an aperture through which to make his escape. No hunted deer ever surpassed him in throwing out the intricate windings of his flight, to mislead his sagacious pursuers. Where he unexpectedly found himself stared in the face by some affair, the serious complexion of which he did not like, he would exorcise the apparition away by a profuse sprinkling of witty jests, calculated to lessen the importance of the hated object, or to divert from it the attention of persons interested in its examination. No Ulysses could be more replete than he with expedients to extricate himself out of all difficulties; but the moment he was out of danger, he would throw himself down, panting with his recent efforts, and think of nothing else than to luxuriate on the couch of repose, or to amuse himself with trifles.

Maurepas, in more than one respect, was made up of contrarieties, a living antithesis in flesh and blood, a strange compound of activity and indolence that puzzled the world. Upon the whole, he was generally thought to be, by superficial observers, a harmless, good-natured, easy sort of man. But withal, in spite of his habitual supineness, he could rival the lynx, when he applied the keenness of his eye to detect the weak, ridiculous, or contemptible parts in the formation of his fellow-beings: and no spider could weave such an imperceptible but certain web around those court flies he wanted to destroy, or to use to his own purposes. He was born a trifler, but one of a redoubtable nature, and from his temperament as well as from his vicious education, there was nothing so respected, so august, or even so awful, as not to be laughed or scoffed at by him. There was no merit, no virtue, no generous, no moral or religious belief or faith in any thing, that he would not deride, and he would sneer even at himself, or at his own family, with the same relish, when the mood came upon him. Yet, worthless as that man was in his private and public character, he had such a peculiar turn for throwing the rich glow of health around what was most rotten in the state; he could present to his master and to his colleagues the dryest matter under such an enlivening aspect, when they met in the council-chamber; he could render apparently so simple what seemed so complicated as to require the most arduous labor; and he could solve the most difficult political problem with such ease, that it looked like magic, and made him the most fascinating of ministers.

For such a king as Louis the XVth, who felt with great sensitiveness any thing that disturbed the voluptuous tranquillity which was the sole object of his life, Maurepas, as a minister, had a most precious quality. Born in the atmosphere of the court, he was intimately acquainted with his native element, and excelled in hushing that low buzzing of discontent, so disagreeable to a monarch, which arises from the unsatisfied ambition, the jealousy, and the quarrels of his immediate attendants. None knew better than Maurepas the usages and secrets of the court, and how to reconcile the conflicting interests of those great families that gravitate round the throne. He knew exactly what was due to every one, either for personal merit or for ancestral distinction. His was the art to nip in the bud all factions or cabals, to stifle the grumblings of discontent, or to lull the murmurs of offended pride. He knew how to make the grant of a favor doubly precious by the manner in which it was offered; and the bitterness of refusal was either sweetened by assurances of regret and of personal devotion, or by a happy mixture of reasoning and pleasantry, which, if it did not convince the mind, forced disappointment itself to smile at its own bad luck.

With all his faults, such a minister had too much innate talent not to do some good, in spite of his frivolity. Thus, he made great improvements and embellishments in the city of Paris; he infused new life into the marine department, corrected many abuses, visited all the harbors and arsenals, sent officers to survey all the coasts of France, had new maps made, established nautical schools, and ordered the expeditions of learned men to several parts of the world. Geometers and astronomers, according to his instructions, went to the equator and near the boreal pole, to measure, at the same time and by a concurrent operation, two degrees of the meridian. Thus, La Condamine, Bouguer, Godin, Maupertuis, Clairaut, and Lemonnier, were indebted to him for their celebrity. Also, in obedience to his commands, Sevin and Fourmont visited Greece and several provinces of the East; others surveyed Mesopotamia and Persia, and Jussieu departed to study the botany of Peru.

That frivolous minister did, through his strong natural sagacity, partially discover that commerce ought to be unshackled, and withdrew from the India Company the monopoly of the coffee trade and of the slave trade. By such a wise measure, he largely contributed to the prosperity of the French colonies. But, in such an ele-

vated region of thought, conception, and action, Maurepas was too boyish to remain long. He would confide the labors of his office to those whom it was his duty to guide, and would steal away to the balls of the opera, or to every sort of dissipation. If he remained in the cabinet destined to his official occupations, it was not to think and to act in a manner worthy of the minister, but to write lampoons, scurrilous drolleries, and facetious obscenities. He took a share in the composition of several licentious pieces, well suited to the taste and morals of the time, and contributed to one which attracted some attention, under the title of *The Ballet of the Turkeys*. These things were not, for him, the result of a momentary debauch of the mind, but matters of serious occupation and pursuit. Such a relish did he find in this pastime, which would be called childish if it had not been tainted with immorality, that it took the mastery over his prudence, and he had the indiscretion to write a lampoon on the physical charms of the Marquise de Pompadour, the acknowledged favorite of Louis the XVth. The pruriency of his wit cost him his place, and in 1749, after having been a minister twenty-four years, he was exiled to the city of Bourges, and afterward permitted to reside at his *Chateau de Pontchartrain*, near Paris. There, his princely fortune allowed him to live in splendor, and to attach a sort of mimic court to his person. He appeared to bear his fall with philosophical indifference, observing that, *on the first day of his dismissal, he felt sore; but that on the next, he was entirely consoled.*

On the death of Louis the XVth, his successor sent for Maurepas, to put him at the helm of that royal ship, destined soon to be dashed to pieces in that tremendous storm which might be seen gathering from the four quarters of the horizon. The unfortunate Louis could not have made a poorer choice. Maurepas had sagacity enough to discover the coming events, but he was not the man, even if the power had been in his hands, to prepare for the struggle with those gigantic evils, whose shadow he could see already darkening the face of his country. Such an attempt would have interfered with his delightful suppers and disturbed his sleep; and to the Cassandras of that epoch, the egotistical old man used to reply with a sneer and a shrug of his shoulders, "The present organization of things will last as long as I shall, and why should I look beyond!" This observation was in keeping with the whole tenor of his life; and, true to the system which he had adopted, if he lived and died in peace, what did he care for the rest? He had no children, and when he married in all the vigor of youth, those who knew him intimately, predicted that the bridal bed would remain barren. The prediction proved true, and had not required any extraordinary powers of divination. Is it astonishing that the lineal descendant of a succession of ministers should be without virility of mind, soul, or body? What herculean strength, what angel purity would have resisted the deleterious influence of such an atmosphere, working, for nearly two centuries, slow but sure mischief, from generation to generation?

After having been a minister for six years under Louis the XVIth, Maurepas died in 1781. So infatuated was the king with his octogenarian minister, that he had insisted upon his occupying, at the Palace of Versailles, an apartment above his own royal chamber; and every morning, the first thing that the king did, was to pay a visit to the minister. Pleasant those visits were, because the wily old minister presented every thing to his young master under the most glowing colors, and made him believe that his almost centenarian experience would smooth the rugged path that extended before him. If parliaments rebelled, if fleets were defeated, if provinces were famished, Maurepas had no unpalatable truths to say. Only once, the eaves-droppers heard his voice raised above its usual soft tone. What frightful convulsion of nature could have produced such a change? None but the death of a cat! Distracted with the shrieks of his wife, whose troublesome four-footed favorite, interfering with the king when engaged in his darling occupation of a blacksmith, had been killed by an angry blow of the royal hammer, he loudly expostulated with the murderer for the atrociousness of the deed. What must have been his dread of his wife, when under the cabalistic influence of her frowns, such a courtier could so completely drop the prudential policy of his whole life, as to venture to show displeasure to the king!

When Maurepas died, the king shed tears, and said with a faltering voice, "Alas! in the morning, for the future, when I shall wake up, no longer shall I hear the grateful sound to which I was used—the slow pacing of my friend in the room above mine." Very little deserving of this testimonial of friendship was he, who never loved any thing in this world but himself.

So much for Pontchartrain and Maurepas, who have given their names to those beautiful lakes which are in the vicinity of New Orleans. From Lake Pontchartrain, Iberville arrived at a sheet of water which is known in our days under the name of Lake Borgne. The French, thinking that it did not answer precisely the definition of a lake, because it was not altogether land-locked, or did not at least discharge its waters only through a small aperture, and because it looked rather like a part of the sea, separated from its main body by numerous islands, called it Lake Borgne, meaning something incomplete or defective, like a man with one eye.

On that lake, there is a beautiful bay, to which Iberville gave the patronymic name of St. Louis. Of a more lofty one no place can boast under the broad canopy of heaven.

Louis the IXth, son of Louis the VIIIth of France, and of Blanche of Castile, was the incarnation of virtue, and, what is more extraordinary, of virtue born on the throne, and preserving its divine purity in spite of all the temptations of royal power. In vain would history be taxed to produce a character worthy of being compared with one so pure. Among heroes, he must certainly be acknowledged as one of the greatest; among monarchs, he must be ranked as the most just; and among men, as the most modest. For such perfection, he was indebted to his mother, who, from his earliest days, used to repeat to him this solemn admonition: "My son, remember that I had rather see you dead than offending your God by the commission of a deadly sin." When he assumed the government of his kingdom, he showed that his talents for administration were equal to his virtues as a man. Every measure which he adopted during peace, had a happy tendency toward the moral and physical improvement of his subjects, and in war he proved that he was not deficient in those qualifications which constitute military genius. He defeated Henry the IIId of England at the battle of Taillebourg in Poitou, where he achieved prodigies of valor. He gained another decisive victory at Saintes over the English monarch, to whom he granted a truce of five years, on his paying to France five thousand pounds sterling.

Unfortunately, the piety of the king making him forgetful of what was due to the temporal welfare of his subjects, drove him into one of those crusades, which the cold judgment of the statesman may blame, but at which the imagination of the lover of romance will certainly not repine. In 1249, Louis landed in Egypt, took the city of Damietta, and advanced as far as Massourah. But after several victories, whereby he lost the greater part of his army, he was reduced to shut himself up in his camp, where famine and pestilence so decimated the feeble remnant of his forces, that he was constrained to surrender to the host of enemies by whom he was enveloped. He might have escaped, however; but to those who advised him to consult his own personal safety, he gave this noble answer: "I must share in life or in death the fate of my companions."

The Sultan had offered to his prisoner to set him free, on condition that he would give up Damietta and pay one hundred thousand silver marks. Louis replied, that a king of France never ransomed himself for money; but that he would yield Damietta in exchange for his own person, and pay one hundred thousand silver marks in exchange for such of his subjects as were prisoners. Such was the course of negotiation between the two sovereigns, when it was suddenly arrested by the murder of the Sultan, who fell a victim to the unruly passions of his janizaries. They had rebelled against their master, for having attempted to subject them to a state of discipline irksome to their habits and humiliating to their lawless pride. Some of those ruffians penetrated into the prison of Louis, and one of them, presenting him with the gory head of the Sultan, asked the French monarch what reward he would grant him for the destruction of his enemy. A haughty look of contempt was the only answer vouchsafed by Louis. Enraged at this manifestation of displeasure, the assassin lifted up his dagger, and aiming it at the king's breast, exclaimed, "Dub me a knight, or die!" Louis replied with indignation, "Repent, and turn Christian, or fly hence, base infidel!" When uttering these words, Louis had risen from his seat, and with an arm loaded with chains had pointed to the door, waving the barbarian away with as much majesty of command as if he had been seated on his throne in his royal palace of the Louvre. Abashed at the rebuke, and overawed by the Olympian expression of the monarch's face, the Saracen skulked away, and said to his companions, when he returned to them, "I have just seen the proudest Christian that has yet come to the East!"

After many obstacles, a treaty of peace was at last concluded: Louis and his companions were liberated; the Saracens received from the French eight hundred thousand marks of silver, and recovered the city of Damietta. But they authorized Louis to take possession of all the places in Palestine which had been wrested from the Christians, and to fortify them as he pleased.

When the king landed in France, the joy of his subjects was such, that they appeared to be seized with the wildest delirium. On his way from the sea-coast to Paris, he was met by throngs of men, women, and children, who rushed at him with the most frantic shrieks, and kissed his feet and the hem of his garments, as if he had been an angel dropped from heaven to give them the assurance of eternal felicity. These testimonials of gratitude, extreme as they may appear, were not more than he deserved. He who used to say to his proud nobles, "Our serfs belong to Christ, our common master, and in a Christian kingdom it must not be forgotten that we are all brothers," must indeed have been beloved by the people! How could it be otherwise, when they saw him repeatedly visiting every part of his dominions, to listen to the complaints of his meanest subjects! They knew that he used to sit, at Vincennes, under a favorite oak, which has become celebrated from that circumstance, and there loved, with august simplicity, to administer justice to high and low. It was there that he rendered judgment against his own brother, Le Comte d'Anjou; it was there that he forced one of his most powerful barons, Enguerrand de Coucy, to bow to the majesty of the law. It was he whose enlightened piety knew how to check the unjust pretensions of his clergy, and to keep them within those bounds which they were so prone to overleap. It was he who contented himself with retorting to those who railed at his pious and laborious life, "If I gave to hunting, to gambling, to tournaments, and to every sort of dissipation, the moments which I devote to prayer and meditation, I should not be found fault with."

Louis undertook a second Crusade; and having encamped on the site of old Carthage, prepared to commence the siege of Tunis, to which it is almost contiguous. There, privations of every sort, incessant fatigue, and the malignant influence of the climate, produced an epidemical disease, which rapidly destroyed the strength of his army. His most powerful barons and most skillful captains died in a few days; his favorite son, the Count de Nevers, expired in his arms; his eldest born, the presumptive heir to the crown, had been attacked by the pestilence, and was struggling against death, in a state of doubtful convalescence; when, to increase the dismay of the French, Louis himself caught the infection. Aware of approaching death, he ordered himself to be stretched on ashes · wishing, he, the **great** king, to die with all the humility of a Christian. At the foot of his bed of ashes, stood a large cross, bearing the image of the crucified Savior, upon which he loved to rest his eyes, as on the pledge of his future salvation. Around him, the magnates of France and his own immediate attendants knelt on the ground, which they bathed with tears, and addressed to Heaven the most fervent prayers for the recovery of the precious life which was threatened with sudden extinguishment.

Out of the royal tent, grief was not less expressive. The silence of despair, made more solemn by occasional groans, reigned absolute over the suffering multitude that had agglomerated on the accursed Numidian shore; and the whole army, distracted, as it were, at the danger which menaced its august head, seemed to have been struck with palsy by the horror of its situation. The dying were hardly attended to, so much engrossed were their attendants by heavier cares; and even they, the dying, were satisfied to perish, since they thus escaped the bitterness of their present fate; and their loss elicited no expression of regret from their survivors, so much absorbed were they by the fear of a greater misfortune to them and to France. There appeared to be a sort of frightful harmony between the surrounding objects and the human sufferings to which they formed an appropriate frame. The winds seemed to have departed forever from the earth; the atmosphere had no breath; and the air almost condensed itself into something palpable; it fell like molten lead upon the lungs which it consumed. The motionless sea was smoothed and glassed into a mirror reflecting the heat of the lurid sun: it looked dead. Beasts of prey, hyenas, jackals, and wolves, attracted by the noxious effluvia which issued from the camp, filled the ears with their dismal howlings. From the deep blue sky, there came no refreshing shower, but shrieks of hungry vultures, glancing down at the feast prepared for them, and screaming with impatience at the delay. The enemy himself had retreated to a distance, from fear of the contagion, and had ceased those hostilities which used momentarily to relieve the minds of the French from the contemplation of their situation. They were reduced to such a pitch of misery as to regret that no human foes disturbed the solitude where they were slowly perishing; and their eyes were fixed in unutterable woe on those broken pyramids, those mutilated columns, those remnants of former ages, of faded glories, on those eloquent ruins, which, long before the time when they sheltered Marius, spoke of nothing but past, present, and future miseries.

Such was the scene which awaited Louis on his death-bed. It was enough to strike despair into the boldest heart, but he stood it unmoved. A perpetual smile, such as grace only the lips of the blessed, enlivened his face; he looked round not only without dismay, but with an evangelical serenity of soul. He knew well that the apparent evils which he saw, were a mere passing trial, inflicted for the benefit of the sufferers, and for some goodly purpose; he knew that this transitory severity was the wise device of infinite and eternal benignity, and therefore, instead of repining, he thanked God for the chastisement which served only to hasten the coming reward. The vision of the Christian extends beyond the contracted sphere of the sufferings of humanity, and sees the crowning mercies that attend the disembodied spirits in a better world.

By the manner in which Louis died, this was strikingly illustrated. Calm and collected, after having distributed words of encouragement to all that could approach him, he summoned his son and successor to his bedside, and laying his hands on his head to bless him, he bid him a short and an impressive farewell. "My son!" said he, "I die in peace with the world and with myself, warring only against the enemies of our holy faith. As a Christian, I have lived in the fear, and I depart in the hope of God. As a man, I have never wasted a thought on my own perishable body; and in obedience to the command of our Lord Jesus Christus, I have always forgotten my own worldly interest to promote that of others. As a king, I have considered myself as my subjects' servant, and not my subjects as mine. If, as a Christian, as a man, and as a king, I have erred and sinned, it is unwillingly and in good faith, and therefore, I trust for mercy in my heavenly Father, and in the protection of the Holy Virgin. So I have lived—do thou likewise. Follow an example which secures to me such a sweet death amid such scenes of horror. Thou shalt find in my written will, such precepts as my experience and my affection for thee and for my subjects have devised for thy guidance and for their benefit. And now, my son, farewell! This life, as thou knowest, is a mere state of probation; hence, do not repine at our short separation. Blessed be thou here, and in heaven, where I hope to meet thee in everlasting bliss. So help me God! In the name of the Father, and of the Son, and of the Holy Ghost, Amen!" Thus saying, he devoutly crossed himself, looked upward, and exclaimed: "Introibo in domum tuam, adorabo ad templum sanctum tuum." These were his last words. During his life, he was emphatically the Christian king: shortly after his death, he was canonized by the church, and became a saint.

In spite of these circumstances, which must have been hateful to Voltaire's turn of mind, the recollection of such exalted virtue extorted from that celebrated writer a eulogy which is doubly flattering to the memory of him to whom the tribute is paid, if the source from which it came be considered. That arch scoffer, that systematic disbeliever in so much of what is held sacred by mankind, said of St. Louis, "That prince would have reformed Europe, if reformation had been possible at that time. He increased the power, prosperity, and civilization of France, and showed himself a type of human perfection. To the piety of an anchorite, he joined all the virtues of a king; and he practiced a wise system of economy, without ceasing to be liberal. Although a profound politician, he never deviated from what he thought strictly due to right and justice, and he is perhaps the sole sovereign to whom such commendation can be applied. Prudent and firm in the deliberations of the cabinet, distinguished for cool intrepidity in battle, as humane as if he had been familiar with nothing else but misery, he carried human virtue as far as it can be expected to extend."

Thus, it is seen that the Bay of St. Louis could not borrow a nobler name than that under which it is designated. The magnificent oaks which decorate its shore did perhaps remind Iberville of the oak of Vincennes, and to that circumstance may the bay be indebted for its appellation.

From the Bay of St. Louis, Iberville returned to his fleet, where, after consultation, he determined to make a settlement at the Bay of Biloxi. On the east side, at the mouth of the bay, as it were, there is a slight swelling of the shore, about four acres square, sloping gently to the woods in the background, and on the right and left of which, two deep ravines run into the bay. Thus, this position was fortified by nature, and the French skillfully availed themselves of these advantages. The weakest point, which was on the side of the forest, they strengthened with more care than the rest, by connecting with a strong intrenchment the two ravines, which ran to the bay in a parallel line to each other. The fort was constructed with four bastions, and was armed with twelve pieces of artillery. When standing on one of the bastions which faced the bay, the spectator enjoyed a beautiful prospect. On the right, the bay could be seen running into the land for miles, and on the left stood Deer Island, concealing almost entirely the broad expanse of water which lay beyond. It was visible only at the two extreme points of the island, which both, at that distance, appeared to be within a close proximity of the main land. No better description can be given, than to say that the bay looked like a funnel, to which the island was the lid, not fitting closely, however, but leaving apertures for egress and ingress. The snugness of the locality had tempted the French, and had induced them to choose it as the most favorable spot, at the time, for colonization. Sauvolle, a brother of Iberville, was put in command of the fort, and Bienville, the youngest of the three brothers, was appointed his lieutenant.

A few huts having been erected round the fort, the settlers began to clear the land, in order to bring it into cultivation. Iberville, having furnished them with all the necessary provisions, utensils, and other supplies, prepared to sail for France. How deeply affecting must have been the parting scene! How many casualties might prevent those who remained in this unknown region from ever seeing again those who, through the perils of such a long voyage, had to return to their home! What crowding emotions must have filled up the breast of Sauvolle, Bienville, and their handful of companions, when they beheld the sails of Iberville's fleet fading in the distance, like transient clouds! Well may it be supposed that it seemed to them as if their very souls had been carried away, and that they felt a momentary sinking of the heart, when they found themselves abandoned, and necessarily left to their own resources, scanty as they were, on a patch of land, between the ocean on one side, and on the other, a wilderness, which fancy peopled with every sort of terrors. The sense of their loneliness fell upon them like the gloom of night, darkening their hopes, and filling their hearts with dismal apprehensions.

But as the country had been ordered to be explored, Sauvolle availed himself of that circumstance to refresh the minds of his men by the excitement of an expedition into the interior of the continent. He therefore hastened to dispatch most of them with Bienville, who, with a chief of the Bayagoulas for his guide, went to visit the Colapissas. They inhabited the northern shore of Lake Pontchartrain, and their domains embraced the sites now occupied by Lewisburg, Mandeville, and Fontainebleau. That tribe numbered three hundred warriors, who, in their distant hunting excursions, had been engaged in frequent skirmishes with some of the British colonists in South Carolina. When the French landed, they were informed that, two days previous, the village of the Colapissas had been attacked by a party of two hundred Chickasaws, headed by two Englishmen. These were the first tidings which the French had of their old rivals, and which proved to be the harbinger of the incessant struggle which was to continue for more than a century between the two races, and to terminate by the permanent occupation of Louisiana by the Anglo-Saxon.

Bienville returned to the fort to convey this important information to Sauvolle. After having rested there for several days, he went to the Bay of Pascagoulas, and ascended the river which bears that name, and the banks of which were tenanted by a branch of the Biloxis, and by the Moelobites. Encouraged by the friendly reception which he met everywhere, he ventured farther, and paid a visit to the Mobilians, who entertained him with great hospitality. Bienville found them much reduced from what they had been, and listened with eagerness to the many tales of their former power, which had been rapidly declining since the crushing blow they had received from Soto.

When Iberville ascended the Mississippi the first time, he had remarked Bayou Plaquemines and Bayou Chetimachas. The one he called after the fruit of certain trees which appeared to have exclusive possession of its banks, and the other after the name of the Indians who dwelt in the vicinity. He had ordered them to be explored, and the indefatigable Bienville, on his return from Mobile, obeyed the instructions left to his brother, and made an accurate survey of these two Bayous. When he was coming down the river, at the distance of about eighteen miles below the site where New Orleans now stands, he met an English vessel of 16 guns, under the command of Captain Bar. The English captain informed the French that he was examining the banks of the river, with the intention of selecting a spot for the foundation of a colony. Bienville told him that Louisiana was a dependency of Canada; that the French had already made several establishments on the Mississippi; and he appealed, in confirmation of his assertions, to their own presence in the river, in such small boats, which evidently proved the existence of some settlement close at hand. The Englishman believed Bienville, and sailed back. Where this occurrence took place the river makes a considerable bend, and it was from the circumstance which I have related that the spot received the appellation of the *English Turn*—a name which it has retained to the present day. It was not far from that place, the atmosphere of which appears to be fraught with some malignant spell hostile to the sons of Albion, that the English, who were outwitted by Bienville in 1699, met with a signal defeat in battle from the Americans in 1815. The diplomacy of Bienville and the military genius of Jackson proved to them equally fatal, when they aimed at the possession of Louisiana.

Since the exploring expedition of La Salle down the Mississippi, Canadian hunters, whose habits and intrepidity Fenimore Cooper has so graphically described in the character of Leather-Stocking, used to extend their roving excursions to the banks of that river; and those holy missionaries of the church, who, as the pioneers of religion, have filled the New World with their sufferings, and whose incredible deeds in the service of God afford so many materials for the most interesting of books, had come in advance of the pickaxe of the settler, and had domiciliated themselves among the tribes who lived near the waters of the Mississippi. One of them, Father Montigny, was residing with the Tensas, within the territory of the present parish of Tensas, in the State of Louisiana, and another, Father Davion, was the pastor of the Yazoos, in the present State of Mississippi.

Father Montigny was a descendant from Galon de Montigny, who had the honor of bearing the banner of France at the battle of Bouvines. It is well known that in 1214 a league of most of the European princes, the most powerful of whom were the King of England and the Emperor of Germany, was formed against Philip Augustus. The allied army, composed of one hundred thousand men, and the French army mustering half that number, met at Bouvines, between Lille and Tournay. Before the battle, Philip reviewed his troops, and in their presence, removing his crown from his temples, said to the assembled host, "Peers, barons, knights, soldiers, and all ye that listen to me, if you know one more worthy of the crown of France than I am, you may award it to him." Shouts of enthusiasm declared that he was the worthiest. "Well, then," said he, "help me to keep it." The battle soon began, and raged for some time with alternate success for the belligerents. To the long gilded pole which supported the banner of France, and towered in proud majesty over the plain, the eyes of the French knights, scattered over the wide field of battle, were frequently turned with feverish anxiety. So long as it stood erect, and as firmly fixed in Montigny's iron grasp as if it had taken root in the soil, they knew that the king was safe, it being the duty of the bearer of that standard to keep close to the royal person, and never to lose sight of him. It was an arduous and a perilous duty, which devolved on none but one well tried among the bravest; and it was not long before Montigny had to plunge into the thickest of the fight, to retain his post near Philip Augustus, who felt on that trying occasion, when his crown was at stake, that the king was bound to prove himself the best knight of his army.

On a sudden, a cold chill ran through the boldest heart in the French ranks. The long stately pole which bore the royal banner was observed to wave distressfully, and to rock like the mast of a vessel tossed on a tempestuous sea. That fatal signal was well known—it meant that the king was in peril. Simultaneously, from every part of the field, every French knight, turning from the foe he had in front, dashed headlong away, and with resistless fury forced a passage to the spot where the fate of France was held in dubious suspense. One minute more of delay, and all would have been lost. The king had been unhorsed by the lance of a German knight, trampled under the feet of the chargers of the combatants, and had with difficulty been replaced on horseback. Those that came at last to the rescue, found him surrounded by the corpses of one hundred and twenty gentlemen of the best blood of France, who had died in his defence. His armor was shattered to pieces, his battle-axe, from the blows which it had given, was blunted into a mere club, and his arm, waxing faint, could hardly parry the blows which rained upon his head. Montigny stood alone by him, and was defending, with a valor worthy of the occasion, the flag and the king of France. That occasion, indeed, was one, if any, to nerve the arm of a man, and to madden such a one as Montigny into the execution of prodigies.

To be the royal standard-bearer, to fight side by side with his king, to have saved him perhaps from captivity or death; such were the proud destinies of the noble knight, Galon de Montigny. His descendant's lot in life was an humbler one in the estimation of the world, but perhaps a higher one in that of heaven. A hood, not a crested helmet, covered his head, and he was satisfied with being a soldier in the militia of Christ. But if, in the accomplishment of the duties of his holy faith, he courted dangers and even coveted tortures with heroic fortitude—if, in the cause of God, he used his spiritual weapons against vice, error and superstition, with as much zeal and bravery as others use carnal weapons in earthly causes—if, instead of a king's life, he saved thousands of souls from perdition—is he to be deemed recreant to his gentle blood, and is he not to be esteemed as good a knight as his great ancestor of his torical renown?

Father Davion had resided for some time with the Tunicas, where he had made himself so popular, that, on the death of their chief, they had elected him to fill his place. The priest humbly declined the honor, giving for his reasons, that his new duties as their chief would be incompatible with those of his sacred ministry. Yet the Tunicas, who loved and venerated him as a man, were loth to abandon their old creed to adopt the Christian faith, and they turned a deaf ear to his admonitions. One day the missionary, incensed at their obstinate perseverance in idolatry, and wishing to demonstrate that their idols were too powerless to punish any offence aimed at them, burned their temple, and broke to pieces the rudely carved figures which were the objects of the peculiar adoration of that tribe. The Indians were so much attached to Father Davion, that they contented themselves with expelling him, and he retired on the territory of the Yazoos, who proved themselves readier proselytes, and became converts in a short time. This means that they adopted some of the outward signs of Christianity, without understanding or appreciating its dogmas.

Proud of his achievements, Father Davion had, with such aid as he could command, constructed and hung up a pulpit to the trunk of an immense oak, in the same manner that it is stuck to a pillar in the Catholic churches. Back of that tree, growing on the slight hill which commanded the river, he had raised a little Gothic chapel, the front part of which was divided by the robust trunk to which it was made to adhere, with two diminutive doors opening into the edifice, on either side of that vegetal tower. It was done in imitation of those stone towers, which stand like sentinels wedged to the frontispiece of the temples of God, on the continent of Europe. In that chapel, Father Davion kept all the sacred vases, the holy water, and the sacerdotal habiliments. There he used to retire to spend hours in meditation and in prayer. In that tabernacle was a small portable altar, which, whenever he said mass for the natives, was transported outside, under the oak, where they often met to the number of three to four hundred. What a beautiful subject for painting! The majesty of the river—the glowing richness of the land in its virgin loveliness—the Gothic chapel—the pulpit which looked as if it had grown out of the holy oak—the hoary-headed priest, speaking with a sincerity of conviction, an impressiveness of manner and a radiancy of countenance worthy of an apostle—the motley crowd of the Indians, listening attentively, some with awe, others with meek submission, a few with a sneering incredulity, which, as the evangelical man went on, seemed gradually to vanish from their strongly marked features—in the background, a group of their juggling prophets, or conjurers, scowling with fierceness at the minister of truth, who was destroying their power;—would not all these elements, where the grandeur of the scenery would be combined with the acting of man and the development of his feelings, on an occasion of the most solemn nature, produce in the hands of a Salvator Rosa, or of a Poussin, the most striking effects?

Father Davion had acquired a perfect knowledge of the dialect of his neophytes, and spoke it with as much fluency as his own maternal tongue. He had both the physical and mental qualifications of an orator: he was tall and commanding in stature; his high receding forehead was well set off by his long, flowing, gray hairs, curling down to his shoulders; his face was "sicklied over with the pale cast of thought;" vigils and fasting had so emaciated his form that he seemed almost to be dissolved into spirituality. There was in his eyes a soft, blue, limpid transparency of look, which seemed to be a reflection from the celestial vault; yet that eye, so calm, so benignant, could be lighted up with all the coruscations of pious wrath and indignation, when, in the pulpit, he vituperated his congregation for some act of cruelty or deceit, and threatened them with eternal punishment. First, he would remind them, with apostolic unction, with a voice as bland as the evening breeze, of the many benefits which the Great Spirit had showered upon them, and of the many more which he had in store for the red men, if they adhered strictly to his law. When he thus spoke, the sunshine of his serene, intellectual countenance would steal over his hearers, and their faces would express the wild delight which they felt. But, anon, when the holy father recollected the many and daily transgressions of his unruly children, a dark hue would, by degrees, creep over the radiancy of his face, as if a storm was gathering, and clouds after clouds were chasing each other over the mirror of his soul. Out of the inmost recesses of his heart, there arose a whirlwind which shook the holy man, in its struggle to rush out: then would flash the lightning of the eye; then the voice, so soft, so insinuating, and even so caressing, would assume tones that sounded like repeated peals of thunder; and a perfect tempest of eloquence would he pour forth upon his dismayed auditory, who crossed themselves, crouched to the earth and howled piteously, demanding pardon for their sins. Then, the ghostly orator, relenting at the sight of so much contrition, would descend like Moses from his Mount Sinai, laying aside the angry elements in which he had robed himself, as if he had come to preside over the last judgment; and with the gentleness of a lamb, he would walk among his prostrate auditors, raising them from the ground, pressing them to his bosom, and comforting them with such sweet accents as a mother uses to lull her first-born to sleep. It was a spectacle touching in the extreme, and angelically pure!

Father Davion lived to a very old age, still commanding the awe and affection of his flock, by whom he was looked upon as a supernatural being. Had they not, they said, frequently seen him at night, with his dark, solemn gown, not walking, but gliding through the woods, like something spiritual? How could one, so weak in frame, and using so little food, stand so many fatigues? How was it, that whenever one of them fell sick, however distant it might be, Father Davion knew it instantly, and was sure to be there, before sought for? Who had given him the information? Who told him whenever they committed any secret sin? None; and yet, he knew it. Did any of his prophecies ever prove false? By what means did he arrive at so much knowledge about every thing? Did they not, one day, when he kneeled, as usual, in solitary prayer, under the holy oak, see from the respectful distance at which they stood, a ray of the sun piercing the thick foliage of the tree, cast its lambent flame around his temples, and wreath itself into a crown of glory, encircling his snow-white hair? What was it he was in the habit of muttering so long, when counting the beads of that mysterious chain that hung round his neck? Was he not then telling the Great Spirit every wrong they had done? So, they both loved and feared Father Davion. One day, they found him dead at the foot of the altar: he was leaning against it, with his head cast back, with his hands clasped, and still retaining his kneeling position. There was an expression of rapture in his face, as if, to his sight, the gates of paradise had suddenly unfolded themselves to give him admittance: it was evident that his soul had exhaled into a prayer, the last on this earth, but terminating, no doubt, in a hymn of rejoicing above.

Long after Davion's death, mothers of the Yazoo tribe used to carry their children to the place where he loved to administer the sacrament of baptism. There, these simple creatures, with many ceremonies of a wild nature, partaking of their new Christian faith and of their old lingering Indian superstitions, invoked and called down the benedictions of Father Davion upon themselves and their families. For many years, that spot was designated under the name of *Davion's Bluff*. In recent times, Fort Adams was constructed where Davion's chapel formerly stood, and was the cause of the place being more currently known under a different appellation.

Such were the two visitors who, in 1699, appeared before Sauvolle, at the fort of Biloxi, to relieve the monotony of his cheerless existence, and to encourage him in his colonizing enterprise. Their visit, however, was not of long duration, and they soon returned to discharge the duties of their sacred mission.

Iberville had been gone for several months, and the year was drawing to a close without any tidings of him. A deeper gloom had settled over the little colony at Biloxi, when, on the 7th of December, some signal guns were heard at sea, and the grateful sound came booming over the waters, spreading joy in every breast. There was not one who was not almost oppressed with the intensity of his feelings. At last, friends were coming, bringing relief to the body and to the soul! Every colonist hastily abandoned his occupation of the moment, and ran to the shore. The soldier himself, in the eagerness of expectation, left his post of duty, and rushed to the parapet which overlooked the bay. Presently, several vessels hove in sight, bearing the white flag of France, and, approaching as near as the shallowness of the beach permitted, folded their pinions, like water-fowls seeking repose on the crest of the billows.

It was Iberville, returning with the news that, on his representations, Sauvolle had been appointed by the king, Governor of Louisiana; Bienville Lieutenant-Governor, and Boisbriant commander of the fort at Biloxi, with the grade of Major. Iberville, having been informed by Bienville of the attempt of the English to make a settlement on the banks of the Mississippi, and of the manner in which it had been foiled, resolved to take precautionary measures against the repetition of any similar attempt. Without loss of time, he departed with Bienville, on the 17th of January, 1700, and running up the river, he constructed a small fort, on the first solid ground which he met, and which is said to have been at a distance of fifty-four miles from its mouth.

When so engaged, the two brothers one day saw a canoe rapidly sweeping down the river, and approaching the spot where they stood. It was occupied by eight men, six of whom were rowers, the seventh was the steersman, and the eighth, from his appearance, was evidently of a superior order to that of his companions, and the commander of the party. Well may it be imagined what greeting the stranger received, when, leaping on shore, he made himself known as the Chevalier de Tonti, who had again heard of the establishment of a colony in Louisiana, and who, for the second time, had come to see if there was any truth in the report. With what emotion did Iberville and Bienville fold in their arms the faithful companion and friend of La Salle, of whom they had heard so many wonderful tales from the Indians, to whom he was so well known under the name of "Iron Hand!" With what admiration they looked at his person, and with what increasing interest they listened to his long recitals of what he had done and had seen on that broad continent, the threshold of which they had hardly passed!

After having rested three days at the fort, the indefatigable Tonti reascended the Mississippi, with Iberville and Bienville, and finally parted with them at Natchez. Iberville was so much pleased with that part of the bank of the river, where now exists the city of Natchez, that he marked it down as a most eligible spot for a town, of which he drew the plan, and which he called Rosalie, after the maiden name of the Countess Pontchartrain, the wife of the Chancellor. He then returned to the new fort he was erecting on the Mississippi, and Bienville went to explore the country of the Yatasses, of the Natchitoches, and of the Ouachitas. What romance can be more agreeable to the imagination than to accompany Iberville and Bienville in their wild explorations, and to compare the state of the country in their time with what it is in our days?

When the French were at Natchez, they were struck with horror at an occurrence, too clearly demonstrating the fierceness of disposition of that tribe, which was destined, in after years, to become so celebrated in the history of Louisiana. One of their temples having been set on fire by lightning, a hideous spectacle presented itself to the Europeans. The tumultuous rush of the Indians—the infernal howlings and lamentations of the men, women, and children—the unearthly vociferations of the priests, their fantastic dances and ceremonies around the burning edifice—the demoniac fury with which mothers rushed to the fatal spot, and, with the piercing cries and gesticulations of maniacs, flung their new-born babes into the flames to pacify their irritated deity—the increasing anger of the heavens blackening with the impending storm, the lurid flashes of the lightnings, darting as it were in mutual enmity from the clashing clouds—the low, distant growling of the coming tempest—the long column of smoke and fire shooting upward from the funeral pyre, and looking like one of the gigantic torches of Pandemonium—the war of the elements combined with the worst effects of the frenzied superstition of man—the suddenness and strangeness of the awful scene—all these circumstances produced such an impression upon the French, as to deprive them, for the moment, of the powers of volition and action. Rooted to the ground, they stood aghast with astonishment and indignation at the appalling scene. Was it a dream?—a wild delirium of the mind? But no—the monstrous reality of the vision was but too apparent; and they threw themselves among the Indians, supplicating them to cease their horrible sacrifice to their gods, and joining threats to their supplications. Owing to this intervention, and perhaps because a sufficient number of victims had been offered, the priests gave the signal of retreat, and the Indians slowly withdrew from the accursed spot. Such was the aspect under which the Natchez showed themselves, for the first time, to their visitors: it was an ominous presage for the future.

After these explorations, Iberville departed again for France, to solicit additional assistance from the government, and left Bienville in command of the new fort on the Mississippi. It was very hard for the two brothers, Sauvolle and Bienville, to be thus separated, when they stood so much in need of each other's countenance, to breast the difficulties that sprung up around them with a luxuriance which they seemed to borrow from the vegetation of the country. The distance between the Mississippi and Biloxi was not so easily overcome in those days as in ours, and the means which the two brothers had of communing together were very scanty and uncertain. Sauvolle and his companions had suffered much from the severity of the winter, which had been so great that in one of his dispatches he informed his government that "*water, when poured into tumblers to rinse them, froze instantaneously, and before it could be used.*"

At last, the spring made its appearance, or rather the season which bears that denomination, but which did not introduce itself with the genial and mild atmosphere that is its characteristic in other climes. The month of April was so hot that the colonists could work only two hours in the morning and two in the evening. When there was no breeze, the reflection of the sun from the sea and from the sandy beach was intolerable; and if they sought relief under the pine trees of the forest, instead of meeting cool shades, it seemed to them that there came from the very lungs of the trees a hot breath, which sent them back hastily to the burning shore, in quest of air. Many of the colonists, accustomed to the climate of Canada and France, languished, pined, fell sick, and died. Some, as they lay panting under the few oaks that grew near the fort, dreamed of the verdant valleys, the refreshing streams, the picturesque hills, and the snow-capped mountains of their native land. The fond scenes upon which their imagination dwelt with rapture, would occasionally assume, to their enfeebled vision, the distinctness of real existence, and feverish recollection would produce on the horizon of the mind, such an apparition as tantalizes the dying traveler in the parched deserts of Arabia. When despair had paved the way, it was easy for disease to follow, and to crush those that were already prostrate in mind and in body. To increase the misery of these poor wretches, famine herself raised her spectral form among them, and grasped pestilence by the hand to assist her in the work of desolation. Thus, that fiendish sisterhood reigned supreme, where, in our days, health, abundance, and wealth, secured by the improvements of civilization, bless the land with perpetual smiles.

Sauvolle, from the feebleness of his constitution, was more exposed than any of his companions to be affected by the perils of the situation; and yet it was he upon whom devolved the duty of watching over the safety of others. But he was sadly incapacitated for the discharge of that duty by physical and moral causes. When an infant, he had inherited a large fortune from an aunt, whose godson he was. With such means at his future command, the boy, who gave early evidence of a superior intellect, became the darling hope of his family, and was sent to France to be qualified for the splendid career which parental fondness anticipated for him. The seeds of education were not, in that instance, thrown on a rebellious soil; and when Sauvolle left the seat of learning where he had been trained, he carried away with him the admiration of his professors and of his schoolmates. In the high circles of society where his birth and fortune entitled him to appear, he produced no less sensation; and well he might, for he appeared, to an eminent degree, capable of adorning any station which he might wish to occupy. Nature had been pleased to produce another Crichton, and Sauvolle soon became known as the *American prodigy*. Racine called him a poet; Bossuet had declared that there were in him all the materials of a great orator; and the haughty Villars, after a conversation of several hours with him, was heard to say, "Here is a Marshal of France in embryo."

The frivolous admired his wonderful expertness in fencing, in horsemanship, and his other acquirements of a similar nature; artists might have been proud of his talent for painting and for music; and those friends that were admitted into his intimacy were struck with his modesty and with the high-toned morality which pervaded the life of one so young. The softer sex, yielding to the fascination of his manly graces, was held captive by them, and hailed his first steps on the world's stage with all the passionate enthusiasm of the female heart. But he loved and was loved by the fairest daughter of one of the noblest houses of France, and his nuptials were soon to be celebrated with fitting pomp. Was not this the acme of human felicity? If so, whence that paleness which sat on his brow, and spoke of inward pain, moral or physical? Whence those sudden starts? Why was he observed occasionally to grasp his heart with a convulsive hand? What appalling disclosure could make him desert her to whom his faith was plighted, and could so abruptly hurry him away from France and from that seat where so much happiness was treasured up for him? That it was no voluntary act on his part, and that he was merely complying with the stern decree of fate, could be plainly inferred from that look of despair which, from the ship that bore him away, he cast at the shores of France when receding from his sight. So must Adam have looked, when he saw the flaming sword of the angel of punishment interposed between him and Paradise.

Sauvolle arrived in Canada at the very moment when Iberville and Bienville were preparing their expedition to Louisiana; and he eagerly begged to join them, saying that he knew his days were numbered, that he had come back to die in America, and that since his higher aspirations were all blasted, he could yet find some sort of melancholy pleasure in closing his career in that new colony, of which his brothers were to be the founders, and to which they were to attach their names forever.

Poor Sauvolle! the star of his destiny which rose up at the court of Louis the XIVth with such gorgeousness, was now setting in gloom and desolation on the bleak shore of Biloxi. How acute must his mental agony have been, when, by day and by night, the comparison of what he might have been with what he was must have incessantly forced itself upon his mind: Why had Nature qualified him to be the best of husbands and fathers, when forbidding him, at the same time, to assume the sacred character which he coveted, and to form those ties, without which, existence could only be a curse to one so exquisitely framed to nourish the choicest affections of our race? Why give him all the elements of greatness, and preclude their development? Why inspire him with the consciousness of worth, and deny him time and life for its manifestation? Why had such a mind and such a soul been lodged in a defective body, soon to be dissolved? Why a blade of such workmanship in such an unworthy scabbard? Why create a being with feelings as intense as ever animated one of his species, merely to bruise them in the bud? Why shower upon him gifts of such value, when they were to be instantly resumed? Why light up the luminary which was to be extinguished before its rays could be diffused? Was it not a solemn mockery? What object could it answer, except to inflict extreme misery? Surely, it could only be a conception or device of the arch-enemy of mankind! But how could he be allowed thus to trifle with God's creatures? Were they his puppets and playthings? or, was it one of God's inscrutable designs? Was it an enigma only to be solved hereafter?--These reflections may be supposed to have passed through Sauvolle's mind, as he, with folded arms, one day, stood on the parapet of the fort at Biloxi, looking sorrowfully at the scene of desolation around him, at his diseased and famished companions. Overwhelmed with grief, he withdrew his gaze from the harrowing sight, heaved a deep sigh and uplifted his eyes toward heaven, with a look which plainly asked, if his placid resignation and acquiescent fortitude had not entitled him at last to repose. That look of anguish was answered: a slight convulsion flitted over his face, his hand grasped the left side of his breast, his body tottered, and Sauvolle was dead before he reached the ground.

Such was the fate of the first governor of Louisiana. A hard fate indeed is that of defective organization! An anticipated damnation it is, for the unbeliever, when spiritual perfection is palsied and rendered inert by being clogged with physical imperfection, or wedded to diseased matter! When genius was flashing in the head, when the spirit of God lived in the soul, why did creation defeat its own apparent purposes, in this case, by planting in the heart the seeds of aneurism? It is a question which staggers philosophy, confounds human reason, and is solved only by the revelations of Christianity.

What a pity that Sauvolle had not the faith of a Davion, or of a St. Louis, whose deaths I have recorded in the preceding pages! He would have known that the heavier the cross we bear with Christian resignation in this world, the greater the reward is in the better one which awaits us : and that our trials in this, our initiatory state of terrestrial existence, are merely intended by the infinite goodness of the Creator, as golden opportunities for us to show our fidelity, and to deserve a higher or lesser degree of happiness, when we shall enter into the celestial kingdom of spiritual and eternal life, secured to us at the price of *sufferings* alone: and what sufferings! Those of the Godhead himself! He would not then have repined at pursuing the thorny path, trod before, for his sake, by the divine Victim, and with Job he would have said : " Who is he that hideth counsel without knowledge? Therefore have I uttered that I understood not ; things too wonderful for me, which I knew not. The Lord gave, and the Lord hath taken away ; blessed be the name of the Lord!"

I lately stood where the first establishment of the French was made, and I saw no vestiges of their passage, save in the middle of the space formerly occupied by the fort, where I discovered a laying of bricks on a level with the ground, and covering the common area of a tomb. Is it the repository of Sauvolle's remains? I had with me no pickaxe to solve the question, and indeed it was more agreeable to the mood in which I was then, to indulge in speculations, than to ascertain the truth. Since the fort had been abandoned, it was evident that there never had been any attempt to turn the ground to some useful purpose, although, being cleared of trees, it must have been more eligible for a settlement than the adjoining ground which remained covered with wood. Yet, on the right and left, beyond the two ravines already mentioned, habitations are to be seen ; but a sort of traditionary awe seems to have repelled intrusion from the spot marked by such melancholy recollections. On the right, as you approach the place, a beautiful villa, occupied by an Anglo American family, is replete with all the comforts and resources of modern civilization; while on the left, there may be seen a rude hut, where still reside descendants from the first settlers, living in primitive ignorance and irreclaimable poverty, which lose, however, their offensive features, by being mixed up with so much of patriarchal virtues, of pristine innocence, and of arcadian felicity. These two families, separated only by the site of the old fort, but between whose social position, there existed such an immense distance, struck me as being fit representatives of the past and of the present. One was the type of the French colony, and the other, the emblem of its modern transformation.

I gazed with indescribable feelings on the spot where Sauvolle and his companions had suffered so much. Humble and abandoned as it is, it was clothed in my eye with a sacred character, when I remembered that it was the cradle of so many sovereign states, which are but *disjecta membra* of the old colony of Louisiana. What a contrast between the French colony of 1700, and its imperial substitute of 1848! Is there in the mythological records of antiquity, or in the fairy tales of the Arabian Nights, any thing that will not sink into insignificance, **when compared with the romance of such a history?**

THIRD LECTURE.

Situation of the Colony from 1701 to 1712—The Petticoat Insurrection—History and Death of Iberville—Bienville, the second Governor of Louisiana—History of Anthony Crozat, the great Merchant—Concession of Louisiana to him.

SAUVOLLE had died on the 22d of July, 1701, and Louisiana had remained under the sole charge of Bienville, who, though very young, was fully equal to meet that emergency, by the maturity of his mind and by his other qualifications. He had hardly consigned his brother to the tomb, when Iberville returned with two ships of the line and a brig laden with troops and provisions. The first object that greeted his sight, on his landing, was Bienville, whose person was in deep mourning, and whose face wore such an expression as plainly told that a blow, fatal to both, had been struck in the absence of the head of the family. In their mute embraces, the two brothers felt that they understood each other better than if their grief had vented itself in words, and Iberville's first impulse was to seek Sauvolle's tomb. There he knelt for hours, bathed in tears, and absorbed in fervent prayer for him whom he was to see no more in the garb of mortality. This recent blow reminded him of a father's death, whom he had seen carried off, bleeding, from the battle-field; and then his four brothers, who had met the same stern and honorable fate, rose to his sight with their ghastly wounds; and he bethought himself of the sweet and melancholy face of his mother, who had sunk gradually into the grave, drooping like a gentle flower under the rough visitations of the wind of adversity. On these heavy recollections of the past, his heart swelled with tears, and he implored heaven to spare his devoted family, or, if any one of its members was again destined to an early death, to take *him*, Iberville, as a free offering, in preference to the objects of his love. But there are men, upon whom grief operates as fire upon steel: it purifies the metal, and gives more elasticity to its spring; it works upon the soul with that same mysterious process by which nature transforms the dark carbuncle into the shining diamond. These men know how to turn from the desolation of their heart, and survey the world with a clearer, serener eye, to choose the sphere where they can best accomplish their mission on this earth—that mission—the fulfilment of duties whence good is to result to mankind, or to their country. One of these highly gifted beings Iberville was, and he soon withdrew his attention from the grave, to give it entirely to the consolidation of the great national enterprise he had undertaken—the establishment of a colony in Louisiana.

According to Iberville's orders, and in conformity with the king's instructions, Bienville left Boisbriant, his cousin, with twenty men, at the old fort of Biloxi, and transported the principal seat of the colony to the western side of the river Mobile, not far from the spot where now stands the city of Mobile. Near the mouth of that river, there is an island, which the French had called Massacre Island, from the great quantity of human bones which they found bleaching on its shores. It was evident that *there* some awful tragedy had been acted; but tradition, when interrogated, laid *her choppy finger upon her skinny lips*, and answered not. This uncertainty, giving a free scope to the imagination, shrouded the place with a higher degree of horror, and with a deeper hue of fantastical gloom. It looked like the favorite ball-room of the witches of hell. The wind sighed so mournfully through the shriveled up pines, whose vampire heads seemed incessantly to bow to some invisible and grisly visitors: the footsteps of the stranger emitted such an awful and supernatural sound, when trampling on the skulls which strewed his path, that it was impossible for the coldest imagination not to labor under some crude and ill-defined apprehensions. Verily, the weird sisters could not have chosen a fitter abode. Nevertheless, the French, supported by their mercurial temperament, were not deterred from forming an establishment on that sepulchral island, which, they thought, afforded some facilities for their transatlantic communications. They changed its name, however, and called it Dauphine Island. As, to many, this name may be without signification, it may not be improper to state, that the wife of the eldest born of the King of France, and consequently, of the presumptive heir to the crown, was, at that time, called the Dauphine, and her husband the Dauphin. This was in compliment to the province of Dauphiné, which was annexed to the kingdom of France, on the abdication of a Count of Dauphiné, who ceded that principality to the French monarch in 1349. Hence the origin of the appellation given to the island. It was a high-sounding and courtly name for such a bleak repository of the dead!

Iberville did not tarry long in Louisiana. His home was the broad ocean, where he had been nursed, as it were; and he might have exclaimed with truth, in the words of Byron:—

   — "I have loved thee, Ocean! and my joy
   Of youthful sports was on thy breast to be

> Borne, like bubbles, onward: from a boy
> I wantoned with thy breakers—they to me
> Were a delight; and if the freshening sea
> Made them a terror—'twas a pleasing fear,
> For I was as it were a child of thee,
> And trusted to thy billows far and near,
> And laid my hand upon thy mane."

But, before his departure, he gave some wholesome advice to his government:—" It is necessary," said he, in one of his dispatches, "to send here honest tillers of the earth, and not rogues and paupers, who come to Louisiana solely with the intention of making a fortune, by all sorts of means, in order to speed back to Europe. Such men can not be elements of prosperity to a colony." He left those, of whom he was the chief protector, abundantly supplied with every thing, and seeing that their affectionate hearts were troubled with manifold misgivings as to their fate, which appeared to them to be closely linked with his own, he promised soon to return, and to bring additional strength to what he justly looked upon as his creation. But it had been decreed otherwise.

In 1703, war had broken out between Great Britain, France and Spain; and Iberville, a distinguished officer of the French navy, was engaged in expeditions that kept him away from the colony. It did not cease, however, to occupy his thoughts, and had become clothed, in his eye, with a sort of family interest. Louisiana was thus left, for some time, to her scanty resources; but, weak as she was, she gave early proofs of that generous spirit which has ever since animated her; and, on the towns of Pensacola and San Augustine, then in possession of the Spaniards, being threatened with an invasion by the English of South Carolina, she sent to her neighbors what help she could, in men, ammunition, and supplies of all sorts. It was the more meritorious, as it was the obolus of the poor!

The year 1703 slowly rolled by, and gave way to 1704. Still, nothing was heard from the parent country. There seemed to be an impassable barrier between the old and the new continent. The milk which flowed from the motherly breast of France could no longer reach the parched lips of her new-born infant; and famine began to pinch the colonists, who scattered themselves all along the coast, to live by fishing. They were reduced to the veriest extremity of misery, and despair had settled in every bosom, in spite of the encouragements of Bienville, who displayed the most manly fortitude amid all the trials to which he was subjected, when suddenly a vessel made its appearance. The colonists rushed to the shore with wild anxiety, but their exultation was greatly diminished when, on the nearer approach of the moving speck, they recognized the Spanish, instead of the French flag. It was relief, however, coming to them, and proffered by a friendly hand. It was a return made by the governor of Pensacola, for the kindness he had experienced the year previous. Thus, the debt of gratitude was paid: it was a practical lesson. Where the seeds of charity are cast, *there* springs the harvest in time of need.

Good things, like evils, do not come single, and this succor was but the herald of another one, still more effectual, in the shape of a ship from France. Iberville had not been able to redeem his pledge to the poor colonists, but he had sent his brother Chateaugué in his place, at the imminent risk of being captured by the English, who occupied, at that time, most of the avenues of the Gulf of Mexico. *He* was not the man to spare either himself, or his family, in cases of emergency, and his heroic soul was inured to such sacrifices. Grateful the colonists were for this act of devotedness, and they resumed the occupation of those tenements which they had abandoned in search of food. The aspect of things was suddenly changed; abundance and hope reappeared in the land, whose population was increased by the arrival of seventeen persons, who came, under the guidance of Chateaugué, with the intention of making a permanent settlement, and who, in evidence of their determination, had provided themselves with all the implements of husbandry. We, who daily see hundreds flocking to our shores, and who look at the occurrence with as much unconcern as at the passing cloud, can hardly conceive the excitement produced by the arrival of these seventeen emigrants among men who, for nearly two years, had been cut off from communication with the rest of the civilized world. A denizen of the moon, dropping on this planet, would not be stared at and interrogated with more eager curiosity.

This excitement had hardly subsided, when it was revived by the appearance of another ship, and it became intense, when the inhabitants saw a procession of twenty females, with veiled faces, proceeding arm in arm, and two by two, to the house of the governor, who received them in state, and provided them with suitable lodgings. What did it mean? Innumerable were the gossipings of the day, and part of the coming night itself was spent in endless commentaries and conjectures. But the next morning, which was Sunday, the mystery was cleared by the officiating priest reading from the pulpit, after mass, and for the general information, the following communication from the minister to Bienville: "His majesty sends twenty girls to be married to the Canadians and to the other inhabitants of Mobile, in order to consolidate the colony. All these girls are industrious, and have received a pious and virtuous education. Beneficial results to the colony are expected from their teaching their useful attainments to the Indian females. In order that none should be sent except those of known virtue and of unspotted reputation, his majesty did intrust the bishop of Quebec with the mission of taking these girls from such establishments, as, from their very nature and character, would put them at once above all suspicions of corruption. You will take care to settle them in life as well as may be in your power, and to marry them to such men as are capable of providing them with a commodious home."

This was a very considerate recommendation, and very kind it was, indeed, from the great Louis the XIVth, one of the proudest monarchs that ever lived, to descend from his Olympian seat of majesty, to the level of such details, and to such minute instructions for ministering to the personal comforts of his remote Louisianian subjects. Many were the gibes and high was the glee on that occasion; pointed were the jokes aimed at young Bienville, on his being thus transformed into a matrimonial agent and pater familiæ. The intentions of the king, however, were faithfully executed, and more than one rough but honest Canadian boatman of the St. Lawrence and of the Mississippi, closed his adventurous and erratic career, and became a domestic and useful member of that little commonwealth, under the watchful influence of the dark-eyed maid of the Loire or of the Seine. Infinite are the chords of the lyre which delights the romantic muse; and these incidents, small and humble as they are, appear to me to be imbued with an indescribable charm, which appeals to her imagination.

Iberville had gone back to France since 1701, and

the year 1705 had now begun its onward course, without his having returned to the colony, according to his promise, so that the inhabitants had become impatient of further delay. They were in that state of suspense, when a ship of the line, commanded by Ducoudray, arrived soon after the opening of the year, but still to disappoint the anxious expectations of the colonists. No Iberville had come: yet there was some consolation in the relief which was sent—goods, provisions, ammunition; flesh-pots of France, rivaling, to a certainty, those of Egypt: sparkling wines to cheer the cup; twenty-three girls to gladden the heart; five priests to minister to the wants of the soul and to bless holy alliances; two sisters of charity to attend on the sick and preside over the hospital of the colony, and seventy-five soldiers for protection against the inroads of the Indians. This was something to be thankful for, and to occupy the minds of the colonists for a length of time. But life is chequered with many a hue, and the antagonistical agents of good and evil closely tread, in alternate succession, on the heels of each other. Thus, the short-lived rejoicings of the colonists soon gave way to grief and lamentations. A hungry epidemic did not disdain to prey upon the population, small as it was, and thirty-five persons became its victims. Thirty-five! This number was enormous in those days, and the epidemic of 1705 became as celebrated in the medical annals of the country, as will be the late one of 1847.

The history of Louisiana, in her early days, presents a Shaksperian mixture of the terrible and of the ludicrous. What can be more harrowing than the massacre of the French settlement on the Wabash in 1705; and in 1706, what more comical than the threatened insurrection of the French girls, who had come to settle in the country, under allurements which proved deceptive, and who were particularly indignant at being fed on corn? This fact is mentioned in these terms in one of Bienville's dispatches: "The males in the colony begin, through habit, to be reconciled to corn, as an article of nourishment; but the females, who are mostly Parisians, have for this kind of food a dogged aversion, which has not yet been subdued. Hence, they inveigh bitterly against his grace, the Bishop of Quebec, who, they say, has enticed them away from home, under the pretext of sending them to enjoy the milk and honey of the land of promise." Enraged at having thus been deceived, they swore that they would force their way out of the colony, on the first opportunity. This was called the *petticoat insurrection*.

There were, at that particular time, three important personages, who were the hinges upon which every thing turned in the commonwealth of Louisiana. These magnates were, Bienville, the governor, who wielded the sword, and who was the great executive mover of all; La Salle, the intendant commissary of the crown, who had the command of the purse, and who therefore might be called the controlling power; and the Curate de la Vente, who was not satisfied with mere spiritual influence. Unfortunately, in this Liliputian administration, the powers of the state and church were sadly at variance, in imitation of their betters in larger communities. The commissary, La Salle, in a letter of the 7th of December, 1706, accused Iberville, Bienville, and Chateaugué, the three brothers, of being guilty of *every sort of malfeasances and dilapidations*." "They are rogues," said he, "who pilfer away his Majesty's goods and effects." The Curate de la Vente, whose pretensions to temporal power Bienville had checked, backed La Salle, and undertook to discredit the governor's authority with the colonists, by boasting of his having sufficient influence at court to cause him to be soon dismissed from office.

On Bienville's side stood, of course, Chateaugué, his brother, and Major Boisbriant, his cousin. But Chateaugué was a new man (novus homo) in the colony, and consequently had, as yet, acquired very little weight. Boisbriant, although a zealous friend, had found means to increase the governor's vexations, by falling deeply in love. He had been smitten, perhaps, for the want of something better, with the charms of a lady, to whose charge had been committed the twenty girls selected by the Bishop of Quebec, and who had been appointed, as a sort of lay abbess, to superintend their conduct on the way and in Louisiana, until they got provided with those suitable monitors who are called husbands. That lady had reciprocated the affections of Boisbriant, and so far, the course of love ran smooth. But, as usual, it was doomed to meet with one of those obstacles which have given rise to so many beautiful literary compositions. Bienville stoutly objected to the match, as being an unfit one for his relation and subordinate, and peremptorily refused his approbation. Well may the indignation of the lady be conceived! Boisbriant seems to have meekly submitted to the superior wisdom of his chief, but she, scorning such forbearance, addressed herself to the minister, and complained, in no measured terms, of what she called an act of oppression. After having painted her case with as strong colors as she could, she very naturally concluded her observations with this sweeping declaration concerning Bienville: "It is therefore evident that he has not the necessary qualifications to be governor of this colony." Such is the logic of

Love, and although it may provoke a smile, thereby hangs a tale not destitute of romance.

These intestine dissensions were not the only difficulties that Bienville had to cope with. The very existence of the colony was daily threatened by the Indians; a furious war, in which the French were frequently implicated, raged between the Chickasaws and the Choctaws; and the smaller nations, principally the Alibamons, that prowled about the settlements of the colonists, committed numerous thefts and murders. It seemed that all the elements of disorder were at work to destroy the social organization which civilization had begun, and that the wild chaos of barbarian sway claimed his own again. Uneasy lay the head of Bienville in his midnight sleep, for fearfully alive was he to the responsibility which rested on his shoulders. In that disturbed state of his mind, with what anxiety did he not interrogate the horizon, and strain to peep into the vacancy of space, in the fond hope that some signs of his brother's return would greet his eyes! But, alas! the year 1707 had run one half of its career, and yet Iberville came not. To what remote parts of heaven had the eagle flown, not to hear and not to mind the shrieks of the inmates of his royal nest? Not oblivious the eagle had been, but engaged in carrying Jove's thunderbolts, he had steadily pursued the accomplishment of his task.

Dropping the metaphorical style, it will be sufficient to state, that during the five years he had been absent from Louisiana, Iberville had been, with his usual success, nobly occupied in supporting the honor of his country's flag, and in increasing the reputation which he had already gained, as one of the brightest gems of the French navy. If the duration of a man's existence is to be measured by the merit of his deeds, then Iberville had lived long, before reaching the meridian of life, and he was old in fame, if not in years, when he undertook to establish a colony in Louisiana. From his early youth, all his days had been well spent, because dedicated to some useful or generous purpose. The soft down of adolescence had hardly shaded his face, when he had become the idol of his countrymen. The foaming brine of the ocean, the dashing waters of the rivers, the hills and valleys of his native country and of the neighboring British possessions, had witnessed his numerous exploits. Such were the confidence and love with which he had inspired the Canadians and Acadians for his person, by the irresistible seduction of his manners, by the nobleness of his deportment, by the dauntless energy of his soul, and by the many qualifications of his head and heart, that they would, said Father Charlevoix, have followed him to the confines of the universe. It would be too long to recite his wonderful achievements, and the injuries which he inflicted upon the fleets of England, particularly in the Bay of Hudson, either by open force, or by stealth and surprise. When vessels were icebound, they were more than once stormed by Iberville and his intrepid associates. Two of his brothers, Ste. Hélène and Mèricourt, both destined to an early death, used to be his willing companions in these adventurous expeditions. At other times, when the war of the elements seemed to preclude any other contest, Iberville, in a light buoyant craft, which sported merrily on the angry waves, would scour far and wide the Bay of Hudson, and the adjacent sea, to prey upon the commerce of the great rival of France, and many were the prizes which he brought into port. These were the sports of his youth.

The exploits of Iberville on land and at sea acquired

for him a sort of amphibious celebrity. Among other doings of great daring, may be mentioned the taking of Corlar, near Orange, in the province of New York. In November, 1694, he also took, in the Bay of Hudson, the fort of Port Nelson, defended by forty-two pieces of artillery, and he gave it the name of Fort Bourbon. In 1696 he added to his other conquests, the Fort of Pemkuit in Acadia. When Chubb, the English commander, was summoned to surrender, he returned this proud answer: "If the sea were white with French sails, and the land dark with Indians, I would not give up the fort, unless when reduced to the very last extremities." In spite of this vaunt, he was soon obliged to capitulate. The same year, Iberville possessed himself of the Fort of St. John, in Newfoundland, and in a short time forced the rest of that province to yield to his arms. The French, however, did not retain it long. But his having revived La Salle's project of establishing a colony in Louisiana, constitutes, on account of the magnitude of its results, his best claim to the notice of posterity. We have seen how he executed that important undertaking.

After a long absence from that province, the colonization of which was his favorite achievement, he was now preparing to return to its shores, and arrived at San Domingo, having under his command a considerable fleet, with which he meditated to attack Charleston in South Carolina; from whence he cherished the hope of sailing for Louisiana, with all the pomp, pride, and circumstance of glorious victory. He had stopped at San Domingo, because he had been authorized to reinforce himself with a thousand men, whom he was to take out of the garrison of that island. The ships had been revictualed, the troops were embarked, and Iberville was ready to put to sea, when a great feast was tendered to him and to his officers, by the friends from whom he was soon to part. Loud the sound of revelry was still heard in hall and bower, when Iberville, whose thoughts dwelt on the responsibilities of the expedition which had been intrusted to his care, withdrew from the assembly, where he had been the observed of all, leaving and even encouraging his subordinates to enjoy the rest of that fairy night, which he knew was soon to be succeeded for them by the perils and hardships of war. He was approaching that part of the shore where his boat lay, waiting to carry him to his ship, when, as he trod along, in musing loneliness, his attention was attracted by the beauties of the tropical sky, which gleamed over his head. From that spangled canopy, so lovely that it seemed worthy of Eden, there appeared to descend an ambrosial atmosphere, which glided through the inmost recesses of the body, gladdening the whole frame with voluptuous sensations. Iberville's pace slackened as he admired, and at last he stopped, rooted to the ground, as it were by a sort of magnetic influence, exercised upon him by the fascinations of the scene. Folding his arms, and wrapt up in ecstasy, he gazed long and steadily at the stars which studded the celestial vault.

O stars! who has not experienced your mystical and mysterious power! Who has ever gazed at you, without feeling undefinable sensations, something of awe, and a vague consciousness that ye are connected with the fate of mortals! Ye silent orbs, that move with noiseless splendor through the infiniteness of space, how is it that your voice is so distinctly heard in the soul of man, if his essence and yours were not bound together by some electric link, as are all things, no doubt, in the universe? How the eyes grow dim with rapturous tears, and the head dizzy with wild fancies, when holding communion with you, on the midnight watch! Ye stars, that, scattered over the broad expanse of heaven, look to me as if ye were grains of golden dust, which God shook off his feet, as he walked in his might, on the days of creation, I love and worship you! When there were none in the world to sympathize with an aching heart, with a heart that would have disdained, in its lonely pride, to show its pangs to mortal eyes, how often have I felt relief in your presence from the bitter recollection of past woes, and consolation under the infliction of present sufferings! How often have I drawn from you such inspirations as prepared me to meet, with fitting fortitude, harsher trials still to come! How often have I gazed upon you, until, flying upon the wings of imagination, I soared among your bright host, and spiritualized myself away, far away, from the miseries of my contemptible existence! Howsoever that ephemeral worm, cynical man, may sneer, he is no idle dreamer, the lover of you, the star-gazer. The broad sheet of heaven to which ye are affixed, like letters of fire, is a book prepared by God for the learned and the ignorant, where man can read lessons to guide him through the active duties and the struggles of this life, and to conduct him safely to the portals of the eternal one which awaits mortality!

Thus, perhaps, Iberville felt, as he was spying the face of heaven. But death was around him—it was in the very air which he breathed. The soft balmy breeze in which he luxuriated, was impregnated with an insidious poison, fatal to those not born in tropical climates. The pestilence so well known under the name of yellow fever was sweeping over the land. Giving no warning of its presence, it was among yonder revellers whom Iberville had just left, and whose music and mundane mirth still reached his ears. Morning came, and Iberville fell ill, and on the third day was gathered to his forefathers' bosom. Thus died this truly great and good man, in compliment to whose memory the name of Iberville was given to one of our most important parishes.

Ill was the wind that carried to Louisiana the melancholy information of Iberville's death. It blasted the hearts of the poor colonists, and destroyed the hope they had of being speedily relieved. Their situation had become truly deplorable: their numbers were rapidly diminishing: and the Indians were daily becoming more hostile, and more bold in their demands for goods and merchandise, as a tribute which they exacted for not breaking out into actual warfare. Bienville convened the chiefs of the Chickasaws and of the Choctaws, in order to conciliate them by some trifling presents of which he could yet dispose, and to gain time by some fair promises as to what he would do for them under more favorable circumstances. With a view of making an imposing show, Bienville collected all the colonists that were within reach: but notwithstanding that display, a question, propounded by one of the Indian chiefs, gave him a humiliating proof of the slight estimation in which the savages held the French nation. Much to his annoyance, he was asked if that part of his people which remained at home was as numerous as that which had come to settle in Louisiana. Bienville, who spoke their language perfectly well, attempted, by words and comparisons suited to their understanding, to impart to them a correct notion of the extent of the population of France. But the Indians looked incredulous, and one of them even said to Bienville, "If your countrymen are, as you affirm, as thick on their native soil as the leaves of our forests, how is it that they do not send more of their warriors here, to avenge the death of such of them as have fallen by our hands? Not to do so, when having the power, would argue them to be of a very base spirit. And how is it that most of the tall and powerful men that came with you, being dead, are replaced only by boys, or cripples, or women, that do you no credit? Surely the French would not so behave, if they could do otherwise, and my white brother tells a story that disparages his own tribe."

Thus Bienville found himself in a very critical situation. He was conscious that his power was despised by the Indians, who knew that he had only forty-five soldiers at his disposal, and he felt that the red men could easily rise upon him and crush the colony at one blow. He was aware that they were restrained from doing the deed by their cupidity only, bridled as they were by their expectation of the arrival of some ship with merchandise, which, they knew from experience, would soon have to come to their huts to purchase peace, and in exchange for furs. Bienville felt so weak, so much at the mercy of the surrounding nations, and entertained such an apprehension of some treacherous and sudden attack on their part, that he thought it prudent to concentrate his forces, and to abandon the fort where he kept a small garrison on the Mississippi.

On the other hand, the death of Iberville had encouraged the hostility of Bienville's enemies. They knew that he was no longer supported by the powerful influence of his brother at court, and they renewed their attacks with a better hope of success. The commissary La Salle pushed on his intrigues with more activity, and reduced them to a sort of systematic warfare. He divided the colony into those that were against and those that were for Bienville. All such persons as supported the governor's administration were branded as felons: and those that pursued another course, whoever they might be, were angels of purity. At that time, there was in the colony a physician, sent thither and salaried by the government, who was called the king's physician. His name was Barrot: from the circumstance of his being the only member of his profession in the country, and from the nature of his duties, he was in a position to exercise a good deal of influence. La Salle attempted to win him over to his side, and having failed in his efforts, he immediately wrote to the minister, "that Barrot, although he had the honor of being the king's physician in the colony, was no better than a fool, a drunkard and a rogue, who sold the king's drugs and appropriated the money to his own purposes."

Authors, who have written on the structure of man, have said that if his features were closely examined, there would be found in them a strange resemblance with some of the animals, of the birds, or of the reptiles that people this globe. I remember having seen curious engravings exemplifying this assertion with the most wonderful effect. In a moral sense, the resemblance is perhaps greater, and the whale, the lion, the eagle, the wolf, the lamb, and other varieties of the brutish creation, may, without much examination, be discovered to exist, physically and spiritually, in the human species. Among the bipeds that are reckoned to belong to the ranks of humanity, none was better calculated than La Salle to personate the toad. His mission was to secrete venom, as the rose exhales perfumes. Nature delights in contrarieties. Fat, short, and sleek, with bloated features and oily skin, he was no unfit representative of that reptile, although certainly to him the traditionary legend of a jewel in the head could not be applied. Puffed up in self-conceit, an eternal smile of contentment was stereotyped on the **gross** texture of his lips, where it was mixed with an expression of bestial sensuality. His cold grayish eyes had the dull squint of the hog, and as he strutted along, one was almost amazed not to hear an occasional grunt. This thing of the neuter gender, which, to gift with the faculty of speech, seemed to be an injustice done to the superior intellect of the baboon, did, forsooth, think itself an orator. Whenever this royal commissary had a chance of catching a few of the colonists together, for instance, on all public occasions, he would gradually drop the tone of conversation, and sublimate his colloquial address into a final harangue. Thus, the valves of his brazen throat being open, out ran the muddy water of his brain, bespattering all that stood within reach. Pitched on a high and monotonous key, his prosy voice carried to his hearers, for hours, the same insane, insipid flow of bombastic phrases, falling on the ear with the unvaried and ever-recurring sound of a pack-horse wheel in a flour-mill. A coiner of words, he could have filled with them the vaults of the vastest mint; but if analyzed and reduced to their sterling value, they would not have produced a grain of sense. This man, contemptible as he was, had actually become a public nuisance, on account of the impediments with which he embarrassed the administration of Louisiana. He was eternally meddling with every thing, under the pretext of correcting abuses, and although he was incapable of producing any thing of his own that could stand on its legs for a minute, he was incessantly concocting some plan, as ill-begotten as his own misshapen person. He was, in his own delirious opinion, as complete a financier, as skillful a statesman, as great a general, and, above all, as profound a legislator, as ever lived; so that this legislative Caliban had even gone so far as to imagine he could frame a code of laws for the

G

colony; and, because all his preposterous propositions were resisted by Bienville, he had conceived for him the bitterest hatred. To do him justice, it must be said that he was in earnest, when he reproached others with malversation and every sort of malfeasances. There are creatures whose accusations it would be wrong to resent. They see themselves reflected in others, and, like yelping curs, pursue with their barkings the sinful image: it would be as idle to expect them to understand the workings of a noble heart and of a great mind, as it would be to imagine that a worm could raise itself to the conception of a planet's gravitations.

So, perhaps, thought Bienville, and he passed with silent contempt over La Salle's manœuvers. Was he not right? He who thinks himself your adversary, but who, if you were to turn upon him with the flashes of honest indignation, with the uplifted spear of physical and mental power united, with the threatening aspect of what he does not possess and dreams not of, a soul, convulsed into a storm, would shrink into an atom and flatten himself to the level of your heels, can not be a real adversary: his enmity is to be regarded as a vain shadow, the phantom of impotent envy. This is no doubt the most dignified course to be pursued, but perhaps not the most prudent; and Bienville soon discovered that, however it may be in theory, there is, in practice, no attack so pitiful as not to require some sort of precautionary defense. Thus on the 13th of July, 1707, the minister dismissed Bienville from office, appointed De Muys in his place, and instructed this new governor to examine into the administration of his predecessor, and into the accusations brought against him, with the authorization of sending him prisoner to France, if they were well founded. A poor chance it was for Bienville, to be judged by the man that pushed him from his stool, and whose continuance in office would probably depend upon the guilt of the accused! This was but a sorry return for the services of Bienville and for those of his distinguished family. But thus goes the world!

La Salle had no cause to triumph over the downfall of Bienville, for he himself was, at the same time, dismissed from office, and was succeeded by Diron d'Artaguette. Nay, he had the mortification of seeing Bienville retain his power, while he lost his; because De Muys never reached Louisiana, having died in Havana, on his way to the colony of which he had been appointed governor. To increase his vexation, he saw that most of the colonists, even those who had been momentarily opposed to Bienville, became suddenly alive to his merits, when they were on the eve of losing him, and with spontaneous unanimity subscribed a petition, by which they expressed their satisfaction with Bienville's administration, and supplicated the minister not to deprive them of such a wise and faithful governor. This was sufficiently distressing for La Salle's envious heart; but his spleen was worked into a paroxysm of rage, when he was informed that his successor, the royal commissary, Diron d'Artaguette, had made a report to the king, in which he declared, that all the accusations brought against Bienville, were mere slanderous inventions, which rested on no other foundation than the blackest malice. Writhing like a snake under the unexpected blow, he still attempted to sting, and he wrote to France, "that d'Artaguette was not deserving of any faith or credit; that he had come to an understanding with Bienville, and that they were both equally bad and corrupt."

It was by such misunderstandings among the chiefs of the colony, that its progress was checked so long. In 1708, its population did not exceed 279 persons.

To this number must be added sixty Canadian vagabonds, who led a wandering and licentious life among the Indians. Its principal wealth consisted in 50 cows, 40 calves, 4 bulls, 8 oxen, 1400 hogs, and 2000 hens. This statement shows the feebleness of the colony after an existence of nine years. But the golden eggs had been laid in the land, and although kept torpid and unprofitable for more than a century, by the chilling contact of an imbecile despotism, they, in the progress of time, were hatched by the warm incubation of liberty into the production of that splendid order of things, which is the wonder of the present age.

But, at that time, the colony seemed to be gifted with little vitality, and the nursling of Bienville threatened to expire in his hands at every moment. The colonists were little disposed to undertake the laborious task of securing their subsistence by the cultivation of the soil, and they expected that the mother country would minister to all their wants. Servile hands would have been necessary, but Indian slavery was not found to be profitable, and Bienville wrote to his government to obtain the authorization of exchanging Indians for negroes with the French West India Islands. "We shall give," said he, "three Indians for two negroes. The Indians, when in the islands, will not be able to run away, the country being unknown to them, and the negroes will not dare to become fugitives in Louisiana, because the Indians would kill them." This demand met with no favorable reception. Bienville was so anxious to favor the development of the colony, that he was led by it into an unjust and despotic measure, as is proved by the following extract from one of his dispatches. "I have ordered several citizens of La Rochelle to be closely watched, because they wish to quit the country. They have scraped up something by keeping taverns. Therefore it appears to me to be nothing but justice to force them to remain in the country, on the substance of which they have fattened." This sentiment, howsoever it may disagree with our modern notions of right and wrong, was not repugnant to the ethics of the time.

In spite of the spirited exertions of Bienville, famine reappeared in the colony, and in January, 1709, the inhabitants were reduced to live on acorns. As usual under such circumstances, the intestine dissensions of which such a melancholy description has been already given became more acrid. The minds of men are not apt to grow conciliating under the double infliction of disappointment and famine, and the attacks upon Bienville were renewed with more than usual fierceness. La Salle, although now stripped of the trappings of office, still remained in the colony, to pursue his game, and to force the noble lord of the forest to stand at bay. His associate in persecution, the Curate de la Vente, hallooed with him in zealous imitation, and it is much to be regretted that they were joined in the chase by Marigny de Mandeville, a brave and noble-minded officer, lately come to the country, who informed his government " that the colony never would prosper. until it had a governor with an honest heart and with an energetic mind ;" which meant that Bienville was deficient in both. It was an error committed by Marigny de Mandeville, and into which he was no doubt led by the misrepresentations of La Salle and of the Curate de la Vente.

Bienville had so far remained passive, but was at last stung into angry recriminations, which he retorted on all his adversaries, particularly on the Curate de la Vente, who, said he, "*had tried to stir up every body against him by his calumnies, and who, in the mean time, did not blush to keep an open shop, where his mode of trafficking showed that he was a shrewd compound of the Arab and of the Jew.*"

The scarcity of provisions became such in 1710, that Bienville informed his government that he had scattered the greatest part of his men among the Indians, upon whom he had quartered them for food. This measure had been more than once adopted before, and demonstrates that the Indians could hardly have been so hostile as they have been represented; otherwise, they would have availed themselves of such opportunities to destroy the invaders of their territory. Be it as it may, the colony continued in its lingering condition, gasping for breath in its cradle, until 1712, when, on the 14th of September, the King of France granted to Anthony Crozat the exclusive privilege, for fifteen years, of trading in all that immense territory which, with its undefined limits, France claimed as her own under the name of Louisiana. Among other privileges, were those of sending, once a year, a ship to Africa for negroes and of possessing and working all the mines of precious metals to be discovered in Louisiana, provided that one fourth of their proceeds should be reserved for the king. He also had the privilege of owning forever all the lands that he would improve by cultivation, all the buildings he would erect, and all the manufactures that he might establish. His principal obligation, in exchange for such advantages, was to send every year to Louisiana, two ships' loads of colonists, and, after nine years, to assume all the expenses of the administration of the colony, including those of the garrison and of its officers; it being understood that, in consideration of such a charge, he would have the privilege of nominating the officers to be appointed by the king. In the **mean time, the annual sum of fifty thousand livres**

($10,000) was allowed to Crozat for the king's share of the expenses required by Louisiana. It was further provided that the laws, ordinances, customs, and usages of the Prevostship and Viscounty of Paris should form the legislation of the colony. There was also to be a government council, similar to the one established in San Domingo and Martinique.

This charter of concessions virtually made Crozat the supreme lord and master of Louisiana. Thus Louisiana was dealt with, as if it had been a royal farm, and leased by Louis the XIVth to the highest bidder. It is a mere business transaction, but which colors itself with the hue of romance, when it is remembered that Louisiana was the farm, Louis the XIVth the landlord, and that Anthony Crozat was the farmer.

Anthony Crozat was one of those men who dignify commerce, and recall to memory those princely merchants, of whom Genoa, Venice, and Florence boasted of yore. Born a peasant's son, on the estate of one of the great patricians of France, he was, when a boy, remarked for the acuteness of his intellect; and having the good fortune of being the foster brother of the only son of his feudal lord, he was sent to school by his noble patron, received the rudiments of education, and at fifteen was placed, as clerk, in a commercial house. Then, by the protection of that nobleman, who never ceased to evince the liveliest interest in his fate, and particularly by the natural ascendency of his strong genius, he rose, in the course of twenty years, to be a partner of his old employer, married his daughter, and shortly after this auspicious event, found himself, on the death of his father-in-law, one of the richest merchants in Europe. He still continued to be favored by circumstances, and having had the good fortune of loaning large sums of money to the government in cases of emergency, he was rewarded for his services by his being ennobled and created Marquis du Chatel.

So far, Crozat had known but the sunny side of life; but for every man the hour of trial must strike, sooner or later, on the clock of fate, and the length or intenseness of the felicity that one has enjoyed, is generally counterbalanced by a proportionate infliction of calamity. Happy is he, perhaps, whom adversity meets on the threshold of existence, and accompanies through part of his career. Then, the nerves of youth may resist the shock, and be even improved by the struggle. The mind and body, disciplined by the severe trial through which they have passed, have time to substitute gains for losses in the account book of life. At any rate, when the tribute of tears and sufferings is early paid, the debtor may hope for a clear and bright meridian; and when the sun of his destiny sinks down in the west, he has some right to expect, if clouds should gather round the setting orb, that it will only be to gladden the sight by the gorgeousness of their colors. But if smiling fortune, after having rocked her favorite in his cradle, gives him her uninterrupted attendance until his manhood is past, she is very apt to desert him on the first cold approach of old age, when he is most in need of her support; for, the stern decree that man is born to suffer, must be accomplished before the portals of another life are open; and then, woe to the gray-headed victim, who, after long days of luxurious ease, finds himself suddenly abandoned, a martyr in the arena of judgment, to the fangs and jaws of the wild beasts of an unfeeling and scoffing world. Woe to him, if his Christian faith is not bound to his heart by adamantine chains, to subdue physical pain, to arm his soul with divine fortitude, and grace his last moments with sweet dignity and calm resignation!

Crozat was doomed to make this sad experiment. The first shaft aimed at him fell on his w.fe, whom he lost, ten years after the birth of his only child, a daughter, now the sole hope of his house. Intense was his sorrow, and never to be assuaged, for no common companion his wife had been. Looking up to him with affectionate reverence as one, whom the laws, both divine and human, had appointed as her guide, she had lived rather in him than in herself. She had been absorbed into her husband, and the business of her whole life had been to study and to anticipate his wishes and wants. Endowed with all the graces of her sex, and with a cultivated intellect chastened by modesty, which hardly left any thing to be desired for its perfection, she rendered sweeter the part of ministering angel which she had assumed, to bless him in this world. With feminine art, she had incorporated herself with his organization, and gliding into the very essence of his soul, she had become the originating spring of all his thoughts and sentiments. It was beautiful to see, how, entwining herself round his conceptions, his volition and actions, she had made herself a component part of his individuality, so that she really was flesh of his flesh and bone of his bone. Is it to be wondered at, that when she died, he felt that the luminary which lighted up his path had been extinguished, and that a wheel had suddenly stopped within himself? From that fatal event, there never was a day when the recollections of the past did not fill his soul with anguish.

Crozat's only consolation was his daughter. The never-ceasing anxiety with which he watched over her, until she grew into womanhood, would beggar all description; and even then she remained a frail flower, which, to be kept alive, required to be fanned by the gentlest zephyrs, and to be softly watered from that spring which gushes from the deep well of the heart, at the touch of true affection. She was exquisitely beautiful, but there was this peculiarity in her beauty, that although her person presented that voluptuous symmetry, that rich fullness of form, and that delicate roundness of outline which artists admire, yet soul predominated in her so much over matter, that she looked rather like a spirit of the air, than an incarnation of mortality. She produced the effect of an unnatural apparition: forgetting the fascinations of the flesh, one would gaze at her as something not of this world, and feel for her such love as angels may inspire. She appeared to be clothed in terrestrial substance, merely because it was necessary to that earthly existence which she wore as a garment not intended for her, and which had been put on only by mistake. She was out of place: there was something in her organization, which disqualified her for the companionship of the sons of Eve: she looked as if she had strayed from a holier sphere. Those who knew her were impressed with an undefinable feeling that she was a temporary loan made to earth by heaven, and that the slightest disappointment of the heart in her nether career, would send her instantly to a fitter and more congenial abode. Alas! there are beings invested with such exquisite sensibility, that the vile clay which enters into their composition, and which may be intended as a protecting texture, without which human life would be intolerable for the spirit within, imbibing too much of the ethereal essence to which it is allied, ceases to be a shield against the ills we are heirs to, in this valley of miseries. It is a mark set upon them! It is a pledge that the wounded soul, writhing under repeated inflictions, will wear out its frail tenement, and soon escape from its ordeal. Such was the threatened fate of Andrea, the daughter of Crozat. And he knew it, the poor father! he knew it, and he trembled! and he lived in perpetual fear: and he would clasp his hands, and in such agonies as the paternal heart only knows, kneeling down, humbling himself in the dust, he would pour out prayers (oh, how eloquent!) that the Almighty, in his infinite mercy, would spare his child!

Crozat had sedulously kept up the closest relations with his noble friend and patron, to whom there had also been born but one heir, a son, the sole pillar of a ducal house, connected with all the imperial and royal dynasties of Europe. A short time after his wife's death, Crozat had had the misfortune to follow to the grave the duke, his foster brother; and his daughter Andrea, who was known to lack at home the gentle nursing of a mother, had been tendered the splendid hospitality of the dowager duchess, where she had grown up in a sort of sisterly intimacy with the young duke. There she had conceived, unknowingly to herself at first, the most intense passion for her youthful companion, which, when it revealed itself to her dismayed heart, was kept carefully locked up in its inmost recesses. Poor maiden! The *longum bibere amorem* was fatally realized with her, and she could not tear herself from the allurements of the banquet upon which she daily feasted her affections. Unknown her secret, she lived in fancied security, and, for a while, enjoyed as pure a happiness as may be attained to—the happiness of dreams!

One day, a rumor arose that a matrimonial alliance was in the way of preparation for that lineal descendant of a princely race, for the young duke, who was the concealed idol of her heart. There are emotions which it would be too much for human endurance to hide from a sympathetic eye, much less from parental penetration.

and on that day the terrible truth burst upon Crozat, and stunned him with an unexpected blow. It was a hurricane of woes sweeping through his heart: he felt as if he and his child were in a tornado, out of which to save her was impossible. Too well he knew his Andrea, and too well he knew that she would not survive the withering of her hopes, wild as they were! "Time!" exclaimed he, as he paced his room with hurried steps, holding communion with himself, "Time, that worker of great things, must be gained! But how?" A sudden thought flashed through his brain! Thank God, he clutched the remedy! Was it not currently reported and believed that the betrothed of the duke loved one, of equally noble birth, but whose proffered hand had been rejected by an ambitious father, merely because fortune, with her golden gifts, did not back his pretensions? That was enough! And Crozat, on that very day, had sought and found the despairing lover. "Sir!" said he to the astonished youth, "in the civil wars which desolated France during the minority of Louis the XIVth, and which ruined your family, several millions were extorted from your father by one, who then had the power. Here they are—it is a restitution—ask no name—I am a mere agent and bound to secrecy." The strange tale was taken as true, and in a short time the betrothed of the young duke was led to the hymeneal altar by a more successful rival.

Crozat had been a traitor and a liar!—a traitor to his friend and benefactor's son! But he was a father! —and he saw his daughter's tomb already wide open and gaping for the expected prey! And was she not to be rescued at any cost? And was he to stand with folded arms, and to remain passive, while, in his sight, despair slowly chiseled the cold sepulchral marble destined for his child? No!—he saved her, and did not stop to inquire whether the means he employed were legitimate. Now, he saw her smile again and resume, as it were, that current of life which was fast ebbing away!—and he was happy! And had he not a sufficient excuse to plead at that seat of judgment which every man has within his breast, when the shrill voice of conscience rose against him in accusation, and said, "Thou hast done wrong! to save thyself, or thine, thou hast been recreant to thy trust—thou hast injured thy neighbor, and acted dishonorably?" Crozat, however, was not the man to lay a flattering unction to his soul. There was in him no false logic of a corrupt mind to argue successfully against the plain voice of truth: his were not the ears of the wicked, deaf to the admonitions of our inward monitor. However gently conscience might have spoken her disapprobation, he heard it, and stood self-condemned.

He went to his patron's widow, to the duchess, and told her *all*—and prostrating himself at her feet, awaited her sentence. She raised him gently from her humble posture, and self-collected, soaring as it were above human passions, while she riveted upon him the steadfast look of her calm, blue eyes, thus she spoke with Juno-like dignity, and with a sweet, musical voice, but seeming as cold to the afflicted father, in spite of its bland intonations, as the northern wind: "Crozat, this is a strange and a moving tale. You stand forgiven, for you have acted as nature would prompt most men to do, and even if your error had been more grievous, your manly candor and frank confession would redeem the guilt Therefore, let it pass; let your conscience be relieved from further pangs on this subject. My esteem and friendship stand the same for you as before. What grieves me to the heart, is the deplorable situation of your Andrea, who is mine also, and whom I love like a daughter, although she can not be permitted to assume such a relation to me in the eye of the world. She is young, and it shall be our special care, by gentle means, to cure her by degrees of the wild passion which has possessed her soul, poor child. As this, our first conversation on this painful topic, shall be the last, I wish to express my sentiments to you with sufficient fullness, that I may be clearly understood. I wish you to know, that my heart is not inflated with vulgar pride. I do not think that my blood is different from yours in its composition, and is noble solely because I descend from a particular breed, and that yours is vile, because the accidental circumstance of birth has placed you among the plebeians and what we call the base and the low-born. A peasant's son, if he be virtuous and great in soul and in mind, is more in my estimation than a king's, if an idiot or a wicked man. Thus far, I suppose, we understand each other. There is but one valuable nobility—that in which hereditary rank is founded on a long succession of glorious deeds. Such is the case with our house. It has been an historical one, trunk and branches, for much more than twelve centuries. Kings, emperors, claim a kindred blood with ours. Our name is indissolubly bound with the history of Europe and Asia, and the annals of the kingdom of France, in particular, may be said to be the records of our house. We have long ceased to count the famous knights, the high constables, the marshals, generals, and other great men who have sprung from our fruitful race. This is what I call nobility. To this present day, none of that race has ever contracted an alliance which was not of an illustrious and historical character. It is a principle, nay more, Crozat, it is a religion with us, and it is too late for us to turn apostates. **It is to** that creed, which we have **cherished** from time immemorial, that we are indebted for what we are. If once untrue to ourselves, there is an instinctive presentiment which tells us that we shall be blasted with the curse of heaven. Right or wrong, it is a principle, I say; and there is such mysterious vitality and power in a principle, be it what it may, that if strictly and systematically adhered to for ages, it will work wonders. Therefore the traditions of our house must stand unbroken forever, coeval with its existence, and remain imperishable pyramids of our faith in our own worth.

"I know that your daughter, whom I have raised in my lap, and whose transcendent qualities I appreciate as they deserve, would be the best of wives, and bless my son with earthly bliss. But, Crozat, those of my race are not born to be happy, but to be great. This is the condition of their existence. They do not marry for themselves, but for the glorification of their house. It is a sacred mission, and it must be fulfilled. Every animated thing in the creation must follow the bent of its nature. The wooing dove may be satisfied with the security of its lot in the verdant foliage of the forest, but the eagle must speed to the sun, even if he be consumed by its rays. Such being the fate of our race, a hard one in many respects, you see, my dear Crozat—and I say so with deep regret at the consequences which you anticipate, not however without a hope that they may be averted—you must clearly see that an alliance between our families is an impossibility. It would be fatal to your daughter, who would be scorched by ascending, Phaeton-like, into a sphere not calculated for her; and it would be also fatal to my son, who would be disgraced for his being recreant to his ancestors and to his posterity. You deserve infinite credit for having risen to the summit where you now stand. You have been ennobled, and you are one of the greatest merchants of the age, but you are not yet a Medici! You have not forced your way, like that family, into the ranks of the potentates of the earth. If, indeed—but why talk of such idle dreams? Adieu, Crozat, be comforted—be of good cheer.—Things may not be as bad as you think for your daughter. Her present attachment not being encouraged, she may in time form another one. Farewell, my friend, put your faith in God: he is the best healer of the wounds of the heart!"

Crozat bowed low to the duchess, whose extended hand he kissed reverentially, and he withdrew from the chilling frigidity of her august presence. Crouching under the weight of his misfortune, and under the consciousness of the invincible and immortal pride he had to deal with, he tottered to his solitary room, and sinking into a large gothic chair, buried his feverish head into his convulsive hands. Hot tears trickled through the contracted fingers, and he sobbed and groaned aloud, when he recalled, one by one, all the words of the duchess, as they slowly fell from her lips, burning his soul, searing his brains, filtering through his heart like distilled drops of liquid fire. Suddenly he started up with fierce energy; his face was lighted with dauntless resolution: he ground his teeth, clenched his fist, as if for a struggle, and shook it in defiance of some invisible adversary, while he moved on with expanded chest and with a frame dilating into the majesty of some imaginary command. " O Daughter," he exclaimed, " thou shalt be saved, and if necessary, I will accomplish impossibilities. Did not the proud duchess say that if I were a Medici! . . . the ruler of provinces!—if I had an historical name? She did! and I know that she would keep her word. Well then! ye powers of heaven or hell, that helped the Medici, **I bow** to ye, and call ye to my aid, by the only incantation which I know, the strong magic of an energetic mind. I invoke your assistance, be the sacrifice on my part whatever it may:—I will sign any bond ye please—I will set my all on the cast of a die—and gamble against fate. My daughter is the stake, and death to her and to me the forfeit!" This was a sinful ebullition of passion—the only excuse the paroxysm of a delirious mind. But still it was impious, and his protecting angel averted his face and flew upward. Alas! poor Crozat!

Hence the origin of that charter, by which Louisiana was ceded, as it were, to Crozat. He flattered himself with the hope that, if successful in his gigantic enterprise, a few years might ripen the privileges he had obtained into the concession of a principality, which he would form in the New World, a principality which, as a great feudatory vassal, he would hold in subjection to the crown of France. Then he would say to the proud duchess, "I am a Medici. My name outweighs many a haughty one in the scales of history:—my nobility rests not only on title, but on noble deeds. These were your words—I hold you to them—redeem your pledge—one of your blood can not be false—I claim your son—I give him a princess for his bride, and domains ten times broader than France, or any kingdom in Europe, for her dowry!"

So hoped the heart of the father—so schemed the head of the great merchant! What man ever had stronger motives to fire his genius? What ambition more sacred and more deserving of reward than his? And yet none, save one, guessed at the motives which actuated him! He was taxed with being insatiable of wealth: people wondered at his gigantic avidity. Some there were, who shrugged their shoulders, **and** said that he was tempting fate, that it was time for him to be satisfied with what he had, without exposing his present wonderful acquisitions for the uncertainty of a greater fortune. Such are the blind judgments of the world! Crozat was blamed for being too ambitious, and envy railed at the inordinate avidity of the rash adventurer, when pity ought to have wept over the miseries of the broken-hearted father. On the dizzy eminence whither he had ascended, Crozat, when he looked round for sympathy, was met by the basilisk stare of a jealous, cold-blooded world, who stood by, calculating his chances of success, and grinning in anticipation at the wished-for failure of his defeated schemes. At such a sight, his heart sank within his breast, and elevating his hands, clasped in prayer, "Angels and ministers of grace," he said, "ye know that it is no ambitious cravings, but the racked feelings of a father, that urge me to the undertaking, upon which I call down your blessings. Be ye my friends and protectors in heaven, for Crozat has none on this earth."

FOURTH LECTURE.

LAMOTHE CADILLAC, GOVERNOR OF LOUISIANA—SITUATION OF THE COLONY IN 1713—FEUD BETWEEN CADILLAC AND BIENVILLE—CHARACTER OF RICHEBOURG—FIRST EXPEDITION AGAINST THE NATCHEZ—DE L'EPINAY SUCCEEDS CADILLAC—THE CURATE DE LA VENTE—EXPEDITION OF ST. DENIS TO MEXICO—HIS ADVENTURES—JALLOT, THE SURGEON—IN 1717 CROZAT GIVES UP HIS CHARTER—HIS DEATH.

WHEN Crozat obtained the royal charter, granting him so many commercial privileges in Louisiana, the military forces which were in the colony, and which constituted its only protection, did not exceed two companies of infantry of fifty men each. There were also seventy-five Canadians in the pay of the king, and they were used for every species of service. The balance of the population hardly came up to three hundred souls, and that population, small as it was, and almost imperceptible, happened to be scattered over a boundless territory, where they could not communicate together without innumerable difficulties, frightful dangers, and without delays which, in these our days of rapid locomotion, can scarcely be sufficiently appreciated. As to the blacks, who now have risen to such importance in our social polity, they did not number more than twenty heads. It is probable, that of this scanty population, there were not fifty persons in the present limits of the State of Louisiana, and the contrast, which now presents itself to the mind, affords a rich treat to the imagination, and particularly to our national pride, since we were the wonder-working power.

The possession of the province of Louisiana, if possession it can be called, France had secured by the construction of five forts. They were located at Mobile, at Biloxi, Ship Island, Dauphine Island, and on the bank of the Mississippi. These fortifications were of a very humble nature, and their materials were chiefly composed of stakes, logs, and clay. They sufficed, however, to intimidate the Indians. Such were the paltry results, after fifteen years, of the attempt made by a powerful government to colonize Louisiana; and now, one single man, a private individual, was daring enough to grapple and struggle with an undertaking, which, so far, had proved abortive in the hands of the great Louis the XIVth!

It must be remembered that De Muys, who had been appointed to supersede Bienville, had died in Havana in 1707, and that the youthful founder of the colony had, by that event, remained Governor ad interim of Louisiana. But on the 17th of May, 1713, a great change had come over the face of things, and the colonists stood on the tiptoe of expectation, when they were informed that a ship had arrived with Lamothe Cadillac, as Governor, Duclos as Commissary in the place of D'Artaguette, who had returned to France, Lebas as Comptroller, Dirigoin and La Loire des Ursins, as the agents of Crozat in the colony. Bienville was retained as Lieutenant Governor, and it was expected that, in that subordinate office, he would, from his knowledge of the state of affairs in the province, be of signal use to his successor, and be a willing instrument, which the supposed superior abilities of Lamothe Cadillac would turn to some goodly purpose. This certainly was a compliment paid to the patriotism of Bienville, but was it not disregarding too much the frailties of human nature? Cheerfully to obey, where one formerly had nothing to do but to issue the word of command, is not an every-day occurrence, and it is a trial to which politic heads ought not to expose the virtue of man.

The principal instructions given by Crozat to Lamothe Cadillac were, that he should diligently look after *mines*, and endeavor to find out an opening for the introduction of his goods and merchandise into the Spanish colonies in Mexico, either with the consent of the authorities, or without it, by smuggling. If he succeeded in these two enterprises, Crozat calculated that he would speedily obtain inexhaustible wealth, such wealth as would enable him to throw a large population into Louisiana, as it were by magic, and to realize the fond dreams of his paternal heart. Impatient of delay, he had, in order to stimulate the exertions of Lamothe Cadillac, secured to him a considerable share in the profits which he hoped to realize. Lamothe Cadillac had fought with valor in Canada, and as a reward for his services (so, at least, his commission declared), had been appointed by the king, governor of Louisiana. Had Crozat known the deficiencies of that officer's intellect, he, no doubt, would have strongly remonstrated against such a choice.

Lamothe Cadillac was born on the banks of the Garonne, in the province of Gascony, in France. He was of an ancient family, which for several centuries, had, by some fatality or other, been rapidly sliding down from the elevated position which it had occupied. When Lamothe Cadillac was ushered into life, the domains of his ancestors had, for many past generations, been reduced to a few acres of land. That small estate was dignified, however, with an old dilapidated edifice, which bore the name of *castle*, although, at a distance, to an unprejudiced eye, it presented some unlucky resemblance to a barn. A solitary tower dressed, as it were, in a gown of moss and ivy, raised its gray head to a height which might have been called respectable, and which appeared to offer special attraction to crows, swallows, and bats. Much to the mortification of the present owner, it had been called by the young wags of the neighborhood, "*Cadillac's Rookery*," and was currently known under this ungenteel appellation. Cadillac had received a provincial and domestic education, and had, to his twenty-fifth year, moved in a very contracted sphere. Nay, it may be said that he had almost lived in solitude, for he had lost both his parents, when hardly eighteen summers had passed over his head, and he had since kept company with none but the old tutor to whom he was indebted for such classical attainments as he had acquired. His mind being as much curtailed in its proportions, as his patrimonial acres, his intellectual vision could not extend very far, and if Cadillac was not literally a dunce, it was well known that Cadillac's wits would never run away with him.

Whether it was owing to this accidental organization of his brain, or not, certain it is that one thing afforded the most intense delight to Cadillac:—it was, that no blood so refined as his own ran in the veins of any other human being, and that his person was the very incarnation of nobility. With such a conviction rooted in his heart, it is not astonishing that his tall, thin, and emaciated body should have stiffened itself into the most accurate observation of the perpendicular. Indeed, it was exceedingly pleasant and exhilarating to the lungs, to see Cadillac, on a Sunday morning, strutting along in full dress, on his way to church, through the meager village attached to his hereditary domain

His bow to the mayor and to the curate was something rare, an exquisite burlesque of infinite majesty, thawing into infinite affability. His ponderous wig, the curls of which spread like a peacock's tail, seemed to be alive with conscious pride at the good luck it had of covering a head of such importance to the human race. His eyes, in whose favor nature had been pleased to deviate from the oval into the round shape, were possessed with a stare of astonishment, as if they meant to convey the expression that the spirit within was in a trance of stupefaction at the astounding fact that the being it animated did not produce a more startling effect upon the world. The physiognomy which I am endeavoring to depict, was rendered more remarkable by a stout, cocked up, snub nose, which looked as if it had hurried back, in a fright, from the lips, to squat in rather too close proximity to the eyes, and which, with its dilated nostrils, seemed always on the point of sneezing at something thrusting itself between the wind and its nobility. His lips wore a mocking smile, as if sneering at the strange circumstance that a Cadillac should be reduced to be an obscure, penniless individual. But, if Cadillac had his weak points, it must also be told that he was not without his strong ones. Thus, he had a great deal of energy, bordering, it is true, upon obstinacy;—he was a rigidly moral and pious man;—and he was too proud not to be valiant.

With a mind so framed, was it to be wondered at that Cadillac deemed it a paramount duty to himself and to his Maker, not to allow his race to become extinct? Acting under a keen sense of this duty, and impressed with a belief that he might, by a rich alliance, restore his house to that ancient splendor which he considered as its birthright, but of which evil tongues said, that it was indeed so truly ancient, that it had long ceased to be recorded in the memory of man, he, one day, issued in state and in his gayest apparel, from his feudal tower, and for miles around, paid formal visits to all the wealthy patricians of his neighborhood. He was everywhere received with that high-bred courtesy, which those of that class extend to all, and particularly to such as belong to their own order, but he was secretly voted a quiz. After a few months of ineffectual efforts, Cadillac returned to his pigeon-hole, in the most disconsolate mood; and, after a year's repining, he was forced to content himself with the hand of a poor spinster, who dwelt in a neighboring town, where, like Cadillac, she lingered in all the pride of unsullied descent and hereditary poverty. Shortly after her marriage, the lady, who was a distant relation to the celebrated Duke of Lauzun, recommended herself and her husband to the patronage of that nobleman, who was then one of the brightest of that galaxy of stars that adorned the court of Louis the XIVth. Her letter was written in a quaint, fantastic style, and Lauzun, who received it on his way to the king's morning levee, showed it to the monarch, and was happy enough, by the drollery of his comments, to force a smile from those august lips. Availing himself of that smile, Lauzun, who was in one of his good fits, for the kindness of his nature was rather problematical, and the result of accident rather than of disposition, obtained for his poor connection the appointment of captain to one of the companies of infantry, which had been ordered to Canada.

The reception of this favor, with a congratulatory letter from Lauzun, added stilts to Cadillac's pomposity, and his few dependents and vassals became really astounded at the sublimity of his attitudes. On that occasion, the increased grandeur of his habitual carriage was but the translation of the magnificence of his cogitations. He had heard of the exploits of Cortez and Pizarro, and he came to the logical conclusion, in his own mind, that Canada would be as glorious a field as Peru or Mexico, and that he would at least rival the achievements of the Spanish heroes. Fame and wealth were at last within his grasp, and the long-eclipsed star of the Cadillacs would again blaze out with renewed luster!

The dreams of Cadillac were soon put to flight by sad realities, when he landed in Canada, where hardships of every kind assailed him. The snows and blasts of Siberian winters, the heat of summers equal to those of Africa, endless marches and counter-marches after a wary and perfidious enemy, visible only when he could attack with tenfold chances in his favor, the sufferings of hunger and thirst which were among the ordinary privations of his every-day life, the wants of civilization so keenly felt amid all the destitution of savage existence, days of bodily and mental labor, and nights of anxious vigil, hair-breadth escapes on water and on land, the ever-recurring danger of being tomahawked and scalped, the war-whoops and incessant attacks of the Indians, the honorable distinctions of wounds and of a broken constitution in the service of his country—these were the concomitants and the results of Cadillac's career in Canada during twenty years! All this Cadillac had supported with remarkable fortitude, although not without impatience, wondering all the time that something or other did not happen to make him what he thought nature and his birth intended and entitled him to be—a great man!

But twenty years had elapsed, and at their expiration, he found himself no better than a lieutenant-colonel. To increase his vexation, he had no other issue by his marriage than a daughter, now eighteen years of age, and thus he remained without the prospect of having an heir to continue his line, and to bear his noble name. The disappointment of his hopes in this respect was the keenest of all his afflictions; he was approaching the trying climacteric of fifty-four, and he was as poor as when he departed from the banks of the Garonne. A lieutenant-colonel he was, and would remain, in all probability. His superior officer seemed to be marvelously tenacious of his post and of life, and would neither die nor advance one step beyond his grade: bullets spared him, and ministers never thought of his promotion. Thus it was clear, from all appearances, that Cadillac was not in a position soon to become a marshal of France, and that Canada was not the land where he could acquire that wealth he was so ambitious of, to enshrine his old gray-headed tower, as a curious relic of the feudal power of his ancestry, within the splendid architecture of a new palace, and to revive the glories of his race. Hence he had imbibed the most intense contempt for the barren country where so much of his life had been spent in vain, and he would sneer at the appellation of *New France* given to Canada; he thought it was a disparagement to the beautiful and noble kingdom of which he boasted to be a native, and he frequently amused his brother officers with his indignation on this subject. " This world may revolve on its axis to all eternity," he would say, " and Canada will no more be made to resemble France, than a dwarf will ever be the personification of a giant!" This was a favorite phrase with which he loved to close his complaints against the object of his abomination, whenever he was betrayed into an expression of his feelings; for of late, he had become silent and moody, and only talked when he could not do otherwise. It was evident that his mind was wrapped up within itself, and absorbed in the solution of some problem, or the contemplation of a subject which taxed all its powers of thought. What could it be? But at last it was discovered that the object of Cadillac's abstracted cogitations was the constant blasting of all his hopes, in spite of his mighty efforts to realize them. So strange did it appear to him, that he could come to no other conclusion than that, if he had not risen higher on the stage of life, it was necessarily because he was *spell-bound*.

Cadillac, since his arrival in Canada, had kept up, with the great connection he had acquired by his marriage, the Duke of Lauzun, a regular correspondence, in which, to the infinite glee of that nobleman, he used to enumerate his manifold mishaps. Now, acting under the impression that he was decidedly the victim of fate or witchcraft, he wrote to Lauzun a long letter, in which he surpassed himself in his bombastic style, and out-heroding Herod, poured out on paper, in incoherent declamations, the vexed spirit which ailed him, and cut such antics in black and white, that Lauzun, on the perusal of this epistolary elegy, laughed himself into tears, and almost screamed with delight. It happened, at that time, that the ministry was in search of a governor for Louisiana, and the mischievous Lauzun, who thought that the more he exalted Cadillac, the greater source of merriment he prepared for himself, had sufficient power to have him appointed to that office. This profligate nobleman never troubled his wits about what would become of Louisiana under such an administration. Provided he found out a fit theater, and had it properly illuminated, to enjoy, at his ease, the buffooneries of a favorite actor, what cared he for the rest?

Before taking possession of his government, Cadillac went to France to receive the instructions of the ministry, and to visit his paternal domain. His return produced no slight sensation within a radius of forty miles round his so long-deserted hearth. If the waggish boys who used to torment him with their pranks had grown into manhood, tradition had handed down so much of Cadillac's peculiarities to their successors, that when he appeared before them, it was not as a stranger, but rather as an old acquaintance. Dressed in the fashion which prevailed at the time he left his native province, twenty years before, and which at present helped to set off with more striking effect the oddities of his body and mind, he was, as before, an object of peculiar attraction to the mischievous propensities of the juvenility of his neighborhood. One of them, still fresh from the university, where he had won academical honors, availing himself, in order to display the powers of his muse, of Cadillac's reappearance at home, composed a ballad which he called "*The Return of the Iroquois Chief*," and which was a parody of a celebrated one, well known as "*The Knight's Return from Palestine.*" It met with great success, and was sung more than once under the Gothic windows of Cadillac's tower. But he listened to the sarcastic composition with a smile of ineffable contempt. "Let them laugh at my past misfortunes," he would say to himself; "the future will avenge my wrongs, and my enemies will be jaundiced with the bile of envy. I am now governor of Louisiana, of that favored land, of which so many wonders are related. This is no longer the frozen climate of Canada, but a genial region, which, from its contiguity, must be akin to that of Mexico, where the hot rays of the sun make the earth teem with gold, diamonds, and rubies!" Working himself into a paroxysm of frenzied excitement, he struck passionately, with the palm of his hand, the wall of the room he was pacing to and fro, and exclaimed, "O venerable pile, **which** derision calls *Cadillac's Rookery*, I will yet **make** thee a tower of strength and glory! I will gild each of thy moss-coated stones, and thou shalt be a tabernacle for men to wonder at and to worship!" As he spoke, his eyes became suffused with tears, and there was so much feeling and pathos in his action, and in the expression of his aspirations, that, for the first time in his life, not only he momentarily ceased to be ridiculous, but, to one who had seen him then, would have appeared not destitute of a certain degree of dignity, and perhaps not unworthy of respectful sympathy. Such is the magic of deep sentiment!

When Cadillac landed on the bleak shore of Dauphine or Massacre Island, what he saw was very far from answering his expectations. From the altitude of flight to which his imagination had risen, it is easy to judge of the rapidity of its precipitate descent. The shock received from its sudden fall, was such as to produce a distraction of the mind, bordering on absolute madness. As soon as Cadillac recovered from the bewildered state of astonishment into which he had been thrown, he sent to the minister of the marine department a description of the country, of which I shall only give this short abstract: "The wealth of Dauphine Island," said he, "consists of a score of fig-trees, three wild pear-trees, and three apple-trees of the same nature, a dwarfish plum-tree, three feet high, with seven bad-looking plums, thirty plants of vine, with nine bunches of half-rotten and half-dried-up grapes, forty stands of French melons, and some pumpkins. This is the terrestrial paradise of which we had heard so much! Nothing but fables and lies!"

It will be recollected that Lamothe Cadillac had arrived on the 13th of May. He had since been exploring the country, and with his usual sagacity, he passed this remarkable judgment on Lower Louisiana:

"This is a very wretched country, good for nothing, and incapable of producing either tobacco, wheat, or vegetables, even as high as Natchez." It is fortunate that from this oracular decision there has been an appeal, and we now know whether it has been confirmed or annulled.

The 1st of January, 1714, had come in due time, and Cadillac had not allowed his unfavorable opinions of Louisiana to depart with the expiring year, if we may judge from the dispatch in which he said: "The inhabitants are no better than the country; they are the very scum and refuse of Canada, ruffians, who have thus far cheated the gibbet of its due, vagabonds, who are without subordination to the laws, without any respect for religion or for the government, graceless profligates, who are so steeped in vice that they prefer the Indian females to French women! How can I find a remedy for such evils, when his Majesty instructs me to behave with extreme lenity, and in such a manner as not to provoke complaints! But what shall I say of the troops, who are without discipline, and scattered among the Indians, at whose expense they subsist?" Cadillac went on in this strain, in no sparing style, and summed up the whole with this sweeping declaration: "The colony is not worth a straw for the moment; but I shall endeavor to make something of it, if God grants me health."

God granted the worthy governor as robust health as he could have wished, but without enabling him to redeem his word, with regard to bettering the condition of the colony; and at the expiration of the year 1714, Cadillac found out that his situation, as an administrator, was far from being an enviable one. He had quarreled with Dirigoin, one of Crozat's agents, because, if we take his representations as true, that agent was a fool; and with the comptroller, Lebas, because he, Lebas, was dissipated; with the inhabitants, because they were dissolute and had hitherto refused to build a church, which was a thing not yet to be found in the whole colony; with the soldiers, because they were without discipline; with the officers, and particularly with Bienville, Boisbriant, Chateaugué, and Sérigny, because they neglected to apply for the holy sacrament, even at Easter; with the commissary, Duclos, because the views of that dignitary had differed from his own on more than one occasion; with Richebourg, a captain of dragoons, who had come with him in a ship of the line, because that officer had seduced most of the girls who had embarked with them for Louisiana, and who ought to have been respected; with the girls themselves, because they had suffered their virtue to be seduced, which was the cause of their remaining on his hands, inasmuch as every one refused to marry them on account of their own misconduct. Is it astonishing that, under such untoward circumstances, Cadillac's displeasure at his situation should have swelled into such gigantic proportions as to induce him to allow his gathering indignation to embrace the whole of America within the scope of his animadversion? Is it not to be supposed that his understanding must have been a little confused by his perplexities, when he wrote to the ministry—" Believe me, this whole continent is not worth having, and our colonists are so dissatisfied that they are all disposed to run away?"

The feud between the magnates of the land grew every day more fierce, and the colony presented the aspect of two hostile camps, Trojans and Greeks, tugging in irreconcilable enmity. On one side, there was the governor who was the Agamemnon of his party, and who was backed by Marigny de Mandeville, Bagot, Blondel, Latour, Villiers, and Terrine, scions of noble houses, and all of them young and brilliant officers, who would have joined in any strife merely for the sake of excitement. The fanatic Curate de la Vente was their Calchas, and stimulated them to the contest. On the other side stood Lieutenant-Governor Bienville, the Hector of the opposition, with the king's commissary Duclos, Boisbriant, Chateaugué, Richebourg, Du Tisné, Sérigny, and others of some note or influence, who were at least fully a match for their antagonists. Thus, on this small theater, the human passions were as keenly at work, and there was as hot a struggle for petty power, as if the stage for their display had been a more elevated one, and the objects of contention more exciting to ambition.

From the annals of the Dutch settlements of New York, or rather from the overflowing richness of his own imagination, which, to be prolific, had only to alight on and to be connected with a favorite subject, Washington Irving drew those humorous sketches, which first gave celebrity to his name. But in the early history of Louisiana, which has nothing to borrow from the fields of fiction, there spring up characters and incidents, fraught with as much originality, and tinged with as much romance, as any so felicitously described by him in his productions, or by other authors in any work of fancy. What writer could pretend, in his most whimsical creations, to produce a being more fantastical than Lamothe Cadillac? What powers of invention could match his style and the sentiments expressed in his letters? But let us follow the erratic course pursued by this eccentric personage.

He had come to Louisiana to acquire sudden wealth by the discovery of mines, and not to superintend and foster the slow and tedious progress of civilization. Hence, it is not to be wondered at, that, on his receiving, one day, positive orders to assist the agents of Crozat in establishing trading settlements or posts on the Wabash and on the Illinois, he got out of humor, and in a fit of impatience, had the hardihood to write back to the ministry, in these terms: "I have seen Crozat's instructions to his agents. I thought they issued from a lunatic asylum, and there appeared to me to be no more sense in them than in the Apocalypse. What! Is it expected that, for any commercial or profitable purposes, boats will ever be able to run up the Mississippi, into the Wabash, the Missouri, or the Red River? One might as well try *to bite a slice off the moon!* Not only are these rivers as rapid as the Rhone, but in their crooked course, they imitate to perfection a snake's undulations. Hence, for instance, on every turn of the Mississippi, it would be necessary to wait for a change of wind, if wind could be had, because this river is so lined up with thick woods, that very little wind has access to its bed."

As to the ministerial expectations that he should devote most of his time to favoring agricultural pursuits among the colonists, Cadillac took it in high dudgeon, that such recommendations should ever be addressed to him, as if he had not something better to attend to—the discovery of gold, diamonds and pearls! To trouble himself about conceding and locating lands, was a thing concerning which he never admitted the possibility of his being seriously employed, and he treated the matter very lightly in one of his dispatches, in which he said to the ministry, "Give the colonists as much land as they please. Why stint the measure? The lands are so bad that there is no necessity to care for the number of acres. A copious distribution of them would be cheap liberality."

Thus, agriculture and commerce had failed to engage

the sympathies of Cadillac, who, since the first day he landed in Louisiana, had bent all his energies and all the means at his command toward the discovery of mines. He had sent Canadians in every direction to explore for the hidden treasures of the earth, but months had elapsed without gratifying the cravings of Cadillac's appetite for gold. Some of the Canadians had been killed by the Indians:—others found so much amusement in their favorite avocations of fishing and hunting, that they forgot the duties imposed upon them, and for the discharge of which they were paid:—there were more than one who, having gone so far as the Illinois and the Missouri, suddenly bethought themselves of some love-sick maid, some doting mother or aged father, whom they had left pining on the banks of the St. Lawrence, and instead of returning down the Mississippi, to give to Cadillac an account of their mission, they pursued their way up to their native villages. It must be confessed that all were little competent and too ignorant to investigate properly the object of their inquiries. The few who came back had but "a beggarly account of empty boxes" to lay before Cadillac. But if he had been favored with a romantic turn of mind, he would have found some indemnification in the recital of their marvelous adventures.

Cadillac came at last to the conclusion that he was in a sorry predicament. Sancho, when assailed with the cares of his insular government, never felt the tenth part of his embarrassment. So much so, that Cadillac deeply regretted that he could not be forever asleep; because, when awake, he could not but be aware that he had spent all the funds he could command, and had no more left to consecrate to his favorite scheme. The sad reality stared him in the face:—his purse was empty, and his Canadians were gone. But when he was asleep, his dreams beggared the wonders of the Arabian Nights. Then Queen Mab would drive, four in hand, her tiny cobweb carriage through his brain: some merry elf of her court would tickle his nose with a feather from a humming-bird's tail, and instantly Cadillac would see a thousand fairy miners, extracting from the bowels of the earth and heaping upon its surface enormous piles of gold and silver, having a fantastic resemblance to those Indian mounds which, in our days, make such strong appeals to our curiosity. Heated by these visions, Cadillac addressed himself to Duclos, the king's commissary, for more funds to prosecute his researches after the precious metals for which he thirsted. Duclos replied that the treasury had been pumped dry. "Borrow," answered Cadillac. "I can not," observed Duclos. "Well, then!" said the governor very pithily, "what is the use of your being a financier, if you can not raise money by borrowing, and what is the use of my being a governor, if I have no funds to carry on the purposes of my government!"

Low did Cadillac hang his head, in spite of all his pride, when he found himself so cramped up in his operations. But it would require a more powerful pen than mine to describe his indignation, when Duclos, the king's commissary, requested him to render his accounts for all the funds which had been put in his hands, and for all the goods and trinkets which had been delivered to him for distribution among the Indians. It was long before he could be made to understand what was expected from him, so strange and unnatural to him did *such a pretension*, as Cadillac called it, really seem on the part of the commissary. There was to him something stupendous in the idea that there should ever be the possibility of any such event happening, as that of a commissary calling upon *him*, Cadillac, the noblest among the noble, *him*, the governor, *him*, the representative of the Lord's anointed, to furnish his accounts, just in the same way that such a call might have been made upon any ordinary biped of the human species. Was not such a pretension the forerunner of some extraordinary convulsion of nature? Be it as it may, Cadillac immediately wrote to the ministry to inform them of this astounding fact, which, in his opinion, was a demonstration of the wild notions that had crept into the colony. Evidently, the commissary was "non compos mentis!"

The tribulations of Cadillac were destined to pursue a progressive course, and he was hardly out of one difficulty, when another and still another came in quick succession, like the ghosts that haunted Macbeth. To increase his perplexities, the troops refused to go through all the duties of their regular service, on the ground that they had nothing to eat but corn, when they were entitled to wheat bread. "A deputation of twenty of them," said Cadillac, in his communications to the ministry, "had the impudence to address me on the subject. I immediately sent the spokesman to prison, and having convened the officers, I told them that the troops in Canada were satisfied with corn for their food, that those in Louisiana had, as I had been informed, lived on it three years, and that I saw no reason why they should not continue. None of the officers dissented from me, except the commissary, who expressed a different opinion, which he supported with the most puerile reasoning: but I chid him and gave him a good rapping on the knuckles."

The spirit of discontent was not confined to the soldiery, but had spread through the minds of the colonists themselves. "They have dared to meet without my permission," said he, in another dispatch, "and to frame a petition to demand that all nations should be permitted to trade freely with the colony, and that the inhabitants should have the right to move out of this province, according to their pleasure. Freedom of trade, and freedom of action!—a pretty thing! What would become of Crozat's privileges? The colonists also insist on Crozat's monopoly of trade being confined to the wholesale disposition of his goods and merchandise. They pretend that he should in no case be allowed to retail his goods, and that his gains should be limited to fifty per cent. on the original cost. Their petition contains several other demands equally absurd. In order to cut all these intrigues in the bud, I declared that if this petition was ever presented to me, I would hang the bearer. A certain fellow, by the name of Miragoin, had taken charge of this precious piece of composition, and had assumed the responsibility of its presentation, but on his being informed of my intentions, he tore it to pieces."

One would have thought that Cadillac had *supped full of annoyances, if not of horrors*. But another cause of deep mortification, particularly for one so pious and so strictly moral as he was, had been kept in reserve; which was, his finding himself under the necessity of resisting the solicitations of his friend, the Curate de la Vente, and of the other missionaries, who insisted upon his expelling out of the colony, two women of bad character, that had lately arrived. " I have refused to do so," said he, in one of his dispatches, " because if I sent away all women of loose habits, there would be no females left, and this would not meet the views of the government. Besides (he slyly observed), one of these girls occupies the position of a servant in the household of the king's commissary, who will no doubt reclaim her from her vicious propensities.

After all, I think that the members of the clergy **here** are perhaps too rigid, and too fond of exacting long and repeated confessions. A little more lenity would better suit the place and time. Let me add, in conclusion, that if you do not check the intrigues of Bienville and of the commissary, who have gained over to their side most of the officers and of the inhabitants, Crozat will soon be obliged to abandon his enterprise."

We see that there was a deep feeling of animosity between Cadillac and Bienville, which threatened to be of long continuance. But Cadillac had a daughter, and Bienville was a young man, and one of such as are framed by nature to win the affections of the fair descendants of Mother Eve. Would not a novel-writer imagine, under such circumstances, a love story, either to soothe the two chiefs into a reconciliation, or to fan into more sparkling flames the slow burning fire of their inextinguishable hatred? Is it not strange that what would certainly be devised to increase the interest of the dramatic plot, did actually turn out to be an historical occurrence? But what fact or transaction, commonplace as it would appear anywhere else according to the ordinary run of things, does not, when connected with Louisiana, assume a romantic form and shape?

Thus Cadillac's daughter did really fall in love with Bienville. But although her eyes spoke plainly the sentiment of her heart, Bienville did not seem to be conscious of his good fortune, and kept himself wrapped up in respectful blindness. The lady's love, however, made itself so apparent, that it at last flashed upon Cadillac's mind. This was indeed a discovery! How he did wince at the idea that one whom he looked upon as so inferior to himself in birth and rank, and **particularly** that a *Canadian* should have won the heart of his daughter! Vehemently and long did he remonstrate with his progeny on the unnatural passion which she had conceived; but the love-sick maid thought it perfectly natural, and showed a pertinacity which greatly shocked her equally obstinate parent. Nay, she did what others had done before her, and became so pale and emaciated that she frightened her father's opposition into an acquiescence with her wishes. So much so, that Cadillac brought himself, at last, to think that this match would not be so disproportionate as he had conceived it at first. Bienville, after all, was a gentleman by birth, he was the founder of a colony, and had been a governor!—That was something to begin with, and he might, in the course of time, rise to an eminence which would show him worthy of an alliance with the illustrious Cadillac family. Besides, Cadillac was getting old, and had so far had a poor chance of acquiring the wealth he had been in quest of so long. If he died, what would become of his daughter? These reflections settled the question, and Cadillac said to himself, "Bienville shall be my son-in-law." Never did he, for one single moment, dream of any obstacle. Nothing remained but to encourage Bienville's fancied timidity, and to lift up the curtain which concealed from him the bliss awaiting his unconscious innocence.

One morning, Bienville, much to his astonishment, received a friendly invitation to the governor's closet. There, the great man proffered to his subordinate the olive branch of reconciliation, and by slow degrees, gave him to understand that the god Hymen might seal the bond of their amity. Bienville received this communication with low and reverential obeisance. Much delighted did he show himself at this offer of reconciliation, and much honored with the prospect, **however** distant of an alliance so far beyond his humble aspirations; but, at the same time, he plainly intimated to Cadillac his firm determination, for reasons best known to himself, forever to undergo the mortifications of celibacy! So unexpected this answer was, that Cadillac reeled in his seat, as if he had been stunned by a sudden blow. There he stood in a trance, with his mouth gaping wide, with his eyes starting from their sockets, and with dilating nostrils, while Bienville and the very walls, and every thing that was in the room, seemed to spin and whirl madly around him with electric rapidity. Now, indeed, he had known the worst, fate had entered the lists, and *Birnam wood had come to Dunsinane!* What! his daughter, a Cadillac, to be refused by a Canadian adventurer! No doubt a screw had broken loose in the machinery of the universe, and our whole world was to be flung back into the womb of old chaos again! Before Cadillac had recovered from this paroxysm, Bienville had made his exit, and had gone to tell the anecdote to some confidential friends. The fact which I have related is thus briefly mentioned by Bienville in one of his dispatches: "I can assure your excellency that the cause of Cadillac's enmity to me is my having refused to marry his daughter."

Bienville did not wait long to receive a signal proof of Cadillac's vindictive spirit, and he anticipated a manifestation of it, when summoned a second time to appear before his chief. Nor was he deceived; and when he was ushered into Cadillac's presence, that dignitary's countenance, which looked more than usually solemn and stern, indicated that he had matured his revenge for the insult he had undergone. "Sir," said he to Bienville, "I have received secret information that four Canadians, on their way to Illinois, have been massacred by the Natchez. You must punish the murderers, and build a fort on the territory of that perfidious nation, to keep it in check. Take Richebourg's company of thirty-four men, fifteen sailors to man your boats, and proceed to execute my commands." "What!" exclaimed Bienville, "do you really intend to send me with thirty-four men to encounter a hostile tribe that numbers eight hundred warriors!" "A truce to your observations," continued Cadillac, with a bitter smile, "to hear must be to obey. I can not dispose of a greater force. I have myself good grounds to expect being attacked by the neighboring nations, who, as I am informed, have entered into a conspiracy against us. Yet the offense committed by the Natchez must be instantly requited, or they would be emboldened into the perpetration of worse outrages. Go then, with such means as I can give; in case of success, your merit will be greater, but if you should meet with any reverse, you will be at no loss for an excuse, and all the responsibility shall be mine. Besides, you and Richebourg have such talents and courage as will easily extricate you out of any difficulty. You are a very Hercules, and he is a perfect Theseus, in licentious propensities, at least. What is this mission I send you upon, compared with the twelve labors of the mythological hero, who, like you on this occasion, was sent forth to redress wrongs and punish crimes!" To the studied sarcasm of this set speech, Bienville made no answer. In those days of adventurous and almost mad exploits in America, in an age when the disciplinarian rules of hierarchy commanded such respect and obedience, none, without disgrace, could have questioned the word of his superior, when that word was to brave danger, however foolish and reckless this exercise of authority might be. Moreover, Bienville saw that his ruin had been deliberately planned, and that remonstrance was useless. Therefore, signifying mute assent to Cadillac's wishes, he withdrew to betake himself to the execution of the orders which he had received, and to advise with Richebourg on the best means of defeating Cadillac's malicious designs.

Richebourg was a brave officer, full of intelligence and of cool daring, whose career in Europe, as a military man, had been interrupted by several duels, which at last had forced him to leave his country. He was so amiable, so obliging, so exceedingly conciliatory, that it was difficult for one who did not know a certain eccentric peculiarity of his mind, to understand how he had come to have so many quarrels. Who more gifted than he with suavity of manners and the art of pleasing? He never was fretted by contradiction, and ever smiled at opposition. Popular among men, a favorite with women, he never allowed words of blame to fall from his lips, but on the contrary was remarkable for the good nature of his remarks on all occasions except one. How could this milk of human kindness, which was the dominant element of his disposition, be suddenly soured into offensive acidity, or turned into gall? It was passing strange! But it was nevertheless true, that, for some cause which he never explained, he had conceived the most inveterate hatred for all that smacked of philanthropy. There suddenly sprung up in his heart a sort of diseased aversion for the man, who, in his presence, either went by the name of philanthropist, or expressed sentiments which gave him a claim to that character. Richebourg, on such occasions, would listen with exemplary composure, and, treasuring up in his memory every philanthropic declaration that fell from the lips of the speaker, he would, as soon as he found the opportunity, put him to the test, as to whether his practice corresponded with his theory. Alas! few stood the test, and then Richebourg was not sparing of the words, *humbug, impostor*, and *hypocrite*. What was the consequence? A quarrel; and invariably the philanthropist was run through. On this inexplicable whim, on this Quixotic tilting with all pretenders to philanthropy, Richebourg's friends frequently remonstrated, but found him intractable. No answer would he give to their observations, but he kept steadily on the same course of action. At last it became evident to them, that it was an incurable mania, a crotchet which had got into his brain and was incapable of eradication. With this imperfection they put up with good humor, on account of his many noble qualities, and he became generally known and designated as the philanthropist hater. His companions in arms, who loved him—although with some of them he had actually fought, because, either in earnest or in jest, they had hoisted the red flag that was sure to rouse the bull—had, in a joking manner, convened one day all the officers and inhabitants of Mobile and Massacre Island, and had passed, with mock gravity, a resolution, which was, however, seriously adhered to, and in which they declared that, for the future, no one would allow himself, either directly or indirectly, to be a philanthropist within a radius of three miles of Richebourg. This secured peace; but woe to the imprudent or uninformed stranger who trespassed on that sacred ground, with the slightest visible sign of the heresy which the fanatic Richebourg held in utter abomination!

Such was the officer who was to share with Bienville the dangers of the expedition, which was subsequently known in the annals of Louisiana, as the *first Natchez war*.

On the 24th of April, 1716, Bienville, with the small force which had been allotted to him, encamped on an island, situated in the Mississippi, opposite the village of the Tunicas, at the distance of about eighteen leagues from the Natchez. He immediately sent a Tunica to convey to the Natchez the intelligence that he was coming to establish a factory among them, to trade in furs, and to supply them, in exchange, with all the European merchandise they might want. Bienville had been informed that the Natchez believed that the late murders they had committed on the persons of some French traders had not been discovered, and he resolved to avail himself of this circumstance to accomplish his purposes without the risk of a collision. He affected, therefore, to have come on the most friendly errand, and gave out that he had encamped on the island merely to afford rest to his men, and to minister to the wants of some that were sick. He nevertheless took the precaution to have an intrenchment made with stakes or posts, within which he erected three log-houses. One he intended as a store-house for his provisions and ammunition, the other as a guard-house, and the third for a prison.

On the 27th, three Natchez came, under the ostensible purpose of complimenting Bienville on the part of their tribe, but in reality to act as spies, and they tendered to him the calumet, that mystic pipe which the Indians use for fumigation, as the ensign of peace. Bienville refused to smoke with them, and pretended to consider himself as not treated with the respect to which he was entitled, because their chiefs had not come in person, to greet *him*, the chief of the French. "I see," said he, "that your people are not pleased with the idea of my forming a settlement on their territory, for trading with them. Otherwise they would have expressed their satisfaction in a more becoming manner. Be it so. If the Natchez are so thankless for what I meant to be a favor, I will alter my determination, and give the preference to the Tunicas, who have always shown themselves such great friends to the French."

After this speech, Bienville ordered the three envoys to be well feasted and treated with kindness. The next day, they returned to their villages, with a Frenchman sent by Bienville, and whose mission was to address a formal invitation to the Natchez chiefs to a conference on the Tunicas Island. On this occasion, the Natchez felt greatly embarrassed, and many consultations were had on the best course to be pursued. Some were of opinion, that it would be imprudent for their chiefs to put themselves in the power of the French, who might have received information of what had lately occurred, and who might have come, under the garb of peace, to entrap their great men and wreak vengeance upon them. Others maintained that, from the circumstance of the French having come in such small number, it was evident that they were ignorant of the death of their countrymen, and did not intend to act as foes. "This inference," they said, "was confirmed by the information which had been carefully collected by their spies. They had no pretext to treat the French with indignity, and therefore it was proper for the chiefs of their tribe to go to meet and escort to their villages the wise and valiant pale-faced chief, who had already visited them on preceding occasions. A different course might excite suspicion, and investigation might lead to the discovery of what it was desirable to conceal. At any rate, the chiefs, by refusing to accept Bienville's invitation, would certainly incur his displeasure, and he might, by forming a trading establishment at the Tunicas, enrich that rival nation, to the detriment of the Natchez." These arguments prevailed, and in an evil hour for the Indian chiefs, their visit to Bienville's camp was resolved on.

On the very day Bienville had dismissed the three Indian envoys, he had dispatched one of his most skillful Canadian boatmen, to ascend the river with the utmost secrecy, during the night, and proceeding to a certain distance beyond and above the villages of the Natchez, to give notice to the French who might be coming down the river of the danger that threatened them from the Natchez. That man was provided with a score of parchment rolls, which he was to append to trees in places where they were likely to meet the eyes of those descending the Mississippi, and which bore this inscription: "The Natchez have declared war against the French, and M. de Bienville is encamped at the Tunicas."

On the 8th of May, at 10 o'clock in the morning, the Indian chiefs were seen coming with great state in four pirogues. The chiefs were seated under parasols, and were accompanied by twelve men, swimming. At this sight, Bienville ordered half of his men to keep themselves well armed and concealed in the guardhouse, but ready for sudden action. The other half he instructed to appear without any weapons, to assist the Indians in landing, and to take charge of all their war apparel, as it were to relieve them from an encumbrance, and under the pretext that it would be improper to go in such a guise to the awaiting feast and carousal. He further commanded that eight of the principal chiefs, whom he named, should be introduced into his tent, and the rest be kept outside until his pleasure was made known. All this was carried into execution without the slightest difficulty. The chiefs entered the tent, singing and dancing, and presented the calumet to Bienville. But he waved it off with contempt, and sternly told them that, before drawing one whiff from the smoking pipe, he desired to know what they had to say, and that he was willing to listen to their harangue. At this unexpected treatment, the chiefs were highly disconcerted: they went out of the tent in dismay, and seemed, with great ceremony, to be offering their calumet to the sun. Their great priest, with extended arms, made a solemn appeal to their god, supplicating him to pour his rays into the heart of the pale-faced chief, to dispel the clouds which had there accumulated, and had prevented Bienville from seeing his way and doing justice to the feelings of his red friends. After all this religious display, they returned to the tent, and again tendered their calumet to Bienville, who, tired of all these proceedings, thought proper at once to take the bull by the horns and to come out with his charges. "Before I receive your token of amity," said he abruptly, "and pledge my faith in return, tell me what satisfaction you offer for the death of the Frenchmen you have murdered." The Indians, who had really thought that Bienville knew nothing of that crime, appeared to be struck aghast by this direct and sudden apostrophe: they hung down their heads and answered not. "Let them be carried to the prison prepared for them," exclaimed Bienville impatiently, "and let them be secured with chains, stocks, and fetters."

On this demonstration of hostility, out came the Indians with their death-songs, which, much to the annoyance of the French, they kept repeating the whole day:—they refused all food, and appeared determined to meet their expected doom with the dauntless energy so common in that race of men. Toward evening, Bienville sent for the great chief, called "The Great Sun," and for two of his brothers, whose names were,

"The Stung Serpent" and "The Little Sun." They were the three most influential rulers of the nation. Bienville thus addressed them: "I know that it was not by your order, or with your consent, that the French whose death I come to avenge have been murdered. Therefore, your lives are safe, but I want the heads of the murderers, and of the chiefs who ordered or sanctioned the deed. I will not be satisfied with their scalps:—I wish for the very heads, in order that I may be sure that deceit has not been practiced. This whole night I give you for consultation on the best mode of affording me satisfaction. If you refuse, woe to your tribe! You know the influence which I have over all the Indian nations of this country. They respect, love and trust me, because from the day, seventeen summers ago, when I appeared among them, to the present hour, I have always been just and upright. You know that if I raise my little finger against you, and give one single war-whoop, the father of rivers will hear, and will carry it, up and down stream, to all his tributaries. The woods themselves will prick up their leafy ears, from the big salt lake, south, to the fresh water lakes at the north, and raising their mighty voice as when struggling with the hurricane, they will summon from the four quarters of the horizon the children of the forests, who will crush you with their united and overwhelming powers.

"You know that I do not boast, and that those red allies will gladly march against you, and destroy the eight beautiful villages of which you are so proud, without my risking the life of one single Frenchman. Do you not remember that, in 1704, the Tchioumaqui killed a missionary and three other Frenchmen? They refused to deliver the murderers to me—my wrath was kindled, and I said to the neighboring Indian nations:

• Bienville hates the Tchioumaquis, and he who kills a Tchioumaqui is Bienville's friend.' When I passed this sentence upon them, you know that their tribe was composed of three hundred families. A few months elapsed, and they were reduced to eighty! they sued for peace at last, yielded to my demands, and it was only then that the tomahawk, the arrow and the rifle ceased to drink their blood. Justice was satisfied:— and has Bienville's justice a smaller foot and a slower gait when it stalks abroad in the pursuit of the white man who has wronged the red man? No! In 1702, two Pascagoulas were killed by a Frenchman. *Blood for blood*, I said, and the guilty one, although he was one of my people, no longer lived. Thus, what I have exacted from the Indians, I have rendered unto them. Thus have I behaved, and thus have I deserved the reputation which I enjoy in the wigwams of the red men, because I never deviated from the straight path of honesty. Hence I am called by them the *arrow of uprightness* and *the tomahawk of justice*.

"*Measure for measure!*—this is my rule. When the Indians have invoked my arbitration between themselves, they have been invariably subject to this same rule. Thus, in 1703, two Taouachas having killed a Chickasaw, I obliged their chiefs to put them to death. *Blood will have blood.* When the Choctaws murdered two Chactioumans in 1715, I said, *tooth for tooth, lives for lives*, and the satisfaction was granted. In 1707 the Mobilians, by my order, carried to the Taouachas, the head of one of their tribe in expiation of an offense of a similar nature; and, in 1709, the Pascagoulas having assassinated a Mobilian, '*an eye for an eye*,' was my award, and he who was found guilty forfeited his life. The Indians have always recognized the equity of this law, and have complied with it, not only between themselves, but between them and the French. In 1703, the Coiras made no difficulty to put to death four of their warriors, who had murdered a missionary and two other Frenchmen. I could quote many other instances, —but the cause of truth does not require long speeches, and few words will convince an honest heart. I have done. I do not believe that you will refuse to abide by the law and custom which has always existed among the Indians, and between them and the French. There would be iniquity and danger in the breach of that law: honor, justice, peace and safety lie in its observance. Your white brother waits for an answer."

The Indians listened to this speech with profound attention, but made no reply, and Bienville ordered them to be remanded to prison. The next morning, at daybreak, they requested to speak to Bienville, and they were conducted to his presence. The Indian who was the first of the chiefs by rank, addressed him in these terms: "The voice of the Great Spirit made itself heard within us last night. We have listened to his dictate, and we come to give our white brother whatever satisfaction he desires. But we wish him to observe that we, the great chiefs, being all prisoners, there is no man left behind who has the power to accomplish the mission of bringing the heads thou demandest. Let, therefore, the Stung Serpent be liberated, and thy will shall be done." To this request Bienville refused his assent, because he knew the energy of that chief, and doubted his intentions; but he consented that Little Sun should go in his brother's place.

Five days had elapsed, when Little Sun returned, and brought three heads. After a careful examination of their features, Bienville sent again for all the chiefs, and ordering one of the heads to be flung at their feet; "The eye of the white chief," said he, "sees clear through the fog of your duplicity, and his heart is full of sorrow at your conduct. This is not the head of the guilty, but of the innocent who has died for the guilty. This is not the head of Oyelape, him whom ye call the Chief of the *White Clay*." "True," answered the Indians, "we do not deny thy word, but Oyelape has fled, and his brother was killed in his place." "Even if it be so," observed Bienville, "this substitution can not be accepted."

The next day, the 15th of May, Bienville allowed two other chiefs and the great priest to depart for their villages, and try if they would not be more successful than the Little Sun. They returned on the 25th, and informed Bienville that they could not discover the place of Oyelape's concealment, but they brought along with them some slaves and part of the goods which had belonged to the murdered Frenchmen. In the mean time, twenty-two Frenchmen and Canadians who were coming down the river in separate detachments, having seen the parchment signs posted up along its banks by the order of Bienville, had given a wide berth to the side occupied by the Natchez, and, using proper precaution, had arrived safely at Bienville's camp. Thus he found himself at the head of seventy-one men, well armed, of tried hardihood, and used to Indian warfare. This was a fortunate accession to his forces; for the Indians had almost determined to make, in their canoes, a night attack upon the island, and to rescue their chiefs or perish. The Tunicas had given to Bienville notice of what was brewing among the Natchez, and offered forty of their best warriors to assist the French in the defense of the island. But Bienville, who, although he affected to put great trust in them, feared that they might prove traitors, refused with apparent thankfulness their proffered assistance, and replied that, with his small force, he could make the island good against the whole tribe of the Natchez. This manifestation of confidence in his strength, and the timely arrival of the twenty-two white men, with some Illinois, no doubt prevented the Natchez from carrying their project into execution. It is probable that they were also deterred by the consideration, that the French, if hard pressed, would put their prisoners to death.

The Great Sun, the Stung Serpent, and the Little Sun, who, perhaps, had so far delayed to make any confession, because they entertained the expectation of being rescued, having at last given up this hope, came out with a frank avowal. They maintained that they never had any previous knowledge of the intended murder of the French, and declared that four of the assassins were among Bienville's prisoners. One of them was called the Chief of the *Beard;* the other was named Alahoflechia, the Chief of the *Walnut Village;* the two others were ordinary warriors. They affirmed that these were the only guilty ones, with the exception of Oyelape, the Chief of the *White Clay,* who had fled. "The Great Spirit," they said, "has blinded them, has turned their wits inside out, and they have, of their own accord, delivered themselves into thy hands. It is fortunate that it be so; otherwise the two warriors might have fled, and the two chiefs are such favorites with the nation, that they would have successfully resisted our demand for their heads, and to give thee satisfaction would have been impossible. As it is, it shows that our Great Spirit has shaken hands with the God of the Cross, and has passed on the side of our white brother."

It was then the 1st of June, and the river, which was rising daily, had overflowed the island one foot deep, and made the quarters of the French more than uncomfortable. Humidity, combined with heat, had engendered disease, and half of Bienville's men were stretched on the couch of sickness. It was then high time for him to put an end to the situation he was in. Summoning to his presence all his prisoners, with the exception of the four men who had been designated as the assassins, he said to them: "Your people, after having invited my people to trade with them, suddenly violated the laws of hospitality, and treacherously murdered four Frenchmen who were their guests. They thought the atrocious deed would remain unknown, and that they would quietly enjoy their blood-stained plunder. But the souls of the dead spoke to me, and I came, and I invited you to my camp, as you had invited the French to your villages, and you became my guests, as they had been yours, and I rose upon you, as you rose upon them. Measure for measure. But I shall not butcher you, as you butchered them. You killed the innocent and the confiding—I shall kill only the treacherous and the guilty. Who can say that this is not justice? Now, let us bury the hatchet of war. I am satisfied with and believe your last declarations. Hear, then, on what conditions I consent to release you and grant you peace. You will swear to put to death, as soon as possible, Oyelape, the Chief of the White Clay, and you will bring his head to the French officer whom I shall station among you. You will consent, also, to my putting to death the two chiefs and the two warriors who are in my hands. You will restore every object that you may ever have taken from the French; for what has been lost or wasted, you will force your people to pay the equivalent in furs and provisions. You will oblige them to cut two thousand five hundred stakes of acacia-wood, thirteen feet long by a diameter of ten inches, and to convey the whole to the bank of the Mississippi, at such a spot as it will please the French to erect a fort; and furthermore, you will bind yourselves to furnish us, as a covering for our buildings, with the barks of three thousand trees. This is to be executed before the first day of July; and above all, you will also swear, never, under any pretext or color whatever, to entertain the slightest commercial or friendly relations with the British, whom you know to be the eternal enemies of the French."

The chiefs assented to these terms, swore by the sun that they would, for the future, be the best friends of the French, and urged Bienville to smoke the pipe of peace. Bienville knew well what to think of these hollow protestations, but affected to believe in the return of the Natchez to the sentiments they professed. He refused, however, to smoke, because he considered that the treaty of peace would not be valid, until ratified in a meeting of the whole nation, but he dismissed all the Indians with the exception of the Stung Serpent, the Little Sun, and the four criminals who were doomed to death. With the departing Indians he sent Aid-major Pailloux, accompanied by three soldiers, to be present at the ratification of the treaty. On the 7th of June, nine old men came with great ceremony and pomp, to give to Bienville official information of the expected ratification.

On the 12th, the two Indian chiefs were put to death, the two warriors having already met their fate on the 9th. When the Chief of the Beard saw that the moment had come for the execution of the sentence passed upon him, he ceased his death-song which he had been chanting for some time, and took up a sort of war-song, while he looked fiercely at the threatening muskets of the French, and at the few Indians of his tribe whom Bienville had detained to witness the death of the culprit.

War Song.

I.

"Let there be joy in the hearts of the Natchez! A child is born to them of the race of their Suns. A boy is born with beard on his chin! The prodigy still works on from generation to generation." So sang the warriors of my tribe when I sprung from my mother's womb, and the shrill cry of the eagle in the heavens was heard in joyous response. Hardly fifteen summers had passed over my head, when long and glossy my beard had grown. I looked round, and I saw that I was the only red man that had this awful mark on his face, and I interrogated my mother, and she said:

> Son of the Chiefs of the Beard,
> Thou shalt know this mystery,
> In which thy curious eye wishes to pry,
> When thy beard from black becomes red.

II.

Let there be joy in the hearts of the Natchez! A hunter is born to them, a hunter of the race of their Suns. Ask of the bears, of the buffaloes, of the tigers, and of the swift-footed deer, whose arrows they fear most. They tremble and cower when the footstep of the hunter with beard on his chin is heard on the heath. But I was born too with brains in my head, as well as beard on my chin, and I pondered on my mother's words. One day, when a leopard, whom I strangled, had torn my breast, I painted my beard with my own blood, and I stood smiling before her. She said nothing, but her eye gleamed with wild delight, and she took me to the temple, where, standing by the sacred fire, she thus sang to me:

> Son of the Chiefs of the Beard,
> Thou shalt know the mystery,
> Since, true to thy nature, with thy own blood,
> Thy black beard thou hast turned to red.

III.

Let there be joy in the hearts of the Natchez! for a witted chief, worthy of the race of their Suns, has been born to them, in thee, my son; a noble chief with beard on his chin! Listen to the explanation of this prodigy. In days of old, a Natchez maid of the race of their Suns, was on a visit to the Mobilians. There, she soon loved the youthful chief of that nation, and her wedding-day was nigh, when there came from the big salt lake, south, a host of bearded men, who sacked the town, slew the red chief with their thunder, and one of those accursed evil spirits used violence to the maid, when her lover's corpse was hardly cold in death. She found, in sorrow, her way back to the Natchez hills, where she became a mother; and lo! the boy had beard on his chin! and when he grew to understand his mother's words, she whispered in his ear:

> Son of the Chiefs of the Beard,
> Born from a bloody day,
> Bloody be thy hand, bloody be thy life,
> Until thy black beard with blood becomes red.

IV.

Let there be joy in the hearts of the Natchez! In my first ancestor, a long line of the best of hunters, of chiefs, and of warriors of the race of their Suns, had been born to them, with beard on their chin! What chase was ever unsuccessful, when over it they presided? When they spoke in the council of the wise men of the nation, did it not always turn out that their advice, whether adopted or rejected, was the best in the end? In what battle were they ever defeated? When were they known to be worn out with fatigue, hardships, hunger or thirst, heat or cold, either on land or on water? Who ever could stem, as they, the rushing current of the father of rivers? Who can count the number of scalps which they brought from distant expeditions? Their names have always been famous in the wigwams of all the red nations. They have struck terror into the boldest breasts of the enemies of the Natchez; and mothers, when their sons paint their bodies in the colors of war, say to them:

> Fight where and with whom you please,
> But beware, oh! beware of the Chiefs of the Beard!
> Give way to them, as you would to death,
> Or their black beards with your blood will be red!

V.

Let there be joy in the hearts of the Natchez! When the first Chief of the Beard first trimmed the sacred fire in the temple, a voice was heard, which said, "As long as there lives a chief, of the race of the Suns, with beard on his chin, no evil can happen to the Natchez nation; but if the white race should ever resume the blood which it gave in a bloody day, woe, three times woe to the Natchez! of them nothing will remain but the shadow of a name!" Thus spoke the invisible prophet. Years rolled on, years thick on years, and none of the accursed white faces were seen! But they appeared at last, wrapped up in their pale skins like shrouds of the dead; and the father of my father, whom tradition had taught to guard against the predicted danger, slew two of the hated strangers, and my father, in his turn, killed four!

> Praise be to the Chiefs of the Beard!
> Who knew how to avenge their old ancestral injury!
> When with the sweet blood of a white foe,
> Their black beard they proudly painted red.

VI.

Let there be joy in the hearts of the Natchez! When I saw the glorious light of day, there was born to them a great warrior, of the race of their Suns, a warrior and a chief with beard on his chin! The pledge of protection, of safety, and of glory stood embodied in me. When I shouted my first war-whoop, the owl hooted and smelt the ghosts of my enemies! —the wolves howled, and the carrion vultures shrieked with joy, for they knew their food was coming!—and I fed them with Chickasaw flesh, with Choctaw flesh, until they were gorged with the flesh of the red men! A kind master and purveyor I was to them, the poor dumb creatures that I loved! But lately, I have given them more dainty food. I boast of having done better than my father: five Frenchmen have I killed, and my only regret at dying is, that it will prevent me from killing more!

> Ha! ha! ha! that was game worthy of the Chief of the Beard!
> How lightly he danced! ho! ho! ho!
> How gladly he shouted! ha! ha! ha!
> Each time with French blood his black beard became red!

VII.

Let sorrow be in the hearts of the Natchez! The great hunter is no more! The wise chief is going to meet his forefathers: the indomitable warrior will no longer raise his hatchet in the defence of the children of the sun. O burning shame!—he was betrayed by his brother chiefs, who told his blood. If they had followed his advice they would have united with the Choctaws, with the Chickasaws, and all the other red nations, and they would have slain all the French dogs that came prowling and stealing over the beautiful face of our country. But there was too much of the woman in their cowardly hearts. Well and good! Let the will of fate be accomplished! The white race will soon resume the blood which they gave, and then the glory and the very existence of the Natchez nation will have departed forever with the Chief of the Beard; for I am the last of my race, and my blood flows in no other human veins. O Natchez! Natchez! remember the prophet's voice! I am content to die, for I leave behind me none but the doomed, and I go to revel with my brave ancestors!

> They will recognize their son in the Chief of the Beard;
> They will welcome him to their glorious homestead,
> When they see so many scalps at his girdle,
> And his black beard with French blood painted red!

He ceased, and stood up before the admiring eyes of the French with a look of exulting defiance, and with his fine athletic form measuring seven feet high, and seemingly dilated into more gigantic proportions by the excitement which convulsed his soul. The French officer who commanded the platoon of soldiers chosen on this occasion to fulfill a melancholy duty, gave the word, "*fire!*" and the Chief of the Beard passed into another world.

On the 3d of August, the fortifications ordered by Bienville had been completed, the Indians having strictly complied with the terms of the treaty. They did more: they not only furnished all the materials which had been stipulated, but labored with great zeal in cutting ditches, in raising the parapets and bastions of the fort, and in constructing the buildings required by the French. Stung Serpent even sent one hundred and fifty men to the French, to transport all their baggage, ammunition, and provisions, from the Tunicas to the Natchez. On the 25th of August, Bienville found himself comfortably and securely established in the strong position which he had in such a wily manner obtained, as we know, from the Natchez. However, they appeared to have dropped all resentment at the mode by which Bienville had got such advantages over them, and they behaved as if they were extremely desirous to impress upon him the belief that they were delighted at his forming a settlement among them. Five or six hundred men of that tribe, accompanied by three hundred women, came one day to dance under the walls of the fort, in manifestation of their joy at the termination of their quarrel with the French, and at the determination of the pale faces to establish themselves among their red friends. Bienville invited the chiefs to come into the fort, and treated them with due honors. It is evident that the Indians wished to propitiate the strangers whom they could not shake off, and whom, from instinct alone, they must have regarded as their most dangerous enemies, and as the future cause of their ultimate ruin. But that they felt any satisfaction at the intrusion of these new-comers, the knowledge of human nature forbids us to believe. Two distinct and antagonistical races had met front to front, and at the very moment they appeared to embrace in amity, and joined in the carousing feast, the one was secretly meditating subjugation, and the other resistance and revenge.

On the 28th of August, seeing no signs of hostility from the Indians, Bienville left Aid-major Pailloux in command of the new fort, which was called "Rosalie,' and departed for Mobile, where he arrived on the 4th of October, with the satisfaction of having accomplished the difficult task with which he had been charged. This was one cause of triumph over his adversary, Cadillac, but he there found another cause of gratulation in a letter to him from the minister of the marine department, in which he was instructed to resume the government of the colony, in the absence of De l'Epinay, appointed to succeed Cadillac. This was fortunate for Bienville, for he found his quondam superior in a towering rage at his success, and at what he called Bienville's execrable perfidy in taking forcible possession of the Indian chiefs, as he did. But Bienville contented himself with laughing at his impotent vituperation.

Before closing with Cadillac's administration, I shall briefly relate some other curious incidents, with which it was signalized. In 1715, a man by the name of Dutigné, who loved a joke, wishing to amuse himself with Cadillac's inordinate passion for the discovery of mines, exhibited to him some pieces of ore, which contained certain proportions of silver, and persuaded him that they had been found in the neighborhood of the Kaskaskias. This was enough to fire Cadillac's overheated imagination. Anticipating the realization of all his dreams, he immediately set off for the Illinois, where, much to his mortification, he learned that he had been imposed upon by Dutigné, to whom the deceptive pieces of ore had been given by a Mexican, who had brought them from his country. After an absence of eight months, spent in fruitless researches, he returned to Mobile, where he found himself the laughing-stock of the community. This was not calculated to soothe his mind, and in one of his dispatches, in which he gave an account of the colony, he said:

"There are as many governors here as there are officers. Every one of them would like to perform his duties according to his own interpretation. As to the superior council of this province, allow me to represent to your grace, that its assuming the authority to modify his Majesty's orders is fraught with injury to the royal interest, and precludes the possibility of establishing here a good government, because the language of its members smacks more of the independence of republicans than of the subordination of loyal subjects. '*I will or will not*,'—'*it shall or shall not be*,' are words of daily utterance in their mouths. A governor must be clothed with power superior to any other, in order that he may act with effect, and cause to be executed with prompt exactitude the commands of his Majesty, instead of his being checked by any controlling or opposing influence; which is always the case, when he is forced to consult subaltern officers, who are swayed entirely by their own interest, and care very little for the service of the king, or for the prosperity of the colony." These were stones flung at Bienville, at the commissary Duclos, and at the superior council, who threw obstacles in his way, and interfered with the exercise of the absolute power which he thought that he possessed, because, as governor, he considered himself to be an emanation from, and a representation of the king!

On his way up the river, to search for gold and silver, Cadillac stopped at Natchez. As soon as he was known to approach, the Indian chiefs came out in barbaric state to meet him, and according to their usages, presented to him their calumet, in token of peace and amity. Highly incensed Cadillac was at the presumption of the savages, in supposing that he would contaminate his patrician lips with the contact of their vile pipe. He accordingly treated the poor Indians very little better than he would uncouth animals, thrusting themselves into his presence. His having departed without having consented to smoke with them, had impressed the Natchez, who could not understand the nature of his pride, with the idea that he meditated war upon their tribe. Then, they resolved to anticipate the expected blow, and they secretly massacred some Frenchmen who happened to be in their villages. Hence the origin of the first quarrel of the Natchez with the French, to which Bienville put an end with such signal success, but with a little sprinkling of treachery.

It was not the Natchez alone whom Cadillac had offended. He had alienated from the French the affections of the Choctaws, who had always been their friends, but who, latterly, had invited the English to settle among them. Cadillac ordered them to expel their new guests, but the Choctaws answered that they did not care for him, nor for the forty or fifty French rogues whom he had under his command. This was the kick of the ass, and Cadillac resolved not to bear it, but to show them that the lion was not yet dead. After deep cogitations, he conceived, for their punishment, a politic stroke, which he carried into execution, and of which he informed his government with Spartan brevity: "I have persuaded," said he, "the brother of the great chief of the Choctaws to kill his sovereign and brother, pledging myself to recognize him as his successor. He did so, and came here with an escort of one hundred men. I gave him presents, and secured from him an advantageous peace."

Thus it is seen that Cadillac, with a very bad grace, pretended that his tender sensibilities were shocked at the treatment of the Natchez chiefs by Bienville. In his case it was the eye with the beam finding fault with the mote in his neighbor's eye.

On the 22d of June, 1716, the exasperation of Cadillac, who found himself in a hornet's nest, had become such, that he vented his feelings in these terms, in one of his dispatches: "Decidedly, this colony is a monster without head or tail, and its government is a shapeless absurdity. The cause of it is, that the fictions of fabulists have been believed in preference to the veracity of my declarations. Ah! why is there in falsehood a charm which makes it more acceptable than truth? Has it not been asserted that there are mines in Arkansas and elsewhere? It is a deliberate error. Has not a certain set of novel-writers published that this country is a paradise, when its beauty or utility is a mere phantasm of the brain? I protest that, having visited and examined the whole of it with care, I never saw any thing so worthless. This I must say, because my conscience forbids me to deceive his Majesty. I have always regarded truth as a queen, whose laws I was bound to obey, like a devoted knight and a faithful subject. This is, no doubt, the cause of my having stuck fast in the middle of my career, and not progressed in the path of promotion, while others, who had more political skill, understood how to frame, at my expense, pleasing misrepresentations. I know how to govern as well as any body, but poverty and impotence are two ugly scars on the face of a governor. What can I do with a force of forty soldiers, out of whom five or six are disabled? A pretty army that is, and well calculated to make me respected by the inhabitants or by the Indians! As a climax to my vexation, they are badly fed, badly paid, badly clothed, and without discipline. As to the officers, they are not much better. Verily, I do not believe that there is in the whole universe such another government."

It is not surprising that, under such circumstances, and with the ideas which fermented in his head, Cadillac should have thought that a terrible crisis was at hand. Laboring under this impression, he took refuge in Dauphine Island, where he issued a proclamation, in which he stated that, considering the spirit of revolt and sedition which reigned in the colony, and the many quarrels and duels which occurred daily, and were produced by hasty or imprudent words, by drunkenness, or by the presence of loose women, he prohibited all plebeians from wearing a sword, or carrying other weapons, either by day or by night, under the penalty of one month's imprisonment and a fine of 300 livres, to be applied to the construction of a church. As to persons of noble birth, they were to prove their right to wear a sword, by depositing their titles in the archives of the superior council, to be there examined and registered. Cadillac's enemies, and he had many, availed themselves of this proclamation to turn him into ridicule. They fabricated every sort of mock papers of nobility, to submit them to the superior council, the members of which, from ignorance or from a desire to annoy Cadillac, referred the whole of them to him, who, as governor, was their president. Sadly puzzled was Cadillac on these occasions, and his judgments afforded infinite amusement to the colonists. His waggish tormentors went farther, and, pretending to have formed an order of chivalry, they elected him, in a solemn meeting, grand master of that order, under the title of the *Knight of the golden calf*. They declared, with feigned gravity that this was done in commemoration of the wonderful achievements and labors of their illustrious governor in his researches for precious metals. This piece of pleasantry stung him to the quick; but he winced particularly at a song which, in alternate couplets, compared the merits of the *Knight of the golden calf* with those of the celebrated *Knight of the doleful countenance*, and gave the preference to the first.

Cadillac was preparing to repress these rebellious and heinous disorders, when he received a letter from Crozat.

in which the great merchant told him bluntly, that all the evils of which he complained originated from his own bad administration. At the foot of the letter, the minister of the marine department had written these words: "The governor, Lamothe Cadillac, and the commissary, Duclos, whose dispositions and humors are incompatible, and whose intellects are not equal to the functions with which his Majesty has intrusted them, are dismissed from office." I leave it to a more graphic pen to describe Cadillac's look and Cadillac's feelings when this thunderbolt fell on his head. Suffice it to say, that he contemptuously shook off his feet the colonial dust which had there gathered, and bundling up his household gods, removed himself and them out of Louisiana, which he pronounced to be hell-doomed.

At that time, there were only a few negroes in the colony, and they were all to be found about Mobile or in Dauphine Island. These were the only persons in whom some sympathy was discovered for the departing governor. This sympathy arose from a ludicrous cause. Cadillac had carried to America the fondest remembrance of his home in Europe, and he loved to dilate on the merits of France, of his native province of Gascony, of the beautiful river Garonne, and particularly of his old feudal tower, in which he pretended that one of his ancestors had been blessed with the inestimable honor of receiving the famous Black Prince, the boast of England. There was hardly one day in the week that he did not harp upon this favorite theme, which he always resumed with new exultation. There was not a human creature in the colony, with the exception of the Indians, who was not familiar with this oft-repeated anecdote, which had gained for Cadillac the nickname of the *Black Prince*. It became a sort of designation by which he was as well known as by his own family name; and the poor Africans, who frequently heard it, had supposed that Cadillac drew his origin from a prince of their blood and color. This was to them a source of no little pride, and to the colonists a cause of endless merriment.

There was another person who highly appreciated Cadillac, and who keenly regretted his dismissal from office: that person was the Curate de la Vente. No Davion was he, nor did he resemble a Montigny. With a pale face and an emaciated body; with a narrow forehead, which went up tapering like a pear; with thin compressed lips, never relaxed by a smile; with small gray eyes, occupying very diminutive sockets, which seemed to have been bored with a gimlet; and with heavy and shaggy eyebrows, from beneath which issued, habitually, cold and even stern looks; he would have struck the most unobserving, as being the very personification of fanaticism. When he studied, to qualify himself for his profession, he had, several times, read the Bible and the Gospels through; but his little mind had then stuck to the letter, and had never been able to comprehend the spirit, of the holy books. Like a fly, it had moved all round the flask which contained the sweet liquor, without being able to extract the slightest particle of it. When ordained a priest, the Bible and the Gospels were consigned to oblivion. For him, kneeling was prayer, and prayer was religion. Christianity, which is the triumph of reason, because it exacts no belief but that which flows from rational conviction, was, according to his conception, nothing but a mysterious and inexplicable hodge-podge of crude and despotic dictates, to be accepted on trust and submitted to without reflection, discussion, or analysis of any kind: for him, thought in such matters would have been a grievous sin; his breviary was the only book which he had read for many years, and he laid to his soul the flattering unction that he was a pious man, because he minutely complied with the ritual of his church. He fasted, did penance, and never failed reciting, in due time, all the litanies. Thus, observing strictly all the forms and discipline of the Roman Catholic faith, he thought himself a very good Christian. But every man who did not frequently confess to a priest, and did not receive the sacraments as often as the catechism of his creed required, was, in his opinion, no better than a pagan, and was entirely out of the pale of salvation. Animated with the fierce zeal of a bigot, he would not have scrupled, if in his power, to use the strong hand of violence to secure converts, and to doom to the stake and to the fagot the unbeliever in all the tenets, whether fundamental or incidental, of Catholicism: for his religion consisted in implicit belief in all the prescriptions of his church, and his church was God. Hence, all government which was not theocratical, or bordering on it, he looked upon as an unlawful and sinful assumption of power, which the church, by all means, was bound to take back, as its legitimate property.

With such dispositions, the Curate de la Vente soon became the terror of his flock, whose frailties he denounced with the epileptic violence of a maniac, and whose slightest delinquencies he threatened with eternal damnation. A fanatic disciplinarian, he had been shocked at the laxity with which the soldiers, the officers, the Canadian boatmen and traders, and the other colonists, performed their religious duties. He did not take into consideration that a judicious allowance ought to be made for the want of education of some, for the temptations which peculiar circumstances threw in the way of others, and for the particular mode of life to which all were condemned, and which might be received in extenuation, if not in justification of many faults. He might have reclaimed some by the soothing gentleness of friendly admonition: he discouraged or disgusted all by the roughness of intemperate reproach. Aware of the aversion which he had inspired, and indignant at the evil practices in which some indulged openly from inclination, and others, out of vain bravado to a minister they detested, he had supported Cadillac in all the acts of his administration, in all his representations of the state of the country; and he had himself more than once written to the ministry, that God would never smile upon a colony inhabited by such demons, heathens, and scoffers at the Holy Church; and he had recommended, not a Saint Bartholomew execution, it is true, but a general expulsion of all the people that were in the colony, in order to replace them with a more religious-minded community. As to the Indians, he considered them as sons of perdition, who offered few hopes, if any, of being redeemed from the bondage of Satan.

Seeing that the Ministry had paid no attention to his recommendations, he had determined to make, out of the infidels by whom he was surrounded, as much money as he could, which he intended to apply to the purpose of advancing the interests of the church, in some more favorable spot for the germination of ecclesiastical domination. With this view, he made no scruple to fatten upon the Philistines, and he opened a shop, where he kept for sale, barter, or exchange, a variety of articles of trade. He disposed of them at a price of which the purchasers complained as being most unconscionable; and he also loaned money to the Gentiles, at a rate of interest which was extravagantly usurious. As a salvo to his conscience, he had adopted the comfortable motto that the end justifies the means. The benighted Indians and the unchristian Christians (to use his own expressions) were not spared by him. When the circumstance was too tempting, and he had to deal with notorious unbelievers, he would even indulge in what he would have called actual cheating, if coming from a Christian dealing with a Christian. On these occasions, he would groan piteously, cross himself devoutly, fall on his knees before the image of our Savior, and striking his breast with compunction, he would exclaim, "O sweet Jesus, if this be an infraction of thy law, it is at least a trifling one, and it is done for the benefit of thy church: forgive me, O Lamb of mercy, and I will, in expiation, say twelve paters and twelve aves at the foot of the altar of thy Virgin Mother, or I will abstain a whole day from all food, in thy honor." After this soliloquy, he would get up, perfectly reconciled with himself and with his Maker, to whom, in these cases, he always took care to keep his plighted word. Many a time, his worldly transactions for the glorification of the church, and for the increase of church property at the expense of those he considered as infidels, forced him to enter into such strange compromises with his conscience and with his God. Hence the origin of the accusation brought against him by Bienville, in one of his dispatches, and which I have already reported, "that he kept open shop, and was a shrewd compound of the Jew and of the Arab." The truth is, that he was sincere in his mistaken faith, pious to the best of his understanding, a Christian in will although not in fact, a zealous priest in his way, which he thought a correct one, and a lamentable compound of fanaticism and imbecility.

In August, 1716, a short time before the recall of Cadillac, there had returned to Mobile a young man named St. Denis, who was a relation of Bienville, and whom, two years before, Cadillac had sent to Natchitoches, to oppose the Spaniards in an establishment which it was reported they intended to make in that part of the country. His orders were, to proceed afterward to New Mexico, to ascertain if it would not be possible to establish in that direction internal relations of commerce between Louisiana and the Mexican provinces, where it was hoped that Crozat would find a large outlet for his goods. When St. Denis arrived at the village of the Natchitoches, hearing no tidings of the supposed expedition of the Spaniards, he left there a few Canadians, whom he ordered to form a settlement; and, accompanied by twelve others, who were picked men, and by a few Indians, he undertook to accomplish the more difficult part of his mission.

I would recommend this expedition of St. Denis, and his adventures, to any one in search of a subject for literary composition. It is a fruitful theme, affording to the writer the amplest scope for the display of talent of the most varied order. St. Denis is one of the most interesting characters of the early history of Louisiana.

> "He hither came, a private gentleman,
> But young and brave, and of a family
> Ancient and noble."

He was a knight-errant in his feelings and in his doings throughout life, and every thing connected with him, or that came within the purview of his existence, was imbued with the spirit of romance. The noble bearing of his tall, well-proportioned, and remarkably handsome person was in keeping with the lofty spirit of his soul. He was one in whom nature had given the world assurance of a man, and that assurance was so strongly marked in the countenance of St. Denis, that wherever he appeared, he instantaneously commanded love, respect, and admiration. There are beings who carry in their lineaments the most legible evidence of their past and future fate. Such was St. Denis, and nobody, not even the wild and untutored Indian, could have left his presence, without at least a vague impression that he had seen one not born for the common purposes of ordinary life.

The laborious journey of St. Denis from Mobile to Natchitoches, the incidents connected with it, the description of the country he passed through, and of all the tribes of Indians he visited, would furnish sufficient materials for an interesting book. But what an animated picture might be drawn of that little band of Canadians, with St. Denis and his friend Jallot, the eccentric surgeon, when they crossed the Sabine, and entered upon the ocean-like prairies of the present state of Texas! How they hallooed with joy when they saw the immense surface which spread before them, blackened with herds of buffaloes, that wallowed lazily in the tall luxuriant grass which afforded them such luscious food, and such downy couches for repose! For the sake of variety, the travelers would sometimes turn from nobler to meaner game, from the hunchbacked buffalo to the timid deer that crossed their path. Sometimes they would stumble on a family of bears, and make at their expense a delicious repast, which they enjoyed comfortably seated on piled-up skins, the testimonials of their hunting exploits. Oh! there is sweetness in the prairie air, there is a richness of health and an elasticity of spirit,

"Which bloated ease ne'er deigned to taste.'

But these pleasures, exciting as they were, would perhaps have palled upon St. Denis and his companions, and might in the end have been looked upon as tame by them, from the frequency of their repetition, if they had not been intermingled with nobler sport, which consisted in oft-recurring skirmishes with the redoubtable Comanches, upon whose hunting-grounds they had intruded. On these occasions, St. Denis, protected against the arrows of the enemy by a full suit of armor, which he had brought from Europe, and mounted on a small black jennet, as strong as an ox and as fleet as the wind, would rush upon the astonished Indians, and perform such feats with his battle-axe, as those poor savages had never dreamed of. These encounters gave infinite satisfaction to Jallot, who was a passionate lover of his art, and who never was seen in a good humor, except when he was tending a wound. But he had more frequently the chance of dissecting than of curing the poor Indians, for, in most cases, the stroke of the white man's weapon was certain and instantaneous death. Still, he found some compensation in the numerous wounds inflicted by the Indians on his own companions; he had a fondness for arrow wounds, which he declared to be the nicest and genteelest of all wounds. One day, he was so delighted with a wound of this kind, which he pronounced, much to the exasperation of his patient, to be supremely beautiful, that he actually smiled with self-gratulation and cracked a joke!—to do this, his excitement must have been immense. Another day, when an Indian had been struck down by the battle-axe of St. Denis, without, however, being killed outright, he felt such a keen professional emotion at the prospect of probing and nursing a gash which he thought rare and extraordinary, that he franticly jumped upon St. Denis, hugged him with enthusiasm, called him his best friend, passionately thanked him for the most valu able case he had given him, and swore that *his Indian* should be carried on, whatever impediment it might be to their march, until he died or was cured. Who would have thought that this man, when he was not wielding his surgical instruments, was the most humane being in the world, and concealed, under an appearance of crabbed malignity, the tenderest sensibilities of the heart? Such are the mysteries of human nature!

St. Denis and his troop reached at last the Rio Bravo, at a Spanish settlement then called the Fort of St. John the Baptist, or Presidio del Norte. Don Pedro de Villescas was the commander of that place. He received the French with the most courteous hospitality, and informed them that he could not make any commercial arrangements with them, but that he would submit their propositions to a superior officer, who was governor of the town of Caouis, situated at the distance of one hundred and eighty miles in the interior. Spaniards are not famous for rapidity of action. Before the message of Villescas was carried to Caouis, and before the expected answer came back to the Presidio Del Norte, St. Denis had loved, not without reciprocity, the beautiful daughter of the old Don. What a pretty tale might be made of it, which would deserve to be written with a feather dropped from Cupid's wing! But when the lovers were still hesitating as to the course they would pursue, and discussing the propriety of making a full disclosure to him who, in the shape of a father, was the arbiter of their destiny, there arrived twenty-five men, sent by Don Gaspardo Anaya, the governor of Caouis, with secret instructions, which were soon made manifest, to the dismay of the lovers; for these emissaries seized St. Denis and his friend Jallot, and conveyed them to Caouis, where they were detained in prison until the beginning of 1715. From this place of confinement, St. Denis, fearing that the hostility evinced towards him might be extended to the rest of his companions, ordered them to return speedily to Natchitoches.

Ye Bulwers of America, I invite your attention! Here history presents you with the ready-made groundwork for whatever superstructure and embellishments you may choose to imagine for the amusement of your readers.

Don Gaspardo Anaya had been the unsuccessful suitor of Doña Maria, the daughter of Villescas. What must have been his rage, when he was informed by his spies that the new-comer, the brilliant Frenchman, had triumphed, where he had failed! But now he had that hated rival in his clutches, and he was omnipotent, and if the stranger died in the dungeon of Caouis, who, in these distant and rugged mountains, would bring *him*, the *governor*, to an account? Perilous indeed was the situation of St. Denis, and heavy must have been his thoughts in his solitary confinement! But what must have been his indignation when, one day, Anaya descended into his dark cell, and told him that he should be set free on condition that he withdrew his plighted faith to the daughter of Villescas! How swelled the loyal heart of the captive at this base proposal! He vouchsafed no answer, but he gave his oppressor such a look as made him stagger back and retreat with as much precipitation as if the hand of immediate punishment had been lifted up against him.

For six months, St. Denis was thus detained prisoner, and the only consideration which saved his life was the hope, on the part of Anaya, that prolonged sufferings would drive his victim to comply with his request. At the same time, he repeatedly sent secret messengers to

Doña Maria, whose mission was to inforn her that her lover would be put to death if she did not wed Anaya. But the noble Castilian maid invariably returned the same answer: "Tell Anaya that I can not marry him as long as St. Denis lives, because St. Denis I love; and tell him that if St. Denis dies, this little Moorish dagger, which was my mother's gift, shall be planted, either by myself or my agent's hand, in the middle of his dastardly heart, wherever he may be." This was said with a gentle voice, with a calm mien, as if it had been an ordinary message, but with such a gleam in the eye as is nowhere to be seen except in Spain's or Arabia's daughters. The words, the look, and the tone, were minutely reported to Anaya, and he paused!—and it is well that he did so, and a bolder heart than his would have hesitated; he knew the indomitable spirit of his race—he knew the old Cantabrian blood—and that Spain's sweetest doves will, when roused, dare the eagle to mortal combat!

The Spanish maid did not remain inactive, and satisfied with deploring her lover's captivity. She dispatched to Mexico a trusty servant, such as is only found in Spanish households, one of those menials that never question the will of their lord or lady, dogs for fidelity, lions for courage, who will tear to pieces whatever is designated to them, if such be the order of their masters. His mission was to find out the means of informing the Viceroy that a Frenchman, a presumed spy, had been for several months in the hands of the governor of Caouis, who was suspected of concealing his captive from the knowledge of the higher authorities, in order to tamper with his prisoner for a ransom. The object of this false information was to excite the jealous attention of the government, and to withdraw St. Denis, at all risks, from the dangerous situation he was in.

This stratagem succeeded, and much to his astonishment, Anaya received a peremptory order to send his prisoner to Mexico, with a sure escort, and at the peril of his head, if he failed!

One morning St. Denis found himself suddenly seated on a strong, powerful horse, amid a detachment of twenty men, who were evidently prepared for a long journey. He asked whither he was to be carried, and was particularly inquisitive about his friend Jallot, who had been put into a separate dungeon, and of whom he had heard nothing since his captivity, but he was dragged away without any answer being given to his inquiries. Seven hundred and fifty miles did he travel without stopping, except it be for such time as was absolutely necessary to take a hurried rest, when the magnificent city of Mexico burst upon his sight in all its imperial splendor. *There*, he flattered himself that he would obtain justice, but he soon experienced that change of place had been for him no more than a change of captivity. Look at the woe-begone prisoner in that horrible dungeon, where he is chained to the wall like a malefactor! His constitution is completely broken down; his body is so emaciated by his long sufferings, and by the want of wholesome food, that it presents the appearance of a skeleton; his long matted hair shrouds his face, and his shaggy beard hangs down to his breast. Who would have recognized the brilliant St. Denis in this miserable object, in this hideous-looking, iron-bound felon—a felon in aspect, if not in reality!

One day, an unusual stir was observed in front of his prison. The short, brief word of command outside, the clashing of arms, the heavy tramping of horses, St. Denis could distinctly hear in his dismal abode. The noise approached; the doors of his cell turned slowly on their rusty hinges; on came the bustling and obse-

quious jailer, ushering in an officer who was escorted
by a file of soldiers. It was one whom the Viceroy
had ordered to examine into the situation of all the
prisons of Mexico, and to make a report on their unfortunate tenants. "Who have we here?" said the
officer, in an abrupt tone. "I," exclaimed St. Denis,
starting to his feet, " I, Juchereau de St. Denis, a gentleman by birth, a prisoner by oppression, and now a
suitor for justice." On hearing these words, the officer
started back and looked wild with astonishment; then,
rushing to St. Denis, and putting his face close to his
face, removing with his trembling hand the disheveled
locks that concealed the prisoner's features, and scanning every lineament with a rapid but intense look, he
said, with a quivering voice, which, through emotion,
had sunk to a whisper, "You were born in Canada?"
"Yes." "Educated in France, at the Royal College of
Paris?" "Yes." "You left France to seek your fortune in Louisiana?" "I did." "By heaven, jailer, off
with those accursed chains! quick! set those noble
limbs free!" And he threw himself sobbing into the
arms of the astonished St. Denis, who thought himself
the dupe of a dream, but who at last recognized in his
liberator one of the companions of his youth, his best
early friend, the Marquis de Larnage, who, with some
other young Frenchmen, had entered into the Spanish
army, and who had risen to be the Viceroy's favorite
aid-de-camp. What a dramatic scene! And would
not this incident of Louisianian history be welcomed on
the stage by an American audience!

What a change! Here we are in the gorgeous halls
of Montezuma, where the barbaric splendor of the
Aztec emperors has been improved by the more correct
and tasteful application of Spanish magnificence: there
is a festival at the palace of the Viceroy:—

"The long carousal shakes the illumined hall;
Well speeds alike the banquet and the ball."

Noble and beautiful dames!—Silk, brocade, and diamonds!—Gentlemen of high birth—renowned soldiers—glittering uniforms, studded with stars and other decorations—breasts scarred with wounds—brains teeming with aspirations—grave magistrates—sage councillors—subtle diplomatists—scheming heads! What subjects for observation! The walls are alive with paintings which court the eye, or ornamented with mirrors which multiply the reflected beauty of the glorious pageantry. Now and then, scions of the greatest houses of Spain; younger sons, that had been sent to Mexico to better their fortunes; men whose names, when pronounced, sound like a trumpet inciting to heroic exploits, would make their appearance, and to let them pass, the crowd of brilliant guests would reverentially open their ranks. Such is the involuntary respect paid, mechanically as it were, to those who carry round their foreheads the agglomerated rays derived, through the magnifying focus of one thousand years, from the historical distinction of a long, uninterrupted line of illustrious ancestors!

Suddenly, the large folding doors of an inner apartment are thrown open, and the Viceroy is seen at table, with a few favored and envied guests, enjoying the delicacies of the most gorgeous banquet. What an accumulated treasure of gold and silver, under every form that convivial imagination can fancy, and in the shape of plates, dishes, chandeliers, and every sort of admirably chiseled vases! But who is that noble-looking cavalier on the right-hand side of the Viceroy? Can it be St. Denis, the late tenant of a gloomy jail? It is. Presented by his friend, the aid-de-camp, to the representative of the Majesty of Spain, to the Duke of Linares, he has become such a favorite that his daily and constant attendance is required at court. Nay, the affection which the Viceroy had conceived for St. Denis, had so grown upon that nobleman, that he had insisted upon the young Frenchman being lodged in the palace, where every favor was at his command. The whole city of Mexico had been convulsed with astonishment at the unexpected turn of fortune, which was the lot of the foreign adventurer. Marvelous, indeed, and inexplicable did the fascination exercised by St. Denis on the Viceroy seem to the multitude! Instead of attributing it, perhaps to its true cause, to the congenial affinity of mind to mind, and of heart to heart, they indulged in a thousand wild conjectures. At last, these surmises had settled in the belief that St. Denis had saved the life of the Viceroy, in a nocturnal adventure. It was positively ascertained, however, that St. Denis, a short time after his liberation, passing in a secluded street, heard the clashing of swords. Rushing to the spot from which the noise of conflict came, he saw a man with a mask on his face, and with his back to the wall of a house, who was sorely pressed by three other men, masked also, who were attacking him with the greatest fury. St. Denis took side with the weaker party, and put to flight the cowardly assassins. He never said to whom he had rendered such an eminent service, and if he knew—

>——— "He shunned to show,
> As hardly worth a stranger's care to know;
> If still more prying such inquiry grew,
> His brow fell darker, and his words more few."

His secret died with him!

Amid all the festivities of the vice-regal court, St. Denis had but one thought, one aspiration, that of returning to his lady love, and to his friend Jallot. He had even refused the most brilliant proposals from the Viceroy, such as a high grade in the Spanish army, saying, "I can serve but one God and one king. I am a Frenchman, and highly as I esteem the Spaniards, I can not become one." "But," replied the Viceroy, "you are already half a Spaniard, for you have confessed to me that you love a Spanish maid." "True," observed St. Denis, "but it is not certain that I can marry her, because I consider her father's consent as doubtful." "Well, then, accept my offers," exclaimed the Viceroy, "and I pledge my knightly word to remove every obstacle that may be in your way." St. Denis expressed his thanks, as one overwhelmed with gratitude at such kindness, but could not be shaken from his determination. "At least," continued the Viceroy, "do me one favor. Do not depart now. Take two months for reflection on what you reject. When this delay shall have expired, I will again put this question to you—will you attach yourself to my person, and transfer your allegiance from the Bourbons of France to the Bourbons of Spain?" The two months rapidly flew by, and the chivalric St. Denis remained firm to his purpose. "To lose such a man as you are," said the Viceroy, "is a serious trial to me, but I admire, even in its exaggeration, the sentiment by which you are actuated. Farewell, then, and may God bless you and yours forever. My last hope is, that Doña Maria will induce you to adopt New Spain for your country. With regard to the commercial relations, which, in the name of the governor of Louisiana, you have asked me to permit between that province and those of my government, tell him that it is not in my power to accede to his propositions." The preparations of St. Denis for his departure were not of long duration, for the lady of his heart beckoned to him from the walls of the Presidio del

Norte. The Viceroy presented him with a large sum in gold, which, he graciously said, was intended to pay his wedding expenses. He also sent him, for his journey, a superb Andalusian steed, ordering at the same time that he should be escorted by an officer and two dragoons from the city of Mexico to Caouis.

On the forced departure of St. Denis for the city of Mexico, Jallot had been set at liberty, and had ever since remained at Caouis waiting for the decision of the fate of St. Denis. He was known to be a physician, and as he was the only one within a radius of one hundred miles, he was soon in full practice. In the course of a few months, he had performed so many cures and rendered so many services, that he was looked upon as something almost supernatural. One day, he was summoned to the house of the governor, Don Gaspardo Anaya, whither he went with such a grim smile as clearly indicated that his feelings were in a violent state of excitement. He examined with the most minute care the body of that dignitary, and on his being asked his opinion on the situation of his patient, he went into the most luminous exposition of his disease, and declared that if a certain operation, which he described with much apparent gusto, was not performed, the sick man would certainly die within one month. "Well then," said the governor, "go on with the operation, as soon as you please." "It shall never please me," cried Jallot, in a voice of thunder; and shaking his fist at the enemy of St. Denis, whom, in his turn, he had now in his power, he doggedly withdrew from the house of the infuriated governor. Remonstrances, entreaties, large offerings of money, threats, could not bring him back. At last, the governor swore that he would hang Jallot, and sent some soldiers to arrest him. But the people, who loved Jallot, and feared being deprived of his invaluable services, rose upon the soldiery, beat them off, and proclaimed that they would hang the governor himself, if he persisted in his intention of hanging Jallot. Matters were in this ticklish situation, when St. Denis returned to Caouis.

In company with his friend Jallot, who was almost distracted with joy at his safe return, St. Denis immediately waited upon the governor, to whom he communicated a letter patent, by which the Viceroy gave authority to St. Denis to inflict upon Anaya, for his abuse of power, any punishment which he might think proper, provided it stopped short of death. The terror of the governor may easily be conceived, but after enjoying his enemy's confusion for a short time, St. Denis tore to pieces the Viceroy's letter, and retired, leaving the culprit, whom he despised, to the castigation of heaven and to the stings of his own conscience. He did more: he had the generosity to request Jallot to perform the operation which this worthy had hitherto so obstinately refused to do. The surgeon, who was mollified by his friend's return, consented, not however without terrific grumblings, to use his surgical skill to relieve the bedridden governor, and he admirably succeeded in the difficult operation upon which the fate of his patient depended. But he peremptorily and contemptuously refused the fee that was tendered him, and informed the governor, face to face, and with his roughest tone, that he deserved no remuneration for the cure, because he had saved his life merely out of spite, and under the firm conviction that he would ere long die on the gallows.

Let us now rapidly proceed with St. Denis from Caouis to the Presidio del Norte. There he found a great change;—not that the lady of his love was not as true and as beautiful as ever, but the place looked lonesome and desolate. The five Indian villages which formed a sort of belt round the Presidio, at a short distance from its walls, were deserted. A gloomy cloud had settled over the spot which he had known so brisk and thriving:—and Villescas told him, with the greatest consternation, that the Indians had withdrawn on account of their having been molested by the Spaniards, who used to go to their villages, and there commit every sort of outrage; that he confessed he was much to be blamed for not having checked sooner the disorderly practices of his subordinates; and that if the Indians persisted in their intention of removing away to distant lands, the government at Mexico, whose settled policy it was to conciliate the frontier Indians, would be informed of what had happened, and would certainly visit him with punishment for official misconduct, negligence or dereliction of duty. "I will run after the fugitives," exclaimed St. Denis, " and use my best efforts to bring them back." " Do so," replied the old man, "and if you succeed, there is nothing in my power, which I can refuse you." On hearing these words, which made his heart thrill, as it were with an electric shock, St. Denis vaulted on his good Andalusian steed, and started full speed in the direction the Indians had taken. He was followed, far behind, by Jallot, who came trotting along, as fast as he could, on a restive, capricious, ill-looking little animal, for whom he had perversely conceived the greatest affection, perhaps on account of his bad qualities.

The Indians, encumbered with women and children, had been progressing very slowly, with the heavy baggage they were carrying with them, and St. Denis had not traveled long before he discovered from the top of a hill, the moving train; he waved a white flag and redoubled his speed; the Indians stopped and tarried for his approach. When he came up to them, they formed a dense circle around him, and silently waited for his communication. "My friends!" said St. Denis, "I am sent by the governor of the Presidio del Norte, to tell you that he pleads guilty to his red children; he confesses that you have been long laboring under grievances which he neglected to redress, and that you have been frequently oppressed by those whom it was his duty to keep in the straight path of rectitude. This is a frank avowal, as you see. With regard to the governor himself, you know that he has always been kind and upright, and that, personally and intentionally, he has never wronged any one of you: the old chief has been too weak with his own people—that is all you can say against him. But now, he pledges his faith that no Spaniard shall be allowed to set his foot in your villages without your express consent, and that every sort of protection which you may claim shall be extended over your tribe. Do not, therefore, be obstinate, my friends, and do not keep shut the gates of your hearts, when the pale-faced chief, with his gray hairs, knocks for admittance, but let his words of repentance fall upon your souls, like a refreshing dew, and revive your drooping attachment for him. Do not give up your hereditary hunting-grounds, the cemeteries of your forefathers, and your ancestral villages, with rash precipitancy. Whither are you going? Your native soil does not stick to your feet, and it is the only soil which is always pleasant; and the wheat which grows upon it, is the only grain that will give you tasteful bread; and the sun which shines upon it, is the only sun whose rays do not scorch; and the refreshing showers which fall upon its bosom would elsewhere be impure and brackish water. You do not know what bitter weeds grow in the path of the stranger! You do not know how heavily the air he breathes weighs on his lungs in distant lands! And what distant lands will you be permitted to occupy, without fighting desperate battles with the nations upon whose territory you will have trespassed? When you will be no longer protected by the Spaniards, how will you resist the incessant attacks of the ferocious Comanches, who carry so far and wide their predatory expeditions? Thus, my friends, the evils you are running to are certain, and behind them, lie concealed in ambush still greater ones, which the keenest eye among you can not detect. But what have you to fear, if you return to your deserted villages? There, it is true, you will meet some old evils, but you are accustomed to them. That is one advantage; and, besides, you are given the assurance that to many of them a remedy will be applied. Why not make the experiment, and see how it will work? But if you persist in going away, and if you fare for the worse, your situation will be irretrievable. On the other hand, if you return, as I advise you, should the governor of the Presidio not keep his word, and should you not be satisfied, it will always be time enough to resume your desperate enterprise of emigration."

This is the substance of what St. Denis told his red auditory, and the Indians, who, perhaps, were beginning to regret the step they had taken, spontaneously marched back, with St. Denis riding triumphantly at their head. They soon met Jallot, jogging along with impatience, cursing and spurring his favorite with desperate energy. When he saw that St. Denis, about whom he was extremely uneasy, was safe, and had succeeded so well in his embassy, he gave a shout which made the welkin ring; but he was so astonished at his own doing, and at the unusual sound which had so strangely issued from his throat, that he looked round like a man who was not very sure of his own identity. Those who knew him well remained convinced that this shout had settled in his mind as the most extraordinary event of his life.

Now all is joy again at the Presidio, and the smile of contentment has lighted up the face of the country for miles around. From the Spanish battlements banners wave gayly, the cannons crack their sides with innocent roaring, muskets are discharged in every direction, but from their tubes there do not sally any murderous balls; the whole population, white and red, is dressed in its best apparel; whole sheep, oxen, and buffaloes are roasted in the Homeric style; immense tables are spread in halls, bowers, and under shady trees; whole casks of Spanish wines and of the Mexican *pulque* are broached; the milk and honey of the land flow with unrestrained abundance; the Indians shout, dance, and cut every sort of antics. Well may *all* rejoice, for it is the wedding-day of St. Denis and Doña Maria! Here the long and beautiful procession which is slowly moving to the rustic parochial church, might be described with some effect, but I leave the task to future novel writers. I now dismiss this episode, and only regret that I have not done it the justice which it deserves. Let me add, however, that, after an absence of two years, St. Denis, having returned to Mobile with Don Juan de Villescas, the uncle of his wife, was appointed, in reward for the discharge of his perilous mission, a captain in the French army.

On the recommendation of Crozat, another undertaking was made to open commercial relations with the Spanish provinces of Mexico. Three Canadians, Deléry, Lafrénière and Beaujeu, were intrusted with a considerable amount of merchandise, went up Red River, and endeavored to reach the province of Nuevo Leon, through Texas;—but this attempt was as unsuccessful as the one made by St. Denis.

On the 9th of March, 1717, three ships belonging to Crozat arrived with three companies of infantry and fifty colonists, with De l'Epinay, the new governor, and Hubert, the king's commissary. L'Epinay brought to Bienville the decoration of the cross of St. Louis, and a royal patent, conceding to him, by mean tenure in soccage, Horn Island, on the coast of the present State of Alabama. Bienville had demanded in vain that it be erected in his favor into a noble fief.

Hardly had L'Epinay landed, when he disagreed with Bienville, and the colony was again distracted by two factions, with L'Epinay on one side and Bienville on the other. There were not at that time in Louisiana more than seven hundred souls, including the military; and thus far, the efforts of Crozat to increase the population had proved miserably abortive. In vain had his agents resorted to every means in their power, to trade with the Spanish provinces, either by land or by sea, either legally or illegally;—several millions' worth of merchandise which he had sent to Louisiana, with the hope of their finding their way to Mexico, had been lost for want of a market. In vain also had expensive researches been made for mines and pearl fisheries. As to the trading in furs with the Indians, it hardly repaid the cost of keeping factories among them. Thus, all the schemes of Crozat had failed. The miserable European population, scattered over Louisiana, was opposed to his monopoly, and contributed, as much as they could, to defeat his plans. As to the officers, they were too much engrossed by their own interest and too intent upon their daily quarrels, to mind any thing else. There was but one thing which, to the despairing Crozat, seemed destined to thrive in Louisiana—that was, the spirit of discord.

In the beginning of the month of August, 1717, Crozat, finding that under the new governor, L'Epinay, things were likely to move as lamely as before, addressed to the king a petition, in which he informed his Majesty, that his strength was not equal to the enterprise he had undertaken, and that he felt himself rapidly sinking under the weight which rested on his shoulders, and from which he begged his Majesty to relieve him. On the 13th of the same month, the Prince of Bourbon and Marshal D'Estrées accepted, in the name of the king, Crozat's proposition to give up the charter which he had obtained under the preceding reign.

Against his adverse fate Crozat had struggled for five years, but his efforts had been gradually slackening, in proportion with the declining health of his daughter. The cause of his gigantic enterprise had not escaped her penetration, and she had even extorted from him a full confession on the subject. In the first two years of her father's *quasi* sovereignty over Louisiana, she had participated in the excitement of the paternal breast, and had been buoyed up by hope. But although her father tried, with the utmost care, to conceal from her the ill success of his operations, she soon discovered enough to sink her down to a degree of despair, sufficient to undermine in her, slowly but surely, the frail foundations of life; and when Crozat, losing all courage, abandoned to the tossing waves of adversity the ship in which he had embarked the fortune of his house, his daughter could hardly be called a being of this world. On the very day that he had resigned the charter on which reposed such ambitious hopes, and had come back, broken-hearted, to his desolate home, he was imprinting a kiss on his daughter's pale forehead, and pressing her attenuated hands within his convulsive ones, when her soul suddenly disengaged itself from her body, carrying away the last paternal embrace to the foot of the Almighty's throne.

Crozat laid her gently back on the pillow from which she had half risen, smoothed her clothes, joined her fingers as it were in prayer, and sleeked her hair with the palm of his hands, behaving apparently with the greatest composure. Not a sound of complaint, not a shriek of anguish was heard from him: his breast did not become convulsed with sobs; not a muscle moved in his face. He looked as if he had been changed into a statue of stone: his rigid limbs seemed to move automaton-like; his eyeballs became fixed in their sockets, and his eyelids lost their power of contraction. Calmly, but with an unearthly voice, he gave all the necessary orders for the funeral of his daughter, and even went into the examination of the most minute details of these melancholy preparations. Those who saw him, said that he looked like a dead man performing with unconscious regularity all the functions of life. It was so appalling, that his servants and the few attending friends who had remained attached to his falling fortune, receded with involuntary shudder from his approach, and from the touch of his hand; it was so icy cold! At last the gloomy procession reached the solemn place of repose. The poor father had followed it on foot, with his hand resting on his daughter's coffin, as if afraid that what remained of the being he had loved so ardently might flee away from him. When the tomb was sealed, he waved away the crowd. They dared not disobey when such grief spoke, and Crozat remained alone. For a while he stood staring, as in a trance, at his daughter's tomb: then, a slight twitch of the muscles of the face, and a convulsive quiver of the lips might have been seen. Sensibility had returned! He sunk on his knees, and from those eyes, so long dry, there descended, as from a thunder-cloud, a big heavy drop, on the cold sepulchral marble. It was but one solitary tear, the condensed essence of such grief as the human body can not bear; and as this pearly fragment of the dew of mortal agony fell down on the daughter's sepulchre, the soul of the father took its flight to heaven. Crozat was no more!

> "My task is done—my song hath ceased—my theme
> Has died into an echo: it is fit
> The spell should break of this protracted dream—
> The torch shall be extinguished which hath lit
> My midnight lamp—and what is writ, is writ,—
> Would it were worthier! But I am not now
> That which I have been—and my visions flit
> Less palpably before me—and the glow,
> Which in my spirit dwelt, is fluttering, faint and low."
>
> "Farewell! a word that must be, and hath been—
> A sound which makes us linger—yet—farewell!"

NOTE.—Crozat died in 1738, at the age of eighty-three. He had several sons and one daughter, Marie Anne Crozat, who married Le Comte D'Evreux. I hope I shall be forgiven for having slightly deviated from historical truth in the preceding pages with regard to particulars which I deemed of no importance. For instance, I changed the name of Crozat's daughter. Why? Perhaps it was owing to some capricious whim—perhaps there is to me some spell in the name of Andrea.

LOUISIANA;

Its History

AS

A FRENCH COLONY

RERUM COGNOSCERE CAUSAS.

SECOND SERIES OF LECTURES.

PREFACE

TO THE SECOND SERIES.

THE success of my "Romance of the History of Louisiana," from the discovery of that country by Soto, to the surrender by Crozat of the charter which he had obtained from Louis the XIVth, in relation to that French Colony, has been such, that I deem it my duty toward my patrons to resume my pen, and to present the following work to their kind and friendly regard. When I wrote the preceding Lectures, I said, while I mentally addressed the public:

> "Right, I note, most mighty souveraine,
> That all this famous antique history
> Of some th' aboundance of an idle braine
> Will judged be, and painted forgery,
> Rather than matter of just memory."
>
> SPENSER. *Faerie Queene.*

Nor was I mistaken:—for I was informed that many had taken for the invention of the brain what was but historical truth set in a gilded frame, when, to use the expressions of Sir Joshua Reynolds, I had taken but insignificant liberties with facts, to interest my readers, and make my narration more delightful, in imitation of the painter who, though his work is called *history painting*, gives in reality a poetical representation of facts. The reader will easily perceive, that in the present production, I have been more sparing of embellishments, although "*I well noted, with that worthy gentle-*

man, *Sir Philip Sidney*," as Raleigh says in his history of the world, "*that historians do borrow of poets not only much of their ornament, but somewhat of their substance.*"

Such is not the case, on this occasion, and I can safely declare that the *substance* of this work, embracing the period from 1717 to 1743, when Bienville, who, with Iberville, had been the founder of the colony, left it forever, rests on such evidence as would be received in a court of justice, and that what I have borrowed of the *poet* for the benefit of the *historian*, is hardly equivalent to the delicately wrought drapery which even the Sculptor would deem necessary, as a graceful appendage to the nakedness of the statue of truth.

NOTE.—The sea-fight which opens the Second Lecture in the Romance of the History of Louisiana, was supposed to be fictitious, it being deemed impossible that a French vessel should have beaten three English ships of superior force. This fact, however, is related by rather Charlevoix; and manuscripts copied from the archives of the department of marine in France, and now deposited in the office of the Secretary of State at Baton Rouge, will convince the incredulous that the author has not drawn upon his imagination.

LOUISIANA:

ITS

HISTORY AS A FRENCH COLONY

SECOND SERIES OF LECTURES.

FIRST LECTURE.

CREATION OF A ROYAL BANK AND OF THE MISSISSIPPI COMPANY—EFFECTS PRODUCED IN FRANCE BY THOSE INSTITUTIONS—WILD HOPES ENTERTAINED FROM THE COLONIZATION OF LOUISIANA—ITS TWOFOLD AND OPPOSITE DESCRIPTION—HISTORY OF LAW FROM HIS BIRTH TO HIS DEATH.

NOTHING could be more insignificant than Louisiana in the estimation of her European rulers, when Crozat's charter became one of those things that are among the past. But by one of those rapid transitions so common in human affairs, she was suddenly destined to exercise a wonderful influence over the powerful kingdom of which she was the weak progeny. In her very name there was soon to be discovered something as dazzling to the imagination, as the richest diamond is to the eye of woman. A subtle conjurer arose, who, waving aloft his magical wand, and using that name then so obscure, to give more force to his incantations, prepared for France an intoxicating draught which made her reel as in drunkenness, and nearly prostrated her to the ground, despite of her ever-reviving energies. The star of John Law had risen on the horizon of France; and the Company of the Indies, the great Mississippi scheme, of which he was the chief projector, the destinies of France and of Louisiana, the expected results of such commerce as the world had never known before, the reports of hidden treasures concealed in inexhaustible mines of silver and gold, were to be indissolubly united in the annals of history and of folly.

On the 13th of August, 1717, the situation of affairs in the colony of Louisiana having been brought before the Council of State at Versailles, it was decided by that body, presided over by the Duke of Orleans, Regent of France during the minority of Louis the XVth, that, "for many essential reasons which it would be superfluous to recite, because they were known to every one, it was to the interest of France that the colony of Louisiana should be fostered and preserved."—Such were the terms of that decree, which went on saying, that, "whereas it had been demonstrated, in the case of Crozat, that the colonization of the province of Louisiana was an undertaking beyond the strength of any private individual: and whereas this undertaking would not become the King, on account of the commercial details which were its inseparable concomitant, it was resolved that Louisiana should be intrusted to the administration of a company." From this resolution sprang the creation of the Western Company, or Company of the Indies, whose charter of incorporation was registered by the parliament of Paris, on the 6th of September, 1717.

Thus the monopoly granted to Crozat ceased, merely to be transferred to a Company. The government of one ruler was to be succeeded by an oligarchy, and the worst of all, a commercial oligarchy, an association of cunning stockjobbers, of robbing directors, and of silly dupes in the shape of stockholders. There were not men wanting at the time who foresaw that the creation of the famous Company of the Indies, of which Law was the soul, and which became one of the most popular schemes that ever flourished in France, was destined to impart to the colonization of Louisiana only the short-lived appearance of galvanic vitality, but that, ending soon as all delusions do, it would, in its collapse and bursting, be fatal to the speculators engaged in the experiment, and be productive of the most mischievous results to France. Some of these readers of coming events attempted in vain to warn their fellow-citizens against the evils which they predicted. But the weak voice of individual reprobation was drowned in the loud acclamation of the multitude. When the current of the public mind runs impetuously in one direction, when was it ever checked? It sweeps furiously over such obstacles as wisdom or patriotism may interpose, and it even derives fresh impetus from the very attempt to arrest its course.

Who was John Law, to whom the use of the name of Louisiana was destined to give so much celebrity in the beginning of the 18th century? In the romantic city of Edinburgh, the pride of Scotland, he was born in 1671. A checquered and a singularly varied life his was doomed to be, as checquered and varied as the changeful appearance of those ever-flitting clouds which chase each other through the fields of heaven, now assuming fantastic shapes, now dyed in splendor with the morning or evening rays of the sun, or black with the conception of coming storms. Gay halls and gloomy cells there are in the palace of Holyrood, within sight of which that obscure child was cradled, and of which the projecting battlements so often darkened with their shade his curling locks, as he indulged in the gambols of his age. When in his youth he strolled through that antiquated abode of departed royalty, and there gazed with mixed feelings of admiration and awe at the hoary relics of time, did any prophetic spirit shadow forth to him the gay halls and gloomy cells of his future existence, when he should attain to manhood? The boy had in him the seeds of exalted talent and over-wrought passion. Talent and passion—those unruly steeds upon which, when seated, man not unfrequently speeds away in a mad career, faster than he chooses, whither he heeds not or cares not, and oftener for his ruin than his good, if he does not check them with the reins of morality or the curb of religion.

John Law, or Jessamy Law, or Beau Law, as his playmates called him, for he was as handsome as a mother's heart could wish him, was the son of a goldsmith and banker. Did this circumstance have any influence on his future career, and did he inherit his passion for the precious metals and for banking operations? He was educated in Edinburgh, and he is said to have been no mean adept in versification, if not in poetry. But he soon intuitively discovered that a scribbler's lot was not very enviable, and following the natural bent of his genius, he became so remarkably proficient in mathematics that he could, with the greatest facility, solve the most difficult problems of that abstruse science. He also devoted his attention to the study of trade and manufactures, and made himself master of the principles of public and private credit. He minutely investigated the theory and practice of taxation, and all matters constituting the arcana of political economy. Such were the deep laid and solid foundations of his future eminence.

But John Law was a votary of pleasure as well as of study, and whenever he emerged from his closet, it was to attend the gambling-table, the racing-ground, and to indulge in convivial and amorous exploits. To some men, excitement of some sort or other is the very breath of life. It is the air which inflates and expands their intellectual lungs. Without it, the flow of their mind would stagnate. Such was John Law. An orphan at the age of fourteen, free from paternal control, and the heir to an ample fortune, he had within his reach all the means of vicious indulgence, and sadly did he avail himself of them to barter away the very altars of his household gods. In 1694, goaded on by the desire of extending his sphere of enjoyments, he paid a visit to London, that great center of attraction, where his wit, his graces, his manly beauty, his numerous attainments, gained him admittance into the best society. There, however, his profusions of every sort, his love for deep play, and his gallantries, soon rid him of his patrimonial lands of Lauriston and Randleston. Their broad acres were converted into guineas which melted away in the hands of prodigality, and thus, in early life, through his own folly, John Law stands before us a bankrupt!

That bankrupt was also an adulterer, and the acknowledged paramour of a Mrs. Lawrence. That intrigue brought him into collision with a Mr. Wilson, whom he killed in a duel. Tried for murder, he was found guilty, sentenced to death, and pardoned by the crown. But an appeal was taken by a brother of the deceased, and the appeal was pending before the King's Bench, when Law, not deeming it prudent to await the result, escaped from his prison, and fled to the continent. Law was then twenty-three years of age. A bankrupt, an adulterer, a murderer, and an exiled outlaw! If to feel is to live, Law had thus gone through an intensity and variety of feelings, which, in the spring of youth, must have made his soul and mind as gray with age, as if over them a century had passed.

To Holland, Law retired for an asylum:—he could not

have made a choice more congenial to his tastes, and no place in Europe could afford more facilities to his favorite investigations on trade, finances, public credit, and political economy, than that country, which, of all others, was peculiarly indebted to them for its national importance, and even for its existence. During his residence there, he took care to improve every opportunity to make himself thoroughly acquainted with the constitution and the practical operation of the Bank of Amsterdam.

John Law was not the man, even in a foreign country, to remain long without friends or protectors, and he soon contrived to ingratiate himself with the British Resident in Holland, of whom he became the secretary. But the phlegmatic temperament of the Dutch not presenting him with the materials which he wished for the accomplishment of such schemes as were ripening in his brain, and having received the assurance that he had no longer any thing to fear on account of the death of Wilson, he returned to Edinburgh in 1700, and in the following year he published a pamphlet under this title: "Proposals and Reasons for establishing a Council of Trade." The proverbial prudence of the Scotch received this work with coldness. Not discouraged by this failure, Law showed the remarkable aptitude which he had to possess himself of the favor of all those whom he thought proper to propitiate, and gained the support of the Duke of Argyle, his sons, the Marquis of Lorn and Lord Archibald Campbell, the Marquis of Tweeddale, and other persons of rank and distinction.

Under their patronage, he presented to the Scottish parliament, in 1705, a plan for removing the difficulties under which the kingdom had then been suffering from the scarcity of money and from the stoppage of payments by the bank; and in illustration of his views on that subject, he gave publicity to another work, entitled "Money and Trade considered, with a proposal for supplying the nation with money." What could be more tempting! and what a pity that this grand projector did not live in this projecting age of ours! Like other men, he came too soon.

The proposal of Law, says one of his biographers, was that commissioners, created by an act of parliament, and remaining under their control, should be empowered to issue notes, either in the way of loan at ordinary interest, upon landed security, provided the debt should not exceed half, or at the most, two thirds of the value of the lands, or upon land pledges, redeemable within a certain period, to the full value of the land:— or lastly, upon irredeemable sales to the amount of the price agreed upon. Paper money thus issued would, he conceived, be equal in value to gold and silver coin of the same denomination, and might even be preferred to those metals, as not being, like them, liable to fall in value. But this scheme, though powerfully supported by the court party, and by the influence of such men as the Duke of Argyle and others, was rejected by the parliament on the ground that, "to establish any kind of paper credit, so as to oblige it to pass, was an improper expedient for the nation." Wise Scotchmen! They also apprehended that if Law's plan were adopted, all the estates of the kingdom would thereby be brought to a complete dependence upon the bank, or collaterally upon the government, the bank itself being dependent upon the government. It is remarkable that more than a century after, in 1827 and 1833, Law's plan, or one very similar, was put into operation in Louisiana, under the titles of "The Citizens' Bank" and "The Consolidated Association of the Planters of Louisiana," and that it produced the same disastrous effects that were anticipated by the Scotch in 1705.

It soon became evident to Law, that his countrymen and the English were not sufficiently imaginative to allow him to tempt them into his gigantic experiments, and that to better his fortune, it was necessary that he should seek elsewhere for more pliable instruments. Accordingly he returned to the continent, whither let us follow him, as he flits, like an ignis fatuus, from place to place. Now we see him a man of fashion in Brussels, where his constant success at play brought him into unfavorable notoriety. Then he dashes into the vortex of Paris, where it is said that he introduced the game called Faro, and became still more conspicuous than at Brussels by his enormous gains at the gaming-table. His graceful person, the charms of his conversation, his insinuating manners, were rapidly favoring his ascent into the highest regions of society, when D'Argenson, the Lieutenant or Minister of Police, thought proper to cut short his brilliant career, and to order him out of the kingdom, with this pithy observation, "That Scot is *too expert* at the game which he has introduced."

He retired to Geneva, where he gave an extraordinary proof of his power of extracting money from the dryest sources, by gaining large sums at the expense of the sober-minded and close-fisted citizens of that puritanic little commonwealth. In Genoa and in Venice, he gave such evidence of his invariable luck at play, that the magistrates of these two cities deemed it their duty to interfere for the protection of their fellow-citizens, and to banish Law from these over-exhausted theaters of his exploits. At Florence, he became acquainted with the Duke of Vendôme, whom he favored with the loan of a large sum of money. At Neufchatel, ne obtained access to the Prince of Conti, to whom, as to the Duke of Vendôme, he imparted his financial schemes. He was thus skillfully securing protection for the introduction of his plans into France, on the first favorable opportunity. For several years Law rambled over Europe, proposing his financial systems everywhere and to every body. During a short residence at Turin, he pressed the subject on the King of Sardinia, Victor Amadeus—but that prudent sovereign answered: " I am not rich enough to afford being ruined. France is the proper field where your speculative genius ought to cast its seeds, and where you will reap rich harvests. I am sure that your schemes will be to the taste of my mercurial neighbors. To them, therefore, I would advise you to repair."

This advice seemed to Law a sensible one, and acting under it, he returned to Paris with the enormous sum of two millions and five hundred thousand francs, which were the result of his success in gaming, and of his speculations in stocks and public funds. Soon after his arrival Louis the XIVth died, which was a circumstance favorable to his pretensions. He had no longer to deal only with the prudent Desmarets, comptroller-general of the finances of the state, whose wisdom had discarded the tempting propositions of that adventurer in 1708. But now, in 1716, when the Duke of Orleans, as Regent of France, found himself at the head of the government, the financial situation of France had become desperate. The public debt was immense: it was a legacy bequeathed by the military glory of Louis the XIVth, and the other pompous vanities of his long reign. The consequence was that the load of taxation was overwhelming, merely to pay the interest of this debt, without any hope of diminishing the capital. All the sources of industry were dried up: the very winds which wafted the barks of commerce seemed to have died away under the pressure of the time: trade stood still: the manufactures were struck with palsy: the merchant, the trader, the artificer, once flourishing in affluence, were now transformed into clamorous beggars, and those who could yet command some small means were preparing to emigrate to foreign parts. The life-blood that animated the kingdom was stagnating in all its arteries: and the danger of an awful crisis became such, that it was actually proposed in the Council of State to expunge the public debt by an act of national bankruptcy. But the Regent has the credit of having rejected the proposition; and a commission was appointed to inquire into the financial situation of the kingdom, and to prepare a remedy for the evil.

It was at that time, when the wisest heads in France were not able to see their way through the embarrassments of the treasury, that John Law came forward with his panacea. It was to liquidate the debt of the state, to increase its revenue, to diminish taxation: and all these prodigies were to be suddenly produced by the easiest process in the world—the creation of a bank, by which fictitious capital, quite as good as any real one, would be produced at will. The Regent, who was incessantly in want of money, and whose ardent imagination was always easily captivated by every daring and extraordinary conception, eagerly jumped at the conclusions presented by Law, or L'as, as he was called by the French. He became even a favorite of that prince, and was admitted into all the licentious privacies of the *Palais Royal*. Soon after, in May, 1716, in spite of the opposition made by all the financiers of the kingdom, Law obtained letters patent, not, it is true, complying with all his magnificent schemes, but establishing on a very limited scale the bank of which he was the originator, and which was to bear his name with a capital of six millions of livres, divided into shares of five hundred livres. It was to be a private undertaking, and intended by the government as an experiment.

This institution met with so much success, and became so popular, that in April, 1717, the Council of State assumed the responsibility of ordering that its notes be received as specie by the royal treasury, in all its branches. The influence of Law on the Regent was daily on the increase, and it was he who prevailed on that prince to purchase for the king the celebrated diamond, which, from that circumstance, was called the *Regent*, and which is still the property of republican France, and a part of its public domain. It was a curiosity then thought to be unique of its kind; and the Regent, although strongly tempted, had long hesitated to invest millions in such an unproductive manner, when the revenue of the kingdom was far below its expenses. But Law removed his scruples, by persuading him that he had the means not only of remedying the necessities of France, but of making her richer than she had ever been.

Law now began to develop the stupendous projects he had so long meditated. The success of his private bank had gained him so much credit, that the Regent was induced to change its character, and to make it a royal institution. Law's bank was abolished in December, 1718, to give way to the Royal Bank, of which Law was named the director-general. From that fruitful parent trunk sprung branches which were established at Lyons, Tours, La Rochelle, Orleans, and Amiens.

It will be remembered that, as before stated, the charter of the Mississippi Company had been registered by the parliament of Paris on the 6th of September, 1717. The capital of the company was one hundred millions of livres, to be furnished by stockholders, and to be divided into shares of five hundred livres. Aliens were permitted to become members of the company, and their shares were exempted from the "*droit d'aubaine*," and from confiscation in case of war. The "droit d'aubaine" is the right which the king had to inherit all the property which an alien left at his death. To entice subscribers, their shares were made payable in a depreciated paper currency, called "*billets* d'état," or state bonds, which, however, in the hands of subscribers, were taken at par or full value, although their depreciation amounted to between sixty and seventy per cent. This was such a tempting bait, that it was greedily gulped down by the public, and the subscription was soon more than filled up. By this operation of taking the depreciated paper currency of the state in payment of subscriptions, the company became the creditor of the state for a sum of one hundred millions of livres, on which interest was to be paid at the rate of four per cent.

The following were the principal articles of the company's charter:—

It had the exclusive privilege of trading with Louisiana during twenty-five years, and also the monopoly of the beaver trade with Canada, it being understood that the king reserved to himself the right of determining the number of skins that the company should be bound to purchase annually from the Canadians, at the price fixed by the government of his Majesty.

The company was authorized to make treaties with the Indians, and to wage war against them in cases of necessity. It had taken care to secure the absolute ownership of all the mines which it could discover and work, and it is needless to say that much reliance was placed on this article of the charter.

The faculty was given to the company of making grants of land, of levying troops, of raising fortifications, of appointing the governors of the colony and the other officers commanding the troops, provided they should, on presentation, be accepted and commissioned by the king. The right of recalling or altering these appointments was also reserved to the company.

To build ships of war and cast cannon, to appoint and remove judges and officers of justice, except those of the Superior Council, were some of the numerous powers granted to this mighty company.

Military officers in Louisiana and all others in the French service were allowed, with the king's license, to enlist in the pay of the company. While in that service, their respective grades in the navies or land forces of the realm were to be retained, and they had the gracious promise of the king that whatever service they might render to the company would be acknowledged as rendered to himself.

By the consular jurisdiction of the city of Paris, all civil suits to which the company might be a party, were to be determined; with a right of appeal, in cases above a certain amount, to the parliament of Paris.

The company was prohibited from employing other than French vessels and crews in trading with Louisiana, and all goods found on the company's vessels were to be presumed its property, unless the contrary was proved.

Frenchmen, removing to Louisiana, were to preserve their national character, and their children, born there, were to be considered as the natural born subjects of the king. The same privilege was granted to the children of all other European settlers in Louisiana, provided they professed the Roman Catholic religion. To encourage emigration, it was stipulated that during the continuance of the company's charter, the inhabitants of Louisiana were to be exempted from the payment of any tax, duty, or imposition whatever.

To promote the building of vessels in Louisiana, where it was reported that the most magnificent timber existed in its boundless forests, a bounty was to be awarded for every vessel there built, on its arrival in France.

In anticipation of wars with the Indians, it was agreed that forty thousand pounds of powder were to be delivered annually to the company, out of the royal magazines, at the rate of the manufacturing cost.

The stockholders were to have a vote for every fifty shares. During the two first years, the affairs of the company were to be conducted by directors appointed by the king, and afterward, by others, elected triennially by the stockholders.

In order to minister to the religious wants of the colonists, the obligation was laid upon the company to build churches and to provide for a sufficient number of clergymen. It was understood that Louisiana was to remain part of the diocess of Quebec, under whose spiritual authority it had always been since it had been settled by the French.

The company obliged itself to transport to Louisiana, before the expiration of its charter, six thousand white persons and three thousand negroes: but it was stipulated that these persons should not be brought from another French colony, without the consent of the governor of that colony.

In consideration of the charges assumed by the company, its goods were to be exempted from the payment of any duty, and the king promised not to grant any letters of dispensation or respite to any debtor of the company. He also gave the company the solemn assurance of his effectual protection against any foreign nation.

If the company, as it is seen, took special care to keep its debtors irredeemably within its reach, it was no less solicitous to withdraw itself, as much as possible, from the grasp of any one of the creditors of its stockholders, and it had a clause inserted in its charter, by which the effects, shares, and profits of the stockholders could not be seized and sold either in the hands of its cashier, its clerks, or agents, except it be in cases of open and declared bankruptcy, or on account of the death of the party.

All the lands, coasts, harbors, and islands in the colony of Louisiana were granted to the company, as they were to Crozat, on condition of its taking the customary oath of faith and homage, as practiced in such cases, and of furnishing to every King of France, on his accession to the throne, a crown of gold of the weight of thirty marks.

Thus Louisiana was constituted into a sort of commercial fief, and the Mississippi Company rose almost to the dignity of those great feudatory vassals who, in the days of old, had been, alternately, the pride, the support, and the curse of France. It did not spring into existence, it is true, in the shape of a Duke of Burgundy, who, backed by one hundred thousand men, could, if he pleased, set at defiance his liege Lord, and could proudly enter through the battered walls of Paris, with crested helmet on his head, and the truncheon of command in his hand. But it was perhaps a being more powerful and more dangerous—it was a company—an incorporeal conglomeration, an unfathomable, uncontrollable, unaccountable creation—an agent with such divided responsibility that it amounted to nothing, and, as Lord Coke says of corporations—a thing without a soul, to which, nevertheless, a power more efficacious and more fearful than that exercised over armed men was delegated—the power of controlling commerce!

Law was appointed director-general of the Mississippi Company, as he had been of the Royal Bank, and both institutions were merged into one another. That would have been power enough to satisfy a less craving ambition, but Law was not the man to stop short in his career of aggrandizement. Thus, he soon obtained that the farm of tobacco, that is the exclusive privilege of selling this favorite weed, be made over to the company by the government, at an advance of rent exceeding two millions of livres. This was a pretty rich feather in his cap, but it was not enough; and stepping from one acquisition to another, he immediately afterward procured for the company of which he had the absolute control the grant of the charter and effects of the Senegal Company. It was piling up Pelion upon Ossa, and the world stood aghast with astonishment at the extent of the concessions made by the French government to a foreign adventurer. A Royal Bank, the Tobacco farm, the Mississippi Company, and the Senegal Company, with all their millions, rights, privileges, effects and powers, all combined into a gigantic unity!—and that unity put as an instrument into the hands of another unity in the shape of a man! This was something curious to look at and to study in its operations.

Wise people thought that the climax of folly had been reached; but John Law laughed in his sleeve at their inexperience, or their ignorance of his skill, and before they had breathing time to recover from their surprise, he gave another proof of his wonderful legerdemain, by purloining from the French government a still more extraordinary grant than the preceding ones —which was the exclusive privilege of trading to the East Indies, China and the South Seas, together with all the possessions and effects of the China and India Companies, now dissolved, upon condition of liquidating all just claims upon them. It was then that the Company of the West, or Mississippi Company, dropped its original name to take up that of the Company of the Indies, with the privilege of creating additional shares to the amount of twenty-five millions, payable in coin.

This, it seems, ought to have been enough to satiate the most inordinate appetite. Not so with John Law. On the 25th of July, 1719, the mint was made over to the already overgrown Company of the Indies, that huge financial Polyphemus, which owed its existence to the great Scotch projector. This other concession was made for a consideration of fifty millions of livres, to be paid to the king within fifteen months. This time, it might have been permitted to believe that the digestive organs of this boa constrictor, of this king of speculators, were more than overgorged with the accumulation of superabundant nutrition with which they had been so lavishly favored. But John Law asked for something more! Was he shut up in a lunatic asylum for his mad presumption? No!—he obtained what he begged. Will not the dullest mind be stimulated into curiosity, and will not the quick inquiry be: What more could John Law presume to grasp? This:—on the 27th of August, 1719, he obtained for his progeny, the prodigious Company of the Indies, the great farms of the revenues of the kingdom, which the Regent took out of the hands of the farmers general and gave to the company, in consideration of its paying an advance of rent of three millions and a half of livres: and on the

31st of the same month, to cap the climax of all these almost supernatural wonders, Law obtained again for the same company the general receipt or collection of all the other branches of the king's revenues.

Through this curious process of complex annexation and assimilation, John Law had succeeded in erecting the most stupendous financial fabric that has ever been presented to the world. In one company, and through it, in one man, was vested nothing less than the whole privileges, effects and possessions of the foreign trade companies of France, the great farms of the kingdom, the mint, the general receipt of the king's revenues, and the management and property of a royal bank, with an immense capital! Thus, one man, an obscure foreign adventurer, through his creature, the company, had condensed into one lump, which his hands encircled, all the trade, taxes, and revenues of one of the most powerful kingdoms of Europe, and through the Royal Bank he might, according to his will, increase to any amount the circulating medium of that country! Does not this strictly historical sketch smack of the wild conception of a delirious mind? Is not truth often more incredible than fiction, and in reading these lines, would not misanthropy be tempted to exclaim: "Hail to thee, mischievous sorcerer! Three times hail to thee, John Law!"—while poetical fancy would be permitted to inquire if the Weird Sisters, the foul witches of his native heaths, had not furnished him with the spell under the influence of which so many millions of his fellow-beings had been touched with insanity.

It is not astonishing that on the showering of so many grants on the company, its shares gradually rose from 500 to 1000, to 5000 and to 10,000 livres, which was more than sixty times the sum they were originally sold for, if the depreciation of the "*billets d'état,*" or state bonds, with which they were paid, be taken into account. The desire to become stockholder in a company which promised to realize the fable of the hen with golden eggs, was fevered into frenzy. There was a general rush of greedy subscribers, far exceeding the number wanted, and in their struggles to be ranked among the privileged ones whose claims were to be admitted, the greatest interest was exerted, and every stratagem put in practice.

At the same time, the press was teeming with publications on the Mississippi, or the Colony of Louisiana, and France was flooded with pamphlets describing that newly-discovered country, and the advantages which it offered to emigrants. The luxuriant imagination of prolific writers was taxed, to clothe Louisiana with all the perfections they could invent. It was more than the old Eden, so long lost to mankind. There, the picturesque was happily blended with the fertile, and abundance smiled on rocky mountains as on the alluvial plains of the valleys. The climate was such that all the vegetable productions of the globe existed, or could be introduced with success in that favored land. To scratch the soil, would call forth the spontaneous growth of the richest harvests of every kind. All the fruits ever known were to be gathered in profusion from the forests, all the year round, and the most luscious peaches, pears, apples, and other like nutritious delicacies, dropping from their parent boughs, were piled up in heaps under cool shades and on the velvet banks of bubbling streams. There, dust and mud were equally excluded, as the ground was lined in all seasons with a thick carpet of flowers, endless in variety, and perfuming the air with their sweet breath. The finest breed of all domestic or useful animals was there to be found in all the primitive vigor and gentleness of their antediluvian perfection. The poor peasant who, during a long life in France, had never dreamed of eating meat, would there feed on nothing less than wild ducks, venison, pheasants, snipes and woodcocks. The birds kept up a never-ceasing concert, which would have shamed the opera singing of Paris. The rivers and lakes were stocked with fish, so abundant that they would suffice to nourish millions of men, and so delicate that no king ever had any such on his table.

The seasons were so slightly marked that the country might be said to be blessed with a perpetual spring. None but gentle winds fluttered over this paradise, to fan and keep forever blooming its virgin beauties, and in their gamboling flight through boundless prairies and forests, they produced the effect of Eolian harps, lulling enchanted nature to sleep with heavenly music. The sky was brighter, the sun more gorgeous, the moon more chastely serene and pure, and the nights more lovely than anywhere else. Heaven itself seemed to bend down upon earth in conjugal dalliance, and to environ it with circumambient love. There, it is true, it could not be said to have been positively ascertained that the fountain of eternal youth had been discovered, but it was beyond doubt that there was in the atmosphere a peculiar element which preserved from putrefaction;—and the human body, being impregnated with it, was so little worn out by the action of its organs, that it could keep itself in existence almost indefinitely; and the Indians were known to retain the appearance of youth even after having attained five or six hundred years. Those very Indians had conceived such an attachment for the white men, whom they considered as gods, that they would not allow them to labor, and insisted on performing themselves all the work that might be necessary for the comfort of their pale-faced brethren.

It was profanation in their eye not to minister to all the wants of their idolized guests.

More enticing than all that, was the pretended discovery of inexhaustible mines of gold and silver, which, however, it would not be necessary to work by the usual tedious process, because the whole surface of the country was strewed with lumps of gold, and when the waters of the lakes and rivers were filtered, particularly the thick water of the Mississippi, it yielded an invaluable deposit of gold. As to silver, it was so common that it would become of no value, and would have to be used in the shape of square stones, to pave the public roads. The fields were covered with an indigenous plant which was gifted with the most singular property. The dew which gathered within the perfumed cups of its flowers would, in the course of a single night, be converted into a solid diamond: and the soft texture of the flowers bursting open and dropping down under the weight of its contents, would leave the precious gem resting on the stem in unrobed splendor, and reflecting back the rays of the morning sun. What is written on California in our days would appear tame when compared to the publications on Louisiana in 1719: and the far-famed and extravagant description of the banks of the Mississippi given at a later period by Chateaubriand, would, at the time I speak of, have been hooted at, as doing injustice to the merits of the new possession France had acquired.

When the extreme gullibility of mankind, as demonstrated by the occurrences of every day, is taken into consideration, what I here relate will not appear exaggerated or incredible. Be it as it may, these descriptions were believed in France, and from the towering palace to the humblest shed in the kingdom, nothing else was talked of but Louisiana and its wonders. The national debt was to be paid instantaneously with the Louisiana gold, France was to purchase or to conquer the rest of the world, and every Frenchman was to be a wealthy lord. There never had been a word invested with such magical charms as the name of Louisiana. It produced delirium in every brain: to Louisiana every one wished to go, as now to California, and some of the most unimproved parts of that colony were actually sold for 30,000 livres the square league, which, considering the difference in value in metallic currency between that time and the present, makes that sum almost equal to twenty thousand dollars at the present day.

Who could describe with sufficient graphic fidelity the intense avidity with which the shares of the Company of the Indies were hunted up? All ranks were seized with the same frantic infatuation. To be a stockholder was to be reputed rich, and the poorest beggar, when he exhibited the proof that by some windfall or other he had become the owner of one single share, rose at once to the importance of a wealthy man, and could command the largest credit. There was a general struggle to raise money, for the purpose of speculating in the stocks of the marvelous company which was to convert every thing it touched into gold. Every kind of property was offered for sale, and made payable in stocks. Castellated domains which had been for centuries the proudly cherished possessions of the same families were bartered away for a mess of financial porridge, and more than one representative of a knightly house doffed off the warm lining that had been bequeathed to him by his ancestors, to dress himself, like a bedlamite, in the worthless rags of unsubstantial paper. Such rapid mutations in real estate the world had never seen before! Lands, palaces, edifices of every sort, were rapidly shifted from hand to hand, like balls in a tennis-court. It was truly a curious sight to behold a whole chivalrous nation turned into a confused multitude of swindling, brawling, clamorous, frantic stock-jobbers. Holy cardinals, archbishops, bishops, with but too many of their clergy, forgetting their sacred character, were seen to launch their barks on the dead sea of perdition to which they were tempted, and eagerly to throw the fisherman's net into those troubled waters of speculation which were lashed into fury by the demon of avarice. Princes of the royal blood became hawkers of stocks: haughty peers of the realm rushed on the Rialto, and Shylock-like, exulted in bartering and trafficking in bonds. Statesmen, magistrates, warriors, assuming the functions of pedlers, were seen wandering about the streets and public places, offering to buy and to sell stocks, shares, or actions. Nothing else was talked of; the former usual topics of conversation stood still. Not only women, but ladies of the highest rank forgot the occupations of their sex, to rush into the vortex of speculation, and but too many among them sold every thing, not excepting their honor, to become stockholders.

The company having promised an annual dividend of 200 livres on every share of 500 livres, which, it must be remembered, had been originally paid for in depreciated *billets d'état*, or state bonds, making the interest to be received on every share still more enormous, the delirium soon culminated to its highest point. Every thing foreign to the great Mississippi scheme was completely forgotten. The people seemed to have but one pursuit, but one object in life: mechanics dropped their tools, tradesmen closed their shops; there was but one profession, one employment, one occupation, for persons of all ranks—that of speculating in stocks: and the most moderate, the few who abstained from joining in the wild-goose chase, were so intensely absorbed by the contemplation of the spectacle which was offered to their bewildered gaze, that they took no concern in any thing else. Quincampoix Street, where the offices of the company were kept, was literally blocked up by the crowd which the fury of speculation and the passion for sudden wealth attracted to that spot, and persons were frequently crushed or stifled to death. "Mississippi!—Who wants any Mississippi?"—was bawled out in every lane and by-lane, and every nook and corner of Paris echoed with the word, "Mississippi!"

Immense fortunes were lost or acquired in a few weeks. By stock-jobbing, obscure individuals were suddenly raised from the sewers of poverty to the gilded rooms of princely splendor. Most amusing anecdotes might be told of persons thus stumbling by chance into affluence; and heart-rending stories might be related of such as, from the possession of every luxury, were precipitated into the depths of absolute destitution; while those who had become spontaneously rich, being made giddy with their unexpected acquisitions, launched into such profusions and follies that their return to poverty was as rapid as their accession to wealth, through which it might be said they had only passed with the velocity of steam locomotion. He who could write in all its details the history of that Mississippi bubble, so fatal in its short-lived duration, would give to the world the most instructive composition, made up of the most amusing, ludicrous, monstrous and horrible elements that were ever jumbled together.

The distribution of property underwent more than one grotesque change. The tenants of the parlor or saloon went up to the garret, and the natives of the garret tumbled down into the saloon. Footmen changed places with their masters, and the outside of carriages happened to become the inside. Law's coachman made such a large fortune that he set up an equipage of his own. Cookmaids and waiting-women appeared at the opera, bedizened in finery like the Queen of Sheba. A baker's son, who used to carry his father's loaves in a basket to his customers, was, by a sudden turn of the wheel of fortune, enabled to purchase plate to the amount of four hundred thousand livres, which he sent to his wife, with the recommendation of having it properly set out for supper, and with the strict injunction of putting in the largest and finest dish his favorite stew of onions and hog's feet. The Marquis d'Oyse, of the family of the Dukes of Villars Brancas, signed a contract of marriage, although he was at the time thirty-three years of age, with the daughter, three years old, of a man named André, who had won millions at the Mississippi lottery. The conditions of the marriage were, that it should take place when the girl should reach her twelfth year, and that, in the mean time, the marquis was to receive three hundred thousand livres in cash, twenty thousand livres every year until the day of the wedding, when several millions would be paid to the husband by the father of the bride. All these meteors, who were thus blazing in their newly-acquired splendor, were called "Mississippians," on account of the source of their fortune.

Let us now turn from the system, to its inventor—to John Law, who, under such circumstances operating in his favor, was adored by the people; and as usual, they were few indeed who refrained from worshiping the idol of the hour, and from burning incense at his shrine. He was a favorite with the Duke of Orleans, Regent of France, of whom he was known to possess the ear; and on his abjuring in the hands of Abbé Tencin, since a cardinal, the Protestant religion, which was the only obstacle to his advancement to the highest offices of the state, he was appointed, on the 5th of January, 1720 comptroller-general of the finances of the kingdom. To so eminent a personage, England sent, of course, a free and absolute pardon for the murder of Wilson; and Edinburgh, proud of having given him birth, tendered him the freedom of the city in a gold box. Poets, tuning their lyres to sing his apotheosis, declared him to be the Magnus Apollo of the age, and the Academy of Sciences elected him one of its honorary members. It is impossible not to pay a tribute of admiration to the talents of that low-born adventurer, who, in less than four years, by his own unassisted exertions, and even in despite of the most strenuous opposition from formidable adversaries, rose from a suspicious position in private life, to be one of the ministers of one of the most powerful and enlightened nations of the world. The Duke of St. Simon, who knew him well, and who writes of him with partiality in his celebrated memoirs, says, that Law had a strong Scotch accent, but that although there was much English in his French, he was extremely persuasive, and that he had the peculiar tact, by assuming an air of exquisite candor, frankness, straightness, and modest diffidence, to throw off their guard those he wished to seduce. With prodigious powers of insinuation and persuasion he must indeed have been gifted, to have operated all the wonders we have seen!

Law, who had the pretension of enriching every body, did not, as it is very natural to suppose, forget his own pecuniary interest, and had purchased no less than fourteen of the most magnificent estates of France with titles annexed to them, and among which was the Marquisate of Rosny; that domain had been owned, and its splendid castle had been occupied as a favorite residence by the illustrious friend and minister of Henry the IVth, the great Sully, who, before he was created duke of that name, had borne the title of Marquis of Rosny. But Law had attained his highest degree of prosperity, and the wind was already blowing which was to prostrate him to the ground from his towering altitude.

The year 1720, which saw him at the zenith of his prosperity, witnessed also his rapid declension, and his ultimate fall into the abyss of adversity, where he was forever lost. But how dazzling his position was on the 5th day of that year, 1720, when he was appointed comptroller-general of the finances of the kingdom! At that time, he was literally besieged in his splendid palace by a host of applicants and supplicants of every description. His friendship was courted with cringing eagerness by princes, dukes, peers of the realm, marshals and prelates, who reverentially bowed, and bent a supple knee to the upstart, in the mean hope of securing his patronage. Nobles crowded his ante-chambers in democratic conjunction with a motley crew of people of every hue and feather. It was thought to be a lucky accident or a high honor to attract even his passing notice, and ladies of the most exalted rank were not ashamed to ply meretricious smiles to win his favor.

With no very great stretch of the imagination, we may easily conceive the occurrence of such a scene as the following: far from the bustle of the street, and from the crowd which encumbers his apartments of reception, in a retired but richly and tastefully decorated room of his princely residence, John Law is taking his luncheon in the sole company of his son, his daughter, and his pretended wife, who, says the Duke of Saint Simon, was a high-born English lady. Enamored of Law, she had left her family and dignified position in society, to follow him. She was very haughty, and the superciliousness of her manners was such, that it frequently became impertinent. She rarely paid visits except to the chosen few: she received homage as her due, paid none, and exercised in her house a despotic authority. Her well-shaped person looked noble, and she would have been thought handsome, if a horrid stain of the color of red wine had not covered half of her face and one eye. It is well known that Law always treated her with the utmost respect and tenderness.

Sitting in front of her at a table adorned with exquisitely carved gold and silver implements, Law seemed to be enjoying with peculiar relish the quiet atmosphere of his family circle. Now and then his confidential groom of the bed-chamber glided in, and whispered into his ear the arrival of some distinguished personage who had come to swell the retinue that filled his apartments, and anxiously expected his appearance. At each announcement of a high-sounding name, of a duke, a marshal, a great dignitary of the church, a smile of triumph would flit across his face, and he would cast a look of exultation at his wife, whose natural pride appeared to be intensely alive to the enjoyment which was administered to it by her husband. But Law, keeping his self-composure, would answer, with the utmost unconcern, and without hurrying his meal, whenever a new name was brought in to him: "Well! well! let him wait!" On a sudden, the servant entered again, but not with the same measured step, and cried out with a voice which emotion raised far beyond its usual key: "My lord, his highness the Prince of Conti." Law jumped up as if the irresistible action of a spring in his seat had forced him into his erect attitude, his face became flushed, and his limbs trembled. "Ha!" exclaimed he, "a prince of the royal blood under my roof!" But a thought flashed through his brain, he knit his brows, compressed his lips, looked at his wife with an expression of intense pride, and resuming his chair, composedly turned to his servant, and with the same tone of voice with which he had answered every other call, he said: "Let him wait." Here is something to moralize upon, if moralizing was not so flat, stale and unprofitable. A Bourbon, the descendant of a long line of kings, to be kept waiting in the ante-chambers of the son of a Scotch goldsmith! A prince of the royal blood of France to dance attendance on a low adventurer, an exiled outlaw, who had successively and collectively been called the gambler, the swindler, the profligate, the bankrupt, the adulterer, the murderer, the apostate. O the power of gold! Can we not divine the feeling that made Law's blood thrill with excitement! Ours must be one of unmitigated contempt.

Now the scene has shifted, and John Law is rusticating at his castle of Rosny, the once proud seat of Sully, in Normandy. Reclining in a gothic, richly carved chair, with a high back still retaining, chiseled in its oak, the coat-of-arms of Sully, and tapering into a point surmounted by a ducal crown,—in the very chair of state of that haughty feudal baron, and with his feet resting on the lower and more modest chair of the Duchess of Sully, for in those days Sully's wife would not have dared to occupy a seat of equal dignity with that of her lord,—our great financier, John Law, before indulging in his nightly repose, is reckoning up in his mind his acquired wealth, and framing new plans still to increase its already enormous bulk. It is midnight—and the solemn hour of twelve strikes at the big tower's clock! Hist!—a slow, solemn step is heard— it comes from the stair running up the turret which opens into Law's room. What can it be? The light burns blue on his table:—Law's soul is suddenly awed with the consciousness that an unnatural atmosphere is gathering round him. His hair stands erect: a cold chill shoots through his body, and his eyes involuntarily turn to that iron door which the strange visitor is gradually approaching. O wonder! There is no using of the key—no unbarring—and yet the door grates on its rusty hinges—and opens wide. God! can it be true?—can such things be?

It is Sully himself, with his so well-known stern face, and with the same antiquated dress in which he was clad, when in the latter part of his life, being summoned from his retirement to the court of Louis the XIIIth, to give advice on matters of importance, and his unfashionable appearance having provoked a laugh from those butterfly courtiers who surrounded the young king, he frowned them down with an air of inexpressible majesty and contempt, and then, looking at the crowned son of his old friend, Henry the IVth:—"Sire," said he, "whenever the king, your respected father, sent for me, he used to dismiss from his presence all the buffoons, masqueraders and jackanapes of the palace."—It is the same Sully, to whom the king having exhibited a paper which, to the disgrace of royalty, he had signed in a moment of weakness, seized it, tore it to pieces, and on the king having exclaimed: "Are you mad, Sully!" answered, "Would to God that I were the only madman in your kingdom!"—It is he, whose sense of his feudal and personal dignity was such, that he never would descend to his terraced garden, even to indulge in an early morning walk, without having before and behind him a file of halberdiers escorting him in state. A bold man John Law was. But when this apparition met his sight, drops of cold sweat pearled down his forehead, his voice stuck in his throat, and terror fettered him to his seat, as if his limbs had been bound with chains of adamant. Indeed, a stouter heart than his would have been frozen by the gaze which Sully bent upon him, a gaze in which were so vividly expressed intense, indignant surprise at the witnessed profanation, and the scowling threat of condign punishment. Ay, a bolder man than John Law would have sunk to the ground when, with rapid strides, Sully advanced toward him, and lifting up the hunting whip which his hand tightly grasped, exclaimed, " Dog of a stock-jobber ! vile Scotch hound, darest thou pollute—" A shriek !—a fearful shriek was heard—and John Law shook off his agonizing dream. Yea—it was only a dream. But some dreams are prophetic, and these are the scenes in which the imagination of the historian may be permitted to indulge, to give more graphic force to the truths of his narrative.

It must not be supposed that Law had carried on all his projects so far, without encountering incessant opposition. Among his adversaries the parliament of Paris had been the most redoubtable, and that powerful body had been always on the watch to seize a favorable opportunity to crush Law and his system. That opportunity was soon to present itself. Undermined by the intrigues of his other colleagues in the ministry, carried away by the innate imperfections of his system farther than he had intended, terrified at the mighty evolutions of the tremendous engine he had set at work, and could no longer control or stop, the victim of a combination of envy, apprehension, ignorance and avarice, which interfered with his designs, and made him pay too dear for protection or assistance, Law felt that the moment of his fall was approaching, and saw with terror the threatening oscillations of the overgrown fabric he had reared. He tried to conceal his embarrassments by inducing the company to declare that they had such a command of funds as to be able to propose lending any sum on proper security at two per cent. But in vain did they put on this show of confidence in their own resources:—the smiling mask deceived nobody. There were symptoms which too plainly denoted approaching dissolution and death. Among those dark spots was the number of bank notes which had been manufactured, and which, on the 1st of May, 1720, exceeded 2600 millions of livres, while the whole specie in the kingdom amounted only to 1300 millions.

Then happened what has been frequently seen since: the superabundance of paper money produced a scarcity of specie. It became evident to the most obtuse that those bank notes had no representative, and that sooner or later they would be no more than worthless rags. As soon as that discovery was made, every one hastened to convert his shares or bank notes into gold or silver, and to realize the fortune he had acquired. The most keen-sighted, or the most prudent, not only exchanged their notes for specie, but sent it out of France; and it is calculated that in this way the kingdom was drained of 500 millions of livres. To avert the danger with which his system was threatened, Law, in less than eight months, promulgated thirty-three edicts to fix the value of gold and silver, to preserve and to increase the metallic circulation, and to limit the amount of gold and silver which might be converted into plate and jewelry. No payment in specie could be made except for small sums: the standard of coin was kept in the most bewildering state of fluctuation, while the value of bank notes was decreed to be invariable. Rents, taxes, and customs, were made payable in paper only:—and as a climax to these high-handed measures, individuals as well as secular or religious communities were prohibited, under very severe penalties, from having in their possession more than 500 livres in specie. This ordinance established the most intolerable inquisition, and gave rise to the most vexatious researches on the part of the police. The house of no citizen was free from the visits of the agents of power, and every man trembled to see denunciation lurking by his fireside, and to harbor treason by the very altars of his household gods.

The alarm of the public mind became such, that it was thought necessary to equalize the proportion between the bank notes and the coin; and on the 21st of May, 1720, an edict was issued, which, in violation of the pledge of the state, and of the most solemn stipulations, and as a beginning of bankruptcy, reduced the value of the company's bank notes to one half, and cut down the shares from 10,000, and even 20,000, which was their highest ascent, to 5000 livres. The effect of this edict was instantaneous and overwhelming. At once, all confidence was lost in the bank notes:—general consternation prevailed: and no one would have given twenty cents in hard coin for millions in bank paper. There was a rush on the bank for payment, and one will easily form a conception of the fury, despair and distress of the people, when he is informed that on the stopping of payment by the bank, there was paper in circulation amounting to 2,235,085,590 livres. The whole of it was suddenly reduced to zero. In the whole of France there was but one howl of malediction, and guards had to be given to Law, who had become an object of popular abhorrence. Even the life of the Regent himself was put in jeopardy, and it became necessary to station troops in different parts of Paris, where seditious and inflammatory libels had been posted up and circulated, to increase the confusion and tumultuous disorder which reigned everywhere. It was apparent that France had been transformed into a volcano, from which the slightest cause would have produced an eruption.

With regard to Louisiana, there had been also a great revolution in the public estimate of her merits. She was no longer described as the land of promise, but as a terrestrial representation of Pandemonium. The whole country was nothing else, it was said, but a vile compound of marshes, lagoons, swamps, bayous, fens, bogs, endless prairies, inextricable and gloomy forests, peopled with every monster of the natural and of the mythological world. The Mississippi rolled onward a muddy and thick substance, which hardly deserved the name of water, and which was alive with every insect and every reptile. Enormous trunks, branches and fragments of trees were swept down by the velocity of the current, and in such quantity as almost to bridge over the bed of the river, and they prevented communication from one bank to the other, by crushing every bark or canoe that attempted the passage. At one epoch of the year, the whole country was overflowed by that mighty river, and then, all the natives betook themselves to the tops of trees, where they roosted and lived like monkeys, and jumped from tree to tree in search of food, or they retired to artificial hills of shells, piled up by preceding generations, where they starved, or fed as they could by fishing excursions.

In many of its parts, the country was nothing but a thin coat, one foot thick, of alluvial soil, kept together on the surface of the water by the intermingled teguments of bind-weeds and the roots of other plants, so that if one walked on this crust, he made it, by the pressure of the weight of his body, heave up around him, in imitation of the waves of the sea, and great was the danger of sinking through this weak texture.

Temptingly looking fruits and berries invited the taste, it is true, but they were all poisonous. Such portion of the colony as was not the production of the Mississippi, and therefore a mere deposit of mud, was the creation of the sea, and consisted in heaps of sand. Hence it was evident, that the country was neither fit for the purposes of commerce nor for those of agriculture, and could not be destined by the Creator for the habitation of civilized man. The sun was so intensely hot, that at noon it could strike a man dead as if with a pistol shot: —it was called a stroke of the sun. Its fiery breath drew from the bogs, fens, and marshes the most pestilential vapors, engendering disease and death. The climate was so damp, that in less than a week a bar of iron would be coated over with rust and eaten up by its corroding tooth. The four seasons of the year would meet in one single day, and a shivering morning was not unfrequently succeeded by a sultry evening. The ear was, by day and by night, assailed by the howls of wolves, and by the croakings of frogs so big that they swallowed children, and could bellow as loud as bulls. Sleep, sweet sleep, nature's balmy restorer, was disturbed, if not altogether made impossible, by the buz and stings of myriads of mosquitoes, which thickened the atmosphere and incorporated themselves with the very air which the lungs inhaled.

In such a country, the European race of men rapidly degenerated, and in less than three generations was reduced from the best-proportioned size to the dwarfish dimensions of misshapen pigmies. As soon as the emigrant landed, he was seized with disease, and if he recovered, the rosy hue of health had forever fled from his cheeks:—his wrinkled and sallow skin hung loosely on his bones, from which the flesh had almost entirely departed:—his system could never be braced up again and he dragged on a miserable, sickly existence, which fortunately was not of long duration. In such a climate, old age was entirely unknown, and the statistical average of life did not exceed ten years. There, man lost the energies both of his body and mind, and through the enervating and baleful influence of the atmosphere, soon became stultified into an indolent idiot. Even the brutish creation did not escape the inflictions to which humanity was subject, and experienced the same rapid transformations. Thus, in a short time, horses were reduced to the size of sheep, cattle to that of rabbits, hogs gradually shrunk up so as to be no bigger than rats, and fowls dwindled into the diminished proportions of sparrows. As to the natives, they were cannibals, who possessed all the malignity and magical arts of demons, and waged incessant war against the emigrants, whose flesh they devoured with peculiar relish. This delineation of the features of Louisiana was very different from those of the first portrait, so many copies of which had been industriously circulated through France. It had been Hyperion; now it was a Satyr.

It is easy to conceive the startling effects produced on the minds of a people already in a paroxysm of consternation, by such malicious misrepresentations, which the enemies of Law took care to scatter far and wide. Thus, the tide of emigration which was pouring onward rolled back, and the prospect of establishing a powerful colony in Louisiana, which, at first, had appeared so feasible, and loomed out to the imagination of the speculator in such vivid colors, and with such fair proportions, was nipped in the bud, and was looked upon as an impossibility. Under the exaggerated and gloomy apprehensions of the moment, no actual tender of money, and no promises of future reward, could have tempted any body to embark for Louisiana. So universal was the terror inspired by the name of the Mississippi, that (it is a well-known fact) it became even a bugbear of the nursery, and that for half a century after the explosion of Law's great Mississippi scheme, when French children were unruly and unmanageable, and when all threats had proved ineffectual, the mother would, in the last resort, lift up her finger impressively, and in a whispering tone, as if afraid of speaking too loud of something so horrible, would say with a shudder, and with pale lips to her rebellious progeny: "Hush! or I will send you to the Mississippi!" The child looked imploringly into his mother's face, his passion vanished, his cries and sobs were stifled, and under the soft kisses of maternal affection, coupled with the assurance that he never would be sent to the Mississippi, he fell into gentle and undisturbed sleep.

However, the Western or Mississippi Company having contracted the obligation to colonize Louisiana, and to transport thither, within a fixed time, a certain number of emigrants, found itself under the necessity, in order to comply with the terms of its contract, to have recourse to the most iniquitous and unlawful means. As it was indispensable that there should be emigration—when it ceased to be voluntary, it was necessary that it should be forced. Thus violence was resorted to, and throughout France agents were dispatched to kidnap all vagrants, beggars, gipsies, or people of the like description, and women of bad repute. Unfortunately, the power given by the government to these agents of the company was abused in the most infamous manner. It became in their hands an engine of peculation, oppression, and corruption. It is incredible what a number of respectable people of both sexes were put, through bribery, in the hands of these satellites of an arbitrary government, to gratify private malice and the dark passions or interested views of men in power. A purse of gold slipped into the hand, and a whisper in the ear, went a great way to get rid of obnoxious persons, and many a fearful tale of revenge, of hatred, or of cupidity, might be told of persons who were unsuspectedly seized and carried away to the banks of the Mississippi, before their voices could be heard when crying for justice, or for protection. The dangerous rival, the hated wife, or troublesome husband, the importuning creditor, the prodigal son, or the too long-lived father, the one who happened to be an obstacle to an expected inheritance, or crossed the path of the wealthy or of the powerful, became the victims of their position, and were soon hurried away with the promiscuous herd of thieves, prostitutes, vagabonds, and all sorts of wretches of bad fame who had been swept together, to be transported to Louisiana.

Guarded by a merciless soldiery, they, on their way to sea-ports, crowded the public roads of France like droves of cattle, and as they were hardly furnished with means of subsistence or with clothing by their heartless conductors, who speculated on the food and other supplies with which they were bound to provide their prisoners, they died in large numbers, and their unburied corpses, rotting above ground, struck with terror the inhabitants of the districts through which the woe-begone caravan had passed. At night, they were locked up in barns, when any could be found, and if not, they were forced, the better to prevent escape, to lie down in heaps at the bottom of ditches and holes, and sentinels were put round to watch over them. Hunger and cold pinched the miserable creatures, and their haggard looks, emaciated bodies, and loud wailings, carried desolation everywhere. Such sights, added to the horrifying descriptions which were given of Louisiana, made its name more terrific to the minds of the people of France than that of the celebrated Bastile and its dark dungeons. Dull indeed must be the imagination of the novelist, who, out of these strictly historical facts, could not extract the most romantic and heart-rending tales!

Law was considered as the author of all these cruelties and misfortunes, and he became still more odious to the people. The parliament of Paris thought that the moment was come at last to pounce upon Law; and to gratify their long-cherished resentment, he was summoned to appear in person before that high tribunal, to answer for his misdeeds and for his violations of the laws of the kingdom. On his refusal or neglect to do so, the parliament ordered him to be arrested, and had determined, on his being brought to the palace where they sat, to close their doors; and in order to prevent the expected interference of the Regent, their intention was to try summarily the hated foreigner, and to hang him in their court-yard. Thus, if the Regent, as it was anticipated, sent troops to batter down the gates of the parliament-house, to save his favorite, they would arrive too late, and would find there nothing but a gallows and a corpse. Aware of this plan, Law left his residence and fled to the Regent's palace, which was the only place where he felt himself secure against the pursuit of his enemies. There he cast himself at the feet of his august protector, and bathed his hands with tears. What a change!

> "This is the state of man: to-day he puts forth
> The tender leaves of hope, to-morrow blossoms,
> And bears his blushing honors thick upon him:
> The third day comes a frost,—a killing frost:
> And—when he thinks, good easy man, full surely
> His greatness is a ripening—nips his root,
> And then he falls."

The Regent gave to Law assurance of his protection and vouched for his life; but this was all he could do. He had to bow to the force of public opinion, and to bend to the storm which menaced even his royal person It was evident that Law could no longer stay in France. In the mean time, the Regent, irritated at the presumption of the parliament, exiled that body to Pontoise; but public indignation still gathering fresh fuel from that very circumstance, the Duke of Orleans provided Law, who resigned the office of comptroller-general, with the means of escaping out of the kingdom. On the 22d of December, 1720, Law arrived at Brussels, where he waited for some time in the vain expectation of being recalled. Far from it, he discovered, to his dismay, that when a man is sliding down the hill of prosperity, his best friends, instead of endeavoring to arrest his fall, will not unfrequently help him down with a kick. Thus, the Great Western or Mississippi Company, to which he had stood sponsor or godfather, lifted up a parricidal hand against him; and under the allegation that his accounts had not been faithfully kept and rendered, had proceeded to seize all his property, and had thereby deprived him of all means of subsistence. He did not lose however the favor of the Regent, who appointed him minister of France at the court of Bavaria, where he resided until the death of that prince. Then he traveled through many parts of Europe, but found everywhere that dame Fortune was tired of smiling upon him. He became but too sensible that he was a discarded lover, and that her favors were bestowed on some other favorite.

In October, 1721, he returned to England, and at first was received with distinction by persons of high rank: he was even presented to George the Ist. It had been shrewdly suspected that he had retained a considerable portion of his enormous wealth, of which it was presumed that he had been prudent enough, in his palmy days, to send a valuable fraction out of France. But when it was discovered that he was reduced to beggary, people railed at his supreme want of discretion at not providing better for himself, and they felt indignant at the presumptuous cheat, who had been wheedling himself into their society under the false impression that he was rich. As soon as it was ascertained that he was poor, it followed of course that he was nobody, and no longer to be countenanced or noticed. Out of an innumerable host of friends, the Countess of Suffolk was the only one that remained true to him. Let it stand on record in justice to her, and for the honor of woman! This indeed was another of those but too striking instances of the mutability of fortune and of the instability of friendship.

In 1722, John Law turned his back upon England for the last time, and returning to the Continent, retired to Venice, where he lived in obscurity, and where he died on the 21st of March, 1729, in a state of indigence, and in the fifty-eighth year of his age. He had lost his wife and his only son, and there remained with him to solace his last moments but one faithful heart, a sweet Antigone, who closed his eyelids. That was his daughter. She afterward married Lord Wallingford in England. A branch of the family of Law has preserved to this day in France a very honorable position in society. A brother whom he left in that kingdom when he fled from it, was taken under the special protection of the Duchess of Bourbon. Through her favor, two of his sons found employment, in 1741, in the service of the East India Company, and greatly distinguished themselves. The eldest one, Law de Lauriston, rose to the rank of major-general, and to be governor-general of the French possessions in India. He left several sons; two perished in the unfortunate expedition of La Peyrouse, and one of them lived to be known under the reign of Louis the XVIIIth, as Marquis de Lauriston, a lieutenant-general and a peer of France.

We have followed Law through all the phases of his eventful career, until, crossing with him the Bridge of Sighs, we have left him dying in Venice, "that sea Cybele with her tiara of towers—the revel of the earth—the masque of Italy." A fit tomb for such a man! Now that the last act of this varied drama has been played, let the curtain drop, leaving to the judgment of impartial posterity the memory of **John Law of Edinburgh.**

SECOND LECTURE.

BIENVILLE APPOINTED GOVERNOR OF LOUISIANA FOR THE SECOND TIME, IN THE PLACE OF L'EPINAY—FOUNDATION OF NEW ORLEANS—EXPEDITION OF ST. DENIS, BEAULIEU, AND OTHERS TO MEXICO—ADVENTURES OF ST. DENIS—LAND CONCESSIONS—SLAVE-TRADE—TAKING OF PENSACOLA BY THE FRENCH—THE SPANIARDS RETAKE IT, AND BESIEGE DAUPHINE ISLAND—PENSACOLA AGAIN TAKEN BY THE FRENCH—SITUATION OF THE COUNTRY AS DESCRIBED BY BIENVILLE—THE CHEVALIER DES GRIEUX AND MANON LESCAUT—CHANGES IN THE ORGANIZATION OF THE JUDICIARY—EDICT IN RELATION TO COMMERCE—ADVENTURES OF THE PRINCESS CHARLOTTE OF BRUNSWICK, OF BELLE ISLE, AND OTHERS—SEAT OF GOVERNMENT TRANSFERRED TO NEW ORLEANS—MISCELLANEOUS FACTS AND EVENTS FROM 1718 TO 1722.

IN the last lecture, we examined the effects produced in France by the creation of the Mississippi Company, and by the operations of Law's gigantic system of finances. Let us now proceed to ascertain what influence they had on the prosperity and destinies of Louisiana, and to record the series of events accompanying the colonization of the country.

I have already said that Law, who was the director-general of the Royal Bank of France, was also appointed director-general of the Mississippi Company. The other directors were, D'Artaguette, receiver-general of the finances of Auch; Duché, receiver-general of the finances of La Rochelle; Moreau, deputy representative of the merchants of St. Malo; Piou, also the commercial representative and deputy of Nantes; Castaignes and Mouchard, merchants of La Rochelle.

The company, being thus organized, sent three vessels to Louisiana, with three companies of infantry and sixty-nine colonists, who landed on the 9th of March, 1718, and who, by their presence and the information they brought, revived the hope of better days. The office of Governor of Louisiana was definitively, and for the second time, granted to Bienville, as successor to L'Epinay, who exercised his powers only for a few months, during which he made himself very unpopular, by prohibiting the sale of spirituous liquors to the Indians. The humanity of this provision did not seem to strike the colonists as forcibly as their ruler, and failed to outweigh other considerations. They complained of the want of policy displayed in that ordinance, and they represented, no doubt with truth, that the selling of French brandy was the most profitable article of commerce which they could command, and their most powerful source of influence over the Indian nations. It was, therefore, with great satisfaction, that the colonists learned the nomination of Bienville. Besides, he had passed nineteen years in the colony, of which he was one of the founders: and familiar with all its resources and wants, he had endeared himself to all the inhabitants, every one of whom he knew personally.

The first act of Bienville's new administration was an important one. It was to select the most favorable place on the banks of the Mississippi for the location of the principal establishment of the colony. He chose the spot where now stands the city of New Orleans, and he there left a detachment of fifty men to prepare the ground and erect barracks or sheds. The geography of the country shows it to have been the most judicious choice, and the present importance of New Orleans testifies to the sagacity of Bienville. In so doing, he showed not only foresight and perspicacity, but also great firmness and independence: because he dared to act against the predilections of his government, which had a strong leaning for Manchac, where a natural communication was open with the lakes through bayou Manchac and the river Amite.

The space now occupied by New Orleans was then entirely covered with one of those primitive forests with which we are so familiar. Owing to the annual inundations of the river, it was swampy and marshy, and cut up with a thousand small ravines, ruts, and pools of stagnant waters when the river was low. The site was not inviting to the physical eye, but Bienville looked at it with the mind's vision. His intellect hovered over the whole country, from his native valleys of Canada, down the Mississippi, in the footsteps of La Salle, through those boundless regions whose commercial emporium he foresaw that New Orleans was destined to be. Were I a painter, I would delight in delineating and fixing on living canvas the scene which my imagination conjures up.

Bienville had arrived with his sturdy companions on the preceding evening; and now the sun is peeping through his eastern curtains, and flings a glow of radiancy over the dawning beauty of the morning landscape. In obedience to the command received, fifty axes have, in concert, struck fifty gigantic sons of the forest. With folded arms and abstracted look, Bienville stands on the bank of the river, and seems, from the expression of his face, to be wrapped up in the contemplation of some soul-stirring fancies. Perhaps he had glimpses of the rapid growth of the city of his creation, and was blessed with the revealed prospect of its future grandeur. Far aloft, above his head, the American eagle might have been observed towering with repeated gyrations, and uttering loud shrieks which sounded like tones of command. Of the Indian race only one representative was there. It was an old sibyl-looking woman, who had the wild glance of insanity or of divination; and with the solemn gesticulations of prophetic inspiration, she kept singing an uncouth sort of chant, in which she said that the time of which she had been warned by the Great Spirit had come at last: that her death-hour was approaching, which was to be on the day when white men were to take possession of the spot where she had dwelt during a hundred summers and winters, and when they would cut down the oak, under the shade of which she had indulged so long her solitary musings. "The Spirit tells me," so she sang, "that the time will come, when between the river and the lake there will be as many dwellings for the white man as there are trees standing now. The haunts of the red man are doomed, and faint recollections and traditions concerning the very existence of his race will float dimly over the memory of his successors, as unsubstantial, as vague and obscure as the mist which shrouds, on a winter morning, the bed of the father of rivers."

I said before, that, on the return of St. Denis to Mobile, in 1716, after his adventures in Mexico, a vain attempt had been made by Crozat to open commercial relations with the Spanish provinces of North America, and that he had dispatched, with that object in view, three Canadians named Deléry, Lafrénière, and Beaulieu. They were hardly on their way to accomplish their mission, when they were joined by the indefatigable and persevering St. Denis. At Natchitoches they procured mules and horses, and with them continued their march onward. When they reached the first village of the Assinais, where it became necessary for them to rest awhile, and to lay in a stock of provisions, St. Denis, who, it will be remembered, had lately left his wife at the Presidio del Norte shortly after his marriage, and who had reluctantly torn himself from her embraces to discharge the duty of rendering to the French governor at Mobile an account of his expedition, could not brook any further delay, and leaving abruptly his traveling companions, continued to move forward with a small retinue of followers, but with a considerable number of bales of merchandise. The gallant knight, the lately appointed captain in the French army, had assumed the garb and the occupation of a merchant, and thought himself fully adequate to the fulfillment of the duties incumbent on such a combination of characters.

When Beaulieu, Deléry, and Lafrénière arrived at the Presidio, they were informed of the seizure of the goods and merchandise of St. Denis by the Spanish authorities, and of his departure for Mexico in the hope of obtaining the restoration of his property. Dismayed at such a piece of intelligence, and afraid of the seizure of their own goods, they intrusted them for safe keeping to some monks who did not scruple to turn an honest penny by granting their protection to the helpless, and they at last succeeded in selling on credit every thing they had on hand to certain merchants of Bocca de Leon. They were patiently waiting for payment, when they heard the unwelcome news that St. Denis had been imprisoned at Mexico. Deléry, Beaulieu, and Lafrénière no longer thought of securing the payment of the money to which they were entitled, but of saving their persons from the tender mercies of a Spanish jailer. Carrying away paper recognizances and bonds which were never paid, they departed with the utmost precipitation, and had the good luck to arrive in safety at Mobile in 1718, after an absence of nearly two years, and after having encountered all the fatigues and accidents of a long and perilous journey.

Let us now accompany St. Denis to Mexico. He is

one of those men whom it is pleasant for the historian to keep in sight. Unfortunately for him, when he entered the gates of that city, he had no longer to deal with the Duke of Linares, who had treated him formerly with such extraordinary kindness. The successor of the duke was the Marquis of Valero, whose dispositions did not prove to be so favorable. For some time, however, St. Denis entertained the hope that he would obtain an order setting aside the seizure of his goods. But it so happened that he had traversed the province of Texas without presenting his respects to the governor, Don Martin de Alacorne, and without endeavoring to propitiate his favor. This Spanish functionary, who was very punctilious in all matters of etiquette, construed St. Denis' haste, forgetfulness, or want of ceremony into a slight on his dignity and authority; and drawing the inference that a man so deficient in manners and knightly courtesy could not be but some lowborn desperado, he wrote to his government that St. Denis was a suspicious character, fraught with hostile and dangerous designs. This was enough to awaken the jealous susceptibilities of the viceroy, when the settled policy of Spain, as it is well known, was so averse to the introduction of strangers into her colonies. Don Martin's denunciation was believed, and St. Denis was thrown into prison. There he pined for a whole month, but his friends and his wife's relations were active on his behalf, and not only was he released, but he obtained possession of his goods, which were sold very advantageously. They were not only sold, but paid for. This was sunshine at last, but a cloud intervened in the shape of a roguish agent who received the money, and who, thinking it convenient to keep for his own uses what belonged to another, absconded to unknown parts.

St. Denis was a gentleman by birth, a soldier by profession, and a merchant by accident, otherwise he would have been more used to such untoward events, and he would have been less indignant at the gentle, easy, soft and ordinary process of fattening one's purse at the expense of another's. But, exasperated by the series of mishaps which had befallen him, he gave loud vent to his complaints of Spanish treachery and tyranny, and had the imprudence to boast of the desolation he could bring on the frontier provinces of Mexico, if he chose to use the influence he had acquired on the Indians of those regions. The threats of St. Denis were not disregarded, and the government ordered him to be arrested. Fortunately he was advised in time of what was coming, and the numerous relatives of his wife remaining true to him, he was supplied with the means of escape. His flight from Mexico to the Presidio del Norte, with his infinite disguises, his countless adventures, his romantic concealments, his turnings and windings from his pursuers, through the endless length of so many hundred miles of a wild and almost impervious country, would furnish a prolific subject to any driver of the quill who might be in quest of materials. Suffice it for me to say, that leaving the Presidio with his wife, he reached Mobile in safety, and rendered to the company his accounts of the second expedition which he had undertaken under Crozat.

The only benefit which France derived from these daring attempts consisted in the acquisition of correct information concerning the Spanish settlements which existed in the neighborhood of Louisiana. No commonplace man was he who, in those days, could journey twice from Mobile to Mexico, and come back through the same avenue of besetting dangers of every description. He must have been gifted with a singular combination of physical, moral, and intellectual energies. A strong mind endowed with persevering volition, sinews that could command any fatigue, a constitution unconquerable by disease, a heart ignorant of fear,— such were the elements of the organization of St. Denis, who was one of the most remarkable characters of the early history of Louisiana. On his last return from Mexico, he remained ever after in Louisiana, where he became the founder of one of our most respectable families.

Crozat had made vain efforts to trade with the Mexican provinces, and to discover gold and silver mines. The company wisely abstained, for the moment, from committing the same error, and turned its attention to matters which promised better results. It was evident that the monopoly of commerce which had been granted to the company, with a province of an immense extent, it is true, but which had hardly any other inhabitants than Indian tribes, could not, after all, be very profitable; because it is impossible that commerce, whose very breath of life requires the two opposite and equiponderant lungs of exportation and importation, should exist on a large scale, where the wants of civilization are not felt. Agriculture, therefore, was one of the first things to be encouraged in the colony; and the company thought that the most effectual mode of producing such a result, was to make large concessions of lands to some of the most wealthy and most powerful personages of the kingdom. Thus, a concession of twelve square miles on Arkansas River, was granted to Law, who, as we have seen, was at that time growing daily upon the favor of the Regent. There were other grants on Yazoo River to a private company, composed of Le Blanc, Secretary of State, the Count de Belleville, the Marquis d'Auleck, and of Le Blond, who, at a later period, came to Louisiana as commander-in-chief of the engineers of the province. Near Natchez, the company made concessions to Hubert, the king's commissary, or *commissaire ordonnateur*, and to a company of merchants of St. Malo; at Natchitoches on Red River, to Bernard de La Harpe; at Tunicas, to St. Reine; at Pointe Coupée, to de Meuse. The spot where the town of Baton Rouge is now situated, was conceded to Diron d'Artaguette; that part of the right bank of the Mississippi which is opposite Bayou Manchac, to Paris Duvernay; the Tchoupitoulas lands to de Muys; the Oumas, to the Marquis d'Ancenis: the Cannes Brulées, or Burnt Canes, to the Marquis d'Artagnac; the opposite bank of the river to de Guiche, de La Houssaye and de La Houpe; the bay of St. Louis, to Mme. de Mézières, and Pascagoulas Bay to Mme. de Chaumont.

It had been stipulated between the company and Law, that he should settle a colony of fifteen hundred Germans on the lands which had been granted to him, and that he should keep up, at his own expense, a body of infantry and cavalry sufficient to protect that infant colony against the Indians. The condition of all the other grants of lands was also that the grantees should, within a fixed time, colonize those lands with a certain number of emigrants, in proportion to the extent of the grants. This experiment proved abortive in most cases: many of the landholders whom I have named, occupied such a high position in France, that they had no inducement to emigrate, and they contented themselves with sending some scores of destitute peasants to improve their new estates in America. The climate soon swept most of them into early graves, and the rest, not being placed under the immediate supervision of their patrons, who had remained abroad, and whose agents generally turned out to be unfaithful, careless or incapable, became discouraged, and abandoned themselves to habits of idleness and dissipation.

As it was impossible, however, to promote agriculture without hands to cultivate the soil, the company was driven into the necessity of turning its attention to the slave-trade, and to rely chiefly upon its supplies to do all the field-work in Louisiana. It was represented that slave labor would be cheaper than free labor, and would be within the command of the company on easier terms. The profits of the trade itself were a matter of no trifling consideration. Vessels were, therefore, sent to Africa, and from Africa to Louisiana, with their black cargoes. According to rules established by the company, slaves were to be sold to the *old* inhabitants (so were called those who had been two years in the colony), on these terms: one half cash, and the balance on one year's credit. The *new* inhabitants (that is, those who had been less than two years in the colony) had one and two years' credit granted to them.

In the month of June, 1718, colonists, convicts and troops, in all eight hundred souls, arrived in three vessels. By the order of the company, the colonists were distributed in the following manner: 148 at Natchitoches, under the command of De Laire, Bernard de La Harpe and Brossard; on the Yazoo lands, Mess. Scouvion de la Houssaye and their followers, numbering 82. The balance, amounting to 68, were settled at New Orleans.

From a communication addressed to the company by Bienville, on the 25th of September, it is to be inferred that he was not very well satisfied with the qualifications of all the colonists who had been transported to Louisiana. "There are among them," says he, "very few carpenters and plowmen. The consequence is, that mechanics and journeymen exact wages of ten and fifteen livres a day. This is what retards our improvements, and is a source of enormous expenses to the company."

Thus closed the year 1718, without any thing else worth recording. In the month of April, 1719, two ships of the company arrived from France, and brought the exciting news that war had broke out between France and Spain. At the same time, Bienville received from the company a dispatch, by which he was advised to avail himself of the opportunity which that war offered, to take possession of Pensacola.

Bienville acted on this occasion with commendable rapidity. He had received the authorization, on the 20th of April, to attack Pensacola, and all his preparations were completed in a few days. On the 13th of May, his brother, Serigny, who was employed by the French government in making a survey of the coasts of Louisiana, embarked with one hundred and fifty soldiers, on board the Philippe, the Comte de Toulouse, and the Maréchal de Villars, commanded by M. Méchin and the Chevalier des Grieux, and set sail from Dauphine Island. Bienville, on the same day, followed in a sloop with eighty men. On the 14th, they were before Pensacola, when at 4 o'clock in the afternoon, the Spanish governor surrendered, without having attempted any defense. The command of Pensacola was given to Chateaugué, a brother of Bienville. In conformity with the capitulation, in which it was stipulated that the garrison should be sent to the nearest Spanish fort, the Spaniards embarked in the Comte de Toulouse and the Maréchal de Villars, to be transported to Havana.

Bienville, who had left Pensacola under the command of Chateaugué, felt great uneasiness, produced by his apprehensions of not being able to retain his conquest. What had been so easily acquired might be as easily lost. Pensacola was but slenderly fortified;—

the French who composed the garrison were but few in number, and not very select men. It was evident that an overpowering force might be sent from Havana, before any means could be taken by the company to secure its new acquisition. The fears of Bienville were soon realized, and Pensacola only remained about two months in the hands of the French. When the two French vessels, the Comte de Toulouse and the Maréchal de Villars, entered the port of Havana, with the garrison of Pensacola, the captain-general of the island of Cuba, disregarding the articles of the capitulation, and little heeding the laws of nations, made himself guilty of a breach of faith, and took possession of the Comte de Toulouse and the Maréchal de Villars. He put on board Spanish soldiers and equipages, and sent them back to retake Pensacola, with three ships of the line, nine brigantines, and landing forces amounting to eighteen hundred men.

The Spanish fleet hove in sight of Pensacola on the 6th of August, and the landing took place the next day,—of the two French vessels which were in port, one was burned, and the other captured. Fifty French soldiers deserted immediately to join the Spaniards, and informed them that the rest of their companions were ready to deliver up the forts. Elated by this intelligence, the Spaniards summoned Chateaugué to surrender. The French commander, discovering that he was abandoned by his troops, capitulated on condition that he should come out of Pensacola with the honors of war, and be transported to old Spain with the French garrison. Immediately after the surrender of Pensacola, the commander of the Spanish fleet put a heavy force on board of three brigantines, and sent them to take possession of Dauphine Island, and of the French vessel, the Philippe, which was anchored there.

Serigny was in command of Dauphine Island, and on his being summoned to yield to the superior forces that would attack him, he answered in the negative, and added that he had prepared a warm reception for his visitors, when they should think proper to come.

As soon as it was night, two of the brigantines entered the bay of Mobile, and stopping half-way between Mobile and Dauphine Island, landed thirty-five men to plunder and to burn certain establishments there existing. The owner of the premises was asleep, and little dreamed of the danger which was at his doors. Suddenly, the invaders, confident of success, and secure of their coveted booty, uttered three cheers, and rushed forward, intent on their meditated work of destruction. But what was their dismay, when they were answered with the unexpected and terrific war-whoop of Indians! Before they could recover from their surprise, they were assailed by sixty Indians and some Frenchmen, who, by the order of Bienville, were marching to the relief of Serigny, the commander of Dauphine Island. They had arrived at the midway house, between Mobile and Dauphine Island, just in time to save it from ruin. Five of the enemy were killed and scalped by the Indians; six were drowned in attempting to gain their boats, and eighteen were made prisoners: only six escaped to carry away the melancholy tale of that night's disaster. Several of the French deserters were among the prisoners, and but short shrift was allowed them. As there was no hangman at hand, they were shot.

Two days after this event, the whole Spanish fleet appeared before Dauphine Island, which was defended only by one hundred and sixty Frenchmen and two hundred Indians, under the command of Serigny. Of the 160 Frenchmen, 80 were soldiers, and no more to be relied on than those who had deserted from Pensacola. Serigny had ordered the French ship, the Philippe, to anchor within pistol-shot of the shore, and her fire was supported by a powerful barbet battery constructed on the island. These means of defense appeared so formidable, that the Spaniards dared not come to a close attack, but keeping out of the reach of the French projectiles, amused themselves, during fourteen days, with a vain and empty cannonading. Although they did not venture to bear down direct upon the village itself, which was so well fortified, they made more than one attempt to land on several other parts of the island; but they were met and foiled at every point. In these several attempts at landing, their losses proved to be very great. Disheartened by these repeated failures, the Spaniards abandoned the siege of Dauphine Island on the 26th of August, and returned to Pensacola. Considering the disparity of forces, the defense of Dauphine Island by Serigny was a very gallant deed.

The Spanish sails had hardly vanished from the horizon of Dauphine Island, when three French ships of the line, under the command of the Comte de Champmeslin, with two vessels of the company, which they had convoyed across the Atlantic, loomed in sight on the 1st of September. This apparition put to flight two Spanish brigantines which had been left to cut off communication between Dauphine Island and Mobile. Bienville and Serigny his brother went on board of the admiral's ship as soon as they could, and at their request a council of war was immediately convened, in which it was determined to attack the two forts of Pensacola, and the Spanish fleet which was in the bay. On the 14th, half of the cargoes being discharged, the ships having taken in a new supply of provisions, water, and wood, and Bienville having had time to gather, equip, and organize a small army of Indians, the expedition departed for Pensacola. Two hundred and fifty soldiers had been embarked on board of the ships, and Bienville went in boats to Perdido River, with such regulars and volunteers as he could bring together. There he found, agreeably to his instructions, five hundred Indians, headed by M. de La Longueville. Without loss of time, he proceeded to invest what was called the GREAT FORT, situated on the main land, so as effectually to prevent all ingress or egress. On the 17th, M. de Champmeslin entered the bay, and attacked the *Small Fort*, which was on the point of the island of St. Rose, and the four ships and five brigantines which were anchored under the protection of the land fortifications. The fort and the fleet surrendered after a severe fight which lasted two hours. The larger fort, which was besieged by Bienville, no longer thought of further resistance, and opened its gates to the French, who made fifteen hundred prisoners. "The Indians," says Bienville in his dispatch, "were frightened at the number of the forces they had dared to encounter and had contributed to conquer, and could hardly believe the evidence of their own senses. It is clear that they are vividly impressed with the conviction of the irresistible power of our arms and of French valor." The fact is, that it was a glorious victory which elated the whole colony, and for many years what was called the Pensacola war, remained a favorite topic of conversation, and a subject of proud recollection which furnished the theme of more than one tale of valor and military achievements.

On board of the captured Spanish ships thirty-five of the French deserters from Pensacola were found. On their being tried, twelve were sentenced to be hung, and the rest to work for life on the galleys of France.

Bienville availed himself of this opportunity to complain, with great force and truth, of the materials which were put at his disposal to colonize Louisiana. "The Council of State," says he, "will permit me to represent that it is exceedingly painful for an officer, who is intrusted with the destinies of a colony, to have nothing better to defend her than a band of deserters, of smugglers, and of rogues, who are ever ready, not only to abandon their flag, but to turn their arms against their country. Are not most of the people I receive here sent by force? What attachment can they conceive for a colony which they look upon in the light of a prison, and which they can not leave at will? Can it be imagined that they will not use every effort to escape from a position which is odious to them? And is it not known that they can do so with great facility in a country so open as this, and when they can so readily find refuge with the Spaniards or the English? It seems to me absolutely necessary, if it be wished to preserve this colony to the king, to send to it none but those who are willing, and to make life here more attractive than it is for the present. In the first place, in order to accomplish this object, I would recommend to transport here a sufficient number of cattle to supply the colony with fresh meat, and then to transmit provisions of every kind with more regularity and in greater quantity than for the past. If not, the people here will continue to be exceedingly miserable. It must also be taken into consideration that the population and the military forces are so scattered, that in a case of sudden emergency, I have to rely, as means of defense, only on the Indian nations. For the present, I am even deprived of this resource on account of the want of provisions and merchandise to secure their support. But, backed by them, we could resist all the efforts of the Spaniards, although they could act powerfully against us, on account of the proximity of Havana and Vera Cruz. It is to be feared, however, that by cruising with large vessels on our coast, they may cut off our supplies from France. We know this to be their intention, from what we have learned from the French deserters we have retaken. In that case, it would be impossible to preserve the colony."

Thus ended the second expedition against Pensacola. De Lisle, one of the lieutenants of the ships of the line, was put by the French admiral in command of the place, somewhat to the mortification of Bienville, who thought that the disposal of this appointment ought to have been left to him as governor of the colony.

I have spoken of the Chevalier de Grieux or des Grieux, who commanded the Maréchal de Villars in the first expedition against Pensacola. Perhaps he was connected by blood as well as by name with the hero of a beautiful novel well known in the literary world, under the title of Manon Lescaut, and written by an abbe of the name of Prevost. Manon Lescaut was one of those frail creatures who, in such capitals as Paris and London, run a sinful career of alternate splendor and misery. She had become celebrated by the duels and ruinous extravagances of those who had worshiped at her shrine, and who, to use the expression of Demosthenes, had " purchased repentence too dear."

> "Ah, vice! how soft are thy voluptuous ways!
> While boyish blood is mantling, who can 'scape
> The fascination of thy magic gaze?
> A cherub hydra round us dost thou gape,
> And mold to every taste thy dear delusive shape"   BYRON.

Spite, jealousy, revenge, or the desire of protecting youthful inexperience against Manon's fascinations, designated her to the arbitrary hand of power, and she was seized by those agents of the government who were recruiting for the colonization of Louisiana. Torn from the lascivious chambers of luxury, she was thrown into a common cart with a promiscuous company of female wretches, and hurried to a seaport. All the way from Paris to Havre, a young man of distinguished birth, but forgetful of what was due to himself, to his family, and to society, followed on foot the vehicle which contained the being whom he loved with that intensity of feeling which produces madness. To have stolen interviews with his mistress, he had given all the money and all the trinkets he had in his possession to the ruthless soldiery who composed her escort. When he had nothing left him with which he could hope to soften the obduracy of the guards, he attempted to touch them by making passionate appeals to what later sensibility might remain in their breast. He bore patiently with their cruel rebukes and coarse gibes; his meek despair might have disarmed hatred itself. Pale and haggard, this effeminate-looking child of wealth and aristocracy tottered along on the muddy roads, keeping pace with the closely-muffled vehicle which carried away the object of his affection. The frenzy of love sustained him against fatigues, hardships, and contumelies to which he was unused. The soul had absorbed the body and magnetized it into a state of feverish somnambulism. Physical wants became unknown to him, or were not attended to. In that journey, how he appeased hunger and thirst, and tasted of the sweets of sleep, none saw or knew. He seemed to be unconscious of the cold rains of winter which poured down upon his head, or of the snow which stiffened his garments.

All the pitiless elements of an inclement atmosphere pelted him as if in derision, and he heeded them not!

At last, he arrived at Havre, and on his offering to embark as a colonist, his proposition was accepted. On board of a ship, on the broad bosom of the ocean, he found himself reunited to his mistress. Alas! that guilty love should know such transports! What cared des Grieux for the roaring of the winds, for the gathering fury of the waves, and for the black wrath of the coming storm! What cared he for the lurid obscurity of the tempestuous night! Sunshine, the sunshine of paradise, was in his soul. The deep anguish of a mother, the malediction of a father, the blasted hopes of a noble and useful career,—all was forgotten in the bliss of the hour. That bliss, whatever it was, whether perfect in its ecstasy, or whether disturbed by the stings of conscience, whether "*it brought with it airs from heaven, or blasts from hell,*" was not of long duration. Soon after her arrival at New Orleans, Manon Lescaut died a repentant Magdalen, and with her dying breath recommended to des Grieux to return to the path of virtue from which she had induced him to stray but too long. With his own hands, des Grieux dug the grave to which he consigned the body of Manon, and then, with a lock of her hair forever to be worn on his breast, and with her memory indelibly impressed on his soul, he departed for France,

"In helpless—hopeless—brokenness of heart."

But let us turn from the field of sentiment to a dryer one, where the facts to be collected by the historian, although no doubt more deserving of record, are of a less captivating nature: and let us not lose sight of the details of the administration of affairs in Louisiana.

The directors having called the attention of the government to the changes which new circumstances required in the organization of the colony, the Superior Council of the province was modified by a royal edict promulgated in the month of September, 1719. It was decreed that the new council should be composed *ex officio* of such directors of the company as might happen to be in the colony, of the governor, the two " *Lieutenants de Roi*," or lieutenant-governors, the king's attorney-general, and four other persons. In all civil suits, the quorum was fixed at three, and at five in criminal affairs. In case no quorum could be formed, on account of absence or disease, the members present could complete the number required, out of the ranks of the most respectable persons of the colony. In judicial matters, the jurisdiction of the council was to be only an appellate one, and it was bound to meet at least once in every month. Formerly, the Superior Council had been the only tribunal in the country, and had been clothed with original jurisdiction: but population having increased considerably, it was found necessary to establish inferior courts, and to appoint as judges the directors of the company, or their agents in the several localities where they might reside. Every one of them, with two of the chief men of the vicinage, might take cognizance of any civil affair, and also of criminal matters, with the assistance of four inhabitants having the qualifications required to sit in civil affairs. From their judgment there lay an appeal to the Superior Council. It is to be remarked that, by a special and a very liberal disposition of the royal edict, justice was to be administered without costs to the parties.

The first Superior Council, as formed in conformity with this edict, was composed of Bienville, as governor, of Boisbriant and Chateaugué, as lieutenant-governors, or *lieutenants de roi*, of Hubert, the king's commissary, or *commissaire ordonnateur*, who was appointed *senior* member of the council, and as such with priority of rank over his puisne colleagues: the other members were L'Archambault, Villardo and Legas, agents of the company, and the king's attorney-general, Cartier de Baune. Couture was appointed clerk to the council.

Although the governor occupied the seat of honor at the council board, yet the *senior* councilor was the actual president of that body. By collecting the votes, he ascertained the sense of the tribunal, and he pronounced its judgments. In all preliminary proceedings, such as the affixing of seals, inventories, and other acts of the like nature, he discharged the duties of a judge of the first instance.

It was the anxious wish of Bienville to transfer the seat of government to New Orleans, on the banks of the Mississippi. But he met with great opposition from his associates in power. When the matter was under discussion, it happened that there was an overflow of the river, which laid the infant city of New Orleans under water. This circumstance gave additional strength to the opposition. It was argued that the company could not, for the present, command the means of erecting the necessary embankments to prevent the annual inundations with which that settlement would be threatened. Hubert, the king's commissary, pleaded strongly in favor of Natchez, but as he owned large tracts of land in that locality, his arguments were little heeded, because it was supposed that they were prompted by self-interest. L'Archambault, Villardo and Legas, who were agents of the company, thought that the commercial views of those they represented would be better promoted by keeping the seat of government on the sea-shore. Their opinion prevailed, and according to their wishes, a detachment of soldiers and of mechanics was sent to the east side of the Bay of Biloxi, where houses and barracks were ordered to be constructed. That place was called *New Biloxi*, in contradistinction to the first settlement which was made in that bay, and which was ever after known as *Old Biloxi*.

The time had come at last when the colony was beginning to assume the shape of definite existence. It was still very weak, it is true, but it gave stronger signs of vitality than it had done so far. The extreme fertility of the soil had invited the plow and the spade, and had been found admirably adapted to the cultivation of rice, indigo, tobacco, and cotton. It was almost impossible, however, to induce Europeans to attend to the labors of the field, on account of the heat of the climate, and of the diseases which were produced by exposure. The whole agricultural pursuits of the country were therefore carried on, at that time, by one thousand blacks, whom the company had caused to be transported from Africa to Louisiana. It is to be regretted that agriculture and commerce did not solely engross the attention of the directors. But the experience which had been acquired during the twenty preceding years since the foundation of the colony, and which had acted as a check on the wild hopes of *some* of the directors, had not brought to the minds of *all* the conviction that it was wiser to abandon altogether the costly and time-losing researches which had been made for mines of precious metals. Hence the renewal of similar attempts, which proved equally abortive.

On the 26th of November, a royal edict was issued in conformity with the charter granting to the company the privilege of exclusive commerce with Louisiana. That edict declared to the world that any other vessels than those of the company would, on their resorting to the colony for the purposes of trade, incur forfeiture and confiscation. Such were the events of 1719, among which the most considerable was the conquest of Pensacola.

The opening of the year 1720 was signalized by a proclamation of a remarkable nature, issued throughout the colony in the name of the company. That proclamation informed the inhabitants of Louisiana that they might obtain from the stores of the company at Mobile, Dauphine Island, and Pensacola, all the merchandises and provisions necessary to their wants. In case the colonists should make it a condition of their purchase, that those provisions and merchandises should be delivered at New Orleans, they were to pay in addition a premium of five per cent.;—ten per cent. if to be delivered at Natchez;—thirteen per cent. at the Yazoo;—fifty per cent at the Missouri and Illinois settlements. It was made obligatory upon the colonists to send to New Orleans, to Biloxi, to Ship Island, and to Mobile, the produce of their labor, which the company engaged to purchase at the following prices: silk, according to its quality, from 7½ livres to 10 livres; tobacco, first quality, at 25 livres the hundred pounds; rice, 20 livres; superfine wheat flour, 15 livres; rye, 10 livres; barley and oats, 90 cents; deer skins, from 15 to 20 cents per skin; if dressed and without the head and tail, 30 cents; hides, 8 cents the pound.

It is evident that the colony could not prosper under the system adopted by its rulers. What inducements could any set of men have to emigrate to a country, where they had not only to encounter the dangers of a sickly climate and of savage warfare, but where they were sure to associate with the dregs of the population of the mother country, and to be kept in a state of the most oppressive servitude? They could purchase nothing except from the company, at the prices fixed by it: they could sell to none except to the company, and at the prices which suited its conveni ence: and they could not go out of the colony with out its permission. Was it not servitude—a disguised servitude, not in name but in fact—and much worse than the open and barefaced servitude of the blacks? Where was the difference between the white slaves transported from Europe, and the black ones dragged from Africa by the emissaries of the company? If the blacks worked only for the benefit of their white mas ters, both blacks and whites labored only for the uses and purposes of the almighty company.

Common sense and experience pointed to a different course of action. When in the never-ceasing wars of Europe, a city happened to be depopulated and razed to the ground, what was the policy often pursued by the prince within whose territory it was situated? It was one which never failed to be successful. The sovereign would solemnly declare that all those who should come to rebuild the ruined city should, for a considerable number of years, be exempted from taxes, from paying war contributions in money and in men, and should enjoy the benefit of self-government, together with other franchises, immunities and tempting liberties of every kind. There was such vitality in this system, that the destroyed city would rise in a short time from its ashes with more splendor than it had ever possessed. Then, it is true, would the royal eagle, tired of his long abstinence, flap his wings in triumph, and the human cattle upon whose flesh he claimed the right to feed, would perceive too late that they had been allowed to grow fat for other purposes than their own gratification. Nevertheless, the correctness of the policy was not the less demonstrated, and if applied to Louisiana would have produced similar results. All that she wanted was air for her expanding young lungs—franchises and immunities of every sort instead of the shackles of monopoly and of the fetters of absolute government—freedom of conscience—of thought—of action—every liberty of which man is susceptible in a state of civilization. There would have been a rush to Louisiana from every part of the world, and the population would have increased accordingly. This would have been to the interest of the colony, undoubtedly, but it is not so clear that it would have served the selfish and narrow-minded views of the company. Unfortunately, the colony, instead of being fostered by such liberal policy, was kept in leading-strings so tight, that she gasped for breath, and was restrained from developing her energies. The great mistake was, that the company said to the colonists, "Work for me," instead of saying, "Work for your own benefit."

Peace having been concluded between France and Spain, on the 17th of February, 1720, the Mississippi Company made another attempt to establish commercial relations between Louisiana and the Spanish provinces of Mexico, and even endeavored to push on its settlements in that direction. With this object in view, Bernard de La Harpe was sent to Texas, and constructed, in latitude 33° 25′, at the distance of about two hundred and fifty miles from Natchitoches, a small fort, with the assistance of the Indians, who hated the Spaniards. His next step was to send a messenger with his compliments to Don Martin de Alacorne, governor of Texas, to whom he made propositions relative to the trade which might be carried on between the two nations. Don Martin made a courteous reply, but at the same time expressed his astonishment at the determination taken by the French to settle in a province which was a part of the territory of Mexico. He, therefore, requested La Harpe to inform the governor of Louisiana, by whose authority he acted, that if the French did not voluntarily retire, he would resort to force to compel them to keep within their limits. In answer to the astonishment manifested by Don Martin de Alacorne, Bernard de La Harpe declared that he was equally astonished at the pretensions of the Spanish government, considering that France had always looked upon Texas as a part of Louisiana, since La Salle had taken possession of that country, which still retained his mortal remains. He added, that the French government could not admit that the pretensions of Spain could legitimately go beyond the Rio Bravo, because all the rivers which discharge themselves into the Mississippi, and all the lands which they water, ought indisputably to be considered as belonging to France.

It is worthy of remark, that the French government supported La Harpe in the position he had taken, and that the company, with the express authorization of the king, ordered that possession be taken of the Bay of St. Bernard. This order was executed in 1722: but, after a short trial, the French were obliged to give up the settlement which they had established, on account of the implacable hostility of the Indians, whom they could not resist successfully, because their new possession was too far from their chief establishments in Louisiana, to admit of ready relief. It is not the less true that France always called in question the rights which Spain pretended, with so much tenacity, to have to Texas.

Knowing the activity, the energy, and the other qualifications of St. Denis, the company intrusted him with the command of Natchitoches. The rising prosperity of that settlement had excited the jealousy of the Spaniards, and it was believed that they were meditating its destruction.

The company seemed to have taken to heart the obligation to stock Louisiana with the population of which it stood so much in need, and during the year 1720, more than one thousand Europeans, and about five hundred negroes, were transported to that colony. Of the emigrants, about three hundred were to be located at Natchez, sixty on the concessions of De Guiche, one hundred and sixty were destined for the grant of St. Reine, at the Tunicas, two hundred and fifty for the concession of Le Blanc; and the rest were to settle at the Yazoos.

Until now, the colonists had hardly met with any hostility from the Indians, except from the Natchez, as we have seen, under the administration of Cadillac, when Bienville was sent up the river by that governor to demand satisfaction for the murder of several Frenchmen. But the moment was come when their friendship or indifference was to be changed into an animosity productive of ruinous and disastrous wars to the colonists. So long as the colony had remained so weak that she seemed destined to perish prematurely from the radical vices of her imperfect organization, her neighbors, the English, had not thought proper to hasten the work of destruction. But they took umbrage at the more vigorous administration of the company, which, in spite of all its errors of policy, was employing its capital in efforts calculated, if persisted in, to make of Louisiana an important colonial possession to France. England never sleeps when her interest is at stake: and she began to take active but secret steps to check the progress of French colonization on the banks of the Mississippi. Besides, the French and English traders used to meet everywhere among the Indians, and their opposition or competition in commerce soon produced a deep feeling of hostility. Hence originated frequent and partial collisions, in which the Indians always took part, and in which they never failed to be divided among themselves: one nation, or one part of a nation, assisting the English, while the French, on their side, were not lacking in the same kind of support.

This state of things gave rise to repeated murders, the recital of which would be but a bloody and uniform catalogue, producing much excitement at the time, but of very little interest in our days. Thus, this year 1720 was marked by a war of the French with the Chickasaws, who were under British influence. Their first act of hostility was to assassinate a French officer named Sorvidal, who had been stationed among them by Bienville, as a spy and an agent of the company. After long negotiations, backed by fair promises of remuneration in merchandise, Bienville succeeded in opposing the Choctaws to the Chickasaws. These, and the Natchez, were the three most powerful nations with which the colony had to deal, and we shall see what a conspicuous part they were destined to play in its history. The other smaller Indian tribes remained in a state of neutrality.

By a royal ordinance, the military forces of Louisiana were fixed at twenty companies of fifty men each. Such were, with the few colonists scattered over an immense territory, the only means of resistance which Bienville had to oppose to the Indians, and to the other foes who might threaten the colony.

There were two causes of complaint on the part of the inhabitants of Louisiana, which the French government attempted to remedy. The first, that there was not in the colony a sufficient number of women; and the second, that the people who were sent to colonize the country were of a character which made them dangerous or contaminating associates for such men of peaceful habits and honest principles as had voluntarily come to better their fortunes in the colony. Wishing to redress these grievances, the French government authorized three nuns, Sister Gertrude, and under her, Sister Louise and Sister Bergère, to conduct to Louisiana a certain number of girls who were taken from the hospital-general of Paris, on their consenting to emigrate. They were placed under the special supervision of Sister Gertrude, and could not marry without her consent. It was also ordered by the king that convicts and vagabonds should no longer be transported to Louisiana, because "the king is convinced," said the edict, "that their presence is a contagious source of corruption, not only for the Europeans, but also for the aborigines, who are kind-hearted, honest, industrious, and well-disposed toward the French."

On the 3d of January, 1721, a ship of the company arrived with three hundred colonists, who were destined for the lands granted to Mme. de Chaumont, at Pascagoulas, and in February, eighty girls, who had been taken from a house of correction in Paris, called La Salpétrière, were landed in Louisiana. It would seem that dissolute women were not looked upon as being included in the recent royal edict which prohibited the transportation to Louisiana of vagabonds or persons of bad morals; or it may be that this edict, as it is frequently the case with such things, had been issued merely to stand on paper for some particular purpose, but not to be executed.

Good or bad, however, the population of Louisiana was fast increasing, and the French government thought it sound policy that no agricultural produce should be raised in the colony, which might compete with that of the mother country, and issued accordingly an ordinance which prohibited in Louisiana the cultivation of the vine, hemp, flax, &c. &c. Such was the despotic, selfish, and short-sighted policy of what was then called *the colonial system.*

In spite of all the efforts made by the company, what contributed still more powerfully to retard the progress of the colony was the never-ceasing misunderstanding which had existed among its officers since its foundation. They were incessantly counteracting each other by reciprocal opposition. Between their pulling backward and forward, and the struggle of their contention, the distracted colony staggered in its feeble march, and could hardly keep its ground. The reports made by the agents of the company on the situation of its affairs were of the gloomiest character. The disbursements were enormous, and no gains had hitherto accrued to the stockholders, whose dissatisfaction was loudly expressed. The direction was reproached with having made unwise and uncalled-for expenses, which would never be productive, and with having selected officers more solicitous about their own interests than those of the company. The fall of Law, and the crisis which followed, brought down still lower the shares of the stockholders in the Mississippi Company, and their disappointment became excited into clamorous rage. Frightened by the general burst of indignation which assailed them, the directors wrote to Bienville that the Regent had complained of the paucity and inefficacy of his services; that they had excused him with his royal highness on the ground that the very agents of the company had checked or weakened the execution of all his plans; that they would, in consequence, change those agents, and substitute for them such as would be entirely his subordinates; that he would then have a fair opportunity to show what he could do, when left to his own judgment, and to deserve rewards which would be commensurate with the merit of his deeds; that none but *real* services would gain for him the grade of brigadier-general, at which he aimed, and the great cross of St. Louis, which was the object of his wishes, and which the Regent had promised to bestow upon him when deserved. The directors thus hoped to stimulate the ambition of Bienville into the adoption and the carrying on of a system of administration in the colony, which might prove more advantageous to the company than all the plans which had hitherto been pursued without success.

In the month of March, two hundred German emigrants arrived in the colony. They were sent by Law to settle on his Arkansas concessions, and they had departed from France on the eve of his flight from that kingdom. They were soon followed by five hundred negroes transported from Africa by the company. This was a valuable addition to the population of Louisiana, but the time when it came did not happen to be opportune, on account of the great scarcity of provisions under which the country was then suffering. With these German emigrants there was a woman whose destinies, if they be true as related, bid defiance to the inventions of the wildest romance.

Let us go back to 1712. At that time, the Duke of Brunswick Wolfenbuttel had a daughter named Charlotte, who was a paragon of beauty, of virtue, and of talent. Who would not have loved such a being? And so she was—by every inhabitant of that little duchy. What could be more auspicious than the beginning of such a life! But at that time also, it happened that Peter the Great had a son named Alexis, who, although heir-apparent to the crown, and the future ruler of millions of men, was so steeped in vice, so coated over with stupidity, and so thoroughly imbued with wickedness, that his father, as more than one father has done in such cases, sent him on his travels, perhaps in the hope that he would either mend his nature by accidental circumstances, by a change of air or of sights, by a better knowledge of the world and a more extensive acquaintance with mankind, or that he would break his neck on the public roads. In his peregrinations, the Muscovite prince stumbled on the Lilliputian court of Brunswick, and savagely brutish as he was, he felt the charm which the Princess Charlotte exercised on all that appertained to the human creation. The Tzar Peter heard with surprise of the new and strange impression which had been produced on Alexis, and he was led to think that his son was not altogether deprived (a thing which he had always held in doubt) of that organ which is called the heart. Seizing the occasion by the forelock, he ordered the hopeful heir to the Russian throne to marry the German princess. He considered that the bright rays emanating from the perfections of the wife might penetrate into the dark abyss where the imperfections of the husband were pandering to each other, and that the spirit of good might, to some degree, control the spirit of evil, if linked together.

The poor Duke of Brunswick did not venture to give a denial to the demand made by the haughty and powerful despot of the North. But deep was the gloom which, on that occasion, settled over the whole territory of that little duchy, and the marriage ceremony looked more like a funeral than a wedding. Why not? It was the consecration of the union of the dead with the living—nay, something worse—the hideous conjunction of the putrefaction of the charnel with the ambrosial purity of heaven. Amid the general desolation, there **was** one heart, above all, that was riven asunder, as **if** a wedge had been forced into its very core. Look at that pale face sicklied over with grief! What agony is there not in those eyes fixed on that altar, and on that bride, so lovely and so sad! How fearfully the soul works on the human frame, and how indelibly it writes a tale of woe on that expressive and plastic tablet—the forehead of man! He, whose quivering lips denoted the fearful struggle within, was the Chevalier d'Aubant, a young Frenchman, who was attached to the court of Brunswick, as an officer in the Duke's household. Alas! a common one his fate had been since the creation of woman. He had so gazed on the star of beauty—that he had become mad—mad with love!

Now the Princess Charlotte is on her way to St. Petersburg, and fast travelers are those horses of the Ukraine, the wild Mazeppa horses that are speeding away with her! A fast traveler is the Russian bear, who is carrying to his den the prize he has won, but the real merit of which he no more values, than a turkey would know the worth of the diamond picked up by chance, for want of a brickbat, and swallowed to aid its digestion. Among the wild-looking escort of Cossacks who surrounded the princess there was one, however, who seemed fully to appreciate his new sovereign. With his shaggy bonnet pulled down to his eyebrows, and his tartar cloak closely muffled up to his ears, he rode close to the carriage door, with watchful care, and seeming to scan minutely the dangers of the roads. Day and night, he was at his post. Whenever the horses of the vehicle which carried the prince and his bride threatened to become unruly, his hand was always the first to interfere and to check them; and all other services that chance threw in his way, he would render with meek and unobtrusive eagerness; but silent he was as the tomb. Whenever the princess alighted, deeper and more reverential was his obeisance than that of any of his companions. Once, on such an occasion, no doubt as an honorable reward for his submissive behavior and faithful attendance, the princess beckoned to him to lend her the help of his arm to come down the steps of her carriage. Slight was the touch of that tiny hand; light was the weight of that sylph-like form: and yet the rough Cossack trembled like aspen leaf, and staggered under the convulsive effort which shook his bold frame.

Now the cannon booms, the bells ring merrily, the people shout, drums beat, and a thousand other military instruments strain their brazen throats—the bride of Alexis has come, and enters the imperial palace. On the evening of that very day, a confidential servant slipped into the hand of the Cossack, with whom we have become acquainted, a small sealed bundle, containing two pieces of paper. One was a letter; it ran thus:—

"D'AUBANT,

"Your disguise was not one for *me*. It could not deceive my heart. Now that I am the wife of another, know for the first time my long kept secret—I love you. Such a confession is a declaration that we must never meet again. The mercy of God be upon us both !

CHARLOTTE."

The other paper was a passport signed by the emperor himself, and giving to the Chevalier d'Aubant permission to leave the empire at his convenience. Before the sun was up, next morning, the princess' wish had been complied with, and d'Aubant was already journeying far away from St. Petersburg.

Whither he went, no one knew, but in 1718, he arrived in Louisiana with the grade of captain in the colonial troops. Shortly after, he was stationed at New Orleans, where, beyond the discharge of his duties, he shunned the contact of his brother officers, and lived in the utmost solitude. No fault was found with his want of sociability, because although his physiognomy was calm and placid, yet there was in it that indescribable expression which indicated that under it lurked such sorrow as commanded respect and sympathy.

On the bank of Bayou, or river St. John, on the land known in our days as Allard's plantation, and on the very site where now stands the large and airy house which we see, there was a small village of friendly Indians. From the bank opposite the village, beginning where at a much later period was to be erected the bridge which spans the Bayou, a winding path made by the Indians, and subsequently enlarged into *Bayou Road* by the European settlers, ran through a thick forest, and connected the Indian village with the French settlement of New Orleans. With the consent of the Indians, in order the better to indulge in his solitary mood, d'Aubant had there formed a rural retreat, where he spent most of the time he could spare from his military avocations. Plain and rude was the soldier's dwelling; but it contained, as ornament, a full length and admirable portrait of a female surpassingly beautiful, in the contemplation of which d'Aubant would frequently remain absorbed as in a trance. There was in this painting a remarkable feature, no doubt allegorical. Near the figure represented, stood a table on which lay a crown, resting not on a cushion, as usual, but on a heart which it crushed with its weight, and at which the lady gazed with intense melancholy. This painting attracted, of course, a good deal of observation, but no one dared to allude to it. By intuition, every one felt that it was sacred ground on which inquiry ought not to tread.

Where was all the while the Princess Charlotte, the gilded victim of imperial misery? Was she beloved as she deserved by her lord and master, Alexis Petrowitz, the stupid son of Peter the Great? No! the brute had been true to his groveling nature; the swine had gone back to its sty; the gross and sensual appetite of the man, who knew naught beyond the gratification of lustful passion, had turned away from the ethereal charms of the goddess; the prince had bestowed his affections, such as they could be, on one of the female scullions of his kitchens,—a Cossack maid,—a she bear worthy of her mate. One day, entering his wife's apartments, in a state of half-inebriation, he insisted upon her receiving his paramour into her household among her maids of honor. Mild was her negative answer, but decisive and dignified in its tone. Heated by the fumes of his deep potations, fiercely impetuous by the nature which he inherited from his father, and which education had not modified, excited by such contradiction as he was not used to meet, the barbarian prince gradually worked himself into a paroxysm of frantic rage, foamed at the mouth like an infuriated dog, and with the wild gestures and terrific shrieks of a maniac, rushed upon his wife, whom, with repeated blows, he laid prostrate on the floor, senseless and cold in apparent death. Of the bystanders none dared to interfere to protect the victim of brutality; for although dignified with the names of noblemen and gentlemen, they were slaves, and their master a despot. But the justice of heaven was not asleep; and when, not many years after, Alexis the brute showed an undoubted and immutable determination to arrest, when power should be his, the civilization which Peter the

Great was imparting to Russia, Europe stood aghast on witnessing a father butchering his own son.

But the princess has recovered from her swoon, and she is left alone, with her friend and bosom companion, the Countess of Kœnigsmark. Long did they converse together in subdued tones, and what they said none ever knew. But if one had, with indiscreet eye, observed the expression of their faces and the nervous contraction of their whispering lips, he would have conceived that these feeble beings had been roused into the commission of some deed of desperate energy. It was evident that the cup of bitterness had overflowed; that enough had been meekly, patiently borne with; that the limits of human endurance had been passed; and in those flashing eyes, although they were those of women, there could be seen the deep-seated resolve, the stern decree of immutable fate. That very night, the Countess of Kœnigsmark entered secretly the princess' room, and there was reacted that scene where **Friar Lawrence** says to Juliet:

> "Take thou this phial, being then in bed,
> And this distilled liquor drink thou off:
> When, presently, through all thy veins shall run
> A cold and drowsy humor, which shall seize
> Each vital spirit; for no pulse shall keep
> His natural progress, but surcease to beat.
> No warmth, no breath, shall testify thou liv'st;
> The roses in thy lips and cheeks shall fade
> To paly ashes; thy eyes' windows fall,
> Like death, when he shuts up the day of life
> Each part deprived of supple government,
> Shall stiff, and stark, and cold, appear like death;
> And in this borrowed likeness of shrunk death
> Thou shalt remain full two-and-forty hours,
> And then awake as from a pleasant sleep.
> Now when the bridegroom in the morning comes
> To rouse thee from thy bed, there art thou dead.
> Then, (as the manner of our country is,)
> In thy best robes uncovered on the bier,
> Thou shalt be borne to that same ancient **vault**,
> Where all the kindred of the Capulets lie."

The imperial funeral took place, and according to the plan which had been laid, the whole of Europe was deceived. The Princess Charlotte of Brunswick Wolfenbuttel, the *wife* of Alexis Petrowitz, was no more, but the *woman* was not dead—the Juliet that loved a Romeo had burst out of her tomb—poor indeed, unknown, without rank, without family, without menial attendance, but free, with the whole world before her, and with Love and Hope for her handmaids. That was enough!

With the two hundred emigrants who had arrived in March, 1721, there had come, as I have already said, a woman who, by her beauty and by that nameless thing which marks a superior being or extraordinary destinies, had, on her landing at New Orleans, attracted public attention. She immediately inquired for the Chevalier d'Aubant, to whom she pretended to be recommended. She was informed that he was at his retreat on the Bayou St. John, and that he would be sent for. But she eagerly opposed it, and begged that a guide should conduct her to d'Aubant's rural dwelling.

It was on a vernal evening, and the last rays of the sun were lingering in the west. Seated in front of the portrait which we know, d'Aubant, with his eyes rooted to the ground, seemed to be plunged in deep reverie. Suddenly he looked up—gracious heaven! it was no longer a mere inanimate representation of fictitious life which he saw—it was flesh and blood—the dead was alive again—and confronting him with a smile so sweet and sad—with eyes moist with rapturous tears—and with such an expression of concentrated love as can only be borrowed from the abode of bliss above. " O God!" exclaimed d'Aubant, starting up and convulsively pressing his forehead with his hands, " what phantasy of a fevered brain is this! Mercy on me!—I am mad!" But soon he felt that the being who nestled in his bosom, that the arms folded round his neck, were not creations of a delirious imagination. What pen could do justice to this scene? Away then with description! What need should there be of any effort of the mind to paint what the heart can so easily conceive! Suffice it to say that, on the next day, the Chevalier d'Aubant was married to the mysterious stranger, who gave no other name to the inquiring priest than that of Charlotte. In commemoration of this event, they planted those two oaks, which, looking like twins and interlocking their leafy arms, are, to this day, to be seen standing side by side on the bank of the St. John, and bathing their feet in the stream, a little to the right of the bridge, as you cross it, in front of Allard's plantation.

It is strange how the most secret events will transpire! With the fluidity of gas, they evaporate through thick walls of stone, and are scattered over the whole world. For instance, what gave currency at the time to the circumstances which I have related? By what concealed agency events are known with astonishingly minute precision in distant places, long before they could be carried there by any physical process? Is it second sight, magnetic perception, supernatural intuition, or the electric traveling of the mind? Are there mysterious carriers of news through heaven and earth? Certain it is, that although d'Aubant and his wife kept their own secret and lived in almost monastic retirement, rumors about their wonderful history were so rife in the colony, and the attention of which they became the objects, subjected them to so much uneasiness, that d'Aubant contrived to leave the country soon after, and went to Paris, where his wife having met the Marshal of Saxe in the garden of the Tuileries, and being recognized by him, escaped detection with the greatest difficulty. D'Aubant departed with the grade of major for the Island of Bourbon, where he resided for a considerable time. In 1754, on his death, his widow returned to Paris with a daughter, the only offspring of her union with d'Aubant, and in 1771, she died in a state bordering on destitution. The particulars of this adventure are found in many memoirs of the epoch, and in the notes and papers of Duclos: but Lévesque, in his history of Russia, Grimm, in his correspondence, and the sceptic Voltaire, in a letter which he published on the 19th February, 1781, deny the truth of the story as being too improbable. However, the experience of centuries teaches us that nothing is more probable than improbabilities: and must it not be inferred that there was some foundation for the romantic incidents I have recorded, when they assumed such a substantial shape as to become a subject of serious controversy with men of the highest distinction?

On the 5th of September, a council of administration for the affairs of the company in Louisiana was organized, and composed as follows:—the governor, the lieutenant de roi, or lieutenant-governor, the directeur ordonnateur, or commissary director, the chief director, and sub-director of accounts. This council was to meet every day at New Biloxi, where its members were bound to reside, with the exception of Bienville, the governor, who was permitted to reside at New Orleans. The deliberations of the council were to be faithfully recorded: of which journal, copies were to be sent to France, and it is to be regretted that this record has not been transmitted to us.

It was ordered, by a decree, that the merchandise of the company should be sold at New Orleans, Biloxi, and Mobile, at fifty per cent. profit on their original cost in France; at Natchez and Yazoo, seventy per cent.; at Arkansas, at one hundred per cent.; and at the Alibamons, at fifty per cent., on account, as it was expressed, *of the competition arising from the proximity of British settlements.* On the 27th of the same month, it was determined that negroes should, on an average, be sold to the inhabitants for 660 livres, for which their notes were to be furnished, on three years' credit, payable by equal instalments, either in tobacco or in rice, according to agreement. When two terms became due, if the purchaser could not pay one third of the amount, the negroes were resold, after due publication, and after notice given of the sale to the public. When the result of the sale was not such as to pay the company, and to meet all other expenses, the debtor was liable to imprisonment.

Tobacco, *en feuilles*, or leaf tobacco, fair quality, was to be received in payment of negroes, at the rate of twenty-five cents per hundred pounds, and rice at twelve cents, when delivered at the company's warehouses at New Orleans, New Biloxi, or Mobile. Wine was to be sold by the company at 120 livres per cask, and brandy at the same price for a quarter of a cask.

Louisiana was divided into nine territorial districts, such as New Orleans, Biloxi, Mobile, Alibamons, Natchez, Yazoo, Natchitoches, Arkansas and Illinois. There were to be for each district a commander or governor, and a judge from whose decisions appeals could be taken to the Superior Council, sitting at New Biloxi. This order of things was established, as stated in the decree, *to put justice, with greater ease, within reach of the colonists.*

In the month of June of the year 1721, there remained in the colony six hundred negroes, and four hundred out of the five hundred colonists who were in the country, when Crozat had given up his charter Seven thousand and twenty individuals had been transported by the company in forty-three vessels specially employed for that purpose, from the 25th of October, 1717, to May, 1721. But of this number about 2000 having died, deserted, or returned to France by permission, the remaining white population did not exceed 5420 souls. The expenses of administration, however, although the territory was so thinly peopled, proved very considerable, and amounted, this year, to 474,274 livres.

A ship of the company had left France in 1718, with troops and one hundred convicts, but had never been heard of. Toward the close of the year 1721, there arrived in Louisiana, a French officer who gave some account of the ill-fated vessel. It appears that her captain had mistaken the mouth of the Mississippi, and had entered, by the 29th degree of latitude, into a large bay, where he at last, but too late, discovered his error. Hardly had the ship anchored, when a contagious epidemic broke out among the convicts, and produced such dreadful havoc, that five of the officers, named Belleisle, Allard, De Lisle, Legendre and Corlat, thought that it would be less dangerous for them to land, well provided with arms and with eight days' provisions, than to remain on board in a pestiferous atmosphere. Their hope was to meet with some friendly Indian who could guide them to the French settlements, which they conjectured to be not far off. In the mean time, the ship sailed away, and of her there never was any further tidings. For several days the five adventurers wandered in every direction without discovering any habitation, or meeting any human being. They exhausted their provisions and ammunition, and had to rely altogether on the scanty supply of food they could procure. Unused to the climate, broken down by privations of every kind, Allard was the first to perish;—De Lisle followed;—soon after Legendre dropped into the grave which Corlat and Belleisle dug for him. Then these two men looked at each other with mute despair in that boundless wilderness by which they were encompassed, and they seemed to scrutinize each other's face to ascertain which of the two would bury the other one. A few days had hardly elapsed, when Corlat bade a last farewell to Belleisle, and yielded the ghost. Belleisle covered his companion's corpse with dry leaves, branches and bushes, and then threw himself on the ground with the determination to die. But the love of life is strong in man's breast, and at last he braced up his energies to escape from the death he had but lately coveted. He sought the sea-shore, where he lived on the contents of shells, on fish, and on roots, anxiously passing many a weary day in studying the broad expanse of the Gulf of Mexico, with the hope that some vessel might heave in sight.

Months elapsed—and there was no prospect of relief. His tattered clothes had dropped from his limbs: exposed to all the inclemencies of the weather, living on unwholesome food, sometimes deprived of any, worn out by mental anxiety as well as by bodily sufferings, he was reduced to a frightful state of emaciation;—and with his overgrown shaggy hair and beard, he looked more like a wild beast than a man. His strength was gradually failing, he felt that life was fast ebbing away, and that a slow, lingering death—the death of starvation—was staring him in the face. One day that he was lying on the ground, incapable, as he thought, of motion, and with his feeble vision scanning the horizon which seemed to dance round him, as it receded and faded away from his swimming sight, he fancied he saw a light grayish smoke rising slowly above the distant trees, in the heart of the forest. Oh! how his heart leaped within his breast!—he shaded his eyes with his tremulous hands, and looked again with fearful doubt and agonizing anxiety. Yes!—it was a smoke! And the gladful conviction flashing on his soul, drew a flood of tears down his wasted and hollow cheeks. He raised his skeleton hands toward heaven, and with a full heart thanked the Almighty. Then up to his feet he sprang—but he staggered back and fell. Good God! will the miserable remnant of his physical powers, although so powerfully stimulated by the prospect of relief, fail him entirely when most needed—at such a critical moment! Making a desperate effort, he rose again and reeled forward to some distance. Then, he crept along like a snake—now panting with exertion and fatigue—now resting awhile—now again dragging himself painfully, with his eyes stretched and riveted on the merrily curling smoke. Oh! how he trembled that it should suddenly disappear! His excitement grew more intense as he drew nearer, and at last he thought that he was within hearing distance. He shouted, or thought he shouted; but his parched throat emitted no sound which reached his own ears.

Three Indians were quietly seated round a brisk fire and roasting luscious venison, the juice of which falling on the live embers produced a grateful hissing sound, and emitted a savory smell, when a slight cracking—the snapping of a dry twig, caught their attention and awoke their suspicion. With one simultaneous bound they sprung—one with uplifted tomahawk—the other two with raised bows ready to fling their deadly arrows. But they dropped their weapons, when they ascertained what object stood before them. It was Belleisle who, with imploring gesticulations, made appeals to their pity. The Indians looked at each other wonderingly, and as it were, in rapid consultation, when one of them beckoned to Belleisle, inviting him to approach the fire and partake of their fare. There they remained encamped until he could walk, and then they took him to their village, where he was kept in a state of servitude during eighteen months. He swept the cabins of his masters, cleaned their weapons, planted their corn, cooked their victuals, and performed all the other services of a menial. A severe trial he had of it —the half-starved drudge!—the overtasked hewer of wood and drawer of water to barbarian tyrants! At last an Indian of the tribe where he was held in captivity, stole from him a small tin box which his masters had permitted him to retain, and which contained his commission as an officer, and other papers. The thief sold the box to a member of the Assinais tribe. These Indians lived in Texas, not far from the French settlement of Natchitoches, with which they had frequent intercourse. The new owner of the box, thinking that it might be valuable to his white neighbors, and that he might sell it to them with advantage, carried it to that market, where, of course, it attracted attention, and was exhibited to St. Denis, the commander of Natchitoches. It gave rise to inquiry, and St. Denis, being informed of the melancholy situation of one of his countrymen, dispatched some Indians to treat for the ransom of Belleisle, who was safely conducted by them to Natchitoches.

Such were all the remarkable events which occurred in 1721.

In the year 1722, on the 12th of March, the company issued an ordinance which prohibited the inhabitants of Louisiana from selling their negroes, for transportation out of the colony, to the Spaniards, or to any other subjects of a foreign nation, under the penalty of a fine of one thousand livres and confiscation of the negroes.

On the 20th of April, Bienville wrote from Fort St. Louis at Mobile, to the French government, an interesting communication on the difficulties attending the unloading of vessels on the shores of Biloxi, on account of the shallowness of the water; which difficulties he represented as not existing in the Mississippi. "I have had the honor," said he, "to send to the council in my last letter detailed information on the mouths of the Mississippi, and to give the assurance that vessels not drawing more than thirteen feet water could go over the bar with all sail set, without risk of stranding. It would not be difficult to render the pass practicable for larger ships, because the bottom consists of soft and moving mud. I would have already done so, if the engineers who are intrusted with the execution of the public works had shared my opinion. But their attention is engrossed by the improvements which have been attempted at Biloxi, and which I think will have to be abandoned. Should the company persist in sending their vessels to Biloxi, it will materially retard the progress of the colony, and will expose us to considerable expenses. The vessels are forced to stop at Ship Island, which is fifteen miles from the main land where our settlement is situated. To unload these vessels, we are obliged to send to Ship Island packet-boats, which, in their turn, can not approach Biloxi nearer than two miles and a half. Then, other small boats are sent to unload the packet-boats, and these boats, small as they are, strand at a distance of carbine-shot from the shore. This statement of facts ought to be sufficient to convince the council of the importance of ordering all vessels coming from France to enter the Mississippi, where they would discharge their cargoes in two days. I assumed the responsibility of sending thither two *flutes* (small vessels), which crossed the bar with all sails set. I would have done the same with the other vessels, which have just arrived, if we had not received the precise order of unloading them at Biloxi."

It is really astonishing that, in spite of the judicious and self-evident representations of Bienville, backed by the physical structure of the country, the French government should have so obstinately and for so many years clung to the bleak and worthless shores of Biloxi, as the chief settlement of Louisiana, and its most important commercial emporium. But there is very little common sense to be discovered in the administration of most colonies by the mother country, and particularly in that of Louisiana under the French domination.

On the 20th of May, it was decreed that there should be in the Superior Council, five councilors instead of four, and those councilors were, Bruslé, Fazende, Perry, Guilhet and Masclary.

On the 4th of June, a vessel of the company arrived with another band of two hundred and fifty Germans, commanded by the Chevalier d'Arensbourg, a Swedish officer, who had so distinguished himself at the battle of Pultawa, that he had been presented by Charles the XIIth with a sword, which is still in the hands of his descendants in Louisiana. This vessel brought back to the colony Marigny de Mandeville, who, in 1709, it will be remembered, had joined in the systematic opposition made to Bienville by the commissary La Salle and the Curate de la Vente. Marigny had obtained in France the cross of St. Louis and the command of Fort Condé at Mobile.

With this vessel came the confirmation of the utter discomfiture of Law, and of the ruin and desolation which his plans and banking operations had generated in France. It produced a great sensation in the colony, because the inhabitants were afraid of being left to their own resources, and of being lost sight of, on account of the general distress which reigned in France, and which was sufficient to absorb all the attention and resources of the government. Their apprehensions, however, were not immediately realized to the extent which they anticipated, and they continued, through part of the year, to receive some further supplies and assistance. On the 15th of July, Duvergier, who had been appointed *directeur ordonnateur et commandant de la marine*, landed at Pensacola, bearing crosses of St. Louis to Boisbriant, to St. Denis, and to Chateaugué, who, it will be remembered, had been made prisoner at Pensacola by the Spaniards, when they retook that place, and who had lately been exchanged.

Although, as it has been shown in the course of these lectures, many importations of females had been made, the want of them continued to be sensibly felt, and to be a subject of complaint on the part of the colonists. As a specimen of the tone and manners of the time, I think it is not out of place to record here an extract from a letter addressed on that subject to one of the king's ministers in France, by one M. de Chassin. It bears a stamp of originality which is quite characteristic. "You see, my Lord," said he, "that to assure the solidity of our establishment in Louisiana, there is but one thing wanting—a sufficient number of women. However, woman is a piece of furniture which many repent of having introduced into their household, and without which I shall contrive to get along until, as I have had already the honor to inform you, the company shall think proper to send us girls having at least some appearance of virtue. If, by chance, there should be among your female acquaintances one disposed to risk the voyage for my sake, I should certainly be greatly under her obligation, and would most assuredly do my best to give her proofs of my gratitude."

This M. de Chassin, who presumed to write in such a style of familiarity to one of the king's ministers, has left no other trace of his passage in Louisiana than this jocose application for a wife. It is likely, from his name, from the lightness of his tone, and from the perfect ease with which he addresses one of the great dignitaries of the kingdom, that he was a scion of nobility, who had been invited to travel to, and to stay in Louisiana, until his morals or his purse should have recovered from the effect of the commission of youthful follies.

Toward the close of the year, the supplies which used to be sent from France became more scanty on account of the disorderly state into which the affairs of the company were falling. Famine made again its appearance in the colony, as it had frequently done before, and it became necessary, from the want of provisions, to quarter some of the troops, in small squads, among the Indians, and to scatter the rest on the banks of rivers, where they lived as they could, on fish and game. Twenty-six soldiers who constituted the garrison of Fort Toulouse among the Alibamons, being reduced to very short allowance, and suffering too acutely and too long from their wants, butchered their captain, Marchand, and with their arms and baggage departed for South Carolina. Villemont, their lieutenant, who, when the murder of Marchand took place at the fort, happened to be absent, and whose life was saved by that circumstance, on hearing of what had occurred, made an appeal to the Indians as friends of his government, and persuaded them to pursue with him the rebellious deserters. They soon overtook the fugitives, who, knowing the fate they had to expect if they surrendered, fought with desperation, and were killed almost to a man.

Fortunately, toward the latter part of September, the colony was relieved by the arrival of a vessel well stocked with provisions and ammunition. It brought the information that the Duke of Orleans, Regent of France, had intrusted the direction of the affairs of the company to three Commissaries, Ferrand, Faget and Machinet.

The distress of the colony was increased by a hurricane which produced the most extensive damage, and De l'Orme, one of the principal agents of the company, who, in a letter of the 30th of October, renders an account of the effects of that hurricane, speaks of continual desertions among the soldiers, mechanics and sailors, and recommends, as a remedy to the demoralizing influence of such derelictions of duty, to allow, in all the vessels of the company, free passage to those persons who might be disposed to return to France.

The paper currency of the colony had been reduced to such a state of discredit, that it had ceased to pass and to answer its purposes. Hence a complete cessation of business. It was necessary to meet that evil, and the company had recourse to a process which was not deficient in ingeniousness, whatever may be said of its want of good faith. The paper currency to which I allude, consisted in notes signed and issued by the directors of the company in France, or by its commanders, officers, or chief agents in the colony. It was decreed that all these *notes* should be converted into *cards*, to which some fair promises and additional privileges were attached to give them value, and that all the notes which should not be presented at certain places to certain agents, and within a time remarkably short, to be converted into *cards*, as desired, should become null and void in the hands of the bearers. These notes being scattered through an immense extent of country, many could not be brought back, partly through want of time and partly through carelessness or indifference, and became thereby extinct according to the decree. In this way a considerable portion of the company's debt was liquidated at once.

Sheep, mild as they are, will bleat obstreperously when they are sheared too close by the shepherd; and the inhabitants of Louisiana, following this example, complained so loudly that, by an ordinance issued on the 28th of December, they were authorized to send an agent with full powers who would advocate and defend their interests before the Council of State, by which the affairs of the company were to be taken into consideration and adjudicated upon. On the 8th of the same month, the Council of State had dispatched Saunoy and de la Chaise to Louisiana, to force the agents of the company to render an account of the merchandise sent by the company, and of the goods which had been delivered to those agents by the clerks of Crozat, when the company was substituted for him in the government of the province. They were instructed to depart with the utmost secrecy and speed, to show their powers to the Superior Council on their arrival in Louisiana, then immediately to repair to the company's warehouses, to take possession of them, and to put the seals on all the papers of the agents.

Thus it is seen that the situation of affairs was gloomy enough. To make it worse, the Natchez recommenced war against the French. They murdered three of their traders, and attacked the *Kolly Plantation*, which was situated in the neighborhood of their villages, and where they killed a man and destroyed a considerable number of cattle.

The three commissaries, Faget, Machinet, and Ferrand, who had been selected by the Regent to assume the direction of the affairs of the company, had certainly been appointed to no sinecure. They had to cope with the discouragements of the colonists, who were constantly attempting to run away from their miseries—with the desertion, the insubordination, and rebellious disposition of the troops—with a depreciated paper currency, heavy debts, hurricanes, and other calamities—with unfaithful and roguish agents—with the spirit of discord, which had always existed among the officers of the colony;—and now, in addition to these numerous perplexities, they were threatened with a war from the Natchez.

The three new commissaries who had assumed the direction of the affairs of the company, of which they were now the sole administrators, sanctioned the execution of two projects which, for a long while, had been favorite conceptions with Bienville, but which he had never been permitted to carry into operation. He was authorized to transfer the seat of government to New Orleans, and to make at the Arkansas a settlement, the chief object of which was to establish a connecting point between the Illinois and the lower part of the colony, and to facilitate the introduction of horses, mules, and cattle from the Spanish provinces. Bienville, as soon as he received the desired authority, ordered La Harpe, with a detachment of sixteen men, to ascend the Arkansas River as far up as possible, to make an accurate survey of the country, to look for mines, and to inform the Spaniards he might meet, that all the territory watered by the Arkansas River, from its source down to its mouth, was regarded by France as belonging to her, in consequence of the possession taken of it by La Salle when he descended the Mississippi.

Thus closed the year 1722.

THIRD LECTURE.

Origin, Customs, Manners, Traditions, and Laws of the Natchez—Decline of that Tribe—Number and Power of the Choctaws and Chickasaws.

THE soil of the colony of Louisiana had been, from time immemorial, tenanted by an infinite number of small insignificant Indian tribes, the mere recapitulation of which would uselessly occupy more than one page. Suffice it to say, that they had a very similar appearance, like twins fresh from the womb of nature. There were, it is true, some differences in their dialects—some varieties in their customs, laws, and manners—merging, however, in the same uniformity of savage existence and of confirmed barbarism. In the dark twilight of uncivilized ignorance in which they lived, the distinctive shades existing between their moral, intellectual, and physical features were hardly perceptible, and are certainly not of sufficient importance to attract the notice and to call for the investigation of the historian. *De minimis non curat historia.* But an exception is to be made in favor of the three most important nations of that country, on account of their numbers, of their power, and of the considerable and direct influence which they exercised over the destinies of the colony. These nations are the Natchez, the Choctaws, and the Chickasaws.

In 1722, the Natchez could bring into the field six hundred warriors. The time, however, was not far distant, when they could have set on foot four thousand able-bodied men. But from different causes acting with frightful rapidity, their population had been dwindling away, and they seemed to be incompetent to arrest the gradual destruction of their race. If vague and indistinct tradition is to be believed, the cradle of the Natchez nation was *somewhere near the sun*, whence they came to Mexico; which country was their resting-place for some centuries. But they were probably driven from it in consequence of civil wars in which they were defeated. Some of the depositaries of their legendary lore even said, that their nation had been one of those that aided Cortez in overthrowing the empire of Montezuma. But soon perceiving that the Spaniards were disposed to exercise over them a tyranny worse than the one from which they had sought to escape by breaking the power of the great Aztec emperor to whom they were subjected, they determined to seek another clime, where they might enjoy in peace and in perfect freedom their ancient nationality. They followed the rising sun from east to west, and came to those beautiful hills in Louisiana, which they selected for their new home. In those days, the country which they occupied extended from Manchac to Wabash, and they could boast of five hundred Suns, or members of the royal family. Now, in 1722, they were confined to a contracted territory and to a few villages, the principal of which was situated three miles from Fort Rosalie, on a small water-course, at the distance of about two miles and a half from the Mississippi. The other villages were within a short distance of the principal one, where resided the sovereign.

Their government was a perfect Asiatic despotism. Their sovereign was styled the *Great Sun*, and on his death, it was customary to immolate in his honor a considerable number of his subjects. The subordinate chiefs of the royal blood were called *Little Suns*, and when they also paid the inevitable tribute due to nature, there was, according to their dignity and the estimation they were held in, a proportionate and voluntary sacrifice of lives. The poor ignorant barbarians who thus died for their princes, did it cheerfully, because they were persuaded that, by escorting them to the world of spirits, they would, in recompense for their devotion, be entitled to live in eternal youth and bliss, suffering neither from cold, nor from heat, hunger, thirst, or disease, and rioting in the full gratification of all their tastes, desires, and passions. These frequent hecatombs of human beings were one of the causes, it is said, which contributed to a rapid diminution of that race. But as this sanguinary custom appears to have been very ancient, and almost coeval with their formation into national existence, how is it that they should ever have swelled up to be such a powerful and numerous tribe as they are represented to have been at one time? It is alledged that the other causes of destruction were,—a state of constant warfare, the prevalence of affections of the chest or lungs in the winter, and the invasion of the small-pox.

The Natchez were of a light mahogany complexion, with jet-black hair and eyes. Their features were extremely regular, and their expression was intelligent, open and noble. They were tall in stature, very few of them being under six feet, and the symmetry of their well-proportioned limbs was remarkable. The smallest Natchez that was ever seen by the French was five feet in height: considering himself a dwarf, and, therefore, an object of contumely, he always kept himself concealed. Their whole frame presented a beautiful development of the muscles, and men were not seen among them, either overloaded with flesh, or almost completely deprived of this necessary appendage to the human body—no bloated, fat-bellied lump of mortality contrasting in bold relief with a thin and lank would-be representative of a man. The sight was never afflicted by the appearance of a hunchback or some other equally distorted wretch, such as are so often observed among the European race. In common with all the aborigines of Louisiana, they were flat-headed—which was a peculiar shape they liked, and into which they took care to mold the skulls of their offspring when in their infancy. The women were not as good-looking as the men, and were generally of the middle size. The inferiority of the female sex to the male, with regard to the beauty of personal appearance, is a remarkable fact among all the Indian tribes, and is, no doubt, to be attributed to the state of degradation in which their women are kept, and to the painful labors to which they are subjected.

The Natchez had shown a good deal of acute invention in providing themselves with all the implements necessary to their wants. To cut down timber, they had flint axes ingeniously contrived, and to sever flesh, either raw or cooked, they had knives made up of a peculiar kind of keen-edged reed, called *conchac*. They used for their bows the Acacia wood, and their bow-strings were made either with the barks of trees, or the skins of animals. Their arrows, made of reed, were winged with the feathers of birds, and when destined to kill buffaloes, or deer, their points were armed with sharp pieces of bone, and particularly of fish-bone. The Natchez understood the art of dressing, or preparing buffalo, deer and beaver skins, and those of other animals, so as to provide themselves with very comfortable clothing for the winter, and they used, as awls for sewing, small thin bones, which they took from the legs of herons. Their huts were made of rude materials, such as rough timber and a combination of mud, sand, and Spanish moss worked together into a solid sort of mortar and forming their walls, to which they gave a thickness of four inches. The roofs were of intermingled grass and reeds, so skillfully put together, that these roofs would last twenty years without leaking. The huts were square, and usually measured fifteen feet by fifteen;—some, however, such as those of the chiefs, had thirty feet square, and even more. They had no other aperture, for egress or ingress, or for admitting light, than a door which generally was two feet wide by four in height. The frames of the beds of the Natchez, which rose two feet from the floor, were of wood, but the inside was a soft and elastic texture of plaited or weaved up reeds: and those unsophisticated sons of nature had, to rest during the day, nothing but hard and low wooden seats, with no backs to lean against.

Their agriculture, before they became acquainted with the French, who taught them the use of wheat and flour, was limited to the cultivation of corn, which they knew how to grind with a wooden apparatus. Their women had arrived at considerable proficiency in the manufacturing of earthenware, and they made all sorts of pots, pitchers, bottles, bowls, dishes and plates bearing designs, among which it is pretended that Grecian letters and Hebrew characters are plainly to be discovered. Their crockery was generally of a reddish color. They also excelled in making sieves, bottles, and winnowing fans. With the bark of the linden or lime-tree, they made very beautiful nets to catch birds or fish. They knew how to dye skins in several colors, of which those they liked best were the white, the yellow, the red, and the black, and their taste was to use them in alternate stripes. The skins thus dyed, particularly that of the porcupine, they embroidered with considerable art, and the drawings were somewhat of a gothic character. They also made bed-coverings and cloaks with the bark of the mulberry-tree, and with the feathers of turkeys, ducks, and geese. Like the other Indians, the Natchez had not carried very far the science of navigation, and to cross rivers, they had imagined to scoop the trunks of trees, which they shaped into canoes. Some of their largest canoes measured forty feet in length by four in width: they were generally made to carry twelve persons, and were exceedingly light. These boats were propelled by the means of paddles six feet long.

During the summer, men and women were always half naked and bare-footed, except when traveling. Then they would wear shoes made of the skin of deer. For ornaments, they wore rings or painted bones through their ears and noses, and in the shape of bracelets round their arms and legs. They were also very fond of painted glass-beads, which they interwove in their hair, or carried round their necks in the shape of collars, to which they added the teeth of alligators, or the claws of wild beasts. These same painted glass-beads they also used in ornamenting their leather garments, and they composed with them fanciful embroideries. The vermilion with which they painted their bodies was one of their favorite embellishments, together with the hieroglyphic figures, or crude heraldic devices, with which they used to impregnate their skins from head to foot. On being made acquainted with those small bells with which mules are decorated, they became very fond of having them about their persons in as great profusion as they could, and were delighted with the merry ringing which attended the slightest of their motions. They shaved the back part of their heads in the man ner practiced by the religious orders among the Roman Catholics, leaving in the midst of the crown five or six locks of hair, wherewith to tie feathers. The rest of the hair was clipped round, friar-like, with the exception of a long twisted tuft which was left dangling down on the left shoulder, and at the extremity of which feathers were fastened on feast days. The sovereign wore round the head a net-work of black thread, to which adhered a diadem of white feathers eight inches in height on the forehead, and dwindling down to four behind. It was surmounted by a tuft of fur, out of which shot up a small crest of horse-hair, one inch and a half in height, and painted red :—it had a picturesque effect.

As soon as a child was born, the mother rose up, and going to the next stream, washed it thoroughly. Then she came back to her hut, and placed the child in its cradle, which was usually two feet and a half long, by eight or nine inches in width, and six inches in height. This cradle made of reeds was very light, hardly weighing two pounds, and was always placed on the very bed of the mother, so that she might conveniently nurse her child. The motion of the cradle was not sideways, as of those used by Europeans, and which must produce the unpleasant sensation experienced in a ship rolling at sea, but forward and backward like one of our modern rocking-chairs. The most watchful maternal care was bestowed upon the children, who were never allowed to stand on their legs before they were strong enough to make the attempt without too much effort, and they were allowed free access to their milk diet from the parental breast as long as they pleased, unless the mother's health, or her peculiar situation, should have prevented its continuance. Every day, they were rubbed with oil, to render their limbs more flexible, and to prevent the bites of flies or mosquitoes.

When boys reached their twelfth year, they were committed to the charge of the oldest man of their respective families, who was called "*the Ancient.*" He undertook to superintend their education, and to impart to them all necessary knowledge and desired qualifications. Under his tuition, they learned to swim, to run, to jump, to wrestle, and to practice with the bow or other weapons, and they received from his lips those moral lessons or precepts which were to regulate their behavior, when they should be grown into manhood. A bunch of hay, as big as the fist, was generally put at the top of a stick, as a target at which they shot with their arrows. The most successful carried the prize, and received the praise which the *ancient* usually awarded him: and as a pre-eminent distinction, he was styled *the Young Warrior*. The next one in skill was called the *Apprentice Warrior*. It is to be remarked that blows were never given to boys as a corrective, but only moral means were resorted to, and appeals were made to their feelings of pride or of shame. The most profound respect was paid to the oldest member of every family—to the *ancient*, whose decisions were supreme, and received with the most implicit obedience. Thus the head of a family was called *father* by all its members, however distant their blood relations might have been to him: and whenever these Indians meant to speak of him from whom they really derived their existence, they used to say, *my true father*, in contradistinction to the word *father* applied to the chief of the family. In old times, a similar respect was paid by our Caucasian race to the experience and dignity of age, but now it is a custom, the breach of which is much more faithfully adhered to than the observance.

When three years old, the children of both sexes were every morning, summer or winter, taken to some stream to bathe in, and in this way they learned how to swim, and at the same time they fortified their bodies so as to endure with ease the hardships to which they would be exposed in the course of their lives. But as it is the case with all the Indians of North America, the men were educated to be only warriors and hunters, and the women to do all the work and drudgery which were necessary for the comfort of their own existence and that of the lordly sex which kept them sunk down to a state of profound inferiority. In one thing, however, they were superior to more civilized nations— quarrels and fights were exceedingly rare among them. The penalty for such transgressions was to live for a certain time in utter seclusion, apart from the rest of the tribe, the culprits being considered as having forfeited their character, and as being unworthy of associating with decent and respectable people. The fear of the infliction of such a disgrace had always proved to be a very effective preventive. In fact, the education which the Natchez received made them so cautious of trespassing on each other's rights, that the few penal laws which existed among them had seldom to be enforced.

As they were ignorant of the art of writing, their history consisted in tradition handed down from one generation to another; but in order to secure to it as much authenticity as possible, a certain number of their most intelligent, discreet, and trustworthy young men were selected to be educated in the knowledge of their traditionary lore, which they were taught and sworn to respect as sacred, to preserve with religious fidelity, and to transmit in their turn to their successors, with exact minuteness. They were called *the repositories of the voice of the past, of the ancient word;* and from time to time they were requested to recite before the old men of the nation what had been deposited, and was to be treasured up in their memory, in order that it might be ascertained whether they would make themselves guilty either of omissions arising from design, oblivion, indifference, and carelessness, or of additions and interpolations proceeding from the exuberance of fancy, or from the pruriency of invention. This shows a respect for historical truth which can not be too highly commended, and which ought to be set up as an example deserving of imitation by our modern recorders of events.

The Natchez had two languages;—which peculiarity existed also among the Peruvians. One was called the *vulgar*, that is, the dialect reserved for the common people, who were permitted to speak no other. The other one was used altogether by the nobles and by the women. Both these languages were said to be very rich, and had no affinity to each other. For instance, he who would have wished to bespeak the attention of a plebeian, would have said "*aquenan,*" *listen*, and to a noble, "*magani,*" which has exactly the same meaning; to a plebeian, "*tachte cabanacte,*" *is it thou?* and to a noble, "*apape-gouya-iche;*" to a plebeian, "*petchi,*" *sit down*, and to a noble, "*caham.*" In the language of the vulgar, "*coustine*" signified *spirit*, and "*tchite*" meant *great*. In the language of the nobles, the word "*coyocop*" meant *spirit*, and "*cliquip*" *great*. These examples are sufficient to show the want of analogy which existed between these two languages. The women, as I have already said, spoke the language of the nobles, but with an affected and quaint pronunciation, totally different from that of the men. The French, who associated more with the women than with the other sex, had taken their pronunciation; which circumstance provoked a rebuke addressed to one of them by a Natchez magnate: "Since thou hast the pretension to be a man," said the chief to the Frenchman, "why dost thou lisp like a woman?"

The Natchez believed in a Supreme Creator of the universe, and they designated him by the name of Coyocop chile, which meant, *Coyocop, spirit; chile, infinitely great.* They thought that, as they expressed it, "*all they saw, all they might see, and all they were not able to see,*" proceeded from him—that he was so good and kind that he could not do harm if he wished; that mere conception and volition on his part had been sufficient to generate every thing; that there were however subordinate spirits, called *Coyocop techou,* who were perpetually standing in his presence, and implicitly obeying his mandates like slaves; that every thing which was bad and calamitous in this world was produced by evil spirits as invisible as the air in which they lived; that these evil spirits formerly had a chief who worked so much mischief, that the Great Spirit had chained him in a dark cell, since which time the evil spirits, his subjects, were not so constantly bent upon doing injury, particularly when they were softened by respectful prayers. Whenever the Natchez wished for rain or fair weather, they had recourse to fasting, and frequently on such occasions their sovereign, the Great Sun, would, during nine consecutive days, abstain from meat and fish, and live altogether on a little boiled corn. He would also take particular care, during all that time, to have no intercourse of any kind with his wives. The Natchez believed in a deluge which had destroyed mankind with the exception of a few people, who had taken refuge on a high mountain, and who had repeopled the earth.

According to the religious creed of the Natchez, the

Great Spirit had molded the first man out of the same kind of clay with which they made their crockery, and being satisfied with his work, had breathed life into it. As to woman, they did not know exactly how she had been created. There were various traditions on this subject. One of them reported, that a short time after the first man was gifted with existence, he was taken with a violent fit of sneezing, when something in the shape of a woman, as big as the thumb, bolted from his nose, and on falling on the ground, kept on dancing with extreme velocity until it grew into the present size of the female sex.

Many centuries before the Natchez came to the banks of the Mississippi, they were living in a condition of almost brutish ignorance, when there appeared among them a man and a woman who had descended from the sun. They were clothed all over with light, and looked so dazzlingly bright that no human eye could long dwell upon their forms. This man told them that from the realms of the sun he had seen that they were the miserable victims of anarchy, because they had no master, and did not know how to govern themselves, while every one of them, although incapable of self-government, thought that he was competent to rule over the rest of his race. Wherefore, he had taken the determination to come down upon earth to teach the Natchez how to live. His moral precepts were few in number and suited to the circumstances of the people he intended to legislate for. The most important ones were not to kill any human being except in self-defense; to be satisfied with the possession of one's own wife, and not to covet that of any other man; never to tell a lie; never to be inebriated; and never to take the property of another. He also strongly recommended generosity, charity, and the distribution of one's goods among the destitute.

This man spoke with such authority that he produced the deepest impression on the Natchez. While he was reposing with his wife in the hut to which they had conducted him, the old men of that nation met in a solemn conclave in the dead of the night, and the next morning they went in great ceremony to the wonderful stranger to propose to him to be their sovereign. He refused at first, saying, he knew he would not be obeyed, and that, much to his regret, this want of obedience would be death to all the Natchez. But yielding at last to repeated solicitations, he accepted on the following conditions: that the Natchez would emigrate to a better country, which he would point out to them; that they would live strictly according to the laws to be established by him, and that their sovereigns would forever be of his race. "If I have," said he, "any male and female issue, there shall be no intermarriage among them, they being brothers and sisters. But they shall be permitted to wed from the bulk of the people. The first-born of my sons shall be my successor, and then the son of his eldest daughter, or in case he should have no daughter, the son of his eldest sister, or in his default, the eldest son of the nearest female relation of the sovereign, and so on in perpetuity."

Then he went into the minutest details concerning the laws of succession to the throne, and provided for all possible contingencies. He called down fire from the sun, and ordered that it should be eternally kept up with walnut wood, stripped of its bark, in two temples, to be built at the two farthest extremities of the country to be occupied by the Natchez. According to his instructions, a body of eight men was selected out of the nation as ministers or priests for each temple.

Their duty was to watch in turn the sacred fire, and on its being extinguished, the guardian then on the watch was to be punished with death. The mysterious lawgiver that had come from the sun, predicted the most awful calamities to the Natchez, if the sacred fire was ever allowed to go out entirely in both temples. Should it be extinguished in one, the guardians were to relight it by hurrying to the other temple. But they were not to be allowed to borrow the sacred fire peaceably. They were to fight for the holy spark, and were not to carry it away before shedding blood in the contest, on the floor of the temple, as a sort of propitiatory offering to the evil spirits.

Implicit obedience was sworn to all the mandatory dispositions of the new sovereign, and he signified that he wished to be called "*thé*," which meant "*thee*." He lived to very old age, saw the children of his grandchildren, and was the author of all the institutions which prevailed among the Natchez, until that nation was destroyed. He certainly was, in the most emphatic sense of the word, their supreme legislator, their Lycurgus. After his death his children were called *suns*, on account of their origin. He established no sacrifices, no libations, no offerings. The only worship which he prescribed, if it can be so called, was the keeping of the sacred fire, and one of the first duties of the Great Sun was to watch over the strict fulfillment of this charge, and to visit one of the temples every day for this purpose.

The Natchez had great national festivals, which partook of a religious and political character. These festivals were religious in one sense, as being instituted with the object of returning thanks to the Creator for his manifold benefits; and they were also essentially of a political nature, as they were the only sources of the revenue of the sovereign; because, although despotic in his authority, and the absolute master of the lives and property of his subjects, he never imposed taxation nor levied contribution, and he remained satisfied with the presents which were made to him on these great festivals.

For the Natchez, the year opened in March, and was divided into thirteen moons. The thirteenth moon was added to make the course of that planet correspond with that of the sun, and to complete the year. On every new moon a great feast was celebrated, and took its name from the fruits which had been gathered, from the game which had been pursued, or from the usual occupations of the people during the preceding moon. Thus, the year began in March with the celebration of the *moon of the deer*. It was the most joyous and the most important celebration. There was rehearsed a sort of dramatic performance, recalling the memory of an historical event which had left a deep impression upon the Natchez.

In days of old, a Great Sun, having heard the uproar of a sudden tumult in his village, issued precipitately from his dwelling, to appease what he supposed to be a quarrel among his people, and fell into the hands of a hostile nation, by which his capital had been surprised. But the Natchez recovering from their astonishment and dismay, came in time to the rescue, delivered their sovereign, and put to flight their enemies with immense slaughter. In commemoration of this honorable event in their history, their warriors, at the beginning of every year, in the *moon of the deer*, would divide themselves into two bodies, made distinct by the colors of their feathers. Those who represented the Natchez, wore white feathers, and those who acted the enemy, sported red feathers. Both these troops put themselves in ambuscade near the residence of the sovereign. The enemies, commanded by the *Great Chief of the Warriors*, who was always the most distinguished general of the tribe, some such thing as an Alexander, a Cæsar, a Bonaparte, or a Wellington, were the first to issue from their place of concealment, and approached with slow steps the house of the *Great Sun*, but shouting all the while to the full top of their voices, and distorting their bodies into every sort of fantastic contortions. Then the *Great Sun* came out full dressed, but rubbing his eyes as if just awaking. The foes, shouting their death-cry, threw themselves upon him and carried him away.

In their turn, the Natchez came rushing on, and encountered their enemies with terrific howls and shrieks, making an appalling compound of all the tones and exclamations expressive of fear, anger, despair and revenge. Then followed, during half an hour, a scene of mimic warfare, in which both parties displayed all the stratagems they could invent, and all the military skill they possessed. During all that time, prodigies of valor were performed by the *Great Sun*, who stoutly defended himself with a wooden tomahawk. The enemies by whom he was enveloped, fell in heaps under his simulated blows, and strewed the ground with their corpses. At last, the Natchez succeeded in routing the hostile warriors, whom they pursued to a considerable distance; and delighted with such a complete and glorious victory, they returned to their village, bearing aloft in triumph their sovereign, making the welkin ring with their joyous shouts, which were merrily responded to by the echoes of their hills. The old men, the women and children came forward to meet the returning host, and joined with noisy demonstrations in the general jubilation. The French writers report that the spectacle of this mimic battle was exceedingly interesting, and that it was so true to nature in all its incidents, and produced such a complete illusion, that no one could witness it without the liveliest excitement.

The *Great Sun*, being escorted back to his dwelling, retired to rest, and while he was reposing, his subjects, who feigned to be ignorant whether he was wounded or not, rambled about the village, uttering groans and plaintive sighs. After the lapse of about half an hour, the Great Sun came out, bareheaded, and without his crown. He was joyfully and respectfully saluted with shouts and every demonstration of enthusiastic greeting. But profound silence ensued among the people, when they saw their sovereign advancing in the direction of the temple. When in front of the edifice, he bowed with profound reverence, as if in adoration. Then he gathered dust, which he threw back over his head, and turned successively to the four quarters of the world in repeating the same act of throwing dust. After this, he looked fixedly at the temple, extended both his arms horizontally, as motionless as a statue, and praying all the while. His subjects observed the deepest silence while this was going on; and on his returning to his house, the groans of the people recommenced, and ceased only when he reappeared with the royal diadem round his temples. Then, his throne, which was a stool four feet high, decorated with curious devices, and covered with a fancifully painted skin, was brought before his door. On his taking his seat, his warriors threw over his shoulders a choice buffalo hide, and under his feet a carpet of costly furs. The rest of his subjects and the women presented him also with various offerings, according to their means. This was the first tribute of the year paid to the sovereign.

When this ceremony was over, the princes of the royal blood, called the *Little Suns*, entered the palace with the *Great Sun*. On this occasion, if there were strangers of distinction in the village, they were invited to dine with the sovereign. In the evening, dances were executed round the royal dwelling, which was built on an artificial mound, measuring eight feet in height by sixty feet square.

The second moon, which corresponded with our month of April, was called the *moon of strawberries*. The women and children gathered a considerable quantity of this fruit, and did not fail to present to the *Great Sun* his full share of the harvest. On that occasion, the warriors tendered him a liberal offering of wild ducks, which were smoked for preservation. This was the second tribute.

The third moon, in the month of May, was called the *moon of old corn*, in which they feasted on the balance of corn remaining from the preceding year, after having paid to their sovereign what they considered his due. This was the third tribute.

The fourth moon, or June, was called the *moon of water-melons*. To the Great Sun was offered a large supply of this fruit, and of fish caught in the Mississippi, and carefully pickled. This was the fourth tribute.

The fifth moon, or the month of July, was called the *moon of peaches*. Then, the sovereign received his provision of wild grapes and peaches. It was his fifth tribute.

The sixth moon, or the month of August, was called the *moon of blackberries*. Full baskets of this fruit were laid before the Great Sun, and he was abundantly supplied with every kind of domestic fowl. It was the sixth tribute. Every one of those moons was attended with feastings and rejoicings.

The seventh moon, or the month of September, was

the *moon of new corn*, the celebration of which consisted in eating in common, with certain religious ceremonies, a quantity of corn which had been planted and cultivated to that effect. To plant that corn, a space of uncleared, virgin land was selected and prepared for cultivation by the warriors, who used fire to kill the trees, and to remove the grass, furz, canes, or other vegetable rubbish which might encumber the ground. On the land being ready, the corn had to be planted by the warriors, under the command of the *war-chief*. None were allowed to work in the sacred field but the warriors, and it would have amounted to profanation, deserving of death, for any other person to join in that labor. When this corn began to ripen, the warriors chose a well-shaded spot, where they constructed a barn in the shape of a large round tower. They called it "Momo ataop," which signified, *barn of value*. When the barn was filled up with the new corn, the sovereign was informed of that fact, and fixed the day on which, in his presence, it was to be eaten in common. Then, temporary huts, made for the occasion, with the lopped off branches of trees, with sweet-smelling grass, fresh leaves, and green moss, were erected for the Great Sun, and all his people, to protect them against the inclemencies of the weather, during the feast, which always lasted several days. At dawn, on the day appointed, all the old men and the adults, the women and children, departed with the necessary utensils, to make the required preparations. The war-chief placed sixteen warriors, among whom were eight veterans, at the door of the sovereign, and eight others at regular intervals of one hundred paces each, from the royal dwelling to the place of rendezvous. Their duty was to act as sedan-bearers to the Great Sun. After making these dispositions, the war-chief went to the meeting-place, where, putting himself at the head of the rest of the warriors, he patiently waited for the arrival of the sovereign.

Now, the royal sedan is at the door of the palace. Its four arms are painted red, and its body is richly decorated with fancifully painted and embroidered deerskins, with leaves of the magnolia, and with garlands of white and red flowers. Out comes the sovereign in full dress, and with all the marks of his dignity. The sixteen warriors, stationed at his door, utter successive shouts as loud as human lungs will allow. The eight warriors who are placed at a distance of one hundred steps, repeat these shouts with the same vehemence, which shouts are almost instantaneously transmitted from throats to throats to the place where the people are congregated, and where they are informed in this way of the coming of their sovereign. On his issuing from his door, the eight old veterans lift him up into the sedan supported by the eight other warriors, who depart with him full speed, and run as fast as they can. At every hundred steps, the sovereign finds a fresh relay of eight men, and travels with the greatest rapidity, followed by those who have successively borne him, and who utter deafening shouts, which are nothing, however, to those bellowed forth, when he appears in sight of the whole nation assembled. He is first carried in triumph round the barn, which he salutes respectfully with three howls, to which the people respond with nine distinct and measured howls. Then he ascends his throne, and familiarly converses with his nobles. During that time, what is called *new fire*, is made by rubbing two sticks together. Every other kind of fire would be looked upon as profane. When all is ready, the *war-chief* presents himself before the throne of the Great Sun, and says to him, "Speak — I wait for thy command." Then the Great Sun rises.

bows reverentially to the four quarters of the world, beginning with the East. He next raises his hands and eyes toward heaven and says, "Let the corn be distributed." The war-chief thanks him with one prolonged howl, the princes and princesses with three howls, and the common people with nine, with the exception of the women and children, who observe a profound silence.

After a certain lapse of time, when it is supposed that the repast is prepared, the *word-bearer*, or *chancellor* of the Great Sun, says to the master of ceremonies: "See if the victuals are properly cooked." Then, two dishes of corn are brought to the Great Sun, who goes out of his hut, presents them to the four quarters of the world, and sending one of them to the war-chief, says, *Pachcou, eat*,—a command which his subjects joyfully and eagerly obey. The warriors eat first, then the young men and boys, and next, the women and young girls. When the warriors have done, they form themselves into two opposite bands, occupying two sides of a square fitted up for the occasion, and they sing with alternate choruses during about half an hour. Those songs are always of a warlike character. The war-chief puts an end to that concert, by striking with his tomahawk the red post which is erected in the midst of the square, and which is called the *Warrior's post*. Then begins what may be called the *declamation scene*, which is opened by the war-chief. With an emphatic tone he relates his exploits, and boasts of the number of foes he has killed. He concludes by making an appeal to the bystanders in confirmation of the truth of his assertions, to which they assent with a loud *ululatus* or howl. All the warriors follow the example of their chief, according to their rank, and like him recite their heroic deeds. In their turn, the young men are allowed to strike the painted post, and to say, not what they have done (their military career not having yet begun), but what they intend to do. The youths that speak well are encouraged with a howl from the warriors, who, when they disapprove, show it by hanging down their heads, and remaining silent. The desire to elicit the approbation of their superiors excites the warmest emulation among the young men, and taxes to the utmost all the energies of their minds.

When night comes, two hundred torches made of dry reeds, and frequently renewed, illumine the square, where the Indians dance until daylight. There is great monotony in these dances. A man sits down with a large kettle in which there is a little water, and which is covered over with deer-skin drawn as tight as possible. With one hand, he holds the kettle between his legs, and with the other he beats time on this kind of rude drum. The women form a circle round him at a certain distance from each other, and have their hands thrust into a ring of feathers which they twirl round their wrists, while they move in cadence from left to right. The men form another circle next to the one of the women, and keep at a distance of six feet from each other. Every one of them has his *chichicois*, with which he keeps time. The *chichicois* is a sort of oblong gourd bored at both extremities: through these holes a stick is run, the longest outside part of which serves as a handle. In the gourd there are small stones, or dry beans, which, when shaken, produce a considerable noise. As the women turn in dancing from left to right, the men move from right to left. The dancers, when fatigued, withdraw, and are often replaced by others. In proportion as the number of dancers increases or diminishes, the circles grow larger or smaller.

The next day, the Indians do not leave their huts

before they are summoned out by the Great Sun, who, at nine o'clock, makes his appearance on the public square, and where, having promenaded for some time with the war-chief, he orders the kettle-drum to be beaten. Then the warriors come out of their huts, and form themselves into two bands, to play at tennis. The one, with white feathers, is headed by the Great Sun, and the other, with red ones, by the war-chief. The game is: for one party to drive the tennis ball in the direction of the hut of the Great Sun, so as to make it strike the hut, and for the other party to oppose it, and to push the same ball toward the dwelling of the war-chief, with a similar intent. The contest generally lasts two hours, and is at an end when the ball strikes either hut. Then come war-dances; and in the evening, to refresh their wearied limbs, the people amuse themselves with bathing. This feast continues until the corn is eaten up, with the exception of what is reserved for the Great Sun, who alone has the privilege of carrying some of it away. It constitutes the seventh tribute.

October is the *moon of the turkeys;* November, the *moon of the buffaloes;* then follow the *moon of the bears*, the *moon of the geese*, the *moon of the chestnuts*, and the *moon of the walnuts*. On each of these moons, the Great Sun receives his monthly tribute.

There were some very remarkable traits in the national character of the Natchez, among which was the pre-eminence allowed to the male over the female sex. In all assemblies, either public or private, even in the privacy of the family circle, the youngest boys had the precedency over the oldest women, and when all the members of one family sat down to their meals, a boy, two years old, received his food before his mother was helped. Whatever impression this circumstance may have produced on the temper of the Natchez women, it is certain that so much docility was inculcated by education into their minds, that a quarrel between husband and wife would have been looked upon as something monstrous.

If the women were docile and very industrious, they were, according to our standard of morality, extremely addicted, when unmarried, to the lowest profligacy. Strange to say, this profligacy was a merit in the estimation of the Natchez. Thus, all their women, while single, were allowed to sell their favors; and she who had acquired the wealthiest marriage portion by this abominable traffic, was looked upon as having the most attraction, and as being far superior to all the females of her tribe. She became an object of competition, and received the homages of the loftiest and most renowned warriors. However, as soon as they were married, these professed courtesans were immediately transformed into as many Lucretias, and both husband and wife became patterns of fidelity. They said, in explanation of this change in their conduct, "that having solemnly given away their persons, they had no longer a right to dispose as they pleased of that which they had pledged to another." The married woman being thus so remarkable for fidelity, industry, and docility, matrimonial happiness was as common among the Natchez as it is rare among other people, and although they had the right of repudiation, they very seldom exercised it; —a thing which is not to be wondered at, since no one must be supposed to be willing to renounce the sweet slumbers which he enjoys under the soft rays of a perpetual honey-moon.

Marriages were never contracted without the unanimous assent of the elder members of the two families. When that was obtained, the two heads of the families, or the two *ancients*, or *fathers*, as they were called, met and settled the preliminary conditions. The young people were never forced into alliances against their will, but at the same time they could not gratify their inclination without its being approved by those members of their families to whom they owed respect and obedience. It was thought that no one had a right to introduce into a family a member that would not be acceptable. It is clear that the philosophy of elopements was not understood by those barbarians, and was reserved for a more refined state of civilization.

When a marriage had been determined upon, the head of the family of the bride, *the ancient*, went with her and her whole family to the residence of the bridegroom, who there stood surrounded also by his own family. The oldest man on the side of the bridegroom welcomed his compeer in age on the side of the bride, with this brief salutation: "*Cabanacté*"—*is it thou?* "*Manatté*"—*yes*, answered the other. "*Petchi*"—*sit down*, replied the first. Then the whole assembly took seats, and the most grave and profound silence followed the laconic dialogue which I have related. After a lapse of a quarter of an hour, the oldest man rose, and ordering those who were to be united to stand before him, he addressed to them an allocution, in which he recapitulated all the duties they voluntarily assumed, and gave them abundant and wholesome advice. When this sermon was over, the father of the bridegroom handed to his son the present which he was to make to the family of his future wife, and the father of the bride stepped forward and put himself by the side of his daughter. Then the bridegroom said to the bride, "Wilt thou have me for thy husband?" She answered, "With all my heart; love me as much as I love thee, for thou art and thou shalt be my only love." When these words were uttered, the bridegroom held over the head of his bride the gift which he presented to her family, and said, "I love thee: therefore do I take thee for my wife: and here is the present with which I buy thee from thy parents." Then he delivered the present to the father of the bride.

The bridegroom wore a tuft of feathers at the top of the plaited lock of hair which fell down on his left shoulder, and at the lower end of which was tied an oak twig with its leaves. In his left hand he held a bow and arrow. The tuft of feathers was an emblem of the power and command which he had the right to exercise in his household; the oak twig signified that he was not afraid of going to the woods in quest of game; the bow and the arrows meant that he would always be ready to meet a foe, and to defend his wife and children.

The bride had in her left hand a green twig of the laurel tree, and in her right hand an ear of corn. The laurel twig signified that she would preserve her fame ever fair, and smelling as sweet as the laurel leaf; the ear of corn meant that she would know how to prepare it for her husband's food, and to fulfill the other duties imposed upon her as a loving and a dutiful wife.

When the bridegroom and the bride had exchanged the words which I have recited in the preceding paragraphs, the bride dropped the ear of corn which she held in her right hand, and tendered that hand to the bridegroom, who took it and said, "I am thy husband." She replied, "I am thy wife." Then the bridegroom went round, and grasped the hand of every member of the family of his wife. When this was over, he took her by the arm and led her to every member of his own family, to whom she was introduced by him, and with whom she shook hands. In conclusion, he walked with her to his bed, and said to her, "Here is our bed; keep it undefiled."

Does not the simple relation of their marriage rites carry the mind back to those antique customs which Herodotus has described in such bewitching style? Are they not impregnated with the soft graces of the poetry of Greece?—and, at the same time, do they not assume a character of scriptural austerity and beauty! To me the whole scene is redolent with the atmosphere of Arabia, and conjures up in my imagination the glows and tints of the patriarchal days so beautifully described in the Holy Book.

The nation of the Natchez was composed of three classes: the Great Sun, or the sovereign, and the Little Suns who constituted the nobility; then came the men of consideration or gentry. The plebeians were known under the appellation of "miche quipy," or the *stinking*. The Natchez, in order to be sure that their sovereigns should always be of the blood of the man who had come from the sun to civilize them, had established as a fundamental law of their national polity, that the right of succession to the throne should be imparted to the men only through the female line. Thus the female descendants of a Great Sun always remained noble, and retained the privilege of giving birth to the sovereign; but the grandson of a Great Sun was no more than a *man of consideration*, and his great-grandson became a plebeian—one of the *stinking*—while nobility was perpetual in the female line. After some generations the nobles, although from the same parent stock, were not related at all, or not at least within those degrees which prevented matrimonial alliances; and yet they could not intermarry on account of two fundamental laws: one prescribing that none of the nobility should be put to death, and the other ordaining that, after the death of a male or female noble, his wife or her husband should be immolated. The nobles were therefore obliged to abstain from marrying among their equals; which obligation was revolting to the pride of many. There are very few women who have not a leaning to aristocracy, and this may be owing to the innate distinction of their nature. Thus it appears that this custom, which forced them to marry among the plebeians, or stinking, had become offensive to their proud and delicate nostrils. Le Page du Pratz relates a singular attempt made by one of them to produce a revolution, or a change in the organic laws of her tribe.

Le Page du Pratz had lived eight years in the French settlement near the Natchez, and had become well known among those Indians, who held him in high esteem. One day a female Sun entered his room with her daughter, a girl of eighteen; she locked the door carefully, and sat down for a few minutes in deep and dignified silence. Le Page, knowing the gravity of Indian manners, wondered all the while at the meaning of this mysterious visit, but said nothing, and patiently waited for the communication which would be made at last. After having rested in silence as long as she thought becoming, she rose and thus addressed Le Page: "We all know, and I know better than any body else, that thou art a true man; that falsehood abideth not in thy heart, and that thy tongue hateth the profusion of words. Thou speakest our language. We love thee as a brother, and we regret that thou art not one of our Suns. I have matters of deep import to communicate—wherefore open thy ears and thy heart to receive the impression of my words. But close thy mouth, and never trust to the winds what I am to say to thee in secrecy!" Here she stopped again, and after a short silence observed, as if in doubt, "But shall I be listened to?" Now she remained mute for a considerable time, and seemed buried in profound meditation. Le Page, whose mind was teeming with conjectures about this strange scene, broke the silence he had preserved so far, and said, "My ears are open as thou wishest, and yet I hear nothing but the whistling of the wind."

Then she resumed her discourse in this manner: "My daughter, whom thou seest here, is young; but if she has the weak body of a woman, she has the strong mind of a man. Therefore, knowing that her lips are sealed, I have not feared to bring her with me, and to let her hear my words to thee. When thy countrymen speak, I listen, because although many are light-headed, some are wise and know much. I have heard them say that some of our customs are bad and wrongful; that in their country the noble marries with the noble, and the ignoble with the ignoble, and that each class fares the better for it; that it is cruel to force the wife to die with her husband, and the husband with the wife; that the Great Spirit, whose laws the French follow as they are communicated to them by the '*speaking bark*' which he gave them, frowns on such a barbarous custom; that it is an error to believe that husband and wife can continue to live as such in the world of spirits, because spirits have no solid bodies and no sexes, wherefore they can not cohabit and procreate; and that it is foolish in the Natchez to believe that they will have *there* the same pleasures and avocations which they pursue *here*. I have pondered on their remarks concerning these matters and many others, and I think they talk with wisdom. Our customs are bad, and lead to the destruction of our race. But how are we to change them? Who will have the energy and power to make the attempt, and to crush all opposition? Therefore have I come to thee whom I love, trust, and respect. Marry my daughter; she is the nearest of kin to the Great Sun, and thy son, if she brings one to thee, will be our sovereign on a future day. Educated by thee, and supported by the French, he will have the mind, the will, and the power to change those laws which you look upon as nefarious."

Le Page was taken by surprise, and at first was at a loss for an answer. He knew that there are certain propositions of which women never forgive the rejection; and as he was not willing to incur deadly hostility, he sought to frame an answer which would make his refusal palatable. "Thy daughter," said he, "is as fair as the rainbow, and my heart leaps toward her. But far away, at the place where I was born, is a blue-eyed woman, to whom I am married, and to whom I must return as soon as I can. While she lives, the God whose laws I obey, forbids that I should take unto my bosom another wife. It is an obstacle, as thou seest, which can not be removed. Therefore, be satisfied with my thanks and my gratitude." The old female Sun listened with evident disappointment, and hung down her head as if in sorrow; but she gave no sign of ill-feeling or resentment. Saluting Le Page with truly royal dignity, and putting meaningly her index on her lips, she departed with her daughter. This anecdote has a raciness which vouches for its authenticity, and is an interesting illustration of the ideas which were originating from the association of the Natchez with the French.

The Natchez, when they had causes of war, pursued, before they began hostilities, a certain preliminary course, which, being almost general among the Indian tribes, must be looked upon as proceeding from a custom which must have been their *law of nations*. The old warriors composed what was called the council of war, to deliberate on that question. If they came to the conclusion that their nation had been injured, they sent an embassy to seek redress. If that redress was granted, they smoked the calumet of peace, which was a pipe ornamented with a variety of decorations, and with feathers of the white eagle set in the shape of a fan. If satisfaction was refused, the ambassadors speedily returned home, and the warriors assembled for the war-dance, a ceremony during which they smoked the calumet of war, which was shaped like the calumet of peace, but with the exception, that its ornaments and colors were different, and that its fan was composed of the feathers of the flamingo. Their warriors were divided into three classes: the *true warriors*, or those whose courage had been tried on all occasions, and had invariably been found the same at all times; the *ordinary warriors;* and the *apprentice warriors*, or young men, who were beginning their military career. A formal declaration of war consisted in a hieroglyphic picture, executed in a rude manner, an left by the nation declaring war, near the principal village of the nation against which war was declared. It was intended, I suppose, for some such manifesto as is published in our days, on the like occasions, by the civilized nations of Christendom.

When war was resolved on, they painted their bodies in various colors, so as to make themselves as frightfully-looking devils as possible, and prepared for battle by feasting: a practice which they held in common with the Spartans. On a day solemnly fixed, they gathered in circles round all the delicacies which they could command, such as fish, deer, buffalo, or bear meat, either fresh or smoked, and particularly a roasted dog, which was a dish as much esteemed by them as a roasted peacock by the Romans: corn was liberally used, and was dressed in various ways, of which the most relished was one which is still in fashion among the old French population of Louisiana, and which is called "*sagamité*." They drank on this occasion an exhilarating beverage, which consisted in a fermented liquor, made with the leaves of the Cassia berry-tree. To this feast the warriors always came fully equipped, and with their weapons in the best order. Before the warriors partook of the repast set before them, the oldest among them, so old as to be incapable of active service in the field, holding the calumet of war in his right hand, made a speech, in which he recited his exploits, and exhorted his companions to emulate his deeds. One of them once concluded his address in this way: I give it as a sample of this kind of oratory

"Now, my brothers," said he, "depart with confidence. Let your courage be mighty, your hearts big, your feet light, your eyes open, your smell keen, your ears attentive, your skins proof against heat, cold, water, and fire. If the enemy should be too powerful, remember that your lives are precious, and that one scalp lost by you is one cause of shame brought upon your nation. Therefore, if it be necessary, do not hesitate to fly, and in that case, be as wary as the serpent, and conceal yourselves with the skill of the fox, or of the squirrel. But although you run away, do not forget that you are men, that you are true warriors, and that you must not fear the foe. Wait awhile, and your turn will come. Then, when your enemy is in your power, and you can assail him with advantage, fling all your arrows at him, and when they are exhausted, come to close quarters, strike, knock down, and let your tomahawks be drunk with blood."

This rough kind of eloquence seldom failed to provoke enthusiastic shouts. Satisfied with the effect he had produced, the orator filled the calumet of war with tobacco, drew a puff, and passed the instrument to the war-chief, from whom it circulated among the rest of the warriors. When this was over, the war-chief cut a slice of the roasted dog, the other warriors did the same, and ate while they walked very fast, to signify that a good warrior ought not to stop even to take his food, that he ought to be constantly in motion, and ever watchful like a dog. Then they sat down and began their repast in earnest. But a young man, who was placed in ambuscade at a distance of two hundred or three hundred steps, suddenly shouted the death-cry; spontaneously all the warriors seized their weapons, and ran to the spot from which issued the shout. When they came to it, the same young warrior repeated the same shriek, to which all the warriors responded in the same manner.

Then, they came back together to continue the repast which they had abandoned, but hardly were they at it, when another young man repeated the same operation, which produced the same effects. After several interruptions of this kind, which were intended as practical lessons, the war beverage, composed, as I have already said, with the leaves of the cassia berry-tree, was introduced, to the great satisfaction of the warriors, who partook very freely of the intoxicating liquor. When the eating and drinking was over, the warriors planted the war-post, which was painted red, and the top of which was shaped so as to represent the head of a man. Every warrior, in his turn, rushed furiously at the post and struck it with his tomahawk, in uttering the death-cry. He then recited his exploits with emphasis, and insulted the war-post, which represented the enemy. He concluded his taunting speech with a tremendous howl, which was answered by the other warriors. When every one of them had gone through this monotonous exhibition, they began the war-dance, which they executed in their war-dress, and with all their weapons about their persons. While the warriors were thus engaged, the rest of the nation assumed the garb of affliction, and observed a strict fast. The war feast lasted three days: after which, the warriors marched against the enemy with all the provisions prepared for them by their wives.

Pitched battles among the Indians were of rare occurrence. War with them consisted in ambuscades and surprises. They delighted in picking up some stragglers from the nation against which they were warring —poor wretches who, while fishing, hunting, or engaged in some other peaceful avocations, were startled by the unexpected and terrific whoop of an unmerciful foe. But the greatest of all exploits for them, was, to surprise a village at night, to kill and scalp all the men, to burn down to the ground all the habitations, and to carry away all the women and children, when they did not kill them on the spot, while intoxicated with rage and with the reeking vapors of indiscriminate slaughter. Then, as a recording monument, and in glorification of what they had done, they nailed to a tree a hieroglyphic picture with two bloody arrows, forming the St. Andrew's cross. After this, they retreated from the enemy's territory with the utmost speed, and had recourse to every stratagem to conceal the route they took, in order to escape pursuit. They made slaves of their prisoners when those prisoners were women and children, and they cropped short the hair of such as were thus reduced to slavery. But when it was a man whom they carried back to their homes, their triumph was complete, because the whole tribe was to be entertained with the spectacle of the torments to be inflicted on the prisoner.

On the day fixed for this exhibition, of which the Indians were as fond as the Romans were of the fights of their gladiators, or of the mutilation of human beings by wild beasts in the arena, above which sat sovereignty in the imperial shape of a Cæsar, two posts, ten feet long, were driven into the ground; another post was placed transversely at the distance of two feet from the soil, and another, transversely also, at the distance of five feet from the one below. Then the arms and legs of the patient were tied to the four right angles which were thus formed. Before this was done, however, the warrior whose prisoner he was, stunned him with the blow of a wooden tomahawk, and raised his scalp. A large fire was made up, and every one, lighting a long reed, applied it to some part of the prisoner's body. It was then that the Indians taxed their ingenuity to inflict the keenest torment, and he who succeeded in extracting from the sufferer a cry, or any demonstration of pain, was rapturously applauded. But this satisfaction was very seldom obtained. Commonly, the patient displayed unbroken fortitude, and the impassibility of inanimate matter. Far from weeping or begging for mercy, he sang as if in defiance of his enemies, heaped upon them every opprobrious epithet that he thought calculated to kindle their fury, and never ceased to provoke their resentment until death stopped his voice. It sometimes happened that some tender-hearted woman, wishing to put an end to his prolonged agony, gave him a blow which cheated his tormentors of their prey. Not unfrequently also, a young widow, whose mate had died in the war, took him for her husband, and thus saved him from the horrible death to which he was destined.

FORTIFICATIONS OF THE INDIANS.

The Indians understood the art of making fortifications sufficiently strong to resist the means of assault which were brought to bear upon them. Trunks of trees, of a circumference of six feet, were driven five or six feet into the ground, leaving ten feet out with sharpened tops. The joints of these posts were strengthened inside by the application of other posts of the diameter of one foot. This wooden wall was protected outside by towers erected at the distance of forty steps from one another. Its inside was supported by an elevation or bank of earth three feet wide by three in height, which bank was lined, to keep the earth compact, with green branches and leaves serried together by strong stakes. They showed great intelligence in opening loopholes; and all along their walls, about five feet above the parapet of earth of which I have spoken, they had a sort of pentice made with branches and splinters of wood, as a protection against grenades. In the center of the fort, they planted a tree, the branches of which had been lopped off at about nine inches from the trunk, so that they might serve to go up to the top, where, when necessary, the Indians placed a sentinel to watch the movements of the enemy. Round this tree, or ladder, they constructed several cabins, or sheds, as an asylum for the women and children against falling arrows. Round the fort were several fortified houses, which were its outposts and dependencies: they were useful in times of peace, as relieving the fort from many of its encumbrances; but when a serious attack was made, they were generally abandoned after a short resistance. If you cut the wicker strings which bind the hoop of a barrel, and if you fling that hoop on the ground, the figure which it will form, when both extremities of the hoop lie apart and get loose from each other, will represent the fort and its entrance. This entrance always fronted some stream or spring from which water was procured, and was defended by a truncated tower. In cases of extreme danger, this passage was blocked up with every kind of briers and thorny shrubs.

When a nation was so badly defeated that it feared entire destruction, it applied to another nation, the mediation of which it invoked, through ambassadors who carried presents. If the victor rejected this mediation, the conquered nation abandoned its territory, and incorporated itself with the nation for whose protection it had sued.

I have already said that the Indians, although generally brave, were extremely economical of their lives. In imitation of Diomedes and Ulysses before the walls of Troy, and of other heroes elsewhere, they delighted in murdering their enemies when asleep, but yet, in spite of all their prudence, some of them were killed occasionally; and then they were scalped, when possible, by their own companions, who were anxious not to leave in the hands of their enemies such trophies and proofs of victory. There was another circumstance which contributed to render their wars less destructive than ours, and which would throw some embarrassment in the way of our modern generals. Thus, when the party that had gone on a war expedition returned home with the loss of some warriors, the war-chief paid an indemnity to their families. A very humane and considerate provision for barbarians to think of, and a powerful check on the wanton sacrifice of lives by military leaders.

The Indians were not free from some of those vices which are so prevalent among us, and which a high state of moral and intellectual cultivation has failed so far to eradicate. For instance, gamesters, although held in bad repute, were common among them; and there was one particular game which they preferred above all others. It could be played by two only; one darted a long pole, in the shape of a bishop's cross, and at the same time, before the pole fell to the ground, hurled down on its edge, in the same direction, a heavy circular stone in the shape of a wheel, while the other player also flung his pole. He whose pole was nearest to the stone when it stopped rolling, won a point, and had the throwing of both pole and stone, which was a great advantage, as he could measure their velocity so as to make them meet. As it is with us, the Indians generally began with playing for trifles, but when excited, they raised their stakes, and ended often by losing all their worldly possessions. Human nature is always the same at bottom, however modified it may be at the surface, whether it remains in the original nakedness of barbarism, or conceals itself under the varied garments of civilization.

The women also had their game, but it was a very innocent one, because they never staked any thing for fear of offending their husbands. They played three by three, with three pieces of differently painted reeds, nine inches long, with one side flat and the other convex. One of the players held the three pieces in her open palm; one of the other players struck them with a small rod. They fell to the ground, and if two of the reeds had their convex sides up, it constituted the winning of a point. This certainly was a very sinless way for the Indian ladies of fashion to while away a wearisome hour.

The French, so famous for their politeness, were struck with the innate courtesy of the Indians, and have expressed their admiration in pages which are now lying before us. If an Indian met a Frenchman, he went up to him, took and squeezed his hand, and with a gentle inclination of the head, exclaimed, "*Is it thou, my friend?*" and if he had nothing to say worthy of utterance, he passed on without indulging in idle conversation—a proof of infinite good sense, and a thing well deserving of imitation.

Should an Indian overtake a Frenchman in walking, he never would pass before him, and would patiently follow behind at some distance. But if in a hurry, he would deviate from the path, take a long circuit so as to keep out of the stranger's sight, and come back to his direct way at a considerable distance ahead.

On their receiving a visit, they shook the visitor's hand, and after a few words of greeting, they invited him to sit down, generally on a bed used for this purpose. Then a profound silence was observed, until the visitor, after a few minutes of rest, thought proper to speak. After he had spoken, the wife of the person who was visited brought what victuals she might have ready, and her husband said to the visitor, "*eat.*" It was necessary to taste of every thing that was presented, otherwise it would have been looked upon as a demonstration of contempt or fastidiousness.

However numerous the Indians might be when they met to converse, there was but one who spoke at a time, and he was never interrupted. In their public councils, the greatest decorum prevailed, and each one in his turn, if he chose, addressed the meeting, which was composed of as good listeners as any orator might wish for. When a question had been discussed, and had to be put to the vote, a quarter of an hour was allowed for silent meditation, and then the sense of the assembly was taken. The impetuous volubility of the French was to them a matter of surprise; and they could not help smiling when they saw the French talk together with such vehement gesticulations, all of them speaking at the same time, and none of them listening. Le Page du Pratz relates with great simplicity of heart, that he had remarked the smile which flitted on the lips of the Indians on such occasions, and that for more than two years he had inquired of the Indians for the cause of it, without obtaining any other answer than this one—"*What is it to thee? It does not concern thee.*" At last, one of them yielding to his solicitations, said, "My friend, do not be angry then, if I tell thee the truth, which by thy importunity is forced out of me. If we smile when we see the French talk together, it is because we are exceedingly amused, and because they put us in mind of a cackling flock of frightened geese."

If the French admitted that the Indians were as polite as themselves, it can not be denied that these barbarians were also more careful observers of the rules of hygieine than their mercurial pale-faced brothers. For instance, they never could be persuaded to eat of the skillfully-made dishes of the French, because they said that they were afraid of the ingredients which entered into their composition. They never ate salad nor any thing raw or uncooked except ripe fruit, and they never could relish wine. Unfortunately, these men who were so remarkable for their enlightened sobriety in every thing else, could not resist the fatal allurements of brandy, known in their language as the *fire liquor*, and they thoroughly despised the French for mixing it with water.

In one respect, they were superior to every nation of antiquity, or of modern times. *They ate only when they were hungry*, and therefore had no fixed hour for their meals, nor did they eat together, the promptings of the stomach not being the same with all. The only exception was, when a feast was given: then the men ate by messes or companies, all out of the same dish, and the women, adults, and children stood apart, doing the same among themselves. When the Indians were sick, they refrained to the last moment from calling a physician to their aid, and behaving with as much sense as could have possessed the seven wise men of Greece put together, they abstained from their ordinary food, and lived entirely on gruel water.

But, in some of the preceding pages, I have been describing manners common to all the Indians. I return to the Natchez in particular. The temple of the village where their sovereign resided, was built near a small stream, on a mound eight feet high. This temple was thirty feet square. The corner posts were of one foot and a half diameter, and of one foot for the other posts. The space between the posts was filled up by a mud wall nine inches thick. To secure the solidity of the edifice, the posts, which were twenty feet long, were driven ten feet into the ground, leaving therefore an elevation of ten feet from the floor to the ceiling. The apsis of the temple fronted the east: the inside was divided into two unequal compartments, by a thin wall running from east to west. In the largest room there was a table or altar, six feet in length by two in width, and four feet in height. It supported a reed-basket, or coffin, in which were deposited the bones of the last *Great Sun*. There also the eternal and sacred fire was kept. In the small room, there were sundry small objects of adoration, the nature of which the Indians never would explain to the European visitors, and which the eye could not ascertain on account of the darkness of the room. The roof of the temple went tapering up, and its apex was only six feet long. There, sat three wooden birds, twice as large as a common goose. Their feathers were painted white, with a sprinkling of red. These birds faced the East.

The plebeians were not permitted to enter the temple. It was accessible only to the Suns or nobles, and to such strangers of distinction as were permitted to visit it with the express consent of the Great Sun, who was both the Sovereign and the High Priest of the nation.

The sacred fire was fed by the eight guardians of the temple, with the wood of the white walnut, stripped of its bark. The logs were eight inches in diameter, by eight feet in length. Death to the guilty guardian, or guardians, was the consequence of the extinguishment of the fire.

No nation on the face of the globe ever had more respect for the dead than the Indians of America, and particularly the Natchez. At their funerals, they gave undoubted signs of the truest and most unbounded grief for the departed. They did not, like the Greeks and Romans, practice the usage of burning the dead bodies, so as to keep their ashes in sculptured urns, to be preserved under the domestic protection of household gods. But they temporarily placed the dead in coffins made of reeds, where the necessary process of decomposition was to be undergone, and on which they continued for some time to deposit articles of food as a tribute of love and remembrance, and as a demonstration of their willingness still to minister to wants, which unfortunately no longer existed. When nothing but the dry bones remained, they were transferred to wicker coffers, which were laid up in small temples or private chapels. These temples of the dead were hardly distinguishable from the ordinary dwellings of the Indians, except it be by the wooden imitation of a human head hanging over the door. Nothing can exceed the veneration which they entertained for the cherished relics of their ancestry; and more than one Indian nation, when emigrating, carried away the parental bones, to which they clung with an intenseness of passion, hardly to be conceived in these our days of worldly philosophy.

Who cares now for the dead, except the surgeon, for dissecting purposes, or the sexton, for his fee? Who cares for the dead in this utilitarian age? To what practical use can they be turned, except to make coat buttons, or knife handles, or whistles, with their bones? Who thinks of the dead, except it be to reflect on the direful necessity they impose upon us, of having unhealthy grave-yards, and to devise the means of stripping these places of solemn repose of their frigid aspect, and to convert them into pleasure-gardens, where the tombs, or what purports to be such, are decked in gay colors, pagan ornaments, and a meretricious look: and instead of teaching morality and religion, leave the mind of the visitor free to discuss its ordinary pursuits of pleasure or of gain, and invite the lover's hand to snatch the rose growing out of his father's dust, to present it to his lady love, who stands by, and smiles on the profane donation. Fy! Who cares for the dead? Is it he who sells his ancestral portraits at the auctioneer's shop, or inventories the very sheets of the death-bed, to ascertain their value, and to secure the strict distribution of every dime of their worth among the greedy claimants? There is a land where I have descended into family vaults, in which a solitary lamp cast a dubious light, making darkness visible. There lay, in august repose, twenty generations, side by side. There, the imposing severity of the marble monuments, and the austere-looking statues of the departed, sleeping so solemnly on the top of their own tombs.—There, **the** soul-moving records of the past, often chiseled by the hand of genius.—There, the time-honored inscriptions.—There, that peculiar smell which reminds one of breathing the atmosphere of antiquity.—There, every thing impressive, awfully monitory, and Christian-like! There, profane thought was put to flight, and mundane mirth was chilled into reverential sobriety! As I came out with a heart overflowing with emotion, and my sight rested on the moss-covered, swallow-tenanted turrets of the family mansion, where, for centuries, the same race of people had dwelt in joy or in sorrow, my eyes became suffused with involuntary tears, and this indistinct and half-muttered expression of my feelings rose up to my lips: "Blessed be the land where there are such connecting links between the dead and the living!"

In 1725, *Stung Serpent*, of whom I have spoken when relating the first expedition of Bienville against the Natchez, in 1716, departed from his beautiful native hills overhanging the bed of the father of rivers, and went on his final pilgrimage to the world of spirits. The better to illustrate the manners, laws, and customs of the Natchez, I shall recite what occurred on that occasion. Although I shall confine myself to a strictly historical narrative, I believe it will be found not destitute of dramatic and romantic interest.

Stung Serpent being dangerously ill, the chief of the guardians of the temple came to Fort Rosalie to inform the French of this fact, and to let them know that the Great Sun, the brother of Stung Serpent, according to a mutual promise not to survive one another, had determined to redeem his pledge to the dying man. This was a startling information, because the death of these two chiefs at the same time, was calculated to be a heavy blow to the nation on account of the number of victims that would be sacrificed in their honor. The commander of Fort Rosalie, accompanied by Le Page du Pratz and others, hastened to the chief village, to inquire into the circumstances of the case. They found the Great Sun in his hut, and with him they went to visit Stung Serpent. It soon became evident to the French, that the sick prince had breathed his last. But the Great Sun was still in doubt, and when the French were preparing to retire, he stopped Le Page by the arm, and said: "*Ouitigui-tlatagoup-coheyogo*"—"is he dead truly? What dost thou say?" Le Page answered, "Noco," "I do not know"—in order to prolong an illusion which he did not wish suddenly to destroy.

The French accompanied the Great Sun back to his dwelling, into which he invited them. As soon as he crossed his threshold, he exclaimed, "My brother is dead"—and he squatted down with his head sunk on his breast, and his hands covering his eyes. On hearing these words, the Great Sun's wife uttered fearful shrieks, which were echoed all round, and went multiplying through the village, every hut resounding with wailings and lamentations. Then, muskets were fired to notify the neighboring villages, which in their turn answered the firing. A short time after, the Great Sun's *word-bearer*, or *chancellor*, came in and wept. The Great Sun raised his head and looked meaningly at his wife, who threw water on the hearth and extinguished the fire. At this sight, the *word-bearer* saluted the Great Sun with a howl, and departed. As soon as he was out of the hut, he uttered a frightful shriek, which was taken up by all the people of the village, and it went on wildly spreading from echo to echo, through every village. The shriek of the *word-bearer* had given the Natchez to understand that the Great Sun had ordered the fire of his own hearth to be extinguished, and therefore that every other fire was to be put out: which portended the approaching death of the sovereign. Hence this universal lamentation.

Le Page du Pratz, who, for several years, had been on a footing of intimacy with the Stung Serpent and with the Great Sun, approached that sovereign, who was still squatting on the floor, and tapping him on the shoulder, said: "Hast thou ceased to be a man since thy brother's death? Thy people inform us that thou art resolved to put an end to thy life, through grief, and because thou art too weak to bear thy loss with the heart of a warrior. Thy French friends can not believe that thou art such a coward. Tell them, therefore, that thy people do not understand thee rightly. Swear to us that they are mistaken, and that thou shalt not commit the vile suicide which they suspect." The Great Sun looked up at Le Page, and answered calmly: —"Rest assured that I no longer think of it. Farewell, then, and sleep in peace. The night steals upon us apace." However, there was something in his eye which contradicted his words, and the French, not altogether trusting to his declaration, left at his door a soldier to watch his doings. They went back to the Stung Serpent's dwelling, and they found his corpse stretched in pomp and in full dress on his bed. His face was painted with vermilion, his feet were encased in beautifully embroidered moccasons, and his head was encircled with the crown of white and red feathers, as a prince of the royal blood. His weapons were suspended all round his bed, and consisted of a double-barreled gun, a pistol, a bow, a quiver full of arrows, and a tomahawk. There were also to be seen, ostentatiously displayed, all the calumets of peace which had been tendered to him during his lifetime, to sue for his mercy or protection. At the head of his bed, stood a red pole supporting a chain made of reeds, painted red, and composed of forty-six rings. The rings meant the number of foes he had killed in war.

All the people composing the household of the prince, stood round him in the attitude of mourners. At certain hours, as if he had been alive, food was brought to him: and as, of course, it remained untasted, his body servant would, every time, break out into the same monotonous lamentation: "Why," said he, " wilt thou not accept of our offerings? Dost thou no longer relish thy favorite dishes? Hast thou any reason to be displeased with us, and dost thou reject our services as disagreeable to thee? Ah! thou dost not speak to us as it was thy wont. Wherefore, thou must be dead. Well, then, all is over—our occupation is gone—and since thou leavest us, we will follow thee to the land of spirits." He concluded every time this expostulation with the Indian death-cry, which was repeated by all the people present, and which, from mouth to mouth, outside of the hut, was to be heard swelling up in the distance, leaping from village to village, and ending with one appalling chorus, which congealed the blood within the heart. There also stood in the hut of the Stung Serpent, besides his favorite wife, a second one, whom he used to keep in another village—his woodbearer—his physician—his body-servant—his pipe-bearer—and some old women. They were all destined to be strangulated at his funeral, to keep company with the dead in the other world, whither he had gone.

A woman of noble birth, who had carried on an amour with Stung Serpent, whom she had not been able to marry, since, as it will be recollected, the nobles could not marry any one of their class, put herself voluntarily among the number of those who were to accompany the dead to the world of spirits. She was called by the French "*La Glorieuse,*" or "*the proud,*" on account of her majestic figure, of the haughty expression of her face, and because she consented to hold intercourse with none of the French except those of noble birth. She was acquainted with the virtues of a great many medicinal plants, and this female Esculapius had saved the lives of many of the sick among the French. The Stung Serpent's favorite wife seeing how sadly impressed the French were with the spectacle which was offered to them, addressed them in these terms: "Chiefs and nobles of France, I see how much you regret my husband. Truly, his death is of much consequence for the French as well as for our nation, because he carried them all in his heart. Whenever the French chiefs spoke to him, their words dwelt forever in his ears. He trod the same path with the French, and he loved them more than his own self. Now, he has ascended to the world of spirits; in two days I shall be with him, and tell him that I have seen your hearts grow heavy at the sight of his dead body. When I am gone, Frenchmen, remember that my children are orphans, remember that you have loved their father, and let the dew of your friendship fall plentifully on the children of him who has always been the friend of the French." After this speech, she resumed her seat with dignified composure.

The night being far advanced, the French retired to a lodge which had been prepared for them, but they requested the servants of the Great Sun to watch him closely, and if they saw any thing suspicious, to give them timely information. At daybreak, a breathless messenger, trembling with agitation, rushed into the apartment where the French slept, woke them up, and told them that the Great Sun was attempting his life. Hastily dressing themselves with such of their clothes as they could put their hands on in the dark, they ran to the Great Sun's dwelling. There, every thing was in the wildest uproar and confusion. The presumptive heir to the throne was struggling with the sovereign, and trying to wrest from his hands the gun with which, it appears, he had shown the intention to put an end to his life. A number of nobles and men of consideration, whom the excess of fear seemed to have palsied into a trance, stood looking on without daring to interfere. Le Page went up to the Great Sun, laid his hand gently on the gun, and said, " What! yesterday the noble sovereign of the Natchez swore to me, his friend, that he would not kill himself; that he was a man, and that I might rely on his word. To-day, what has become of that word? What has become of that man? Art thou both a liar and a coward? Speak!" At these words he dropped the gun, stared at Le Page with a vacant look, then rubbed his eyes as if awaking from a dream; and as if consciousness had suddenly returned, he extended his hand to him, covered his face and wept.

When the nobles saw the success obtained by Le Page, they advanced one after the other to shake him by the hand, but without uttering one word. The silence became so deep that, although the room was crowded to suffocation, the light buzzing of a fly would have been heard.

Looking round, Le Page saw that the wife of the Great Sun still continued to be in a state of great perturbation. He approached her and inquired if she was sick. She answered, "*yes;*" and then sinking her voice into a whisper, she said: "Stay awhile with us. If not, my husband dies, and then woe to the Natchez. Remain by his side, for it is to thy voice alone that he listens. Thy voice is weighty, and at the same time it is as pointed as an arrow. Who would have dared to speak to him as thou didst? Who would have succeeded half so well? But he knows thee to have been the true friend of his brother, and to be now his own best friend. We all respect thee, for thou art not eternally laughing, as the French always do. When thou spokest to the Great Sun, didst thou observe how all eyes feasted on thee, and how all ears drank thy words? Yes; thy words have all been garnered up in our hearts."

In compliance with this touching appeal, Le Page du Pratz moved silently to the side of the Great Sun, who extended his hand to him, and said in a loud voice so as to be heard by the whole assembly, "My friend, there is so much grief in my heart that my eyes, although open, have not seen that the French were standing up. My mouth has forgotten to invite them to sit down. What will they think of this churlish want of courtesy? I pray thee to excuse me with them, and to tell them to take seats."

Le Page answered that no apology was necessary; that the French were well acquainted with his good breeding, and would leave him for the present to enjoy the rest of which it was evident that he stood in need. "But," added he, "I shall cease to be thy friend, if thou dost not order fire to be lighted on thy hearth, and if thou dost not command the same to be done in the dwelling of every one of thy people. If thou compliest with my request, I shall stay to be present at the funeral of thy brother; and when it is over, I must insist on thy coming to my house to break the fast of grief and eat the meal of consolation." The Great Sun pressed the hand of Le Page in silent acquiescence, and drawing himself up to his full height, looked round with inexpressible majesty, and said: "Since the chiefs and nobles of France love me and wish me to live, be it so; my life is safe in my own keeping; let all the fires be relighted. I will wait until natural death reunites me to my brother. I am old and can not tarry long. In the mean time, I will walk in the path of the French. Had it not been for them, I should have been now with my brother, and to do me honor, the hills of the Natchez would have been strewed with the dead."

Emboldened by their success, the French strongly remonstrated against the absurd, inhuman, and fatal custom so long observed by the Natchez, to sacrifice so many lives on the death of one of their chiefs. But all that they obtained was, that the number of victims should be restricted to the two wives of the dead chief, to his physician, his word-bearer, his body-servant, his pipe-bearer, and some old women. "All the people composing my brother's household must die," said the Great Sun, "because they are his *meat and victuals*. It can not be otherwise." On that day, an old woman who was called *the wicked*, and who had committed some crime or other, was put to death, and a plebeian child was strangled by its own father and mother. Strange to say, this horrible crime raised the murderers above the class of the *stinking*, to which they belonged, and transformed them into nobles. On that day also there was twice, in the morning and in the evening, a minute rehearsal of the tragedy which was to be acted on the day of the funeral. Thus, the grand master came out in full official costume from the hut of Stung Serpent, accompanied by the two widows, the word-bearer, the pipe-bearer, the physician, the body-servant, and the old women who were destined to die. They moved in solemn procession, each of the victims being attended by eight of his nearest kinsmen or relations, whose duty it was to put them to death. One carried an uplifted tomahawk, with which he now and then threatened to strike the victim;—another one, the mat on which the *doomed* was to sit down;—a third, the rope for strangling;—the fourth, carried the deer skin which was to be thrown over the head and shoulders of the victim;—the fifth, a wooden bowl with five or six large pills of tobacco, which were administered to the patient before undergoing strangulation;—the sixth, a small earthen bottle containing a pint of water, which the victim was allowed to drink to facilitate the passage of the pills. The two other persons who followed, were destined to put themselves on the right and left of the poor suffering wretch, in order to draw the rope tight, and to make the operation as quickly effective as possible.

The eight persons who attended in this way every one of the victims, became nobles; and therefore to be one of them was an advantage which was much coveted. These executioners and future nobles walked two by two in the rear of the victims, whose hair was painted red, and who held in the right hand the shell of a river *muscle*, usually measuring seven inches in length by three or four in breadth. As to the executioners, they wore red feathers tied to the long tuft of plaited hair which hung down on their left shoulder, and their hands were painted red. On reaching the public square where the temple stood, the persons who were to die, and their executioners, shouted together the death-cry;—every victim put himself on his mat and executed on it the death dance, while the executioners did the same round them. It was the most appalling spectacle that the imagination could conceive. After each rehearsal, the procession returned in the same order to the hut of the deceased.

On that day, a half serious, half ludicrous accident took place. An Indian, named Ette-Actal, was led to the Great Sun, under the escort of thirty men. This Indian had married a female Sun, and on her death, his fate was to be sacrificed, according to the good old custom of his nation. But Ette-Actal's mind happened to be in advance of the age in which he lived, and he thought that to run away and to save his life, was a philosophical innovation to which it might be profitable to call the attention of the Natchez, and of which, at any rate, he ought to make the experiment. Putting into action his ideas of reform, he took to his canoe and paddled lustily down the Mississippi to New Orleans, where he placed himself under the protection of Bienville of whom he became the voluntary slave. But the love of country was strong in him, and now and then, he obtained permission to visit his friends and relations among the Natchez, after he felt assured that from the lapse of time since the funeral of his wife, and on account of the situation he occupied in relation to Bienville, the governor of Louisiana, he had no longer any thing to fear from his countrymen. But now that Bienville had been recalled to France, and that the presence of Ette-Actal in the village of the Natchez had reminded them of the old debt he had omitted to pay, they had arrested him with the intention of putting him to death at the funeral of the Stung Serpent.

When this Indian found himself a prisoner in the hut of the deceased, without any hope of escape, he began to give the most unequivocal signs of despair. At this sight, the favorite wife of Stung Serpent strode up haughtily to him, and said: "Art thou not a warrior?" "Yes," answered he, with a fresh gush of tears. "And yet thou weepest," continued she. "Is life so dear to thee? If it be so, it is not meet that thou shouldst come with us. Hence—begone—go, thou coward, and live among women." "Certainly," exclaimed Ette-Actal, "life is dear to me, and I wish to keep it for my own uses and purposes, and I should be happy to live among women, as thou sayest, in the hope of leaving a large posterity of children." Greatly incensed at this cynical retort, the princess repeated with increased vehemence: "Hence, cowardly dog! It is not decent that thou shouldst pollute us with thy company in our way to the world of spirits. Thy soul belongs to the earth, and there let it rot with thy body. Hence—let me not see thee again!" Never was order obeyed with more alacrity, and Ette-Actal vanished with the rapidity of lightning. But on that day, three decrepid old women, who were related to him by blood, and whose infirmities had disgusted them with life, offered to die in his place, and that substitution was accepted. This voluntary sacrifice of these three kinswomen of Ette-Actal's, not only secured to him his life for the future, but from a plebeian, or *stinking*, that he was, raised him to be a *man of consideration*. Thus, being borne onward by the tide of fortune, says Le Page du Pratz, Ette-Actal became insolent, like an upstart that he was, and availing himself of the instructions he had received among the French, he went on cheating his countrymen without stint, and showed himself a most accomplished rogue.

On the day of the funeral, the French proceeded to the dwelling of the Great Sun, to pay him a ceremonial visit; and Stung Serpent's favorite wife, knowing that they were there, came to bid them a last adieu. She had brought her children with her, and she addressed them in these words in the presence of the French:— "The death of your father is a severe loss. He tarries for me to accompany him to the world of spirits, and I must not keep him waiting long. I am anxious to depart, because since my husband's death, I walk on this earth with a heavy step. With regard to you, my children, you are very young, and you have before you a long path, through which you must journey with prudence in your minds, and boldness in your hearts, taking care not to tear your feet with the brambles of duplicity, and the sharp-edged flints of dishonesty. I leave to you the keys, bright as you see, and free from rust, of the inheritance of your father, and of my own worldly possessions. Take them: you will find our coffers full of corn. Never speak with an evil tongue of the French: walk in their path without deceit, as your father and myself have done: treat them, and love them as we have. Be true to them, and they will supply your wants:—if they do not, abstain from complaint, and wait until justice opens their hearts to your merits. They were the friends of your father; therefore, if they wrong you, let forgiveness tread on the heels of the offense. And you, French chiefs, continue to befriend the Natchez: be liberal and kind to them: do not be too harsh, and too exacting in your barters and exchanges with your red brothers, and look with the eye of the dove on the errors which they may commit." Perceiving that one of the French was so moved, that tears came into his eyes, she said,—" Do not weep: —it is womanly—although you may well regret the loss of such friends as my husband and myself. Instead of weeping, let us feast together. So far, I have never tasted meat with the French, because it would not have been becoming in a woman: but I am at liberty to do so, now that I am going to the world of spirits." And turning to her attendants: "Let victuals be brought plentifully," she said, "Stung Serpent's wife and the French chiefs must eat together, before parting forever." The French were struck with admiration at the surprising firmness, the extraordinary elevation of sentiments, the queen-like dignity of manner displayed by this woman, and they wondered at the infinite tact and skill with which she was contriving to secure for her children their protection and friendship.

The temple, the hut of the Stung Serpent, and that of the Great Sun, were situated in front of a public square, which was in the center of the village. On the day of the funeral, the French took their stand on the artificial mound on which the hut of the Great Sun was built; and from that elevated position they had a full view of all the ceremonies. The Great Sun did not make his appearance, and remained wrapped up in the privacy of grief. At the hour appointed for the obsequies, the master of the ceremonies, with a semi-crown of red feathers on his brows, presented himself at the door of the Great Sun. He held in his right hand a red pole in the shape of a bishop's cross, from the head of which hung down a garland of black feathers. The upper part of his body was painted red, with the exception of his arms; which signified that his hands were never dipped in blood. He wore from his waist to his knees, a sort of half tunic, which was ornamented with alternate rows of white and red feathers. After having taken the commands of the Great Sun for the ceremony, the grand master went to the dwelling of Stung Serpent, which he saluted with a howl, in token of respect, and he then shouted the death-cry, which was echoed back by the whole village. The corpse of Stung Serpent, carried on a litter by eight men, of whom six were the guardians of the temple, came out in state. The grand master of ceremonies took the lead, followed by the oldest warrior of the nation, who carried on a pole the chain of reeds which recorded the number of men killed in battle by Stung Serpent. In the other hand, he held a calumet of war, as a sign of the princely dignity of the deceased. Then came the body:—after which, the victims. The whole train went three times round the dwelling of Stung Serpent, and then proceeded direct toward the temple, describing a series of small intersecting circles, so that if their steps had been imprinted on the ground, they would have formed to the eye something like a chain of rings, extending from the dwelling of Stung Serpent to the temple. Every time the carriers of Stung Serpent had completed one ring, and were entering into another, the man whom I have mentioned as having strangled his child, threw down its corpse, so that the dead body of Stung Serpent should pass over it, and picking it up again by one foot, he continued the same operation until the funeral train reached the temple. By this hellish deed the unnatural father became a member of the nobility.

When the procession arrived at the temple, the tragedy which had been rehearsed twice on the preceding day, was acted in earnest, and the victims were put to death according to the programme. The body of Stung Serpent was deposited inside of the temple on the right, and his two wives slept in the same tomb. *La Glorieuse*, or *the proud*, was buried outside of the temple, to the right, and the word-bearer to the left. The other bodies were transported to the villages to which they respectively belonged. To conclude the ceremony according to the ancient rites of the tribe, fire was set to the dwelling of Stung Serpent, and it was burnt to the ground.

The French wended their way back to Fort Rosalie, reflecting and commenting on the strange scenes to which they had stood witnesses. One of them, Philippe de Chamilly, a beardless officer, celebrated for the recklessness of his disposition, the sprightliness of his conversation, the exuberance of his animal spirits, but who, under apparent thoughtlessness and the utmost carelessness of deportment, concealed steadiness of purpose, well-digested plans of ambition, and the keen-sighted, far-seeing sagacity of a shrewd and strong mind, had remained moody and silent. It was so foreign to his habits, that it struck his companions, who rallied him on his extraordinary taciturnity, and asked him whether he had been crossed by the apparition of Stung Serpent's ghost. "No," said he, "gentlemen; it would not have produced such a painful impression upon me as the daily demonstration of a fact which puzzles my philosophy. How is it that man never obeys the impulses of his heart without doing something which his reason reprobates, as calculated to interfere with his welfare, his safety, and prosperity? Although my assertion is not conducive to morality, and although I confess that it sounds like a libel on the divine goodness, yet, as I do not stand here in the pulpit of theology, or do not speak from the mountain as a lawgiver, I do affirm, much to my regret, that according to my short experience, a man who begins his career has to choose between these two guides—the heart and the head. They never agree; and one leads to ruin as surely as the other to success in this world, however different it may be after death. For instance, when we interfered to prevent that mahogany-looking blockhead of a barbarian, the Great Sun, from butchering half of his people in honor of his dead brother, and persuaded him not to commit suicide, which would have been also a death-warrant for a good many of his subjects, we acted according to the dictates of our hearts. We have been sentimental and romantic, to be sure, but have we behaved with common sense? We lay our hands on our hearts, and we say with self-complacency—what generous, noble, humane fellows we are! But what says reason, that sound little politician we have in the head? It cries out to us, ye are fools! and is it not true? Is it not our interest to destroy, or to weaken as much as we can, those untamable wild beasts, who have to this day so materially interfered with our purposes of colonization, and who may one day lap our blood like tigers, if they ever have a favorable opportunity? Which of us is simple enough to believe that those Indians do not see, with secret but deadly hostility, our gradual encroachments on their lands? Do you think that they do not feel that their existence and ours can not continue long side by side, and that one must, sooner or later, make way for the other. If this be the decree of fate, why not facilitate its execution, and thereby avert the dangers and bloodshed which may be the result of our maudlin generosity or bastard humanity, so suicidal for us, and so fruitless for those it was intended to benefit. What course then had we to pursue on this occasion? Why—a plain one—it was, in order to diminish the number of our enemies, to encourage those stupid savages in their nefarious practices, to stimulate their pride, and to show great admiration at the magnanimous courage with which they are ever ready to sacrifice themselves on the tombs of their chiefs. We ought to have assisted in tying the ropes round the necks of half of those red devils, and in making the other half pull the murderous strings, while we should have stood by enjoying the joke and cracking our sides with laughter. Such would have been the policy of Louis the XIth, a pretty wise statesman of ours, who said, that 'the smell emanating from the corpse of a foe was the sweetest of perfumes.' O, shame! This would have been cruel and barbarous! I do not deny it. But, finally, to achieve the destruction of those people must be the inevitable consequence of the position you have assumed toward them. A man, if he be not a fool, must be a logician in virtue, or in crime. If he makes up his mind to rob and to oppress, he ought, in self-defense, to take away life from the oppressed, when he can turn his victim to no better use. Mark the words of him whom you take for a thoughtless, inexperienced stripling. As we have acted with Christian charity, and *obeyed the heart*, we may be rewarded for it in the kingdom of bliss above; but as we have *disregarded the head*, and been politically foolish, we shall be punished and suffer for it on this side of the grave. So the conclusions of my speech keep tune with its premises. But a truce to my gravity—Fort Rosalie is in sight. Supper, thank God, a French supper—not an Indian one, must be ready. I cheerfully drop the soothsayer to be no more than a boon companion over a merry cup." Four years had hardly elapsed, before the prediction was accomplished. The white flag was pulled down from Fort Rosalie by the hand of an Indian warrior, and the whole French colony at Natchez was visited with complete destruction.

The advanced state of the medical art, which is presumed always to keep pace with the other arts and sciences, may therefore be received as a criterion of the degree of civilization to which nations have arrived. If we judged of the Natchez by that test, we might be tempted to believe and to say, without much sarcastic exaggeration, that the French could hardly claim any superiority in that respect over those barbarians. For many diseases to which the Natchez were subject, their physicians were quite as skillful as the French, if not more so. If they were powerless against the small-pox, by which they were threatened to be annihilated, and which was a recent European importation against which, until lately, they had never felt the necessity of guarding themselves, they did not, it may be justly observed, show themselves more ignorant than our modern physicians, who, in spite of their profound studies, and of the written information which comes to them from every part of the world, and from the experience of so many centuries, are invariably bewildered and miserably impotent, whenever humanity is attacked by one of those unknown diseases which, from time to time, are so suddenly and so mysteriously generated. The Natchez understood the art of blood-letting and scarifying in many ways, not omitting the application of the moxa, just as well as any Esculapius of the present day, although not exactly by the same process. The system of hydropathy was not unknown, and cold bathing and vapor-baths were much in practice. In provoking perspiration, in using frictions, in administering drastics, and in applying other devices of the healing art, they were not so inferior to our race as might at first be thought by those learned men who hold their diplomas from the medical faculties of London and Paris.

It may not be without interest to enumerate here a few of their remedies. Thus, in cases of diarrhea and dysentery, they used with much effect a kind of bread made with the pounded fruit of the persimmon-tree, which they dried up either in an oven or by exposure to the sun. They had discovered the balsam of the copal-tree to be an excellent febrifuge. First purging the patient, they administered to him ten or twelve drops of this balsam several times a day, and an hour or two before the patient had eaten any thing. If they were troubled with ulcers, wounds, sores, &c., they applied for several days on the diseased parts a poultice of the ground ivy, well pounded, and afterward they washed and dressed those wounds, ulcers, &c. with the balsam of copal, which was also very powerful in the affections of the chest and bowels, in cases of obstructions, of relaxations, &c. &c. In fact, it was for the Indians a universal panacea, and like good wine, it is said to have gladdened the heart. Another febrifuge of great virtue and as efficacious as quinine, was the red grain of the magnolia. The grain of the wax-tree boiled in water gave an astringent beverage which produced all the good effects of ipecacuanha. For ordinary cuts or gashes, the root of the cotton-tree afforded them a precious remedy. If they suffered from the stomach, they took, as tea, an infusion of the leaves of the cassia berry-tree. If they had the tooth-ache, they chewed a piece of "*bois d'amourette*," or of the acacia, and the pain was gone; so that dentists would have starved among them. With the leaves of the elder and with hog's lard they relieved their pains, when proceeding from piles; and no ague could resist one or two purgatives, followed by a strong decoction of the *Liane barbue*, or bearded withwind.

When the Natchez wished to perspire, so as to cure a cold, or to re-establish the functions of the skin, they drank hot infusions of the China radix. It is said that an infusion of the root of the same plant was also used by them as a specific to prevent the hair from falling, or to make it grow again with more profusion than ever. I here mention the fact for the benefit of those who are threatened with baldness. The leaves of the China radix were likewise employed in the curing of wounds.

The Natchez were acquainted with the medicinal qualities of sassafras, sarsaparilla, and maiden-hair. But their most powerful sudorific was the plant called by the French *plat de bois*.

They possessed an antidote against the bite of the

rattlesnake. It consisted in chewing the onion or root of a plant which the Indians called oudla-coudlo-gouille, and the French *l'herbe à serpent à sonnettes*, or *rattlesnake plant*, which is a literal translation of the Indian appellation. After having chewed the onion, they applied the residue to the wound. The poison was promptly checked, and the patient recovered entirely in four or five hours. An application to the forehead of the pounded green leaves of the ground ivy cured every headache. The old colonists used to extract from it a salt, which they put in arquebusade water, and it was thought to be an infallible remedy for the megrim. Those Indians astonished the French by their rapid cures of the most dreadful wounds produced by firearms. One of their curative ingredients was the plant known to this day in Louisiana as the Choctaw root. They possessed the most invaluable secrets to cure the dropsy, the sciatica, and the fistula lachrymalis. I could name many other diseases which, if what is reported is to be taken as true, they could master better than if they had studied old Hippocrates. This sketch is sufficient, however, to show what proficiency those Indians had attained in the healing art, the most important of all to mankind. It certainly speaks much in favor of their powers of observation, of investigation and of discrimination: that they should have arrived at discovering more than three hundred medical plants, of which the king's commissary, De la Chaise, sent a collection to France with a memoir written on the subject by Le Page du Pratz. The physicians ranked very high among the Natchez, and were looked upon as inspired. Those people believed, that for every disease the Great Spirit had provided a remedy in the shape of a plant, and that he never refused to point it out to the physician, when supplicated in the proper manner. Hence, if they awarded the most liberal fees to the physician in cases of success, they frequently put him to death, when his patient did not recover, on the ground that it must have been his fault if he did not find out the curing remedy.

When the French became acquainted with that interesting nation, it is said it had much degenerated from its former state of power, population, and civilization. The Natchez were then thought to be in the last stage of decline, and doomed to approaching and inevitable destruction. They knew it, and crouched gloomily under that fatality which, in the days of antiquity, hung with such terrific perseverance over certain individuals, certain families, and even whole nations. A century had hardly elapsed, when the sacred fire being accidentally extinguished, the guardians concealed the fact to escape death, and relighted the altar with profane and ordinary fire. A short time after, the same accident happened in the other temple, and on its being discovered, fire was procured, according to the old custom, from the first temple. But it was *profane fire;* so that the nation was thus deprived of that celestial flame which their great lawgiver and first sovereign had brought down with him from the Sun. The sacrilegious guardian of the sacred fire, who had concealed the truth, being on his death-bed, and racked with remorse, made at last the awful confession of his guilt—a confession which sounded in the ears of the Natchez as their death-knell. From the day when they had lost the fire from the sun, calamities on calamities had rained down on their tribe; and although they had sought to remedy the evil, by taking fire from a tree struck and ignited by lightning, they felt that their prosperity was withering and fast dropping its yellow leaves, and that there would soon remain nothing but its naked and lifeless trunk to blacken and rot away under the wrath of heaven. Nothing could wipe away from their souls the belief that the entire annihilation of their race was at hand; and their tradition said that the guilty guardian, who had to answer for the destruction of a whole nation, was locked up by the Great Spirit in one of those large mounds which are to this day to be seen in the vicinity of the present city of Natchez. There he is doomed to languish forever, and to be eternally barred from entering the world of spirits, unless he can make fire with two dry sticks, which he is ever rubbing together with desperate eagerness. Now and then a light smoke issues from the sticks—the wretch rubs on with increased and lightning rapidity;—and just as a bright spark begins to shoot up, the sluices of his eyes open against his will, and pour out a deluge of tears, which drown the nascent fire. Thus he is condemned to a ceaseless work, and to periodical fits of hope and despair. It is Ixion's ever-rolling rock, or the bottomless tun of the Danaides.

The Choctaws occupied a very large territory between the Mississippi and the Tombecbee rivers, from the frontiers of the Colapissas and of the Biloxis, on the shores of lakes Pontchartrain and Borgne, up to the frontiers of the Natchez, of the Yazoos, and of the Chickasaws. They owned more than fifty important villages, and it was said that at one time, they could have brought into the field twenty-five thousand warriors. Chacta, Chatka, or Choctaw, spelling it according to the various pronunciations, means *charming voice* in the Indian dialect. It appears that the Choctaws had a great aptitude for music and singing. Hence the name that was given to them. Very little is known about their origin, although some writers pretend that they came from the province of Kamtschatka. It is said that they suddenly made their appearance, and rapidly overran the whole country. That appearance was so spontaneous, that it seemed as if they had sprung up from the earth like mushrooms. With regard to their manners, their customs, and their degree of civilization, it is sufficient to say, that they had many characteristic traits in common with the other Indian nations. However, they were much inferior to the Natchez in many respects. They had more imperfect notions of the divinity, and were much more superstitious. They were proverbially filthy and stupid in the estimation of all who knew them, and they were exceedingly boastful, although notoriously less brave than any other of the red tribes.

What the Choctaws were most conspicuous for, was their hatred of falsehood and their love of truth. Tradition relates that one of their chiefs became so addicted to the vice of lying, that, in disgust, they drove him away from their territory. In the now parish of Orleans, back of Gentilly, there is a tract of land, in the shape of an isthmus, projecting itself into Lake Pontchartrain, not far from the Rigolets, and terminating in what is called " Pointe aux herbes," or *herb point*. It was there that the exiled Choctaw chief retired with his family and a few adherents, near a bayou which discharges itself into the lake. From that circumstance, this tract of land received, and still retains the appellation of " *Chef Menteur*," or " *Lying Chief*."

The Chickasaws ruled over a fertile region, which extended from the Mississippi to the Tombecbee, in the upper part of the state of Mississippi, and near the frontiers of the present state of Tennessee. They numbered from two to three thousand warriors, and were by far the most warlike of all the Louisiana tribes. They had numerous slaves, well-cultivated fields, and numerous herds of cattle. They never deviated in their attachment to the English, and they became exceedingly troublesome to the French. With some shades of difference, they had, on the main, the invariable and well-known attributes of the Indian character. Therefore, to pursue the subject into further details would, perhaps, be running the danger of falling into the dullness of monotonous and uninteresting description. Suffice it to say, that they were the Spartans, as the Natchez were the **Athenians,** and the Choctaws the Bœotians of Louisiana.

FOURTH LECTURE.

TRANSFER OF THE SEAT OF GOVERNMENT TO NEW ORLEANS—ITS POPULATION AND APPEARANCE IN 1724—BOISBRIANT, GOVERNOR AD INTERIM—BLACK CODE—EXPULSION OF THE JEWS—CATHOLIC RELIGION TO BE THE SOLE RELIGION OF THE LAND—PERIER APPOINTED GOVERNOR—LEAGUE OF ALL THE OFFICERS OF GOVERNMENT AGAINST DE LA CHAISE, THE KING'S COMMISSARY—HE TRIUMPHS OVER THEM ALL—REPUBLICANISM OF THE COLONISTS—THE URSULINE NUNS AND THE JESUITS—PUBLIC IMPROVEMENTS MADE OR CONTEMPLATED BY GOVERNOR PERIER—CENSUS IN 1727—EXPENSES OF THE COLONIAL ADMINISTRATION—EDICT OF HENRY THE SECOND AGAINST UNMARRIED WOMEN—OTHER FACTS AND EVENTS FROM 1723 TO 1727—TRADITIONS ON THE MUSIC HEARD AT THE MOUTH OF PASCAGOULA RIVER, AND ON THE DATE TREE AT THE CORNER OF DAUPHINE AND ORLEANS STREETS.

IN 1723, the seat of government was at last and definitively transferred to New Orleans, much to the satisfaction of Bienville. That city, now so populous and so flourishing, contained at that time about one hundred very humble buildings, and between two and three hundred souls. All the streets were drawn at right angles, dividing the town into sixty-six squares of three hundred feet each. The city thus presented a front on the river of eleven squares, by six in depth. The squares were divided into lots of sixty feet front on the street, with a depth varying from one hundred and twenty to one hundred and fifty. The name of New Orleans was given to the city in compliment to the Duke of Orleans, Regent of France, and Chartres-street was called after the Duke of Chartres, son of the Regent:—Maine, Condé, Conti, Toulouse, and Bourbon streets were also named after the princes of the royal blood, such as the Prince of Conti, Duke of Maine,

Prince of Condé, Count of Toulouse, and Duke of Bourbon. One of the streets was honored with the name of Bienville, the founder of the city, and deservedly has that name been lately bestowed on one of the parishes of this state. The only establishments which then existed between New Orleans and Natchez, were those of Mezières and St. Reine,—a little below Point Coupeé; that of Diron d'Artaguette, at Baton Rouge; that of Paris Duvernay, near Bayou Manchac; of the Marquis d'Ancenis, near Bayou Lafourche; of the Marquis d'Artagnac, at the Cannes Brulées, or Burnt Canes; of De Meuse, a little lower, and of the Brothers Chauvin, at Tchoupitoulas. With the exception of the Chauvins, these aristocratic possessors of the virgin soil of Louisiana were not destined to strike deep roots in it, and their names soon disappeared from the list of the landholders in the colony.

In that year, however, another settlement, which was to grow rapidly in importance, was made on that portion of the banks of the river which now forms the parishes of St. Charles and St. John the Baptist. Large tracts of land were conceded to those Germans, whom Law had sent from Alsatia, to settle on the twelve square miles of territory which had been granted to him on Arkansas River, by the India Company. When these German families were informed of the fate of Law, and saw themselves abandoned to their own resources in that distant part of the colony, they broke up their establishment, and descended the Mississippi in a body, with the intention of returning to their native country. But, fortunately, they were prevailed upon to settle at a distance of about thirty miles from New Orleans, on a section of the banks of the river, which, from that circumstance, drew the appellation of the *German Coast* under which it was long known. Every Saturday, they were seen floating down the river in small boats, to carry to the market of New Orleans the provisions which were the result of their industry. From this humble but decent origin, issued some of our most respectable citizens, and of our most wealthy sugar planters. They have, long ago, forgotten the German language, and adopted the French, but the names of some of them clearly indicate the blood that flows in their veins, although more than one name has been so Frenchified, as to appear of Gallic parentage. The *German Coast*, so poor and beggarly at first, became in time the producer and the receptacle of such wealth, that, a century after, it was called the *Gold Coast*, or *Côte d'or*.

In the very year when these industrious people came to reside at the *German Coast*, and before they could show what rich harvests could spring from the prolific soil of Louisiana, the colony suffered extremely from the want of provisions, and, in a dispatch of the 24th of January, the Superior Council informed the French government " that the colonists would absolutely starve, if the India Company did not send by every vessel an ample supply of salt meat." From 1699 to 1723, such representations, however incredible they may appear, had been made every year, and had forced the French government into heavy expenses, so that it is calculated in a memoir of that epoch, that the few individuals scattered over Louisiana had, at an average, cost annually to France, in provisions alone, about one hundred and fifty thousand livres. There must certainly have been much abuse and malversation at the bottom of this state of things, and it is evident that there was in the organization of the colony a defect, which, if it starved some, fattened others. Be it as it may, the existence of the colony was nothing but a prolonged agony. The principle of life seemed to be wanting in her.

Thus, the colonists in Louisiana, during the year 1723, were dragging along, sluggishly and miserably, a rickety sort of existence, when, on the 11th of September, there burst upon them a tremendous hurricane, which lasted three days. The church, the hospitals, and thirty houses in the modest little hamlet of New Orleans, were pulled down by the wind. Three ships that were in port were completely wrecked: the crops were destroyed: very few of the edifices on the embryo farms of the colonists could withstand the fury of the hurricane, and were swept away like chaff, or autumn leaves. The desolation was so widely spread, and so intensely felt, that the first impulse of the people in their despair was to quit the colony forever: and, no doubt, they would have executed their design, if they could have procured means of transportation. A company of infantry that had embarked at Biloxi for New Orleans, availed themselves of this favorable opportunity for escape, took possession of the vessel, and forced her captain to sail for Charleston, where they landed safely with their arms and baggage.

It frequently happens that both the excess of misery and of prosperity, has a tendency to develop the evil propensities of the human heart. It was, on this occasion, strikingly exemplified by the colonists, who, at all times, had been strongly addicted to gaming, but who now, seeking perhaps for artificial excitement, to lose the consciousness of their wretchedness, went on playing with such wanton recklessness at all kinds of games of chance, that the authorities found it necessary to interfere, and to prohibit with stringent penalties their indulging in this culpable and dangerous passion.

In spite of all the misfortunes which had befallen the

country, its agriculture had been developing itself to some extent, although checked by many obstacles. The number of negroes, or slaves, was gradually increasing, and, this year, it was determined by an ordinance, that the negroes introduced by the India Company from Africa, should be sold for 676 livres per head, on a credit of one, two, and three years, payable in rice and tobacco. The price of rice was fixed at 12 livres the barrel, and tobacco at 26 livres per hundred pounds. Wine was to be supplied to the colonists for 26 livres the cask, and brandy at 120 livres. Another ordinance fixed the value of the Spanish pistoles and dollars, which, from the proximity of the Spanish provinces, had become current in the colony.

The spiritual concerns of the colony were not neglected. Louisiana was divided into three grand ecclesiastical districts. The first was intrusted to the Capuchins, and extended from the mouth of the Mississippi to the Illinois. The Carmelites had jurisdiction over all that section of country which spread from the Alibamons to Mobile;—the Wabash and Illinois district was the lot of the Jesuits. Orders were given and provisions were made for the construction of churches and chapels, the colonists having complained of their being obliged, for want of proper places of worship, to assemble in the open air round wooden crosses erected in the fields, or public thoroughfares and roads.

The necessity of deepening the mouth of the Mississippi, had attracted the attention of the French government at the earliest period of the establishment of the colony, and the engineer Pauger made, in this year, 1723, a very interesting report on the practicability of arriving at this desired result. He represented that it was easy and not expensive to *fix* (fixer) or to control the current of the Mississippi, so as to make it subservient to the plan of operating upon the sand-banks which obstructed the several mouths of the river, and so as to give admittance to the largest ships, whatever might be the depth of water they drew; that, if necessary, a fine artificial harbor with quays might be created at the Balize, with the numerous resources which the nature of the locality offered, and that it might be effectually protected by such fortifications as he indicated. He recommended to shut up all the mouths of the river, except one, in order to force a greater volume of water into the remaining channel, which would, consequently, acquire more depth; and he calculated that the increased velocity and power of the current would sweep away the whole of the mud or sand-bank which barred the entrance of the Mississippi. He suggested that the immense quantity of drift-wood which it carried down, might be secured and fastened to its banks to give them greater solidity, and to narrow the bed of the river. He also stated that, for the execution of the works he described, the government had at hand inexhaustible cypress forests, furnishing an incorruptible kind of wood, which, without much expense, might be used to any extent and with incalculable advantages and results.

In 1849, when I write these lines, there is no such thing as a French colony in North America, but there is in it a gigantic empire composed of thirty sovereign states, having in the aggregate a population of twenty-five millions of souls, and a commerce more extensive than that of any nation in the world except Great Britain. The limits of that empire, known under the appellation of the United States of America, extend from the frozen banks of the St. Lawrence to the sun-burnt hills of New Mexico and the golden Californian shores of the Pacific. The thousands of miles of country which the Mississippi waters in its course belong exclusively to this mighty people, and, consequently, the deepening of the mouths of the Mississippi, and the giving a free access to what has justly been called *an inland sea*, on the shores of which stand such cities as New Orleans and St. Louis, in a boundless region where several millions of the human race are already domiciliated, and where countless millions will reside in the future, would be one of the most important national works which the government of the United States could undertake; and yet it is no more thought of than if it was not recommended by the eloquence of its own magnitude, and if it had not repeatedly been brought before Congress by more than one legislative resolution of the State of Louisiana. True it is, that it would not cost perhaps one hundred thousand dollars a year, to have forty feet of water at the mouths of the Mississippi, through which pass annually so many millions of importation and exportation in every sort of goods and produce;—that it would stimulate and increase commerce, by the affording of new facilities and the diminishing of obstacles, risks, and expenses to ship-owners and merchants; that it would be investing money that would return the highest interest;—that it would procure to the people the precious advantage of studding the banks of the Mississippi with navy yards, at points teeming with infinite resources, far from the guns of hostile fleets;— and that it would make of that mighty stream a harbor, an asylum, and a home for our winged monarchs of the ocean. True it is, that the expenses attending the accomplishment of such a vast object, would be microscopical when compared with the results of every kind which would be attained, and that large sums have been lavishly spent in more favored states, because they were of more political importance. But, long ago, would this much-needed improvement have been carried into execution, which, for more than a century, by its immense importance, its easy feasibility, and the imperious necessity which demands it, has struck with the force of self-demonstration every mind that has bestowed the slightest attention on the subject, if Louisiana had been blessed, like New York, with a large congressional representation. Let us hope that the time will come, when, to secure the success of some move on the political chess-board of the day, and to gain the complement of certain votes required to fill up the scale of power, that great national work shall be done, which was delayed so long when it was demanded only by the wants of commerce, the sense of justice, and the voice of public interest.

A treaty of peace having been concluded between Spain and France, Pensacola, which had been taken by the French in 1719, was restored to the Spaniards. This peace dissipated the fears and feelings of insecurity which existed in the colony from the neighborhood of Cuba and of the other Spanish possessions on the continent; and a successful campaign which the Choctaws had undertaken against the Chickasaws, at the instigation of the French, gave such a crushing blow to this warlike tribe, as to secure the country for a while against their depredations. Bienville said, in one of his dispatches, "The Choctaws, whom I have set in motion against the Chickasaws, have destroyed entirely three villages of this ferocious nation, which disturbed our commerce on the river. They have raised about four hundred scalps, and made one hundred prisoners. Considering this state of things, it is a most important advantage which we have obtained—the more so, that it has not cost one drop of French blood, through the care which I took of opposing those barbarians to one another. Their self-destruction, operated in this manner, is the sole efficacious means of insuring tranquillity to the colony." Bienville also wrote that there were thirteen feet water on the bar at the Balize, and that he was actively engaged in fortifying that pass, and in preparing lodgings for a small garrison.

The Chickasaws had hardly been disabled from doing further mischief, when Bienville was informed that the Natchez, in consequence of some difficulties which had sprung up between them and the French, had murdered two or three of the latter and plundered their habitations. He immediately went up the river with an army of seven hundred men, and having obtained the sacrifice of some heads, in atonement for those of the French who had been killed, he smoked the calumet of peace with the Indians, and only three days after his arrival at Natchez, he had the satisfaction of speeding back to New Orleans, after having put an end to hostilities which threatened a protracted and a dangerous war.

But the Indians were not the worst enemies he had to cope with. He had active and ever-plotting adversaries in the colony, and no vessel returned to France without carrying back heavy accusations against the Governor of Louisiana. Hubert, the king's commissary, was one of the foremost, and kept repeating to the French government that Louisiana was the finest country in the world; that if it had a fault, it was that its virgin soil was too rich, which was injurious to agriculture, the first harvests being too luxuriant to be productive; but that if the colony did not prosper more, it was owing to the mal-administration of Bienville, and to his favoritism for his numerous relations and allies. The fact is, that the colony, as for the past, was divided into two factions, and the quarrels of its officers and administrators waxed so hot and so acrimonious, that almost every day, anonymous and defamatory writings were stuck up at every street corner in New Orleans, and satirical compositions were clandestinely circulated, which produced much irritation and many duels. The Superior Council had to publish an ordinance on the subject, and to inflict heavy penalties on those who participated in the composition and publication of these libels.

On the 16th of January, 1724, Bienville had the mortification of receiving a dispatch from the French government, by which he was called to France to answer the charges brought against him. Perhaps to soften the blow, his cousin Boisbriant was appointed governor *ad interim*. This was the second time that his enemies had succeeded against him, and forced him to visit France in self-defense. But before leaving the colony, he published, in the month of March of the year 1724, a *Black Code*, containing all the legislation applicable to slaves. It remained in force until after the cession of Louisiana by Spain to France, and by France to the United States, and some of its provisions have been incorporated into the Black Code which is now the law of the land. As it embodies the views, feelings, and legislation of our ancestors more than a century ago, on a subject which has been daily growing in importance, I have deemed it of sufficient interest to lay the whole of it before the public.* Its first and its third articles were, it must be confessed, strangely irrelevant to the matter in consideration. Thus, the first declared that the Jews were forever expelled from the colony; and the third, that the Roman Catholic religion was the only religious creed which would be tolerated in Louisiana. By what concatenation of causes or of ideas, these provisions concerning the su-

* See the Appendix.

premacy of the Roman Catholic religion and the expulsion of the Jews came to be inserted into the Black Code, it is difficult to imagine.

I transcribe here a short royal ordinance, which shows the nature of the morality of the country at the time, and which demonstrates the state of distraction and of bitter conflict with which the colonists were afflicted, instead of working harmoniously for their mutual welfare.

"Royal ordinance concerning the breaking up of seals, and the violation of the secrecy of letters.

"Whereas the directors of the India Company have represented to us, that in our province of Louisiana many breaches of trust are committed with regard to the letters and packages which are received from Europe, and those which are destined to be transported from said colony to our kingdom; that some evil-minded persons, either through malicious intentions or a guilty curiosity, intercept said letters and packages, and after having opened them, make public what they contain, whereby quarrels and animosities are produced in our colony, we have deemed it expedient to stop the course of an abuse so prejudicial to commerce and so repugnant to good faith: and to this effect, we have declared and ordained that all persons, officers, clerks, inhabitants, or others, on being convicted of having detained or intercepted one or several letters or packages, shall be sentenced, to wit: the officers or clerks, to a fine of five hundred livres, to be deprived of their office or offices, and to be forever incapable of holding any other under our government; and that the inhabitants (habitants) and others shall be sentenced to the iron collar (carcan), and to a fine of five hundred livres."

The affairs of the company, far from improving, were rapidly becoming worse. Louisiana was losing ground in the estimation of the French government, and it was thought necessary to diminish the expenses of such an unprofitable possession. Thus, by an ordinance of he 7th of September, the military forces of the colony vere reduced from twenty companies to ten, commanded by Marigny de Mandeville, De la Tour, D Artaguette, Du Tisné, Lamarque, Le Blanc, Des Liettes, Marchand de Courcelles, Renault d'Hauterive, and Pradel. Such being the economical views of the French government with regard to Louisiana, the excellent observations and plans presented by the engineer Pauger, concerning the improvements to be made at the mouth of the Mississippi, could not be carried even into partial execution; but as a reward for his labors, he was appointed member of the Superior Council.

The colony had always greatly suffered from the want of surveyors. The grantees of lands experienced much difficulty and long delays to be put in possession of their grants, and frequently, these surveys being made by persons who were incapable, and not legally empowered to officiate, much confusion and uncertainty ensued, and promised future litigation when the country should be more thickly settled. To remedy this evil, two brothers, named Lassus, were sent to Louisiana with full powers to act as engineers in the name of the company.

One of the curses of the colony was the constant fluctuation of its monetary circulation. Not only its paper currency underwent rapid depreciation as soon as a new one succeeded that which fell into discredit, but the company, for the most nefarious jobbing purposes, used to change, by repeated edicts, the standard of the Spanish dollars and pistoles, which were the chief metallic currency of the country. Thus, by an edict of the

23d of February of the preceding year, the company had suddenly raised the value of the dollar from 4 livres to 7 livres 10 centimes; and twelve months after, on the 26th of February, 1724, the pistole was reduced from 30 to 28 livres, and the dollar from 7 livres 10 centimes to 7 livres. On the 2d of May, there was another reduction for the dollar from 7 livres to 5 livres 12 centimes, and for the pistole, from 28 to 22 livres 8 centimes. On the 30th of October, there came a further reduction. Thus, from 22 livres 8 centimes, the pistole was brought down to 18 livres, and the dollar, from 5 livres 12 centimes to 4 livres 10 centimes. It would be tedious to go into all the details of these financial operations, and to investigate their real causes. It is evident that there must have been at the bottom of them some dark fraud, greedy corruption, and thieving speculation, which enriched some individuals at the expense of the sheepish multitude. To give an idea of the perturbation which was produced in the affairs of the colony, it is sufficient to state that, in the course of two years, there was, by successive arbitrary ordinances, a rise and fall of nearly fifty per cent. in the value of the metallic currency of the country. An indescribable confusion was the consequence of such measures. The pecuniary situation of every colonist was changed; the ruin was almost general, but some large fortunes sprung up from the vast wreck. Comments are unnecessary, when facts speak so loudly and so distinctly. The mere statement of these facts suffices to show what was the spirit which presided over the administration of that miserable colony. Under such an incubus, how could it prosper without a miracle, when suffering from the violation of all the laws of nature, of common sense, of civilization, and of political economy?

In 1724, the white population of Louisiana, says La

Harpe, amounted to about 1700 souls, and the black population to 3300. If La Harpe's statement be true, it shows an astonishing diminution of the white population, which, in 1721, was computed at 5400. There were in the colony, 1100 cows, 300 bulls, 200 horses and mares, 100 sheep, 100 goats, some hogs, and a considerable number of domestic fowls of every kind. In New Orleans and its vicinity, there were about 1000 souls, including the troops, and the persons employed by the government.

This year, 1724, was made remarkable by the promulgation of a law for the protection of domestic animals, and by its Draconic severity. Thus, the king, at the request of the Superior Council of the colony, issued a royal edict, declaring that the voluntary killing or maiming of a horse, or of a horned animal, by any one but the owner, should be punishable with death, and that any person who, without leave from a competent authority, should kill his own horse, his own cow, and sheep, or their young ones, if of the female sex, should pay a fine of 300 livres.

The enacting of such a law was no doubt prompted by the necessity of preserving against wanton destruction, animals which were so useful to the colony, and which it was extremely important to multiply. But as the human race was quite as scarce in the colony, and of a nobler and more precious nature, it seems that some scale of proportion should have been observed between the degrees of punishment to be inflicted for the killing of an ox, or of a man, and that the bipeds and quadrupeds should not have been assimilated under the same ægis of protection. What a wonderful change has taken place in our legislation, in our manners and customs, in the whole state of the country, and in its very bones and sinews since 1724! This change is so great, that we can hardly admit the reality of the evidence that, only a little better than a century ago, one might have been broken on the wheel, or decapitated in Louisiana, for having maimed or wounded a horse or a cow. It shows that blue-laws were not confined altogether to the soil of Connecticut.

On his arrival in France, Bienville laid his defense, in 1725, before the French government. He represented that he had honorably served the king for thirty-four years, during the greater part of which he had acted as the governor, or one of the chief officers of Louisiana:—that as an officer of the Navy, he had served seven years, and gone through seven campaigns at sea:—that during these seven campaigns, he had been present at all the sea-fights of his brother Iberville, on the coasts of New England, of Newfoundland, and in the bay of Hudson, and among other engagements, at the one which took place between one single French ship of 42 guns, commanded by Iberville, against three English ships, of which one was of 54 guns, and two of 42, when, after a struggle of five hours, Iberville sunk the fifty-four, took one of the 42, and dismasted the other, which escaped under the protection of the dark shades of night; in which fight, he, Bienville, was dangerously wounded in the head. He further represented, that it was he, who, in 1699, jointly with his brother Iberville, had discovered the mouth of the Mississippi, and established a colony in Louisiana; that, for twenty-seven consecutive years, he had devoted himself exclusively to the colonization of that province; that he had sacrificed in favor of this public spirited enterprise the brilliant career which was open for him in his majesty's navy, in which many members of his family had distinguished themselves, seven of his brothers having died naval officers; that his father had died on the battle-field, in the service of his country; that there still remained in the navy three of his brothers: De Longueil, governor of Montreal, in Canada, De Sérigny, captain of a ship of the line, and De Chateaugué, naval ensign. He then reviewed what he had done since he arrived in Louisiana, the unceasing hardships and difficulties of every sort it had been his lot to struggle against,—the causes which excited the jealousy and hostility of his adversaries; and he labored to prove that all his acts had been in conformity with the laws, with his instructions, with the interest of the colony, and of the king's service, and that it was to his unremitted exertions and devotion, that the colony was indebted for the continuation of its existence. Bernard de la Harpe, who, in his *historical journal*, warmly supports Bienville against his accusers, says pithily, that the best proof that Bienville had always been more mindful of the colony's interest and welfare than of his own, was, that during the twenty-seven years he had resided in the colony, and wielded power, he had not acquired in property more than 60,000 livres worth (or $12,000), which was more than could be said of his traducers.

But if Bienville had implacable enemies, he had friends, blood relations, and allies, whose fidelity and active zeal were a compensation equal to the hostility from which he had to suffer. One of them, De Noyan, his nephew, presented to the Superior Council a petition, in which he stated, that he wished to disprove an assertion which had been advanced by his uncle's enemies, who had assured the French government that the Indian nations, having been oppressed by Bienville, were rejoiced at his departure from Louisiana. The Superior Council acceded to the prayer of the petition, and De Noyan brought before them deputations from the Oumas, Tunicas, Natchez, Choctaws, and other tribes, who declared that Bienville had always been their best friend, and that, during his absence, their hearts would ever be clad in mourning. Nevertheless, Bienville, in spite of his own exertions, and of those of his friends, was dismissed from office, and Périer was appointed governor in his place on the 9th of August, 1726. The success of Bienville's enemies was so complete, that Chateaugué, his brother, who had long been acting as "*Lieutenant de Roi*," or lieutenant-governor in the colony, was also removed, and that the two Noyans, both his nephews, one a captain, and the other an ensign in the army, were broken, and the order was given to send them to France. The object of these measures, besides the gratification of private malice, was to destroy the influence of Bienville, to sweep away all the obstacles of a foreseen opposition from the path of his successor, and to make level ground for the new administration.

This change, and the other modifications which were expected in the administration, produced considerable perturbation, ill-blood, and fears, in the colony. The excitement was increased by the anticipation of a war, and the proclamation of Boisbriant, the governor ad interim, and De la Chaise, the king's commissary, which invited all the colonists to carry to the king's warehouses at New Orleans and Mobile, all the ammunition and provisions they could command, to provide for the contingencies of a war likely to break out between Spain and England, and in which France would be called to take a part, in virtue of her treaty of alliance with Spain.

It will be recollected that De la Chaise had been sent by the India Company, in 1723, with Du Saunoy, to exercise inquisitorial powers over the affairs of Louisiana, to take informations on the conduct of all the officers and administrators of the colony, and to report thereon to the government. Du Saunoy having died shortly after his arrival, De la Chaise had remained clothed with all the authority of the joint commission. As soon as he entered upon his duties, the old intestine war had immediately ceased by mutual consent between the officers, clerks, agents of the colonial administration, and they had leagued themselves against the common enemy—against the spy whom the government had set *in terrorem* over them all. De la Chaise soon found himself in a hornet's nest, and met fierce opposition in every thing, and from every quarter. He was a nephew of the celebrated Jesuit, Father de la Chaise, the confessor to Louis the XIVth, and of patrician birth, the ancient feudal castle of his family, the *Chateau d'Aix*, being situated among the mountains of the province of Forez, in France. His father was the son of George d'Aix, Seigneur de la Chaise, who was distinguished for his military services, and had married Renée de Rochefort, daughter of one of the noblest houses of the province. Members of the De la Chaise family continued to occupy high rank in the army, and in the king's household, and one of them, during the regency of the Duke of Orleans, died a lieutenant-general. He had acquired reputation for his uncompromising integrity, and his unflinching attachment to duty, but, says the Duke of St. Simon, in his memoirs, he was so deficient in intellect, that he frequently met with unlucky accidents, in his military career.

De la Chaise, the king's commissary in Louisiana, was not gifted with a superior intellect; but he was a solid square block of honesty, who neither deviated to the right nor to the left from the path of duty, and who, possessing a considerable share of energy, moved stoutly onward in the accomplishment of his mission, regardless of persons and of consequences. The never-ceasing repose of his handsome features was an unmistakable indication of the unruffled serenity of his soul: and the dignity of his person, the measured propriety of his deportment and actions were such, that it checked in others the ebullition of passion, forced discussion to be courteous, and anger itself to be respectful. With the blandest urbanity, but with unwavering firmness, he called every one to account, and the opposition, which he goaded into fury by his steadiness of purpose, and his unsparing investigations, became such, that the government thought it necessary to act with vigor. Boisbriant, the governor ad interim, Perrault, Perry, the engineer Pauger, the attorney-general Fleuriau, all members of the Superior Council, were censured with severity by the government. Moreover, Governor Boisbriant, Bienville's cousin, was summoned to France, to justify his acts: Perrault, Fazende, and Perry, members of the council, were dismissed from office: Fleuriau, the attorney-general, was invited to throw up his commission, and the office itself was suppressed for the moment. They had the mortification to receive the imperative order to appear respectfully before De la Chaise, and the new governor, Périer, or before whomsoever these dignitaries might choose to designate, and then to account to them for all their official acts. After that, Perrault and Perry were to be transported to France. With regard to Fazende, the other councillor, he was permitted to remain in Louisiana as a private citizen. Through the influence of Boisbriant, the governor ad interim, who was violently opposed to De la Chaise, a spirit of insubordination having infected the troops themselves, the king had issued an ordinance on the 20th of November, to prohibit all assemblies of officers. It was a complete revolution in miniature, but these were thought to be mighty events in the lilipu-tian colony of Louisiana.

Thus, De la Chaise and Périer remained the supreme masters in Louisiana. The India Company, thinking it good policy that Périer should have a personal interest in the prosperity of the colony, and anxious to secure his zealous co-operation, even if it were on selfish grounds only, granted him, over and above his regular salary as governor, a concession of ten acres of land, fronting on the river, with the ordinary depth, and decreed that he should receive the donation of eight negroes a year, as long as he should retain his office.

The India Company gave to Périer the minutest instructions, to serve as rules for his administration. They informed him that they expected he should keep up the best understanding with De la Chaise, the king's commissary, whose integrity, zeal, and intelligence were well known to the company, and that there should be no jealousy and no clashing of authority between them; that from the sad experience of the past, they had come to the conclusion that power should be divided in the colony between two persons only, each one responsible for his acts in his respective department; that one should be the executive officer and the military commander of the colony, and the other should have the supervision of its police, its commerce, and its judicial administration; that they should remain completely independent of each other, in order to prevent the dissensions and quarrels which had hitherto been so fatal to the prosperity of the country; that he, Governor Périer, and the commissary, De la Chaise, would find, in the company's instructions, their powers and functions clearly defined and kept distinctly apart; that De la Chaise having made many enemies in consequence of his zeal for the interests of the company, Governor Périer was required to back and to support him with all the means which would be in his hands; and that, in concert with this colleague in authority, he was expected to take all the measures necessary to punish, according to their deserts, those who had opposed the exercise of the authority conferred upon the king's commissary.

One of the articles of the instructions ran thus:— "Whereas it is maintained that the diseases which prevail in New Orleans during the summer, proceed from the want of air and from the city being smothered by the neighboring woods, which press so close around it, it shall be the care of M. Périer to have them cut down, as far as Lake Pontchartrain." This paragraph shows two things:—1. That, at that remote time, the summer was a sickly season in New Orleans, as it is to this day; and 2. That to make it more healthy, the government was, as far back as 1726, struck with the necessity of an improvement which, for many years past, has in vain been urged upon the public authorities of New Orleans. To procure to this city a free and pure ventilation from Lake Pontchartrain, there remains to be removed only a thin curtain of wood, which might soon be withdrawn; and there being no other impediment to prevent a mutual exchange of breezes between the Mississippi and the lake, gentle drafts of invigorating air would daily sweep through our streets, and make of New Orleans, during the summer, the safest and most agreeable urban residence in the Union. When it should be once known that New Orleans is as much blessed with health as any other part of these United States, its rapid aggrandizement would be almost without limits, and it would, with the advantages it possesses, become at once the pride and the wonder of the American continent. In 1844, under the administration of Governor Mouton, this enlightened chief magistrate of the state of Louisiana proposed to the mayor of the city, to put at his disposal from eighty to one hundred black convicts, sentenced to hard labor, on condition that they should be employed by the municipal councils of New Orleans, in cutting down the forest which lies between the lake and New Orleans, and on condition that, during that time, they should be fed and clothed at the expense of the city. This liberal offer was not accepted for some futile causes, and a very important public improvement was indefinitely delayed. But he who studies some of the designs of Providence, as they are stamped on the map of the world, can see, however feeble his vision may be, that it is not in the power of the apathy, the stupidity, or the malice of man, materially to affect the destinies which are in store for the noble city now rising so proudly on the bank of the mighty father of rivers in the Egypt of the New World. Time will do all that is necessary—time! that great destroyer and beautifier of things!

> "Hæc igitur formam crescendo mutat, et olim
> Immensi caput orbis erit. Sic dicere vates. OVID.

In another article of the instructions, the company impressed upon Périer's mind the importance of his visiting, as soon as possible after his arrival in Louisiana, the powerful tribe of the Natchez, in order to become well acquainted with their dispositions, and the nature of their relations with the neighboring French settlement, to which it was the intention of the company to give as full a development as it was susceptible of. He was informed that the Natchez had three important villages in close contiguity with the French settlement; which circumstance had been and was expected to be the cause of incessant misunderstandings and quarrels; and that it was the desire of the company that he should look into this state of things, and that, if he should be of opinion, after a thorough investigation, that there was danger in keeping so close together two antagonistic races, then to tender to the Natchez chiefs, presents sufficiently persuasive to induce them to remove farther. These instructions, which, no doubt, became known to the French settlers, and leaked out among the Indians, and the feelings and acts to which they must have given rise, were probably one of the main causes that produced the horrible tragedy which marked with letters of blood the annals of Louisiana in 1729.

The new governor, Périer, had, when accepting his office, undertaken a task which, to be performed with credit to himself and to the India Company, required capacities of mind and soul of no inferior order; for, he had to contend with difficulties, for which mediocrity was no match. To appreciate his position, it is sufficient to read the description which Drouot de Valdeterre, who had commanded at Dauphine Island and Biloxi, gives of the colony in 1726.

"The inhabitants of this country," said he, "whose establishment in it is of such recent date, not being governed in the name of his majesty, but in that of the company, have become republicans in their thoughts, feelings, and manners, and they consider themselves as free from the allegiance due to a lawful sovereign. The troops are without discipline and subordination, without arms and ammunition, most of the time, without clothing, and they are frequently obliged to seek for their food among the Indian tribes. There are no forts for their protection; no places of refuge for them in cases of attack. The guns and other implements of war are buried in sand and abandoned; the warehouses are unroofed; the merchandise, goods, and provisions are damaged or completely spoiled; the company as well as the colonists are plundered without mercy and restraint; revolts and desertions among the troops are authorized and sanctioned; incendiaries who, for the purpose of pillage, commit to the flames whole camps, posts, settlements, and warehouses, remain unpunished; prisoners of war are forced to become sailors in the service of the company, and by culpable negligence or connivance they are allowed to run away with ships loaded with merchandise; other vessels are willfully stranded or wrecked, and their cargoes are lost to their owners; forgers, robbers, and murderers are secure of impunity. In short, this is a country which, to the shame of France be it said, is without religion, without justice, without discipline, without order, and without police." What a picture! It wants no finishing stroke.

In this energetic enumeration of the imperfections of the colony at the time, there is one thing which is deserving of notice. It is the innate spirit of republicanism which stuck to it from its origin: a spirit, of which Governor Cadillac complained so bitterly in 1717, and which, in 1726, was not much more to the taste of Drouot de Valdeterre.

It must be confessed that the company itself was the first, in some instances, to give bad examples by the violation of contracts and of the laws of morality and justice. Thus, on the 31st of October, the Council of State, at the instigation of the company, issued an ordinance decreeing that all creditors should accept in satisfaction of their claims, and that all holders of promissory notes and letters of credit should receive in payment of those obligations (any contrary stipulations notwithstanding) the copper currency which had been introduced in the colony, and for the value affixed to it, instead of Spanish dollars or other Spanish coin. Any person violating this ordinance was declared to be guilty of peculation or extortion, sentenced to pay a fine of three hundred livres, one half of which for the benefit of the informer, and the other for the relief of the charity hospital, and further to be whipped and branded by the public executioner. The Spanish dollars or coin paid in violation of this edict were confiscated on behalf of the government.

Nothing could have justified this violent interference with private contracts; and it seems to us, modified as we are by the political atmosphere we live in, that those who framed and issued the ordinance we have mentioned, were much more deserving of the hangman's whip and brand than those who, in conformity with their pledged faith in contracts which were lawful at the time they were made, would have disregarded and disobeyed such retrospective and barbarous legislation.

Beyond this act of arbitrary and unjust legislation, nothing else marked the close of the year 1726, which had winged its flight over the colony without having dropped from its pinions one feather which Louisiana might have added to her stores of acquisitions and prosperity. For her there had been no progress. Time and the world had stood still.

In 1727, some Ursuline nuns and some Jesuits, in conformity with a contract, which, in the preceding year, they had passed with the India Company, came to Louisiana, where they were to reside permanently. The Ursulines were seven in number, and were to take charge of the charity hospital in New Orleans. According to previous stipulations, they were transported at the cost of the company with four servants, and they had received each, before their departure, as a gratuity, the sum of five hundred livres. They were immediately put in possession of the hospital, in which they were to reside until a more convenient dwelling should be built up for them. The company was to concede to the hospital a lot of ground measuring eight acres, fronting on the Mississippi by the usual depth of forty. The object of this concession was the establishment of a *plantation*, capable of supplying the wants of the Ursulines, and of affording to them a sufficient remuneration for their services in the hospital. Those eight acres were to be located as near New Orleans as possible. Each of the nuns was to receive six hundred livres a year, until their plantation should be in full cultivation, or during five years after they should have been furnished by the company with eight negroes, on the ordinary conditions on which they were sold to the colonists. It was expressly stipulated, that if the nuns ceased to serve in the hospital as agreed upon, they would forfeit their plantation and the immovables attached to the hospital, and would retain only the negroes and other movables.

An edifice, which is still in existence, was constructed for their use on Condé-street, between Barracks and Hospital streets. They took possession of it in 1730, when it was completed, and they continued to occupy it until 1824, when they moved to a more splendid and more spacious convent, which they had caused to be built, three miles below the city, on the bank of the river. After the State House had been burnt in New Orleans, the Legislature sat in the old convent, and in 1831, its sacred walls, one century after they had pealed for the first time with holy anthems, and had heard soft prayers whispered to the sweet Virgin Mary, **were** converted to purposes of legislation, and resounded with fierce oratorical debates. It has since resumed a character more consonant with its original destination, and has become the bishop's palace.

Such is the humble origin of one of the wealthiest religious corporations of the state. The Ursulines have long ceased to be connected with the charity hospital, and have established a convent for the education of females. Heaven has ever after favored them with uninterrupted prosperity, and so far, has spared them those trials and vicissitudes which are the common lot of the human race. In a country where all the laws counteract the permanent accumulation of wealth in private hands, and also where lay corporations of every sort invariably run into debt and end in bankruptcy, the history of these Ursuline nuns is a remarkable demonstration of the vitality, and of the spirit of preservation and of acquisition inherent to religious Catholic associations. It is undeniable that, to husband the terrestrial resources of the world, and to make the most of them, no individuals nor set of people are to be compared with those who deal in religious spirituality, and whose minds are fraught with *thoughts celestial*. Parched deserts, where it seemed that none but the salamander could live, have smiled at the command of monks, and have become the delightful habitations of man. There, stupendous buildings have been erected in the very bosom of sterility, refreshing waters have gushed from the burning sand, luxuriant gardens have sprung into existence, the hot breeze has been made sweet with perfumes, and the gorgeous display of opulence has astonished the pilgrim or the inquisitive traveler, in places which looked as if consecrated by nature to solitude and to famine. . On how many craggy sides of desolate mountains, where the goat itself could hardly find scanty food, have comfortable human abodes been raised, and flourishing institutions been established under the magic spell of religious association! Religious association! It gives even to woman the strength of a giant. There is in it consolidation, duration, infinite power, and almost ubiquity of influence. Truly, it is no transient bauble, as so many of our political or other worldly institutions, but it is something to study and to admire. Its granite organization inspires me with a respect which discourages censure, and I feel little disposed to analyze the good or the evil it has produced, and to indulge in a philosophical examination of its bearings on the destinies of nations, and in a prophetic anticipation of its future doings. To pyramids, the grandeur of which awes my sight, I bow with that innate love I feel in my soul for the stupendous, without enquiring, or caring perhaps, whether harvests profitable to mankind, or rank weeds, will grow within reach of their lengthened shadows.

These reflections lead me by an easy transition to the Jesuits, who landed in Louisiana at the same time with the Ursulines. The Superior of the company of the Louisiana Jesuits was to reside in New Orleans, but could not exercise therein any ecclesiastical functions, without the permission of the Superior of the Capuchins, under whose spiritual jurisdiction New Orleans happened to be placed. The Jesuits had been transported to the colony at the cost of the company; before their departure, and as a gratuity, each one received 150 livres; during the first two years of their residence in Louisiana, they were to be paid severally at the rate of 800 livres annually, and, afterward, that salary was to be reduced to 600 livres. A concession of eight acres of land, fronting on the river, with the usual depth, was made to them in the neighborhood of New Orleans, and they long dwelt on a *plantation*, a little above

Canal-street, in that part of the city which is now called the second municipality. A house and chapel were constructed for them, and they soon became as powerful in Louisiana, as they are destined to be wherever they may have a footing. Thus New Orleans was handsomely provided with spiritual protection, being flanked, on the left, with the Ursulines, and on the right, with the Jesuits.

In the beginning of 1727, the spot where now stands New Orleans, not being protected by a levee, was subject to annual inundations, and presented no better aspect than that of a vast sink or sewer. The waters of the Mississippi, and of Lake Pontchartrain, met at a ridge of high land, which, by their common deposits, they had formed between Bayou St. John and New Orleans, and which was since called the *Lepers' bluff*. The whole city was surrounded by a large ditch, and fenced in with sharp stakes wedged close together. For the purposes of draining, a ditch ran along the four sides of every square of the city, and every lot in every square was also ditched all round, causing New Orleans to look very much like a microscopic caricature of Venice. Mosquitoes buzzed, and enormous frogs croaked incessantly in concert with other indescribable sounds; tall reeds, and grass of every variety, grew in the streets and in the yards, so as to interrupt all communication, and offered a safe retreat, and places of concealment to venomous reptiles, wild beasts, and malefactors, who, protected by these impenetrable jungles, committed with impunity all sorts of evil deeds. It provoked a proclamation from Rossard, the inspector of police, who complained bitterly of the *overstretched obstinacy* with which, in spite of repeated admonitions, the inhabitants of New Orleans persisted in abstaining from removing such nuisances, and therefore he threatened them with condign punishment. It is pleasing to the imagination, to compare the past with the present, the hay standards of primitive Rome with the gold eagles which spread their wings in front of the legions of Cæsar.

Governor Périer signalized the beginning of his administration by some improvements of an important nature. On the 15th of November, he had completed in front of New Orleans a levee, of eighteen hundred yards in length, and so broad that its summit measured eighteen feet in width. This same levee, although considerably reduced in its proportions, he caused to be continued eighteen miles on both sides of the city, above and below. He announced to the company, that he would soon undertake to cut a canal from New Orleans to Bayou St. John, in order to open a communication with the sea through the lakes, and he mentioned the arrangements which he had made with the inhabitants in relation to the negroes they were to furnish for the execution of this work, which was actually begun, but to which subsequent events put a stop. Thus it is seen that the plan of the canal which now bears the name of Carondelet, did not originate with that Spanish governor.

The English, being at war with the Spaniards, were intriguing among the Indians, to set them against their enemies, and at their instigation, the Talapouches had besieged Pensacola. But Governor Périer having sent them word that, if they did not retire, he would cause them to be attacked by the Choctaws, they obeyed his summons. He also gave to the Spaniards all the indirect and secret aid that he could, and he devoted much time and intrigues, to exciting a feeling of hostility among all the Indian nations against the English. Running up the Mississippi, he put an end to several puny wars which existed between small Indian tribes from the Arkansas to the Balize, so that during the year 1727, an almost unprecedented tranquillity prevailed in the colony. He caused a census to be made of the negroes, and found that population amounting to 2600 souls: the whites hardly exceeded that number. Insignificant as this infant colony was, its expenses of administration, this year, rose to 453,728 livres, which, considering the comparative value of the precious metals, was at least equivalent to three times that sum in our days.

On the 29th of July, the Council of State in France, for reasons unknown to us, but which we must suppose to have been weighty at the time, promulgated a decree, putting in force in Louisiana an old edict of Henry IId, which made it a capital crime for unmarried women to conceal their pregnancy. This legislative act was received in the colony with exceedingly marked signs of displeasure; and it is to be hoped that, on account of its severity, it never was carried into execution if any case ever called for its application.

During that summer, Governor Périer, leaving New Orleans, visited the first settlements of the French at the Bay of St. Louis, at Biloxi, Pascagoula, and Mobile. While among the Pascagoulas, or *bread-eaters*, he was invited to go to the mouth of the river of that name, to listen to the mysterious music which floats on the waters, particularly on a calm, moonlight night, and which, to this day, excites the wonder of visitors. It seems to issue from caverns or grottoes in the bed of the river, and sometimes ascends from the water under the very keel of the boat which contains the inquisitive traveler, whose ear it strikes as the distant concert of a thousand Eolian harps. On the banks of the river, close by the spot where the music is heard, tradition says that there existed a tribe different in color and in other peculiarities from the rest of the Indians. Their ancestors had originally emerged from the sea, where they were born, and were of a light complexion. They were a gentle, gay, inoffensive race, living chiefly on oysters and fish, and they passed their time in festivals and rejoicings. They had a temple in which they adored a mermaid. Every night when the moon was visible, they gathered round the beautifully carved figure of the mermaid, and with instruments of strange shape, worshiped that idol with such soul-stirring music, as had never before blessed human ears.

One day, a short time after the destruction of Mauvila, or Mobile, in 1539, by Soto and his companions, there appeared among them a white man, with a long gray beard, flowing garments, and a large cross in his right hand. He drew from his bosom a book, which he kissed reverentially, and he began to explain to them what was contained in that *sacred little casket*. Tradition does not say how he came suddenly to acquire the language of those people, when he attempted to communicate to them the solemn truths of the gospel. It must have been by the operation of that faith which, we are authoritatively told, will remove mountains. Be it as it may, the holy man, in the course of a few months, was proceeding with much success in his pious undertaking, and the work of conversion was going on bravely, when his purposes were defeated by an awful prodigy.

One night, when the moon at her zenith poured on heaven and earth, with more profusion than usual, a flood of light angelic, at the solemn hour of twelve, when all in nature was repose and silence, there came, on a sudden, a rushing on the surface of the river, as if the still air had been flapped into a whirlwind by myriads of invisible wings sweeping onward. The placid water was immediately convulsed; uttering a deep groan, it rolled several times from one bank to the other with rapid oscillations, and then gathered itself up into a towering column of foaming waves, on the top of which stood a mermaid, looking with magnetic eyes that could draw almost every thing to her, and singing with a voice which fascinated into madness. The Indians and the priest, their new guest, rushed to the bank of the river to contemplate this supernatural spectacle. When she saw them, the mermaid tuned her tones into still more bewitching melody, and kept chanting a sort of mystic song, with this often repeated ditty:—

"Come to me, come to me, children of the sea,
Neither bell, book, nor cross shall win ye from your queen."

The Indians listened with growing ecstasy, and one of them plunged into the river to rise no more. The rest, men, women, and children, followed in quick succession, moved, as it were, with the same irresistible impulse. When the last of the race disappeared, a wild laugh of exultation was heard; down returned the river to its bed with the roar of a cataract, and the whole scene seemed to have been but a dream. Ever since that time, is heard occasionally the distant music which has excited so much attention and investigation. The other Indian tribes of the neighborhood have always thought that it was their musical brethren, who still keep up their revels at the bottom of the river, in the palace of the mermaid. Tradition further relates that the poor priest died in an agony of grief, and that he attributed this awful event, and this victory of the powers of darkness, to his not having been in a perfect state of grace when he attempted the conversion of those infidels. It is believed also that he said on his death-bed, that those deluded pagan souls would be redeemed from their bondage and sent to the kingdom of heaven, if on a Christmas night, at twelve of the clock, when the moon shall happen to be at her meridian, a priest should dare to come alone to that musical spot, in a boat propelled by himself, and should drop a crucifix into the water. But, alas! if this be ever done, neither the holy man nor the boat are to be seen again by mortal eyes. So far, the attempt has not been made; sceptic minds have sneered, but no one has been found bold enough to try the experiment.

Since I am dealing in traditionary lore, I may as well close this lecture with another legend, which, when I was a boy, thirty years ago, a man of eighty related to me, as having been handed down to him by his father.

In a lot situated at the corner of Orleans and Dauphine streets, in the city of New Orleans, there is a tree which nobody looks at without curiosity and without wondering how it came there. For a long time, it was the only one of its kind known in the state, and from its isolated position, it has always been cursed with sterility. It reminds one of the warm climes of Africa or Asia, and wears the aspect of a stranger of distinction driven from his native country. Indeed, with its sharp and thin foliage, sighing mournfully under the blast of one of our November northern winds, it looks as sorrowful as an exile. Its enormous trunk is nothing but an agglomeration of knots and bumps, which each passing year seems to have deposited there as a mark of age, and as a protection against the blows of time and of the world. Inquire for its origin, and every one will tell you that it has stood there from time immemorial. A sort of vague but impressive mystery is attached to it, and it is as superstitiously respected as one of the old oaks of Dodona. Bold would be the axe that should strike the first blow at that foreign patriarch; and if it were prostrated to the ground by a profane hand, what native of the city would not mourn over its fall, and brand the act as an unnatural and criminal deed? So, long live the *date-tree* of Orleans-street— that time-honored descendant of Asiatic ancestors!

In the beginning of 1727, a French vessel of war landed at New Orleans a man of haughty mien, who wore the Turkish dress, and whose whole attendance was a single servant. He was received by the governor with the highest distinction, and was conducted by him to a small but comfortable house with a pretty garden, then existing at the corner of Orleans and Dauphine streets, and which, from the circumstance of its being so distant from other dwellings, might have been called a rural retreat, although situated in the limits of the city. There, the stranger, who was understood to be a prisoner of state, lived in the greatest seclusion; and although neither he nor his attendant could be guilty of indiscretion, because none understood their language, and although Governor Périer severely rebuked the slightest inquiry, yet it seemed to be the settled conviction in Louisiana, that the mysterious stranger was a brother of the Sultan, or some great personage of the Ottoman empire, who had fled from the anger of the vicegerent of Mohammed, and who had taken refuge in France. The Sultan had peremptorily demanded the fugitive, and the French government, thinking it derogatory to its dignity to comply with that request, but at the same time not wishing to expose its friendly relations with the Moslem monarch, and perhaps desiring, for political purposes, to keep in hostage the important guest it had in its hands, had recourse to the expedient of answering, that he had fled to Louisiana, which was so distant a country that it might be looked upon as the grave, where, as it was suggested, the fugitive might be suffered to wait in peace for actual death, without danger or offense to the Sultan. Whether this story be true or not is now a matter of so little consequence, that it would not repay the trouble of a strict historical investigation.

The year 1727 was drawing to its close, when on a dark, stormy night, the howling and barking of the numerous dogs in the streets of New Orleans were observed to be fiercer than usual, and some of that class of individuals who pretend to know every thing, declared that, by the vivid flashes of the lightning, they had seen, swiftly and stealthily gliding toward the residence of the *unknown*, a body of men who wore the scowling appearance of malefactors and ministers of blood. There afterward came also a report, that a piratical-looking Turkish vessel had been hovering a few days previous in the bay of Barataria. Be it as it may, on the next morning the house of the stranger was deserted. There were no traces of mortal struggle to be seen; but in the garden, the earth had been dug, and *there* was the unmistakable indication of a recent grave. Soon, however, all doubts were removed by the finding of an inscription in Arabic characters, engraved on a marble tablet, which was subsequently sent to France. It ran thus: "The justice of heaven is satisfied, and the date-tree shall grow on the traitor's tomb. The sublime Emperor of the faithful, the supporter of the faith, the omnipotent master and Sultan of the world, has redeemed his vow. God is great, and Mohammed is his prophet. Allah!" Some time after this event, a foreign-looking tree was seen to peep out of the spot where a corpse must have been deposited in that stormy night, when the rage of the elements yielded to the pitiless fury of man, and it thus explained in some degree this part of the inscription, "the date-tree shall grow on the traitor's grave."

Who was *he*, or what had *he* done, who had provoked such relentless and far-seeking revenge? Ask Nemesis, or—at that hour when evil spirits are allowed to roam over the earth, and magical invocations **are made**—go, and interrogate *the tree of the dead*.

FIFTH LECTURE.

Arrival of the Casket Girls—Royal Ordinance relative to the Concessions of Lands—Manner of settling the Succession of Frenchmen married to Indian Women—French Husbands—Indian Wives—History of Madame Dubois, an Indian Squaw—Conspiracy of the Natchez against the French—Massacre of the French at Natchez in 1729—Massacre of the French at the Yazoo Settlement in 1730—Attack of the Natchez against the French Settlement at Natchitoches—They are beaten by St. Denis—The French and Choctaws attack the Natchez—Daring and Death of Navarre and of some of his Companions—Siege of the Natchez Forts—Flight of the Natchez—Cruel Treatment of Natchez Prisoners by Governor Perier—Desperation of the Natchez—The Chickasaws grant an Asylum to the Natchez—Conspiracy of the Banbara Negroes—List of the Principal Officers in the Colony in 1730.

In the beginning of 1728, there came a vessel of the company with a considerable number of young girls, who had not been taken, like their predecessors, from houses of correction. The company had given to each of them a casket containing some articles of dress. From that circumstance, they became known in the colony under the nickname of the "filles à la cassette," or "the casket girls." The Ursulines were requested to take care of them until they should be provided with suitable husbands. Subsequently, it became a matter of importance in the colony to derive one's origin from the *casket girls*, rather than from the *correction girls*. What distinctions, however slim they may be, will not be eagerly sought after by human pride?

With great propriety, Governor Périer turned his attention to the encouragement of the agriculture of the country, and by words and deeds excited the colonists to draw out of the fertile soil on which they dwelt, the wealth which was concealed within its bosom. Rice, tobacco, and indigo were cultivated with success by the two thousand six hundred negroes who had been imported, and the fig and orange trees, lately introduced, were thriving everywhere, and ornamenting almost every garden. Land was rising in value, and as surveys had been carelessly made, limits fixed in a very loose or arbitrary manner, and titles of property mostly incomplete from negligence, indifference, or from some other cause, a royal ordinance, in order to check anticipated lawsuits, and to prevent future confusion, was issued on the 10th of August, 1728, and declared:

"That all the orders of concession addressed, before the 30th of December, 1723, by the India Company in France, to its directors in Louisiana, if not as yet presented to said directors for confirmation, or if not as yet followed by the possession and improvement stipulated in the acts of concession, were null and void."

In obedience to this ordinance, every landholder was bound to show his titles to the Superior Council, within a specified time, and to designate the quantity of land he claimed and had cultivated, under the penalty of a fine of 1000 livres, and of the loss of the conceded land, which, in that case, should escheat to the company.

Every concession of land situated on both sides of the Mississippi, below Manchac, was to be reduced to twenty acres, fronting on the river, except it should be proved that a greater number of acres was under cultivation.

The depth of every concession was to vary from between one hundred acres and one hundred an l twenty acres, according to the nature of the locality.

The company was authorized to raise a tax of one

cent for every acre, cultivated or not, and of five livres for every slave. The revenue arising from this tax was to be consecrated to the building of churches and hospitals.

The expenses of the colonial administration had continued to be very great, and had amounted, this year, to 486,051 livres.

The year 1729 dawned on the colony under favorable auspices. Through the harmonious and joint administration of Périer and De la Chaise, tranquillity had been established in the country, which, for the first time, was free from the evils produced by the jealousies and quarrels of the governor, and of the king's commissaries. Unchecked in the exercise of the high authority with which he was clothed, De la Chaise turned his attention to the jurisprudence of the country, and to the settling of disputes and juridical conflicts among the inhabitants. A case presented itself, in which he used his influence much to the satisfaction of the colonists. Father de la Vente, the bigoted curate of Mobile, had demanded that the French be authorized by the government to take Indian wives. This demand had been opposed by the governor, Lamothe Cadillac, and the king's commissary, Duclos. The government had neither sanctioned, nor actually prohibited such marriages, but had merely recommended that they be discouraged as much as possible. However, the church had thought differently, and consecrated a great many alliances of that kind. It was, no doubt, very correct, in a moral point of view, but it gave rise to legal difficulties. Thus, on the death of French husbands, their Indian wives claimed, according to the customs of the Viscounty of Paris, half of their succession: and if they died without issue, the property acquired during marriage went to the Indian heirs of the wife in prefer ence to the French heirs of the husband These Indian heirs frequently ran away with what was left by the deceased, and it was next to an impossibility to force them to pay the debts of the succession, and to subject them to the observance of those formalities required by, and inherent to, the laws of succession. The French were therefore clamorous to prevent Indian wives from enjoying the benefit of *the custom of Paris*, and they urged that, to deviate from it in such cases, would be nothing but an act of justice and of sound policy, on the ground that what had been acquired by the French should remain to the French, and not go to the huts of barbarians, who were their enemies. Taking these complaints into consideration, and on the recommendation of De la Chaise, the Superior Council decreed that, for the future, on the death of a Frenchman married to an Indian woman, the property left by the deceased should be administered, if there were minor children, by a tutor, and if there were none, by a curator to vacant estates, who should pay annually to the widow one third of the revenue of the estate, provided that this pension should cease in case she returned to dwell among her tribe. The expenses of preserving from deterioration, and of keeping up the goods, chattels, and movable or immovable property of the succession, were to be at the charge of the children, or of the other heirs.

The fact is, that the conduct of the Indian wives toward their French husbands was not such as to entitle them to much respect or sympathy, and adultery was one of the frequent offenses of which they became guilty. When brought into the society of the white race, it seems that they lost those qualities which they possessed when pursuing the savage and primitive life of their ancestors, and on the other hand, they acquired none of the virtues and blandishments of civilization. One instance in support of this assertion, among many others which might be cited, will be sufficient.

In the district of the Illinois, in 1720, the French had built a fort, and were living in good intelligence with the Indians, when the commander, or governor of the district, no doubt with the intention of producing a deep impression on those barbarians by the sight of the number, the resources, and the power of the French nation, undertook to induce some of them to pay a visit to the *Great French village across the big salt lake.* He talked so much about the marvelous things to be seen in his own country, that he persuaded twelve of the Indians to follow him to France. One of them was the daughter of the chief of the Illinois, and she is said to have been the paramour of the governor. That officer, leaving the command of his fort to his lieutenant, descended the Mississippi with his twelve Indian attendants, and a sergeant named Dubois, and arrived safely at New Orleans, where they embarked for France. There, they were conducted to Versailles, introduced at court, and presented to the king, as a sample of his red subjects in Louisiana. They amused the *élite* of the aristocracy, by hunting a deer in the *Bois de Boulogne*, according to the Indian fashion; and the women, particularly the daughter of the chief of the Illinois, who was beautiful, were caressed and petted for a week by duchesses and such high-born dames. They even appeared on the floor of the Italian opera in Paris, to perform Indian dances, and they had the honor of being the flitting wonder of a few days. The Indian princess was converted to Christianity, baptized in the splendid gothic cathedral of Notre Dame with great pomp and ceremony, and then married to Sergeant Dubois, who in consideration of this distinguished alliance, was raised by the king to the rank of captain, and commander of the Illinois District. She received handsome presents from the ladies of the court, and from the king himself. Her companions were not forgotten, and came in for their share of petticoats, shining blue coats, and cocked hats lined with gold. They were, of course, very much pleased with their reception by their white allies, and after having seen every thing, and having been exhibited to every body, they left Paris and Versailles, to return to their distant home, and departed in high glee for Lorient, where they took ship. With regard to the officer who had brought them to France, he remained in his native country, gave up forever all thoughts of returning to Louisiana and to Indian paramours, and married a rich widow, who, like Desdemona, had *loved him for the dangers he had passed*, among

> "Cannibals that each other eat,
> The anthropophagi, and men whose heads
> Do grow beneath their shoulders."

The Indians, when they arrived at New Orleans, were entertained in that city at the expense of the India Company. They were also supplied with boats and rowers, and with an escort of soldiers, and thus transported back to the Illinois. Great were the rejoicings among those people, who had long thought they had lost some of their most important and most cherished members. Dubois took possession of the fort as the commander of the district, and there lived for a short time in the full enjoyment of power and peace. His wife, however, used to pay to her relations among her tribe, more frequent visits than he liked. One day, she helped her people to surprise the fort, and Dubois and the whole garrison were butchered without mercy. Madame **Du** bois then renounced Christianity, stripped herself of her cumbersome French dress, and returned to the worship of her old idols, to her early habits, and to the savage life which, it seemed, had lost in her eyes none of its primitive attractions. So much for the attempt to tame lions and tigers!

Périer, on his arrival in the colony, had been struck with its defenseless situation, and with the necessity of fortifying the distant settlements. He had made frequent remonstrances on the subject to the company, and had solicited an additional force of two or three hundred men. But his fears were treated as chimerical, and his motives misunderstood. It was thought that, by asking for more troops, his intention was to give more importance to his command, and to engage in some war in order to display military talents. But subsequent events justified Périer's apprehensions.

In 1729, the French settlement at Natchez was under the command of an officer called Chopart, Chépart, or Etcheparre. He was rapacious, haughty, and tyrannical, and by repeated acts of oppression and injustice, had made himself odious to those over whom he ruled. One day, he ordered a subordinate officer to be put in irons without cause. The officer, who was no other than Dumont, well known for the interesting historical memoirs he has left on Louisiana, having succeeded in escaping from his prison, fled to New Orleans, and laid his complaint before Governor Périer. Chopart was summoned to head-quarters, tried by his peers, and found guilty of an abuse of power. He would even have been broken, if pressing and powerful solicitors had not obtained his pardon from Governor Périer. But he was reinstated in his office, only on condition that he should change his conduct, and treat those under him with more justice and mildness.

Having received a salutary lesson, Chopart, on his return to Natchez, acted toward the white population with more reserve, but made up for it by treating the Indians with insolence and cruelty. Acquainted, no doubt, with the instructions given to Périer by the company, and in which the wish was expressed that the Natchez, to prevent further collisions, should be induced, if possible, to remove farther off, he acted accordingly, and heaped every sort of outrage and insult upon that devoted race, to force them to abandon the spot they had occupied for so many centuries. Seeing that by such means he did not obtain the object he had in view, he went still further. One day, he summoned to his presence the Great Sun, and told that chief that he, Chopart, had received orders from Governor Périer to take possession of the beautiful village of the *White Apple*, which was situated six miles from the French fort, and there to establish a plantation, and to construct certain buildings; wherefore it was necessary that the Natchez should remove to some other place, which they might occupy without prejudice to the French. This intimation was given in an abrupt manner, without the slightest attempt at conciliation. It was the tone of an eastern despot, speaking to a slave. The Great Sun looked at Chopart with a composed but inquisitive eye, and said:—"Surely, my white brother does not speak in earnest, but wishes only to try the fortitude of the red man. Does not my white brother know that the Natchez have lived in that village for more years than there are hairs in the twisted lock which hangs from the top of my head to my waist?" "Foolish barbarian!" exclaimed the French officer, with kindling ire and fierce contempt. "What ties of brotherhood can there be between thy race and mine? I have no explanations or apology to give to such as thou. It is sufficient for thee to know that I obey superior orders—obey mine!"

In spite of the habitual command of an Indian over his muscles and features, and his aversion to any demonstration of his inward feelings, when such language fell on the ears of the Great Sun, his eyes flashed and his breast heaved up with emotion, but he replied with a calm voice: "Brother, we have not been used to such treatment. So far, the French have taken nothing from us by force. What they possess, we gave freely, or they purchased. Wishing to live in peace with thy nation, I say to thee: We have other lands that we can spare—take them!—can we do more? But, as to the village of the White Apple, leave it untouched in the hands of the Natchez. There we have a temple, and there the bones of our ancestors have slept since we came to dwell on the bank of the father of rivers." Chopart listened to this touching appeal with an ironical smile, and said:—" I will not bandy fine sentiments with thee, romantic Indian; but mark my word, and remember that I shall keep it. Toward the latter part of November, I expect a galley from New Orleans. If, when she arrives, the village of the White Apple is not delivered up to me, I will send thee bound hand and foot to our great chief in our great village down the river. Thou seest that I make short work of it. Go."

"Good, I see," replied the Indian; "and I go home to lay thy communication before the old and wise men of the nation."

When all the magnates of the Natchez met in council, at the call of their sovereign, every one of them knew beforehand the subject of their future deliberations. The words of the French chief had been spoken publicly, and had spread like wildfire, causing the utmost indignation, and rousing the slumbering hatred which had been pent up in more than one breast against the insolent intruders. But when what had happened was officially communicated by the Great Sun, there was in the assembly a fresh outburst of indignation, which was hushed up and gave place to profound silence, when the chief of the White Apple was seen to rise. Next to the Great Sun, he was the most influential man among the Natchez, on account of his exploits as a warrior, and of his eloquence as an orator. Majestically rising, he stood up, buried as it were in profound meditation, while all eyes were riveted on his noble form. After the lapse of a few minutes, he thus began:—

"Children of the Sun, old traditions and oracles have long informed us of the approaching doom that awaits our nation. We have had ancestors, but we are destined to be the ancestors of no human beings. If those traditions and oracles are true; nay, if portentous signs and appearances are to be believed, soon this nation, which once was so powerful, will cease to exist. We have been gradually shrinking up into a small and weak population, and our once broad domains, which it required so many moons to travel over, have fast escaped from our grasp, as water oozes through the fingers by which it is clutched. Diseases, frequent human sacrifices in honor of our dead chiefs, and long wars with some of the red tribes by which we are surrounded, had contributed to diminish our numbers, when, on a sudden, there came upon us this hostile race, the pale-faced warriors, who had been announced to us as our future destroyers. Bowing to the decree of the Great Spirit, and yielding to the superior powers which we recognized in these strange men, we tried to conciliate their good-will, and we granted them land and all sorts of supplies. What has been the consequence? Every year they have become more greedy, exacting, and overbearing Every year, between them and our people, quarrels have sprung up, in which blood was shed, and for which we had to make atonement, sometimes at the cost of the heads of our most illustrious warriors. The vic'nage of these men has become at last an intolerable curse upon us. With their merchandise and new wares, they have introduced new wants among our people, corrupted their morals, and changed particularly the manners of our young men, who now despise the rugged virtues of their forefathers to ape the frivolity of the French, and have become effeminate and worthless drunkards. As to our women, their heads have been turned by the silver tongue and the gaudy plumage of these loose strangers. What is the result? Why, that debauchery has crept into every bosom, and that the very blood of the Natchez is tainted in its source. Which of us is sure now of the affections and of the purity of his daughter or of his wife, when yonder thieves are prowling about our dwellings? Before the French settled near us, we were in the full enjoyment of the greatest of blessings—boundless freedom! What are we now?—hardly better than slaves!—are we not controlled in every thing, and dare we move without asking leave from that haughty chief who sits in yonder fort with the white flag? Are they not stripping us every day of the poor remains of our ancient liberty? Do they not frequently strike us with clubs, as they do with the black slaves? Depend upon it, they will soon seize upon us, put us in irons, force us to work for them in their fields, tie us to posts and apply the lash to our backs, as they do with the black faces. Shall we wait for that moment, or shall we not prefer to die before, but satiated with blood, and surfeited with revenge?"

Here a low and half-suppressed growl, forcing its way,

as it were, through clenched teeth, was heard running through that grim-visaged assembly, and some of the young warriors, giving way to their excitement, started up from their seats, and uttering a fierce shout, shook their tomahawks with wild fury. The orator looked round with a grave and rebuking glance, as if disapproving the undignified and premature display of feelings by which he had been interrupted, and waving his hand as if he commanded silence, he thus continued :—
" Have we not met now to deliberate on a peremptory command which the French have ventured to send to us? Have we not before us a sample of their present audacity, and the harbinger of their future daring? Have they not ordered us to relinquish to them the harvests which grow around us, and which are the results of our labors? Do they not order us away from the village of the White Apple, to shift for ourselves in the woods like wild beasts? Will they not soon drive us out of the other villages? What then will become of the tombs of our ancestors and of the cradles of our children? The white faces will run their plows over the bones of our dead, and put their cattle in our temples. Shall we consent to such profanation? Are we not strong enough to prevent it? We are. Shall we wait until the French become so numerous that we shall not be able to resist oppression? For my part, I say—no! We can destroy them all, if we choose, and if we act with proper courage and skill. Should we be doomed in our turn to perish all, and leave none of our race behind, let it not be without having struck a blow worthy of the children of the Sun. Let us not be immolated like bleating sheep, without resistance, but let us die like warriors, after having done a deed that will make the name of the Natchez famous among all the red tribes, however distant they may be from our na-

tive hills. I pause . . . . . to put this question: shall we yield our birth-place, our beautiful valleys, our temples, our sacred mounds, the tombs of our ancestors, and every thing that we hold dear, without a struggle? and shall we only utter impotent wailings like babes, when deprived of their playthings? Shall we move away like a nation of cowardly beggars, to steal from some weaker tribe the land that we shall want for our support? War or submission!—which do you choose? I wait for an answer."

A simultaneous war-cry announced the spontaneous decision of the assembly to the orator, who thus resumed his address, with a grim smile of exultation.

"I see with pride that the contact of the French has not yet turned the Natchez into mean-spirited women. Now, listen to what I propose for the full and secure accomplishment of our design. We have always been reputed to have more mind than the other red nations; let us show it on this occasion. All the Indians—the Yazoos, the Chickasaws, the Choctaws, and others, have equally suffered like us from French insolence, and must be tired of their oppressive domination. Let us invite them to forget our past hostilities, to join with us in a holy alliance against the common enemy, and to free our father-land with one blow from the hated presence of strangers. Let ambassadors be forthwith sent to them, to lay our proposition before their councils of wise men. If they adopt it, let bundles, made up of an equal number of small sticks, be remitted to them, and let one stick be removed every day. The last remaining one will designate the day when this combined attack shall be made against the French, over the whole face of the country. Thus assailed by surprise, and isolated, cut off from the reciprocal succor which the several settlements would give to each other if this plan be not adopted, the French must succumb under the vastly superior numbers that we shall bring against them. But, for the successful execution of this combination, we must gain time, and we must humbly entreat our august sovereign, the Great Sun, here present, to enter into negotiations with the hungry French wolf, the crocodile-hearted chief in yonder fort, to obtain, by dint of presents, that our removal be postponed, and that the delay be sufficiently long to ripen to maturity the good fruit of this day's deliberations. The chief of the White Apple, children of the Sun, has but one more recommendation to make, with a view to secure the success of our enterprise: that is, the observation of secrecy. You know that women are never to be trusted in any thing, much less with designs of importance. They are fickle and indiscreet, and they can no more keep a secret than a sieve will hold water. Besides, many of them love the French, and would certainly betray us. Therefore, let us swear before we separate, to keep our lips sealed, and not to say one word which might give to our women the slightest intimation of what we intend. The chief of the White Apple has done, children of the Sun, and waits for better advice."

The orator sat down amid a universal hum of applause, and all his propositions were accepted by acclamation.

The next day, the Great Sun called at the French fort, and representing to Chopart how ill prepared they were to move so suddenly, without having selected the place whither they could transport their effects, he obtained that the fulfillment of the order of expulsion should be postponed until the latter part of December, provided that the Natchez should pay to Chopart, in the interval, a contribution consisting of one barrel of corn, and a certain quantity of fowls, furs, and bear's oil, for each and every cabin of the White Apple village: which was a pretty considerable and valuable contribution, considering that there were eighty cabins in the village. The Great Sun and the French officer parted, both equally satisfied with the bargain they had made. The one had gratified his appetite for gain, and the other thought that he had secured his revenge.

After some time, the ambassadors of the Natchez returned, and brought back the information, that all the Indian nations to which they had been sent, had eagerly embraced the proposition made to them, and had entered into the league against the French, whom they would attack on the day fixed. Thus, the whole colony was threatened with total destruction, through the imprudence of an avaricious and tyrannical subaltern officer. It is evident that the Indians could, at any time, if united, have crushed the French without much effort, if we believe a statement made by Diron d'Artaguette, in a dispatch dated on the 9th of December, 1728, and in which he estimated that the Indians settled on the banks of the principal rivers of Louisiana could set on foot seventeen thousand men, and said that, with regard to the inland nations, one of them alone, the nation of the Choctaws, could bring into the field ten thousand warriors.

All the movements which I have related, had not taken place among the Natchez without exciting the suspicions of the women; and with that eager curiosity which is said to characterize their sex, they went to work to discover what was in the wind. The Great Sun, whose intended suicide, on the death of his brother Stung Serpent, had been prevented by the French, had since died, and had been succeeded by a young Sun, his nephew, the same who had struggled with the Great Sun, to take possession of the gun with which that prince wanted to blow out his brains. The mother of the new sovereign was a woman distinguished for her intellect. She had a great deal of partiality for the French, and it was even reported that her son was the offspring of an amour she had carried on with a French officer. Disquieted by the observations she had made, she inquired of her son what was the motive of the recent meetings of the nobles and of the embassies which had sped in every direction. He answered her, that the object of these missions was merely to renew the alliances of the Natchez with the other nations, and to smoke with them the calumet of peace. She appeared satisfied with the answer: but when, on the return of the ambassadors, she saw that instead of receiving them publicly, as was the old custom, the nobles met in secret session to listen to their communication, which was not afterward made known to the people, all her fears revived, and she resolved to penetrate into such mysterious proceedings.

She requested the Great Sun to accompany her to a village called the *Corn Village*, where she pretended to have a female relation extremely sick, who required her assistance. On her son complying with her wish, she departed with him, and took the least frequented path, under the pretext that it was the most shady, and the most agreeable. When they arrived at a spot which the princess, from its solitary appearance, thought the most free from unexpected intrusion, and therefore most favorable for the accomplishment of her design, she pleaded fatigue, and begged her son to sit down by her. She then addressed him thus:

"The weariness of my old limbs is not the only cause why I stop here, my son. I wished for an opportunity to speak to thee in private, and without fear of interruption. Open thy ears to admit my words into thy brain, because they are weighty. I have always taught thee to avoid a lie as the most disgraceful of sins, and I have always told thee that a liar did not deserve to be looked upon as a man, much less as a warrior. But were a Sun, and particularly the chief of the Suns, to tell a lie, he would fall even beneath the contempt of women. How can I doubt, therefore, but that thou wilt speak the truth to thy mother? Are not all the Suns bound together with fraternal ties, whether they be males or females? Are not their interests the same? Are they not but one family? And if there be some shadow of an excuse for not trusting one or two young and giddy-headed female Suns, does the same reason exist for the aged and trust-worthy, and, above all, for the gray-haired mother of the sovereign of the Natchez? I have discovered that there is a secret at work in the bosom of the Suns; and yet that secret is kept concealed from me, as if my lips had been cut wide apart, and could no longer be sealed! Do I deserve such treatment? Does it not reflect shame and disgrace on thee? The contempt shown to a mother taints the son through skin, flesh, and bones. Dost thou know me to be vile, and capable of betraying thee and my tribe? Thou dost not dare to harbor the thought that I can intentionally commit such a crime! Well then! Didst thou ever know me to be talking in my sleep? Why therefore am I not trusted, as it is my right? Why am I spat upon by my tribe, and by my son? Where is the cause of such heart-bruising contumely? What! hast thou not come out of my womb? Whence dost thou draw thy blood but from my veins? Whence did flow the milk which fed thy infant lips but from my breast? Wouldst thou be a Sun—nay, the Great Sun, wert thou not my child? Without the tender nursing with which I surrounded thy cradle where wouldst thou be?

By me, and through me, thou art every thing, and to me thou art the most precious and most beloved thing I possess. Yet I stand now by thy side, without being even looked at, and no more noticed by thee, than if I were a worthless cur! Why dost thou not drive me away with thy foot, or thy whip? Is it because in our nation, a son has never been guilty of such an outrage toward his mother? Nay then—why dost thou insult me, in a different, it is true, but no less mortifying manner? To conceal from *me*, the oldest female Sun, *me*, the mother of the sovereign of the Natchez, a great national resolution taken by our nobles, what is it but an affront equivalent to a blow? When the womb of the whole nation is heaving up with the conception of a big design, could such throes escape my motherly penetration? Am I a fool? Am I an idiot? Was it becoming in thee to wait until I should descend to an inquiry? And shouldst thou not, before this time, have opened thy mind to thy mother? Didst thou think that I have lived so long without having acquired sagacity enough to look into thy heart with as much facility as into any of our wells of pure water? The Natchez meditate to rise upon the French.—Is it not the truth? Is not my finger on the sore? Nay; why dost thou start, and why this bewildered look? None of the pale faces listen to us, and dost thou fear that I shall sell thee in bondage to them? What dost thou imagine they could give me, me whose body is bent with age, and whose feet are already sprinkled with the dust of death, in exchange, or as a full price for a son's blood? And now," said she, rising with solemn dignity, and speaking with the deepest emphasis, "farewell forever! The earth refuses to bear the burden of the mother who is despised by her son:—the blessed air which drops from heaven is profaned by entering her lungs.

Dig my grave: for the sight of thy dishonored mother shall not, to-morrow, disgrace any longer the ancestral rays of yonder God, from whom we draw our origin."

Warm tears gushed from the eyes of the young prince when he heard reproaches which racked his heart, but he preserved his composure, and whatever might have been his inward emotion, he calmly rose, and seizing his mother by the arm, he gently forced her to resume her seat. Then, several minutes elapsed, when he seemed to be buried in reflection, and to be struggling against the opposite influences of affection and of prudence. At last he said, mournfully and respectfully:—" Mother, thy reproaches are poisoned arrows which pierce my heart. These reproaches are not deserved. I have never repulsed nor despised thee. But hast thou ever heard that it was permitted to reveal what had been resolved by the wise men of the nation in secret council? Am I not the Great Sun? Must I not set the good example? Wouldst thou persuade thy son to do a base thing? Am I not more bound to secrecy than any body else, from one peculiar circumstance? Is it not darkly rumored" (looking fixedly at his mother) " that my father was a Frenchman? And might I not be suspected of partiality toward them, although the Great Spirit knows that I hate them worse than any red foe our nation ever had! But since thou hast guessed all, what more shall I say? Thou knowest as much as I do. Therefore, close thy lips."

"I approve thy resentment against the oppressors of our race, my son," continued the princess, " but I tremble lest the Natchez should not have taken sufficient precautions to secure their revenge, without exposing our whole nation to destruction. We can not succeed, unless we take the French by surprise. Although their chief has lost his mind, they are wary and brave; if they discover that we meditate aught against them, they have plenty of merchandise to tempt all the other nations to rise against us. If you were painting your bodies in the colors of war to march against a red nation, my sleep would not be disturbed, and I would not have made to thy feelings the appeal which has disquieted them so much. But the pale faces are a fearful race. They know infinitely more than we do, and they have resources that we dream not of. It is not for myself that I tremble; it is for thee; it is for our nation. Old as I am, what care I how soon or how I die? What is it to me whether I am killed by an Indian or a French warrior? But there is more caution in woman than in man, and I may detect some flaw in the net you have spread around the French, and give good advice. For instance, one thing above all strikes me at first sight. Granting you all the success that you may anticipate, and supposing that you destroy every Frenchman, woman, and child that live in the neighborhood of our villages; admitting also that you take possession of yonder thundering fort, would not their countrymen come from their big village down below, with innumerable red allies, and overwhelm us in complete destruction? What would signify our short-lived triumph?"

Thus she artfully went on until she gradually drew from him the whole plot, and she appeared tranquilized when she knew all the details of the conspiracy, which she confessed to have been conducted with the utmost prudence and skill, her son having given her the most positive assurance that all the French in the colony would be destroyed at one blow and on the same day, all the Indian nations having joined the league, with the exception of the Tunicas and the Oumas, who had not been spoken to, because they were known to be too friendly to the French. Therefore the destruction of these two tribes had also been resolved upon. "But," said the old princess, "how can you be sure that among so many distant nations, there will not be some mistake as to the day on which the blow is to be struck." "There can be none," answered her son, who then told her all about the bundles of sticks, and informed her that the bundle reserved by the Natchez was preserved in the Great Temple of the principal village.

The princess, whose name was "*Bras Piqué*," or *Pricked Arm*, was greatly alarmed at the extent of the danger which threatened her friends, the French, but she carefully concealed her feelings from her son, and appeared to enter warmly into the conspiracy. In the mean time, she thought of nothing else but of putting the French on their guard, without exposing the safety of her son and of her nation. She acted under the supposition, that if the suspicions of the French were once aroused, they would assume an attitude and take precautions which would check the Natchez, and prevent the breaking out which they meditated. Thus, by words which she let fall from her lips, as it were carelessly, she excited the fears of some Indian women whom she knew to be attached to the French by more than one tender tie, and who communicated their information to their lovers. The old *Bras Piqué*, or *Pricked Arm*, did more; seeing no sign of precaution taken by the French, notwithstanding the warning she had caused to be given, she one day stopped a French soldier whom she accidentally met, and told him to inform the French chief that the Natchez had lost their minds, and that he had better be on the look out, and increase the strength of his fort.

The soldier repeated this admonition to Chopart, who, instead of inquiring into the causes of this strange piece of information, which was sent to him in such a vague manner, but from such high authority, said that the princess was an old hag, called the soldier a coward and a visionary, put him in the stocks to punish him for spreading false reports, and declared that he would certainly abstain from repairing the fortifications, or from doing any thing which would give the Natchez to understand he was afraid of them, because the secret motive of all these warnings, as he pretended, was to frighten him out of his resolution to force them to evacuate the village of the White Apple.

Indefatigable in her exertions to save the French, *Pricked Arm* penetrated into the temple, and clandestinely withdrew some of the sticks from the bundle, in order to destroy the concert which had been agreed upon among the Indian tribes, and to bring on prematurely the day on which the attack was to be made by the Natchez. She hoped that some of the French, at least, would escape, and have time to put on their guard the rest of the colony. She also contrived to transmit indirect and anonymous warnings to several Frenchmen, who communicated to Chopart what they had learned. But he again branded them with the epithet of cowards, and put some of them under arrest. *Pricked Arm*, astounded at the result of her repeated attempts, and forgetting in her extreme anxiety the resolution she had taken not to expose to danger, by too positive information, her son and her whole nation, went so far as to address one Macé, a sub-lieutenant, and to tell him enough to remove all doubts from minds not unalterably bent on resisting the persuasion of the strongest evidence. She presumed that Macé, being an officer, would have more influence on the French commander. But she was deceived, and Chopart remained wedded to the same fatal incredulity. Bewildered at the sight of such infatuation, the old princess was struck with superstitious awe, and very naturally came to the conclusion, that the French were doomed by the Great Spirit, and abandoned by the very God they worshiped. From that moment she became passive, and seemed to have accepted the decree of fate with the stoical indifference so common to Indians.

Time, however, was flying apace; and on the very eve of the contemplated attack, Chopart took a step which seemed to be the inspiration of some evil spirit determined to treat its victim to the last with mischievous mockery. In order to show in a signal manner his contempt for the alarming reports which had been made to him, and his determination to put a stop to them for the future, he went with several Frenchmen to the *Great Village* of the Natchez, and caroused with them the whole night. The Great Sun, to whom he communicated all the intelligence which, from time to time, had been laid before him, concerning the alledged conspiracy, behaved with great composure and profound dissimulation, notwithstanding his youth, and persuaded the infatuated man that the Natchez were his best friends, and that if he had enemies, it was among his own countrymen. " In confirmation of my declaration," he said, " my people will bring to thee to-morrow more than the amount of the tribute for which thou hast granted us time for our removal, and will then put thee in possession of the White Apple Village." Chopart returned to the fort, late in the night, drunk with pride and the fumes of the potations in which he had freely indulged. Feeling the want of rest, he gave the most precise order that, under no pretext whatever, he should be waked up before nine in the morning.

When that morning came, which was on the 29th of November, the eve of St. Andrew's day, long before

THE MORN OF THE 29TH NOVEMBER.

the rising of the sun there was a great bustling in all the villages of the Natchez. The conspirators had taken their measures with such foresight and precision, that, at the same moment, within a radius of many miles, the house of every Frenchman, however remote it was, found itself full of Indians asking for something or other. Some begged for powder, shot, and brandy, to go on a hunting expedition, promising to make ample returns for the desired loan. Others had a present to make, or an old-remembered debt to pay, or some bargain or other to propose. Motives or excuses of infinite variety were not wanting to remove suspicion. At eight, the Great Sun was seen departing from his village at the head of his nobles and of a troop of warriors. The procession moved with a great noise of instruments, and carried, with as much show as possible, the stipulated tribute of fowls, corn, oil, and furs. The master of ceremonies, gorgeously dressed, and making himself conspicuous above the rest, twirled on high, and with fantastic gestures, the calumet of peace. With demonstrations of joy, they went several times round the fort, and entered the house of the French commander, who, waked up by the noise, made his appearance in his morning gown. Elated at the sight of the valuable presents which were laid before him, laughing in his heart at the credulity of those who had attempted to rouse suspicions in his mind as to the fidelity of his Indian friends, he ordered the *givers of warnings*, as he called them, to be released from their confinement, that they should come to see how futile were their cowardly fears. Then, the Indians began to dance, to sing, and to creep into the fort and everywhere. In the mean time, a chosen band of warriors glided down the hill to the bank of the river, where the long-expected and richly-laden galley, which had arrived the day previous, was moored. There, each warrior having leisurely picked his man and made his aim sure, a simultaneous discharge was heard.

This was the preconcerted signal, which was followed far and wide by discharges of firearms so close on each other, that they seemed to make but one volley. Let us listen to Governor Périer himself, relating that event in one of his dispatches: "Such being the dispositions of the Indians, and the hour having come," says he, "the general assassination of the French took so little time, that the execution of the deed and the preceding signal were almost but one and the same thing. One single discharge closed the whole affair, with the exception of the house of La Loire des Ursins, in which there were eight men, who defended themselves with desperation. They made the house good against the Indians during the whole day. Six of them were killed, and when night came, the remaining two escaped. When the attack began, La Loire des Ursins happened to be on horseback, and being cut off from his house by the intervening foes, he fought to death, and killed four Indians. The people who were shut up in his house had already killed eight. Thus it cost the Natchez only twelve men to destroy *two hundred and fifty* of ours, through the fault of the commanding officer, who alone deserved the fate which was shared by his unfortunate companions. It was easy for him, with the arms and the forces he had, to inflict on our enemies a severer blow than the one we have received, and which has brought this colony to within two inches of utter destruction."

It is said that Chopart had the grief of surviving all his countrymen. Such was the horror and contempt the Natchez had for him, that death inflicted by the hands of a warrior was thought too honorable for the

French chief. None of that class condescended to lay hands upon him, and the lowest among the *stinking*, or plebeians, was sent for, who beat him to death with a club, in his own garden, whither he had fled. A few Frenchmen escaped, as it were by miracle, from the general massacre: among others, Navarre, Couillard, Canterelle, Louette, and Ricard, who succeeded in reaching New Orleans after many perilous adventures. Two men only were spared by the Natchez, one wagoner, named Mayeux, to be employed by them in transporting all the goods, merchandise, and effects of the French to the public square, in front of which stood the palace of the Great Sun, and where that sovereign was to make a distribution of the spoils among his subjects. The other Frenchman, named Lebeau, was a tailor, and owed his life to that circumstance. As the Natchez stood in want of his craft, they preserved him to turn him to profitable account, and employed him in repairing, or reshaping the clothes of the dead, and in fitting them to the bodies of the new owners. Dumont relates that the Natchez were particularly pleased with the variegated, diversified, and highly-colored patches which he adapted to their vestments.

The women and children, with a few exceptions, were spared and destined to be slaves, their number amounting to about three hundred. Many of the blacks, to whom the Natchez had promised their freedom and a share in the booty, had been induced to join them in the conspiracy. Some of them, however, had the credit of remaining faithful to the French, and succeeded in making their way to New Orleans. The Natchez being under the impression that all the French were destroyed throughout the land, that they had no longer any thing to fear from such redoubtable foes, and finding themselves more wealthy than they had ever been, gave themselves up to the wildest exhibitions of joy. They wound up that bloody day of the 29th of November, by a general carousal, and they kept dancing and singing until late at night, around pyramids of French heads, piled up as cannon-balls usually are in an arsenal. The agonies of the wretched women and children who witnessed the slaughter of their husbands and fathers, and who, amid the demoniacal rejoicings which followed, had to bear outrages too horrific to be related, are more easily conceived than described! Long before the next day dawned upon them, the Natchez were in such a state of inebriation, that thirty well-determined Frenchmen, says Dumont, could have destroyed the whole nation.

The Natchez, when they came back to their senses, stationed warriors along the Mississippi, to watch for all canoes and barks navigating on that river, and a few days after the massacre, they descried some travelers coming down stream. They were French, and on being hailed, not suspecting what had happened, they came to landing. They were five in number, and hardly had they touched the bank of the river, when they were received with a discharge of muskets. Three were killed, the fourth fled to the woods, where he concealed himself, and he afterward had the good luck to reach the friendly village of the Tunicas. The fifth was taken prisoner, and carried to the great village of the Natchez, where he was tortured by them in one of the public exhibitions of the kind of which they were so fond, with all the refined ferocity peculiar to the Indians.

The Natchez set fire to all the habitations of the French, which were reduced to ashes, and after the first outburst of riotous excesses in which they indulged to celebrate their triumph, they set to work with intel ligence and activity, to avail themselves to the utmost of the success they had obtained. It appears that, for some reasons unknown, they had not communicated to the Yazoos the rising they meditated against the French. On the very day of the massacre, a deputation of Yazoos, who perhaps suspected what was going on, had arrived among the Natchez. They were present at the performance of that bloody drama, and being easily persuaded to attack the few French people who had settled on their territory, they departed with a certain number of Natchez warriors. The Yazoo settlement was distant one hundred and twenty miles from the Natchez. This united band of Yazoos and Natchez ascended the Mississippi in boats, and, on their way up, discovered on the bank of the river, in a shady spot, some travelers assembled. They proved to be French, and were coming down the river with one of the Jesuit missionaries. When they were descried by the Indians, these people were engaged in the holy occupation of listening to a mass said by the priest. With that stealthy, cat-like step, so familiar to their race, the Indians approached without being observed, and poured upon them their fire at the very moment they were dropping on their knees, at the elevation of the Host; and they aimed particularly at the priest, whose sacerdotal habiliments were the objects most coveted by their cupidity. Strange to say, the murderous volley of balls proved harmless, and the French had time to fly to their boat. But the Indians had also time to reload their muskets, and fired again at the fugitives, who, being all clustered together in a boat, presented a mark which the most inexperienced shooters could hardly fail to hit. Yet, the only one among the French who was hurt, was the man who was pushing the boat from the bank. He received a ball in the thigh, but succeeded in getting into the boat, and was subsequently cured at New Orleans. The French considered their escape as providential, and attributed it to the presence of God among them at the elevation of the host, when they were attacked by the savage heathens. For many years after, the priesthood often mentioned this fact in their preachings.

The fort which the French had built among the Yazoos, was called St. Claude. Its commander, Du Coder, being on a visit to the French at Natchez, when they were butchered, shared their fate. The Yazoos had no difficulty in taking by surprise the fort of St. Claude, which had a garrison only of twenty men, whom they killed, together with the few families who had settled around, under the protection of the fort. The destruction of the French settlements at the Yazoos, took place on the first or second day of January, 1730.

At that time, St. Denis was commander of Natchitoches, where he had made himself so popular, that he led the life of a small, half barbaric, half civilized potentate. For hundreds of miles round that settlement, the Indians had submitted to his sway, and had readily acknowledged him as their great chief. He settled authoritatively all the disputes arising among the different tribes, and ruled over them as if he had been born an Indian, and been their natural sovereign. He had really become a powerful chieftain, and in case of need, with a sufficient allowance of time, might have set on foot from five to six thousand warriors. The Natchez feared him more than any thing else, and knowing his daring and indomitable energy, had no doubt but that, on his hearing of the slaughter of his countrymen, he would march against their assassins at the head of a considerable number of the formidable Texan warriors. Resolving, therefore, to anticipate his blow, and to fall upon him when least expected, they sent one hundred and fifty warriors on that expedition. When these Indians arrived in the vicinity of the French fort at Natchitoches, perceiving that they were discovered by the spies of the vigilant St. Denis, they had recourse to this stratagem. They sent a deputation with the calumet of peace, to inform him that they had been so unfortunate as to have lately had some difficulties with the French settled in their neighborhood, that they wished to take him as arbitrator or umpire, and that they had brought with them a Frenchwoman, whom they wanted to set free, and to deliver to him in token of their good intentions.

St. Denis answered them, that he would accede to their proposition, provided they brought to him the Frenchwoman, with an escort only of ten warriors. The Natchez refused to do so, and insisted upon coming in a body. St. Denis then sent them word, that he saw plainly from their large number, and from their refusal to comply with his demand, that they were traitors and liars bent upon mischief; that he was disposed, however, to allow them to return quietly to their villages, provided they surrendered to him the Frenchwoman, for whom he would pay a ransom. Enraged at the answer of St. Denis, and at the bad result of their expedition, the Natchez burnt the Frenchwoman in sight of the French fort, and hastily intrenched themselves, so as to be protected against any attack from St. Denis, during the approaching night.

St. Denis had at his disposal only forty soldiers, and twenty settlers. But he was not the man to hesitate on any emergency of this kind:—and a little before daybreak, leaving twenty soldiers in the fort, he marched against the camp of the Natchez, at the head of forty Frenchmen, and forty select Natchitoches warriors. He fell upon them so unexpectedly, and with such fury, that, in an instant, he routed them completely, and killed sixty, without having lost one of his men. Of the Natchez who fled, a good many died of their wounds; only a few reached their native hills, and were the bearers of a melancholy tale.

Ricard was the first fugitive from Natchez, who brought to New Orleans the information of the destruction of that important French settlement. He looked so haggard and so bewildered, that he was thought to be deranged in mind, and nobody would believe his statements. But Couillard and a few others reached New Orleans soon after, on the 3d of December, and left no room for doubt. Governor Périer then knew all the extent of the danger he had run, when he had prudently refused to receive the visit of the Choctaws, who, to the number of six hundred warriors, had arrived at the mouth of the Chefuncte River, in Lake Pontchartrain, on the 1st of December, and had sent a deputation to Périer, to ask leave to come and present him with the calumet of peace. Governor Périer thought that, whatever advantages might be derived from this visit, if really friendly, would be more than counterbalanced by the danger of admitting so many Indians in the capital, and sent them word, that he would receive their chief with thirty warriors only. Seeing that they were suspected, they returned to their villages, and contented themselves, on their way home, with killing and stealing some cattle which belonged to the Pascagoula settlement. Which circumstance shows clearly the evil intentions with which they were animated.

A short time after, the Choctaws sent a deputation to the Natchez, to smoke with them the calumet of peace, and to renew their treaty of alliance. But not receiving as valuable presents as they expected from the rich spoils of the French, they upbraided the Natchez with their meanness and perfidy, reproaching them with having hastened prematurely the day of the attack upon the French, and with having, in this manner, robbed the other Indian nations of their chance of plundering their common enemy. They said that it was owing to the indiscreet haste of the Natchez, prompted by their uncontrollable avidity, that the Choctaw expedition against New Orleans had failed, the French having, no doubt, received at that time some information of what had happened at Natchez. The Choctaw deputation at last departed in great anger, after having told the Natchez that they were no better than dogs, and that they would be treated as such. Not long after, there came another Choctaw deputation, who were not better pleased with their reception than the first. Having been informed that the Natchez were deliberating on the expediency of killing all their French prisoners, women and children, who, they thought, proved to be rather an expensive encumbrance, the Choctaws went in ceremony to the public square, struck at the warriors' red post, which stood there according to immemorial custom, and told the Natchez that the French were the allies of the Choctaws, who would march with all the forces of their numerous nation against the Natchez, if they dared to make away with a single one of their prisoners. This energetic demonstration produced great effect upon the Natchez, and probably saved the lives of the French captives. After having uttered these solemn threats, the Choctaw ambassadors departed, leaving the Natchez in a violent state of anxiety, which induced them to meet frequently in council, without being able to come to any conclusion, as to what they would ultimately do in an emergency which looked so critical.

Governor Périer, on the very day that he was informed of the Natchez massacre, sent an officer with a detachment of men up the river in a boat, to put the planters on both sides of the river on their guard, and to order them to construct redoubts at certain convenient distances, wherein to take refuge in case of need, with their families, their goods, and their cattle. This order was complied with in a short time, and the whole *coast*, as it is called, from New Orleans to Natchez, in those parts where it was settled, was put in a state of defense. The same officer was instructed to look closely into what was going on among the small nations on the banks of the river, and to make sure of their fidelity. A courier was sent to two Choctaw chiefs who were shooting ducks on Lake Pontchartrain; and they were informed that Governor Périer wished to have *a talk with them*. The Choctaw nation was by far the most powerful of all the Indian tribes, and great and well-founded doubts existed as to their intended course of action in this dangerous crisis. It had become extremely important to secure their services, and in this way, to remove the exaggerated apprehensions of the colonists. The terror which prevailed was so intense, that Governor Périer, in one of his dispatches, said:

"I am extremely sorry to see, from the manifestation of such universal alarm, that there is less of French courage in Louisiana than anywhere else. Fear had assumed such uncontrollable domination over all, that the very insignificant nation of the Chouachas, a little above New Orleans, which was composed of thirty warriors, became a subject of terror to all our people. This induced me to have them destroyed by our negroes, who executed this mission with as much promptitude as secrecy. This example, given by our negroes, kept in check all the small nations higher up the river. If I had been inclined to avail myself of the good dispositions of our negroes, I could have destroyed by them all those nations which are of no service to us, and which, on the contrary, may stimulate our blacks to revolt, as the Natchez have done. But certain prudential considerations prevented me, and in the situation in which I was, I felt that it was safe to trust none but the few French I had at hand. I therefore called a general meeting of them, and provided them with arms. I have raised one hundred and fifty men in New Orleans, and divided them into four companies, each commanded by a member of the council. I have chosen the lieutenants among trusty persons employed by the government. At the head of the companies which I have formed on the banks of the river, I have put the most influential planters, and I have ordered that a certain number of negroes be sent to make intrenchments around the city of New Orleans." It is probable that one of the reasons which prompted Périer to have the throats of the Chouachas cut by the negroes, was to produce a state of hostility between the red and black races, of which the whites were equally distrustful. It was an act of policy, cruel, it is true, but not without its logic.

On the 5th of January, 1730, Governor Périer sent a vessel to France to inform the government of the precarious situation of the colony, and to ask for the assistance which was so much required. He had also dispatched a detachment of soldiers and planters, under the engineer Broutin, to join Loubois, who commanded at Point Coupée, and these officers were requested to try, by a bold and sudden stroke, to carry off the

French women and children, the negroes and all the canoes the Natchez had in their possession. Captain de Lassus was sent, by the way of Mobile, to the Choctaws, to ascertain whether or not that nation was disposed to side with the French.

Every day there came to New Orleans the alarming report of some traveler being murdered on his way down the Mississippi. On the 8th of January, Father Doutreleau, a Jesuit, who, having been attacked at the mouth of Yazoo River, had received two wounds in the arm and lost three men, reached New Orleans. To prevent the recurrence of such events was extremely desirable; and on the 15th, Governor Périer dispatched a bark with twenty white men and six negroes, to carry ammunition to the Illinois settlement, and to pick up on the way, protect and escort to New Orleans, all the French travelers they might meet.

On the 16th, the governor received a piece of intelligence which removed a load of anxieties from his mind. It was, that the Choctaws, to the number of seven hundred warriors, commanded by a French officer named Le Sueur, had marched against the Natchez, and that one hundred and fifty warriors of that nation had set off to throw themselves between the Natchez and the Yazoos, to prevent the former from sending away to the latter any portion of the French prisoners, or of the negroes, as it was reported they would do, if they were attacked.

The rendezvous-general of the French who were to operate against the Natchez was at the Tunicas, and that expedition was put under the command of Loubois. While the French were still gathering at that spot, it was deemed expedient to send five men to discover what was going on among the Natchez. They ascended the Mississippi in a boat, and landed, says Le Page du

Pratz, at nine miles from the Great Village of the Natchez, at the mouth of a small stream on which that village was situated, and which discharged itself into the Mississippi at the foot of a hill, from which a canoe might be spied six miles off. The French scouts were not seen, however, and they felt so secure, that after their having landed, night coming on, they went quietly to sleep, as if they were not in the very lap of danger. The next morning, they breakfasted merrily, and drank so much brandy, that their courage worked itself up to the highest pitch of boldness. Thus, they walked straight toward the Great Village of the Natchez, without making any attempt at concealment, and they were within two miles of it, when, on a sudden, yelling Indians started up around them in every direction. The French, instead of crying out that they came with peaceful intentions, and of trying to impress the enemy with that persuasion, presumed to defend themselves against such overwhelming odds; and one of them by the name of Navarre, who had been one of the few that had escaped from the great massacre on the 29th of November, was the first to fire. The Indians, however, appeared disposed to keep altogether on the defensive, and summoned the French to surrender. But these madmen, throwing themselves into a ravine which presented the appearance of a natural intrenchment, continued their fire, which was at last returned by the Indians. Navarre was wounded, and became more furious: speaking the language of the Natchez, he taunted them with every sort of opprobrious epithet, and went on fighting until he was killed.

The four other Frenchmen, who seemed to have been entirely under the influence of Navarre, and who had been fighting also with great courage, surrendered as soon as he was dead. They were conducted to the

Great Sun, and Mesplais, or Mesplet, an officer of noble birth, of the province of Bearn, in France, who ought to have known how to control the imprudent temerity of such a man as Navarre, a mere soldier, destitute of education, was interrogated by the Indian prince. On his being asked what the object of his visit was, Mesplais answered that he had been sent by his chief as the bearer of propositions of peace. "But," observed the Great Sun, "how camest thou to fire at those who merely said to thee to surrender? One of thy companions is killed and thou art wounded, through his and thy own fault. Is this the conduct of peace-bearers?" Mesplais answered that Navarre had taken too much of the *fire-liquor*, and begged the Great Sun to remember that, on the death of this man, he, Mesplais, had ordered his companions to lay down their arms. The Great Sun appeared to be satisfied with this explanation, and ordered them to be released, but to be closely watched. He then sent for one of the female prisoners, a woman by the name of Desnoyers, and said to her: "Write to thy great war-chief, that if he wishes for peace, and desires that all the French prisoners and the negroes be restored to him, he must send me for every one of them so many casks of brandy, so many blankets, muskets, shirts, provisions, &c." . . . . . He wanted so many different things, and in such quantity, that it would have been impossible to find in the whole colony what he had the presumption to ask, even if it had been thought to be an act of expediency and of good policy to yield so much to these barbarians.

Desnoyers wrote down what she was told, and availed herself of this opportunity to inform Loubois of the miserable condition in which the French captives were, and of the dangers which threatened them. She did **not fail** to communicate all she knew about the preparations the Natchez had made for defense, and to impart every other piece of intelligence she thought might be useful to the French.

The Great Sun delivered the letter to one of Mesplais' companions, and ordered him to carry it to the French chief at the Tunicas, and to inform him that if a favorable answer was not sent back in three days, the hostages whom the Natchez had in their possession, would abide the consequences of their anger and disappointment. Eagerly did the French emissary depart on his mission, and "even without looking back," says Le Page du Pratz. So active did he prove himself, that he arrived on that same day at the Tunicas, and handed the letter to Loubois, who vouchsafed no answer.

While the Natchez remained in the expectation of an answer, they treated their prisoners kindly, but on the fourth day after the departure of the French emissary, the Great Sun, having given up all hopes of his return, flew into a violent passion, and sentenced to death the three other Frenchmen. Two of them, one a common soldier, and the other an officer of education and birth, by the name of St. Amand, were killed instantly, without being exposed to much suffering. Unfortunately for Mesplais, he had made himself conspicuous in some of the preceding wars of the French against the Natchez, and he had been for the Indians an object of particular notice, on account of the long flowing hair which curled down on his shoulders, and which made it a very *desirable scalp*. They concentrated, therefore, the fury of their revenge on such a well-known warrior, and swore they would make him weep like a woman. He was tied to the celebrated Indian stake, exquisitely tortured during three days and three nights, and died at last, after having exhibited superhuman fortitude, and without having gratified his torturers by uttering one word of complaint. All the Frenchwomen, prisoners among the Natchez were present, and kneeling round the miserable victim of savage ferocity, addressed loud prayers to heaven during all the time that the lingering execution lasted. The sufferer never shed a tear, nor allowed one groan to escape his lips, but, occasionally, would beg the Frenchwomen for water. That was a boon, however, which they were prevented from giving. It was a horrific spectacle, and a minute description of it would convey to us but a faint idea of the hideous reality, and of the appalling dangers to which our ancestors were exposed, when toiling so painfully to prepare for us the peaceful and glorious home which we now enjoy.

The Avoyelles, Tunicas, and other small nations, had declared themselves against the Natchez, and were harassing them by partial attacks and marauding expeditions. Not unmindful of the threats which the Choctaw delegation had made against them, the Natchez, coming gradually to a more correct appreciation of their situation, began to feel a real desire to accept, or to offer reasonable terms of peace. Thus, one night, when they had met in deliberation, they sent for a Frenchwoman who spoke their language well, and they interrogated her on the practicability of a peace with her nation. "Are not the French of a forgiving nature," said the Great Sun to her, "and do they not often embrace their enemies and eat with them, after having met them in battle?" The Frenchwoman, who was greatly frightened, answered that her countrymen were as mild as lambs, although rather of a pugnacious temperament; that they would frequently feast with their enemies before fighting, and feast again with them after fighting; that they were very fond of such alternate feastings and fightings, and were of all people the most easily pacified. She was skillful enough thus to harp on the right cord, and the Indians, well pleased with her answers, dismissed her with courtesy from their presence.

In spite, or perhaps on account of their fears, and to lose sight of their anxieties, the Natchez had been carousing, almost every day, since the destruction of the French settlement. The temptation was too strong for them to resist, when they had in their possession so much liquor, and so many provisions taken from the French warehouses. On the 27th of January, they were feasting on the banks of St. Catherine's creek, when they were suddenly attacked by the Choctaws, headed by Le Sueur. Their defeat would have been complete, if those negroes who had joined the Natchez in the massacre of the French, had not fought with desperate valor, and, by their fierce resistance, had not given time to their Indian allies to retire within the two forts they had prepared, in anticipation of the expected war which they knew would soon burst upon them. But the Choctaws killed sixty of the Natchez, took from fifteen to twenty prisoners, rescued fifty-four French women and children, and recovered about one hundred of the negroes.

On the 8th of February, half of the French forces arrived at Natchez, and joined the Choctaws on St. Catherine's creek. On the 9th, they left the quarters of the Choctaws, and encamped at a certain distance nearer the Mississippi. The rest of the army came up on that day, which was spent in reconnoitering and skirmishing with the Indians. The 10th, 11th, and 12th were employed in carrying the artillery, ammunition, and provisions from the boats to the French camp. The 13th was consumed in fruitless parleying with the Indians, in approaching nearer to the forts, and in transporting pieces of artillery on the mound on which stood the Great Temple, and which happened to command the two forts. The French protected that position with intrenchments.

On the 14th, at daybreak, the French opened against the forts their fire, which was answered briskly. The four pieces of artillery which the French had, were hardly fit for service, and were wretchedly managed. The Natchez had three pieces, which were still more clumsily handled. At night, the Natchez came through a cane-brake to dislodge the French from the temple. But some grape thrown among them forced them to retreat.

On the 15th, the French, at the distance of five hundred and sixty yards, cannonaded the forts during six hours, without throwing down one single stake, and the Choctaws, to whom they had promised to make a breach in less than two hours, became discouraged, and hooted at the impotency of the French missiles.

On the 16th, a man by the name of Du Parc, was sent with a flag to summon the forts to surrender. He was received with a general discharge of musketry, which made him scamper away in such haste that he left behind him his flag. It would have fallen into the hands of the Indians, had not a soldier, known under the nickname of the *Parisian*, run to the spot and carried away the flag under a heavy fire from the enemy. He was immediately made a sergeant as a reward for his valor. At the very moment when the *Parisian* was rushing to rescue the flag, the Indians had opened their gates to make a sally to take it. Some Frenchwomen availed themselves of that circumstance to rush out pellmell with the Indians, and succeeded in gaining the French camp. But the Indians avenged themselves for their escape in the most atrocious manner

The poor women had left children in the fort, hoping that they would be taken care of by their companions in captivity. The Indians seized these children, and impaled them on the stakes of the fort, to the great horror and rage of the French. On that day, an additional body of men arrived at the French camp, with four pieces of artillery quite as worthless as those the besiegers had already. Despairing to make with such artillery any impression on the forts, the French resolved to have recourse to mining, and went to work accordingly. Some, more impatient and more intrepid than the rest, offered to rush close to the walls and to fling grenades into the forts, but Loubois refused, under the apprehension of doing as much injury to the French captives as to the Indians.

From the 17th to the 22d of February, the French made scientific preparations to attack the forts, and were engaged in erecting gabions and in undermining. On the 22d, during the night, one hundred Natchez attacked the French works in front, and two hundred in the rear, under the protection of a wild cane-field through which they had approached. They broke through the mantelets, penetrated into the last trench or traverse, and assailed with fury the temple and the French battery. They fought with desperation during three quarters of an hour, and retired with considerable loss, but carrying away a good many blankets, spades, and other articles. The Choctaws came to the assistance of the French with great readiness.

On the 23d, the Choctaws threw the French into consternation by threatening to withdraw, if the siege was not carried on with more vigor. This representation had its effect, and on the 24th, a battery of four pieces of the caliber of four pounds was established at three hundred and sixty yards from the forts, and the

French informed the Natchez that they were determined to blow them up at all hazards to the French captives, if they did not surrender. Intimidated by the more active preparations made by the French, the Natchez sent one of their female captives, Madame Desnoyers, of whom it has already been spoken, to make propositions of peace. But she remained in the French camp, and no answer was returned to the Natchez.

On the 25th, the Natchez hoisted a flag as a token that they wished to parley. Alibamon Mengo, one of the most famous Choctaw chiefs, growing impatient at all these parleyings which never had any result, approached one of the forts, and addressed this harangue to the Natchez: "Did you ever hear that such a numerous band of Indians as ours ever remained together two months encamped before forts? From this circumstance so foreign to our customs and habits, you may judge of our zeal and attachment for the French It is therefore perfectly useless in you, who are but a handful of people, when compared to our nation, to persist in refusing to give up to the French their women, children, and negroes. So far, the French have treated you with more leniency than you deserve, considering the quantity of their blood which you have shed. As to us, Choctaws, we are determined to blockade you until you die of hunger." This speech had its effect, and the Natchez promised to deliver to the Choctaws all the captives, provided the French would remove to the bank of the river with their artillery. This was done on the 26th, and thus terminated the siege. The French, whose numbers, as far as we can judge from conflicting statements, amounted to five hundred, lost fifteen men during that siege.

The cowardly and notorious Ecte-Actal acted as negotiator between the French and the Indians, and it had been agreed through him that the French forces would, as I have already said, withdraw to the bank of the river, and that the Natchez, on surrendering to the Choctaws the French captives and spoils, would remain in quiet possession of their lands and forts. This treaty was nothing but the embodiment of mutual deceit. The French commander, thinking himself absolved from adherence to his word by the proverbial perfidy of the Indians, had resolved to recommence the siege, and to complete the destruction of the Natchez, immediately after having got the French prisoners out of their hands; and the Natchez, in their turn, who did not trust the French, had made up their minds to fly with all the spoils they could carry. On the 27th, they delivered to the Choctaws all the French women, children, and negroes, and in the night of the 28th, they made their escape. On the morning of the 29th, the French, much to their surprise, saw the forts deserted, and found in them nothing but worthless rags. Thus finished this expedition, which reflects little credit on the French arms. It was evidently ill-concerted; the French ought certainly to have been as expeditious as the Choctaws, and to have arrived at the same time to strike a crushing blow with their united forces. On the contrary, the undisciplined Choctaws, who had to come by land over three hundred miles, were the first in the field and on the spot, and there had to wait about fifteen days for their white allies, who, when they invested at last the forts of the Natchez, and attacked with light pieces of artillery, almost worthless it is true, and with five hundred men, could do nothing effective in twenty days. In the end, it was the intervention of the Choctaws which succeeded in bringing the Natchez to terms; it was to the Choctaws and not to the French, that they consented to give up their prisoners; and then, eluding the vigilance of the French, or blinding them by the influence of bribery and corruption, they achieved their retreat with honor and without the slightest loss.

Diron d'Artaguette, one of the king's commissaries, commenting on this expedition in one of his dispatches, reflects severely on the want of policy, of judgment, and of activity exhibited by Périer on this occasion. He also blames Loubois for having lost so many days at the Tunicas, where he stopped so long under the apprehension of a general conspiracy, which, if he moved forward, would, as he feared, have put him in the awkward position of having the Natchez in front and other hostile nations in the rear. He speaks in no measured terms of what he calls "*the shameful conclusion of the siege;*" and says, "the Choctaws, it is alledged, wanted to retire, but the truth is, that the French army was the first to give up; and strange stories are told about silver plate, and other valuable articles, which became the subjects of clandestine transactions." He thus goes on, intimating pretty broadly that the Natchez bribed the French into allowing them to escape.

Governor Périer says: "Several causes have prevented our capturing the whole Natchez nation. The first, the weakness of our troops, which were good for nothing; the second, the distrust in which we were of the Choctaws, whom we suspected of treason. This was not without foundation; for the Natchez, during the siege, reproached them a thousand times with their perfidy, after having joined in the general conspiracy of which the Natchez related the circumstances to us. They also boasted that the English and Chickasaws were coming to their rescue. All these circumstances, which were not encouraging for men who had but little experience, forced Loubois, who had served with distinction, to be satisfied with the surrender of our women, children, and negroes. This was the essential point. D'Artaguette (a brother of the commissary of that name) has served with the most brilliant valor, and the planters, with credit, having D'Arensbourg and De Laye at their head. The creoles distinguished themselves particularly; all the officers have done their duty, with the exception of Renault d'Hauterive, De Mouy, and Villainville. Ffteen negroes, in whose hands we had put weapons, performed prodigies of valor. If the blacks did not cost so much, and if their labors were not so necessary to the colony, it would be better to turn them into soldiers, and to dismiss those we have, who are so bad and so cowardly that they seem to have been manufactured purposely for this colony."

The Natchez, on leaving their forts and native hills, crossed the Mississippi to take refuge among the Ouachitas. They were pursued by the chief of the Tunicas at the head of fifty warriors, who kept on their trail in the hope of picking up stragglers. On the territory thus abandoned the French began the erection of a brick fort, the command of which, with a garrison of one hundred men, was given to the Baron of Cresnay, who was also put at the head of all the troops in Louisiana, but who continued to act, however, in a subordinate capacity to Governor Périer. Loubois was rewarded for his successful campaign against the Natchez by being appointed Major and Commander of New Orleans.

When the French and their red allies came to the settlement of their accounts, it was found to be a matter of no small difficulty. The Choctaws proved to be more exacting in their pretensions than the Natchez were, in relation to the delivery of the French women, children, and negroes. The negotiation waxed so hot, that the French and Indians were very near coming to blows. Harmony was at last restored between them, by the interference of the chief of the Tunicas. The French having given up almost every thing they could part with, and promised much more, the Choctaws delivered to them the captives, who were hastily sent down the river, to remove all further pretext for claim or altercation. The Choctaws, on the occasion of this war between the French and Natchez, behaved with consummate skill. They first dealt with the Natchez, and put up their alliance with them at the highest bid, and after playing them off for some time with this delusive hope, and extorting from them every thing they could, seeing that they had pumped the well dry, they turned toward the French, and listened to their overtures, of which they made the most to their own advantage. So that this war ruined the Natchez, empoverished the French, and enriched only the Choctaws. Thus it appears, that, in diplomacy at least, and in national egotism, they were not far behind the most civilized nations of modern times.

Governor Périer availed himself of the fears of the colonists, to push on with activity the enclosing of the city of New Orleans,—and between Natchez and New Orleans, he established eight small forts, as guarantees of protection, and places of refuge in case of need. He also took measures to cause all the small nations which dwelt between the Balize and Natchez, to remove within the year, with the exception of the Tunicas, who had given so many proofs of attachment to the French.

The poor victims of the Natchez massacre were received at New Orleans with great humanity, and entertained at the public expense in the Charity Hospital, where they were nursed by the Ursulines with zeal. De la Chaise made a generous use of the extensive authority with which he was clothed, to satisfy all their wants. Many of the widows were soon married, and concessions of lands were made to them at Point Coupée, where most of them ultimately settled.

Forgetting, it seems, Chopart's provocations, Governor Périer, in his dispatches, and the other French officers, all agreed in taxing the English with having instigated and provoked the war of the Natchez. "The English know," says Périer, "that we are the only barriers between them and Mexico, and that their taking possession of the banks of the Mississippi would soon be followed by their occupation of the Spanish colonies." Thus what has happened one century later, was distinctly foreseen in 1730.

This year, the colony lost De la Chaise, one of the worthiest men it had yet possessed. He left a name deservedly popular among the people, for unflinching integrity, and for the impartiality with which he checked abuses of power, and punished delinquencies among those who hitherto had always been sure of impunity. His sudden death gave rise to some dark rumors of his having been poisoned by those who had cause to fear his investigations. These rumors were long rife in the colony. After having passed a panegyric on his virtues, Le Page du Pratz concludes by saying, "Those orphans and widows who escaped from the Natchez massacre, would be extremely ungrateful if they did not, during all their life, pray for the soul of that good and charitable man."

On the 1st of August, Governor Périer wrote "Those of the Indians who had entered into the general conspiracy, have, since its failure, come back to us, and now help us in daily harassing the Natchez, who have crossed the Mississippi, and retired into the interior of the country. Since their flight, I have succeeded in having fifty of them either killed or taken prisoners. *Latterly, I burned here four men, and two women, and sent the rest to St. Domingo:*—two hundred and fifty warriors of the friendly nations, have been dispatched by me, to watch and blockade the Natchez, until we receive more troops from France."

The burning of two women and of four men was done, no doubt, in retaliation of Indian atrocities. But this imitation of their barbarous manners could do no good. It was not only an act of useless cruelty, but of exceedingly bad policy. It could not serve as a check, because it could not intimidate men who gloried in such practices. On the contrary, it must have looked, in the estimation of the Indians, as an approval of their national custom, by a people who pretended to be so much more enlightened, and therefore it must have operated as an incentive, or encouragement. But what is remarkable and characteristic is the cool, business-like indifference, and the matter of fact tone with which Governor Périer informs his government of the auto-da-fé which has taken place by his orders. He writes on the burning of four men and two women with as much unconcern, as a cook would about the roasting of a leg of mutton!

Although scattered about, the Natchez did not cease to make the French feel occasionally, that they were not all exterminated. One day, they fell on twenty Frenchmen, who were cutting timber in a cypress swamp, to be used in the fort they were constructing, and they killed nineteen, among whom was "*the Parisian,*" who had so much distinguished himself during the siege. Another day, six Natchez warriors had the hardihood to penetrate, under the garb of friendly Indians, into the fort itself, and while there, they rushed, with the fury of mad despair and revenge, on the French, of whom they killed five, and wounded many more. Five of these dare-devils were killed after a desperate fight, and the sixth, being taken prisoner, was *burnt*.

A few days after, the Tunicas carried to New Orleans a Natchez woman they had captured, and Governor Périer allowed them to *burn* her in great ceremony on a platform erected in front of the city, between the city and the Levee. I regret to relate that the whole population of New Orleans turned out to witness that Indian ceremony. The victim supported, with the most stoical fortitude, all the tortures which were inflicted upon her, and did not shed a tear,—on the contrary, she upbraided her torturers with their want of skill, and flinging at them every opprobrious epithet she could think of, she prophesied their speedy destruction. Her prediction proved true:—the Tunicas had hardly returned home, when they were surprised by the Natchez, their village burnt, their old chief, the constant ally of the French, killed, and almost their whole nation destroyed.

These deeds of so much daring show the state of desperation to which the Indians had been reduced, and their thirst for revenge. They were executed by a part of that nation which had taken refuge among the Chickasaws, while the French had thought that the whole nation had crossed the Mississippi, and gone over to Black River.

The Chickasaws, having thus granted an asylum to the Natchez, foresaw that they would be attacked in their turn, and sought to anticipate the blow, by stirring up the Indian nations against the French, and by exciting the blacks to revolt. Fortunately, the conspiracy of the blacks was discovered in time; one woman was hung, and eight men broken on the wheel, among whom was a negro of the name of Samba, who was at the head of the conspirators, and who was a man of the most desperate character. The majority of the negroes then in the colony were Banbaras, and they were the concocters of the rebellion. Their plan was, after having butchered the whites, to keep as their slaves all the blacks who were not of their nation, and to rule the country under leaders periodically elected. It would have been a sort of Banbara republic.

All these events, crowding upon each other, had kept the colonists in a constant fever of fearful excitement. Their apprehensions were a little allayed by the arrival, on the 10th of August, of a small additional corps of troops, commanded by De Salverte, a brother of Périer; so that the forces of the colony could then be set down at about one thousand to twelve hundred regulars, and eight hundred militiamen. It would have been a pretty effective force, if it could have been kept concentrated, instead of being scattered in distant settlements.

The principal officers who were then in active service in Louisiana, were the following:—

THE CHEVALIER DE LOUBOIS,	D'HAUTERIVE,
THE BARON OF CRESNAY,	DE LUSSER,
THE CHEVALIER DE NOYAN,	PETIT DE LIEULLIERS,
" DE ST. JULIEN,	SIMARE DE BELLEISLE,
" D'ARENSBOURG,	MARIN DE LA TOUR,
D'ARTAGUETTE,	DE GRANDPRE,
DE BEAUCHAMP,	THE CHEVALIER D'HERNEUVILLE,
DE BESSAN,	DE L'ANGLOISERIE,
DE ST. DENIS,	DE ST. ANGE,
DE GAUVRIT,	DE LABRUISSONNIERE,
DE PRADEL,	DE COULANGES.
DE COURCELLES,	

They were, all of them, aristocratic scions of noble houses, who had come to better their fortunes in Louisiana, and with the hope of more rapid advancement in their military career, on account of the dangers of the colonial service, in which, for that reason, years counted double for the army, either for promotion, or in support of an application for a retiring pension.

SIXTH LECTURE.

Expedition of Perier against the Natchez—He goes up Red River and Black River in pursuit of them—Siege of their Fort—Most of them are taken Prisoners and sold as Slaves—Continuation of the Natchez War—The India Company surrenders its Charter—Ordinances on the Currency of the Country—Bienville reappointed Governor—Situation of the Colony at that time—The Natchez take Refuge among the Chickasaws—Great Rise of the Mississippi and General Inundation—Extraordinary Number of Mad Dogs—Expedition of Bienville against the Chickasaws—He attacks their Villages—Battle of Ackia—Daring Exploit of the black man, Simon—Bienville is beaten and forced to retreat—Expedition of D'Artaguette against the Chickasaws—His Defeat and Death—History of John Philip Grondel—Other Events and Facts from 1729 to 1736.

The French had at last taken possession of all the ancient domains of the Natchez; but Governor Périer, considering the depredations still committed by that indomitable tribe, came to the conclusion that their complete destruction was indispensable to the prosperity and safety of the colony. Accordingly, he departed for Mobile, to renew treaties of alliance which the French had with the Choctaws, and to take all the measures necessary to secure their neutrality, while he would be engaged in the prosecution of the war of extermination he had determined to carry against the Natchez. The Choctaws were so much pleased with the presents made to them by Périer, that they offered to join him in the new expedition he meditated against the Natchez. But Périer refused, because he thought it good policy to show the Choctaws that the French could, contrary to the belief of these barbarians, do very well without their aid.

On the 13th of November, 1730, Périer returned to New Orleans, where he found that his brother Salverte had almost completed all the preparations necessary for the contemplated expedition. On the 9th of December, Salverte departed with two battalions of marines he had taken from a ship of the line, with instructions to wait for the governor at the village of Carlestin, where he was joined, on the 13th, by that high functionary, with all the ammunition, provisions, &c., which were required, and all the troops of the colony which could be spared.

Before proceeding farther, Périer received the grateful intelligence that the Indian nations on the northern frontiers had remained faithful to the French, and were waging vigorous war against the nation of the Foxes, the hereditary foes of the Illinois, whose friendship to the French had made them valuable allies on all occasions. Périer was officially informed that a great battle had taken place between the Foxes and the Illinois, headed by some Frenchmen; and that the Foxes had been so completely routed, that they had lost from eleven to twelve hundred men. It was one of the fiercest Indian battles which was ever put on record.

On the 14th, Governor Périer proceeded to Bayagoulas, where he stopped four days to wait for the division of planters commanded by Benac, and for the larger boats which contained the provisions, and which were so unwieldy that they could not keep up with the army. The governor had divided his army into three corps, in order to prevent conflicts and to produce emulation. The first, composed of one hundred and fifty marines and forty sailors, was commanded by his brother Salverte. The second, consisting of the troops of the colony, was under the Baron of Cresnay; and the third, the militia, was headed by Benac. This last corps joined the rest, only at Bayagoulas, on the 19th; the whole army moved forward on the 22d, and on the same day encamped at Manchac for the night. There, Périer left the army, and hastened to the Tunicas, in order to accelerate the movements of such of the warriors of that tribe as had survived the defeat they had suffered from the Natchez. On the 27th, Salverte, to whom Périer had left the command of the army, joined his brother at the Tunicas.

On the 28th, the army began its march for the mouth of Red River, where was the general rendezvous, and where the ship, Prince of Conti, had been sent with most of the articles necessary for the campaign. Périer remained until the 3d of January, 1731, with the Tunicas, where his presence was required to make them join the expedition; which they were loth to do, because they were afraid to leave their village, their women and children, exposed to the fury of some of the marauding parties of the Natchez. They had indeed good reasons for apprehension, having just been informed that De Coulanges, whom Périer had sent in a boat, with some Frenchmen and a crew of twenty men composed of Indians and free blacks, to the fort lately built at Natchez, with orders to proceed as high up the river as the Arkansas, had been attacked, and that half of his companions had been killed or wounded. De la Touche, Beaulieu, and Cochart were among the former, and De Coulanges had received two severe wounds. This bold attack on the part of the Natchez had frightened all the small nations, and Périer could not gather round him more than one hundred and fifty of their warriors, but they were of the bravest.

On the 4th of January, 1731, Périer joined the army at the mouth of Red River, where he found all his forces united. The difficulty then was to discover the stronghold where the Natchez had concealed themselves in those unknown regions. The French ascended Red River, went into Black River, from Black River into a stream they called *Silver River*, and from that stream into a small lake, not far from which they had been told the Natchez were. It is not improbable that the stream which is here mentioned is no other than the one now set down on the map as the Ouachita, and that the lake alluded to is the small one which is at a short distance from Trinity, in the parish of Catahoula. The French arrived at that lake on the 19th of January, after having met on that day a party of Natchez, of whom they killed two men and one woman. There, the French had happened to come very close to the stronghold of the Natchez, without as yet being aware of it. But on the 20th, they captured a Natchez boy, who was fishing, and who, under the influence of threats and promises of reward, showed the French the path which led to the Indian fort. Governor Périer sent forward French and Indian scouts and marksmen, supported by two companies of regulars commanded by De Lusser and De la Girouardiere. He next followed with the rest of the army, after having left behind the Baron of Cresnay with one hundred men, to protect the French camp and boats.

Governor Périer had hardly given the order to march, when he heard a brisk fire of musketry kept up between the fort and the skirmishers. After having marched an hour, the army came in sight of the fort. The Tunicas attacked some fortified houses which seemed to be intended as outposts, and drove the Natchez out of them. On the 21st, when the fort was completely invested, Périer ordered the Baron of Cresray to join him. He then sent a flag to the Natchez, and summoned them to give up the negroes who remained in their possession. The Natchez fired at the flag, crying out that the French were dogs, and that they would have nothing to do with them. On this answer, the French began to cast grenades into the fort, and had succeeded in producing considerable effect, when the two mortars which they used, being of wood, bursted, and wounded those who worked them. At half-past five in the evening, the Natchez made a sally, in which they killed a negro, a grenadier of the marines, and wounded a sergeant and De Laye, one of the militia officers. At eight o'clock the same evening, although the weather was very stormy, the French began to mine, and kept up their firing with muskets, one field-piece, and one mortar, which was their last one, and for which they had sent to the boats. The Natchez still retained possession of a fortified outpost, which enfiladed the French workmen engaged in the trenches. On the 22d, Périer ordered it to be attacked by twelve grenadiers and twelve sappers. But on their being repulsed, he sent his brother, who carried it in a quarter of an hour, after a vigorous defense made by the Indians.

On the 23d, the French, under the protection of the redoubt they had taken from the Natchez, pushed on their trenches with more vigor, and approached more closely to the fort.

On the 24th, the Natchez, perceiving that the French were preparing to storm the fort, and fearing the result, made propositions of peace. Périer answered that he would hold no communication with them, unless they did, as a preliminary proceeding, deliver up all the black slaves they had in their possession, and unless their chiefs came out to have a personal interview with him, midway between the fort and the camp. The Natchez immediately gave up nineteen negroes and one negress, and said that there remained only six negroes, who had gone out on a hunting excursion with some of their people. After much hesitation, founded on misgivings which proved to be correct, it was also agreed that Périer's other demand should be complied with; and the Great Sun, the Little Sun, and the chief of the Corn Village came out, at four o'clock in the afternoon, to meet the French chief. After the usual exchange of mutual salutations had taken place, as it began to rain, Périer proposed to the Indian chiefs to enter into a cabin close by, which seemed to be deserted, but as soon as they crossed its threshold, they were surrounded by armed soldiers, and made prisoners. Night came on, the bad weather increased, and, at twelve o'clock, had become a frightful tempest. The chief of the Corn Village availed himself of that circumstance, and, although shut up in a tent under the guard of twelve men, contrived to escape, without being hurt by the shots which were aimed at him.

On the 25th, the storm continued to rage, and interfered very much with the evacuation of the fort, and the complete surrender of the Natchez, which at last had been agreed upon. However, in the course of the day, forty-five men, and four hundred and fifty women and children were, at different intervals, delivered up to the French, with all their baggage and effects. But night having set in, the rest of the Natchez made a sudden sally, and taking the French by surprise, made their escape without one shot being fired at them, so dark the night was, so deluge-like the rain, and so little disposed were the French, and even their red allies, to move from their quarters, and to expose themselves to the pitiless fury of the elements. The next morning, only two sick men and one woman were found in the fort. Périer says, in one of his dispatches, that the party that thus eluded his vigilance and effected such a successful retreat, in front of such overwhelming odds, consisted only of sixteen men and four women. But this was a willful misrepresentation of the truth, the object of which was to conceal his humiliation, and to impress his government with the belief that his success had been greater than it really was. It is not at all probable that the place where the Great Sun had taken refuge with so many women and children, was defended only, according to Périer's statement, by about sixty warriors. Other accounts inform us, that the number of warriors who thus baffled him, and slipped from his grasp, exceeded one hundred and fifty. Périer having, the next morning, sent his Indian allies in pursuit, they killed one Natchez, and took two whom they burned at the stake.

On the 26th and 27th, the army was employed in demolishing the fort, with its fortified outposts, and in burning all their materials. On the 28th, the French began their retrograde march, and encamped on the bank of Silver Bayou, or river. On the 29th, they embarked to return to the Mississippi, through Black River and Red River. In one of his dispatches, Périer bestows much praise on the conduct of all the men he had under his orders, and speaks in high terms of the emulation which existed among the several corps. But he skips very lightly over the manner in which he made the Indian chiefs prisoners. He, no doubt, felt that it was a shameful breach of faith, the mention of which would make him blush, and provoke indignation. However, he was a man of no half-way measures, and at least not over-scrupulous in his dealings with the Indians. As soon as he reached New Orleans, he sent the Great Sun, the Little Sun, the forty-five other male prisoners and the four hundred and fifty women and children to St. Domingo, where they were sold as slaves.

Among them was the princess "*Bras piqué*," who related all the circumstances of the conspiracy of the Natchez, in which she acted a part so friendly to the French.

With such stakes in his hands, it would seem that Périer might have played a better game with the Natchez, and have induced them to emigrate far beyond the French settlements, as a condition of his restoring to them their sovereign, their women and children. It is likely that these would have been considerations sufficiently powerful, to make them subscribe to all the conditions which would have been deemed necessary to secure the future tranquillity of the colony.

However, a different course of policy was pursued, and entailed upon the French a long train of ever-reviving difficulties. The Natchez, driven by their losses to the last stage of despair, instead of being cowed, were nerved to frenzy by their misfortunes. They thought of nothing but revenge, cost what it might, and they committed more depredations than during the past. Diron d'Artaguette, in one of his dispatches, said that the Natchez, far from being destroyed as it had been represented, numbered still three hundred warriors, who had escaped from the grasp of the French, and who panted for their blood. After their last defeat near Black River, some of the scattered remnants of that tribe having incorporated themselves with the Chickasaws, were incessantly engaged in marauding expeditions directed against their white foes. In the month of April, 1731, they attacked four boats which Governor Périer had sent up to Arkansas. At the first fire from the Indians, the commanding officer had two of his men killed and two wounded, and although he had seventy men under his orders, so numerous were the Indians, that he was obliged to fall back, and to avoid the contest. Governor Périer having sent an emissary to the Chickasaws to demand of them, that they should dismiss the Natchez under pain of his displeasure, these Indians answered proudly that they would know how to protect those to whom the hospitality of their tribe had been tendered and pledged. Thus, a Chickasaw war had risen from the ashes of the Natchez war. Attempts were made to induce the Choctaws to pronounce themselves against the Chickasaws. "But," said Diron d'Artaguette on this subject, " how can we ever succeed, when we have nothing in our possession to tempt those Indians to become our allies, when we are without resources, without provisions, and have every thing to fear."

Beauchamp, who commanded at Mobile, writing to his government on this matter, expressed himself thus: " The Choctaws are not disposed favorably, which is the more to be regretted from the fact that, should this nation declare itself against us, we should be obliged to abandon the colony, provided however we had time to do so. Since the departure of Bienville, all the Indians are spoiled. In spite of the augmentation of merchandise we have to supply them with, and of the reduction in the quantity of furs which they give us back in return, they are not satisfied. On the contrary, they are insolent and less tractable. Our war with the Natchez was a source of vexation and danger only to our traders on the Mississippi, but the Chickasaw war is a cause of uneasiness and apprehension to the whole colony. These Indians had sent three emissaries to the Illinois to urge them to side against us, but these emissaries have been delivered into our hands, and M. Périer intends to have them burnt."

To increase the troubles of the French, the Alibamons and Talapouches, at the instigation of the

SITUATION OF THE COLONY. 451

Chickasaws, who had gone over to the British interest, had been on the eve of declaring themselves against the Choctaws, who were the only allies whose assistance the French hoped to have. "If such an event had taken place," continues Beauchamp, "the colony would have been on fire. The English are evidently gaining ground upon us." He then goes on inveighing bitterly against Périer's administration, and the system of policy this officer had assumed toward the Indians. In conclusion, he says: "The evil is now without a remedy, unless M. de Bienville could come back. Perhaps he could succeed in changing the state of things, on account of the consideration which the Indians have always had for him, and of the services which he has rendered them, particularly to the Choctaws."

After a minute description of the situation of the colony, Beauchamp closes thus his remarks to the minister: "You see to what a state of things is reduced this colony, which has so long been groaning under a harsh command. The colonists are in a miserably wretched condition, and are ill supplied with the provisions and the merchandise they want. When flour is sent here, the heads of the colony take hold of it, as they do with all the brandy and cordials which are imported, and they do not part with these articles except at exorbitant prices. It is, after all, what they do for every sort of merchandise. The soldiers, also, have always had just causes of complaint against the company with regard to their food and clothing. I need not speak of the enormous profits made by the company on every thing of which it permitted the sale in the colony." This compendious but graphic description is sufficient to show the disease which preyed on the vitals of Louisiana, and which was keeping her in such a protracted state of consumptive languor. Beauchamp's comments on Périer's harshness were certainly deserved, so far at least as the dealings of this officer with the Indians are taken into consideration. His consigning them to the stake and fagot, or his selling them into bondage, were measures of no soothing character, and it is not astonishing that Beauchamp should have drawn the conclusion, that the return of the mild and humane Bienville, as governor, would be looked upon by the Indians as a boon of conciliation.

Such being the course of events in Louisiana, it is not to be wondered at that the great India Company, the creation of which had produced such a ferment on account of the prodigies it was expected to work in the production of wealth, drooping under the infliction of so many disappointments and the load of so many obligations, should have been anxious to waive the monopoly of trade, and all the other privileges it had obtained to colonize Louisiana. After receiving the melancholy intelligence of the Natchez massacre, the directors of the company and the stockholders, almost unanimously, came to the conclusion that they could no longer support the expenses which were necessary to keep up the colony, and on the 23d of January, 1731, they proposed to the king to return into his hands the charter which they at last found to be too onerous. They alledged in their petition that, in profitless attempts to carry this charter into execution, they had already spent twenty millions of livres, and that they would completely break down under the obligations they had assumed, if the government did not come to their relief. This proposition gave rise to a series of negotiations, and to various transactions between the government and the company, which are not of sufficient interest to be related. But the proposed retrocession became at last final, and the government must be con sidered as having entirely resumed the administration of the colony, on the 15th of November, when it issued several ordinances relative to the winding up of the affairs of the company. Two delegates, Bruslé and Bru, were appointed by the king to proceed to Louisiana, to liquidate and settle the accounts of the company with the government and with individuals; and the creditors of the company in the colony were ordered to present their claims *there* to the delegates, for examination, approbation, and payment, those creditors being prohibited from suing the company in Europe for any debt contracted in Louisiana.

The company had, in payment of its debts, emitted a considerable quantity of bonds, called "*billets de caisse*," which had gradually become part of the currency of the country, and which were in daily use. But on the 15th of November, Governor Périer and the commissary of marine, Salmon, issued an ordinance which declared that, considering that such a currency as the company's bonds or *billets de caisse* interfered with the intrinsic value of the king's coin, and that at the same time it being the wish of his majesty that the holders of these bonds should have the faculty to pay with them the debts contracted while they were the currency of the country, it was decreed that they might still be used during fifteen days from the date of the ordinance, after which time they should be null and void, and withdrawn from circulation. A fine of twenty livres was to be inflicted, for the first offense, on any person convicted of having dealt in these bonds as currency, after the time specified, and corporal punishment was to be the penalty for a second violation of the ordinance by the same person. The effect of this measure was to depreciate these bonds, and their sudden withdrawal from the money-market produced in the currency a vacuum which was sensibly felt. Hence a financial crisis which greatly added to the already existing distress of the colonists.

Thus did the India Company close her career after a laborious existence of fourteen years. She had failed as signally as her predecessor, Crozat, although, having superior means, she had accomplished more for the colony. She had founded New Orleans, which she had so named in compliment to her great patron, the Duke of Orleans, Regent of France, and she had made important settlements at Natchez, at the Tchoupitoulas, Cannes Brulées, Baton Rouge, Manchac, and Pointe Coupée. She had taken Louisiana with a white population of about five hundred souls and twenty negroes, and she left it with a population of five thousand whites and about two thousand five hundred negroes. It is to be remembered, however, that, for the last ten years since 1721, the white population had remained stationary; the negroes alone had increased, their number having swollen from about six hundred to over two thousand. The fact is, that the financial schemes of John Law had given to the colonization of Louisiana by a company, an impetus which was destined to cease by the collapse of the bubbles from which the attempt had originated. Unfortunately, the colonization of Louisiana had not been a great national enterprise, undertaken by patriotism and carried on by enlightened statesmanship. It was a stock-jobbing operation, a mere money-making speculation a bait thrown out to greedy stockholders, and, like most speculations of this kind, it ended in ruin. It had only the honor of being a splendid deception; it blazed out like a meteor, but to be soon swallowed up by obscurity.

The king having agreed to take on his own account all the property of the company in Louisiana, an inventory of what it possessed was made under the direction of Salmon, the king's commissary, and the estimate of what it was found to be worth was fixed at two hundred and sixty-three thousand livres. This property consisted of some merchandise, and of a brick kiln in front of the city, with two hundred and sixty slaves, fourteen horses, and eight thousand barrels of rice. The negroes were valued, on an average, at seven hundred livres a piece, the horses at fifty-seven livres, and the rice at three livres per hundred pounds.

The Superior Council of Louisiana was reorganized by letters patent of the 7th of May, 1732, and was composed in the following manner:—Governor Périer, Salmon, the king's commissary, Loubois and D'Artaguette, *lieutenants de roi*, or the king's lieutenant-governors, Major Benac, commander of New Orleans, Fazende, Bruslé, Bru, Lafreniere, Prat, Raguet, and Fleuriau, who had been reappointed attorney-general. It will be remembered that he had lost his office, in 1726, for having resisted the authority of De la Chaise, the king's commissary. Rossart was appointed secretary of the council.

In order to revive commerce, which had been completely destroyed by the monopoly conceded to the India Company, the king granted several privileges and advantages to such of his subjects as would send vessels to Louisiana. Thus, by an ordinance of the 13th of September, he exempted from duty the merchandise exported from France to Louisiana, and the produce of Louisiana imported into France.

This was, at last, taking one step in the right path, and doing what ought to have been done long before, instead of allowing to one man, or one company, in violation of all the rules of common sense and justice, a monopoly which did not even benefit the grantees.

But as soon as it was known that the trade with Louisiana was open to competition, the merchants of St. Malo, of Bordeaux, of Marseilles, and of the Cap Français began to make preparations to try this new market.

The government fixed the number of regulars to be maintained in the colony at eight hundred men, and, by several ordinances, attempted to prevent the many fluctuations to which the metallic currency of the colony was subject.

Bienville was reappointed governor of Louisiana in the place of Périer, who was subsequently raised to the rank of lieutenant-general as a reward for his services, and his brother Salverte shared the same promotion. Périer had been over six years governor of the colony, and retired with the reputation of a man of integrity and talent, but of stern disposition, and of manners somewhat bordering on roughness. There was at the bottom of his character a fund of harshness from which the Indians had but too much to suffer, and which made itself felt even by his French subordinates.

Bienville, much to his own satisfaction and to the gratification of the colonists, returned to Louisiana in 1733, after an absence of eight years. The surrender of the company's charter, the resumption of the administration of the colony by the king, and the return of Bienville, were circumstances which gladdened their hearts, and inspired them with high hopes of approaching and permanent prosperity.

On the 18th of March, an ordinance of the king fixed the price at which the farmers-general in France were bound to receive the tobacco from Louisiana. The rates were:—35 livres per hundred pounds for 1733; 30 livres for 1734 and 1735; 27 livres for 1736 and 1737; and 25 livres for 1738. Thus the government reserved to itself the right of being the sole purchaser of the tobacco raised in Louisiana, and to pay no more than what it thought proper to give, whatever might be the cost of producing the article, and its intrinsic value in the market. Such was one of the thousand absurdities and flagrant injustices of the suicidal system applied by France to her colonies! The blasting influence which it had on Louisiana can be easily conceived; and it is not astonishing that Diron d'Artaguette, who had gone to France and had returned in company with Bienville, should have found the colony in the situation which he thus describes, in a dispatch of the 23d of April from Mobile. "I have found on my arrival at this place," says he, "two contagious diseases: first, the small-pox, which has carried off and is still killing, every day, a considerable number of persons of both sexes and of every age; and next, a general dearth of provisions, from which every body is suffering, and which has been the result of the destruction of the late crop by a hurricane. Our planters and mechanics here are dying of hunger, and those at New Orleans are in no better situation. Some are clamorous for returning to France; others secretly run away to the Spaniards at Pensacola. The colony is on the eve of being depopulated." Such was the situation of the colony thirty-four years after its foundation, in a country blessed with such fertility as Louisiana! From the very first days of its existence it had continued to struggle against the chilling grasp of famine, and complaints of starvation had been wafted across the ocean by every wind which blew in the direction of the mother country. Such a state of things denotes a profound, a radical vice in the organization and administration of the colony. Active, indeed, must have been the worm concealed in the roots of the tree which had been trans ported into such a luxuriant soil, and which, instead of growing to its natural size and to maturity, instead cf embellishing and enriching the country with its flowers and fruits, could hardly feed its puny trunk with sufficient sap to continue to live in sickly vegetation. It requires, however, no very sagacious eye to discover that what it wanted was the atmosphere of Liberty, which was pumped away by the pneumatic engine of a despotic and imbecile government.

On the 12th of May, Bienville and Salmon, the king's commissary, sent to France a joint dispatch in which they informed the government, that the colonists were very dilatory in producing their titles of concession in order to have them confirmed, as required by the ordinance issued on the 30th of December, 1723, and they recommended that new titles be granted in the name of the king, not only to those who claimed under concessions from the company, but also to those whose claims rested on nothing else but possession. "The country is good," they wrote, " but, like all new countries, is liable to sudden atmospherical changes, and to some confusion of seasons. Besides, the colonists lack experience, and are not sufficiently well settled on their plantations, which are not as yet properly organized. They are in want of negroes, and they complain of their being obliged to pay for the goods they need, two hundred per cent. above what those articles cost the traders. They also complain of the number of useless vagabonds who have been sent here by the company." Speaking of the Ursuline nuns, they said:—"They are very industrious and disinterested; they are much occupied, and live on little." So minute were the details which they went into, that they informed the government that the first child born in the colony, and consequently "*the first Creole*," was named Claude Jousset, and was the son of a Canadian who carried on a small trading business at Mobile.

From a long dispatch which Bienville wrote on the 15th of May, on the situation and disposition in which he found the Indians, it seems that all the tribes in Louisiana were very much disaffected, not excepting even those over whom St. Denis exercised so much influence. "The commander of the fort at Natchitoches," said he, informs me that the Indians have shown an inclination to rebel, and have compelled him to keep himself shut up during six months, and that, although they show themselves more peaceably disposed, yet he still keeps on his guard. In a word it seems that the colony is threatened on every side, and it is, in fact, the custom of the Indian tribes to become hostile in imitation of one another. I hope, however, to restore in Louisiana that tranquillity which she enjoyed when I left her in 1725. Since my arrival, the Natchez have attempted nothing against the French nor against their allies; but they are not destroyed, although we are ignorant of their numbers. The Tunicas have assured me that these indefatigable enemies of the French are divided into three bands: one, the least numerous, has retired into an impracticable country, a little above their ancient villages; the second, which is more considerable, dwells on the banks of the Mississippi, near the Ouatchitas, and opposite the Yazoo River; the third, which is the most numerous, has been received among the Chickasaws, who have granted to these refugees lands on which to build a village. I shall take care that they be constantly attacked and harassed by our Indian allies."

With regard to the Chickasaws, he wrote: "If we can not gain over this nation, it will be necessary to drive it away from the territory of the colony." True to this policy, he induced the Choctaws to set up an expedition against the Chickasaws, and after informing his government of this fact in a communication dated the 26th of July, he added: "It would have been proper to join a body of French troops to the Indians, in order to attack the forts of the Chickasaws, and to achieve some glorious feat, which is an indispensable thing to restore in the colony that healthy tone and self-reliance which it has lost. But we are too poor and without forces, and we must not expose ourselves to fail a second time in any enterprise of the kind. The colony is in such a state of indigence, that, last year, the people were obliged during more than three months to live on the *seeds and grains of reeds*. Much to my regret, therefore, I am condemned to inaction." It is hardly possible to conceive how the country could have been reduced to such a pitch of misery, and such representations can not but be suspected of gross exaggeration. *The seeds and grains of reeds*, of which Bienville speaks, must have been figurative expressions.

On the 10th of August, Bienville informed the French government, that the Natchez who were on the banks of the Mississippi, and who composed the two bands of which it has been spoken, were so effectually harassed by incessant attacks from the Indians he had set upon them, that they were all retreating toward the Chickasaws, to join the third band which had there found shelter and protection.

The whole year 1734 was spent in fruitless negotiations, to induce the Choctaws to make a serious attack upon the Chickasaws, and the dispatches of the time frequently mention a Choctaw chief, called the *Red Shoe*, who acted a conspicuous part in all these transactions, and who, it seems, was constantly oscillating between the French and the English, playing off one interest against the other, selling himself to the highest bidder, and shuffling his cards to his best advantage, in a manner which would have elicited the approbation of Machiavel himself.

Diron d'Artaguette, who commanded at Mobile, asked leave of Bienville to muster one hundred Frenchmen, and with them to put himself at the head of the Choctaws, to march against the Chickasaws; he was greatly irritated at Bienville's refusal on the ground of the want of arms and provisions, and because such forces were too weak to insure success, considering also that the disposition of the Choctaws was doubtful, and therefore that they might prove traitors. It was vainly represented to D'Artarguette, that with such a deficiency of means he would endanger his reputation and that of the French arms. He remained convinced that a feeling of jealousy was at the bottom of this non-compliance with his demand. This conviction was increased when he saw Lesueur, at the head of thirty Frenchmen and one thousand Choctaws, depart to wage war upon the Chickasaws. But Bienville answered his complaints by observing, that if this expedition was defeated, it would bring no discredit or shame on the French, as there were so very few of them engaged in it. The Choctaws had obtained considerable presents from the French to march, and when they arrived in front of the forts of the Chickasaws, being bribed off by those they came to attack, they marched back without striking a blow, with the exception of *Red Shoe*, who showed some conscience, and who, having been paid by the French to fight, resolved to gain his money. At the head of a small band of trusty followers, he stealthily approached one of the villages, and poured a volley of bullets into the cabins. But he was immediately attacked by forces immensely superior to his own, and closely pursued by about two hundred men, the distance of twenty miles. He escaped, however, after having lost four men, among whom was the brother of the great chief of the Choctaws.

On hearing of the unsuccessful termination of this expedition, Bienville convened a meeting of the Choctaws at Mobile, and upbraided them for their want of faith. They all apologized in humble terms for their conduct, with the exception of Red Shoe, who spoke with arrogance, and exalted too much what he had done. Bienville affected to be highly displeased at his presumption, and reprimanded him roughly. However, he made to the chiefs some presents, which were necessarily small on account of the penury in which he was, and he renewed with them the old treaties of alliance. The conditions on which merchandise was to be furnished to the Choctaws were agreed upon, and they, in their turn, solemnly promised to hold no communication with the English. It was exceedingly important for the French to secure the support of this powerful tribe, which Bienville represents as owning fifty-two large villages scattered over a circumference of three hundred miles. Hence Bienville bitterly and incessantly complained of not being supplied with sufficient means to command, by the required presents, the allegiance of these Indians.

Unfortunately for the colony, the misunderstanding which had broken out between Bienville and D'Artaguette became every day more marked and serious in its character. They were both, however, men of distinguished merit, and ought to have understood and appreciated each other. But it seemed, as for the past, that harmony could never exist long between the chiefs of the colony. Thus D'Artaguette, in one of his dispatches, of the 29th of April, 1735, assures his government, that if Bienville is displeased with and complains of him, it is because he, D'Artaguette, has made known the misconduct of Bienville's protégés, or favorites, Lesueur and the Jesuit, Father Beaudoin, *who, to the great scandal of the Choctaws, seduce their women.*

Be it for this cause, or for another, it is certain that, notwithstanding the treaty of alliance which had been recently renewed, and the presents they had received, the Choctaws were divided into two factions, one of which was hostile to the French, and the other in favor of the English, who, for many years, had been struggling to gain over that nation to their interest, and to trade with it exclusively of the French.

In the mean time, the Chickasaws and the Natchez, united in one body, were not inactive, and never failed to attack the French whenever the opportunity was favorable. The imagination may well be permitted to conceive, that the long series of misfortunes heaped upon the Natchez had produced some Hannibal of the wilderness, who sought everywhere for avengers of his nation's wrongs, and who thought that

> "What though the field be lost,
> All is not lost:—the unconquerable will
> And study of revenge, immortal hate,
> And courage never to submit or yield,
> And what is else not to be overcome."
>
> — MILTON.

De Coulanges had been ordered up the river to carry ammunition to young D'Artaguette, who had so distinguished himself when the Natchez were besieged by Loubois, and who had since been intrusted with the command of the Illinois district. He had the imprudence not to obey strictly his orders, and to transport merchandise belonging to some officers, instead of a considerable quantity of powder, which he left behind to make room for the other article. Disappointed at not receiving the ammunition of which he stood much in need, D'Artaguette dispatched in quest of it an officer, named Du Coder, with ten men. Before reaching the Arkansas district, they were attacked by two hundred and forty Chickasaw and Natchez warriors, who killed eight of the soldiers, and made prisoners Du Coder, a sergeant, and a soldier. Speaking of this untoward event, Bienville said: " I have ordered D'Artaguette to imprison De Coulanges for six months in Fort Chartres, and I would have interdicted this officer, if I had not taken into consideration his past services, particularly in the last Natchez war. I hope that this example will be sufficient to moderate the avidity for gain, which some of our officers have imbibed in the service of the company."

It seems, however, that the Chickasaws had become anxious for peace, and they invited Du Coder, their prisoner, to write to that effect to Bienville: they also set free the soldier they had captured. He soon reached New Orleans, and informed Bienville that the Chickasaws had treated kindly their white prisoners, who had been conducted through the Indian villages with a white stick in their hands, and thoroughly washed in public from head to foot, as a token of life being granted to them. Through this soldier they again sued for peace, and begged to be protected against the marauding attacks of the Indian allies of the French. Bienville wrote back to Du Coder to try to escape* with the sergeant his companion, because he could not grant peace to the Chickasaws, and *could not sacrifice the glory and interests of the French nation to the safety of two men.* Thus it is evident that he had taken the resolution, to come to no terms with the Chickasaws, and to drive them away from the colony,

* Du Coder took the advice, and escaped shortly after with his companion.

But though he had determined on a war of extermination, he was obliged to postpone all operations, and he wrote to the French minister of Marine: "I beg your excellency not to forget that I can hardly set on foot two hundred men, and that I can not rely on the Indians, who have given us so many proofs of their cowardice in the expeditions I have induced them to undertake against the Chickasaws. I dare not then, with such means as I have, expose the honor of our arms against a warlike nation, numbering, at least, four hundred and fifty warriors. I have learned from the soldier they sent me back, that they have five palisaded forts, and besides, for every ten cabins in their villages, one that is fortified with three lines or rows of stakes provided with loopholes, and terraced in such a way as to be fire-proof. All these cabins are so situated as to protect one another. The Natchez, who still number one hundred and eighty warriors, have a village of their own contiguous to those of the Choctaws. Besides the fortified cabins and the five forts I have mentioned, the Chickasaws have a larger one with four bastions, which they have constructed with the trunks of trees stuck into the ground, in imitation of the one we had among the Natchez when they revolted. Such are the offensive and defensive means of our enemies. Hence you can judge what we can do. Were I to march against them with the whole colony at my heels, I could not hope for success. I can not therefore undertake any thing lightly. I request, *again and forever*, an augmentation of four companies. I will do however all I can, to continue to harass the Chickasaws with incursions from our red allies. But it is absolutely necessary that some bold and remarkable blow be struck, to impress the Indians with a proper sense of respect and duty toward us."

At that time, it was reported that the British faction among the Choctaws had gained so much ground as to prevail upon that nation to make war upon the French, and to attack Mobile. This gave rise to great alarm in that settlement, where the inhabitants, under the apprehension of immediate danger, never went out of their houses without being well provided with arms, *and even did not go to church to hear mass without having their guns on their shoulders*, as stated in one of Bienville's dispatches. So intense became their fears, that they prepared to abandon the place, and to retire to New Orleans. But Bienville sent them positive orders not to leave their habitations, and assured them that they had nothing to fear. In one of his dispatches he accused Diron d'Artaguette of being the cause of the discontent which had spread among the Choctaws, by the harsh manner in which he had treated some warriors of that nation who had come to Mobile, to have their arms repaired and put in order.

A short time after, on the 16th of July, a smuggling vessel from Jamaica appeared in Mobile Bay, and anchored at twelve miles from the fort. D'Artaguette ordered her to leave the bay, and on her captain delaying to obey, sent Lieutenant De Velles in an armed boat with thirty men, to take possession of the vessel, which had a very inoffensive look, but which, nevertheless, opened such an effective fire on the boat as she approached, that De Velles, having seventeen of his men killed or wounded in an instant, was obliged to retreat, and to allow his enemy to gain the open sea without further molestation. This circumstance again gave to Bienville an opportunity to tax D'Artaguette with gross imprudence and carelessness. In fact, a fierce war of angry accusations and recriminations was now kept up between these two antagonists, and had succeeded the

DIFFICULTY IN SETTLING THE COMPANY'S AFFAIRS.

intimacy which had existed between them during many years.

The settlement of the company's affairs in the colony proved to be of no small difficulty. The stockholders complained that the just debts due to the company could not be recovered, because the debtors were favored by the only judicial tribunal in the country, the members of the council, who themselves were indebted to the company. Considering this state of things, the king, by an ordinance of the 16th of October, 1733, appointed the royal commissary, Salmon, the sole judge to pronounce in the last resort between the company and its debtors or creditors in Louisiana.

Since 1723, when the company had introduced into the colony a paper currency, during the existence of which the dollar had risen in value to 35 livres, a bottle of brandy to 30 livres, a pair of shoes to 35 livres of that paper money, and so on in proportion for every other merchandise, a vast amount of debts had been contracted under that monetary system between the colonists, and between the company and individuals. Now that the government had withdrawn from circulation all the paper money of the company, by receiving it in payment of goods, debtors contended that their debts ought to be reduced to one half, considering that they were under the necessity of making their payments in a currency much more valuable than the one in existence when they had contracted their obligations. Individuals generally submitted to transactions of this kind, but the company, which was much more of a creditor than of a debtor, refused to admit the justice and application of this rule. Salmon was in favor of the proposed reduction, but hesitated to enforce it, and was satisfied with making recommendations to compromise. Thus matters stood for some time.

The French government thought it a heavy burden to provide for the expenses of the colony in hard coin, and, in 1734, consulted Bienville and Salmon on the emission of paper money (papier de cartes). They were opposed to it altogether, but not venturing to express the opinion that it ought not to be emitted at all, they advised that the measure be postponed for two years. In support of this opinion, they described the aversion which existed in the colony against this kind of currency, and the want of confidence with which it would be received; they represented that when the company surrendered its charter, its paper was depreciated to half its original value, and that such had been the fate of every paper currency in the colony since its foundation; that it would drive away the precious metals, make the dollar, as it had been seen once, rise up to 35 livres, and open the door again to the most disastrous stock-jobbing operations, and to the foulest demoralization, and that no more would be required to cause the desertion and total ruin of the country. "We have seen," said Bienville in one of his dispatches, "that one who has paper money in his pocket, will spend it more easily than hard coin, and that, when such is the currency of the country, every one consumes all he earns without any thought of *to-morrow*." Bienville wrote these remarkable lines in 1734. True they were at that time, and that truth was still more energetically demonstrated by what occurred in Louisiana a century later, when it was her curse to be overflooded with a deluge of bank notes. It is easy, however, to conceive the anxiety which the government felt, in 1734, to pay its expenses in paper, when it is known that those expenses amounted, during that year, to 898,245 livres for this puny colony of five thousand souls.

On the 15th of April, 1735, Bienville wrote, on the state of the colony: "One hundred thousand pounds of tobacco are made at Pointe Coupée; two women raise silk-worms for amusement, and succeed very well; eggs should be sent by the government to the Ursulines, who would teach this industry to the orphans whose education is intrusted to them. The cultivation of cotton is advantageous, but the planters experience great difficulty in clearing it from the seeds. Pitch and tar are made in some abundance. I neglect nothing to turn the attention of the inhabitants to agricultural pursuits, but in general they are worthless, lazy, dissolute, and most of them recoil from the labors necessary to improve the lands." To those inhabitants who were represented as lazy and dissolute, the year 1735 was not a favorable one, for Bienville and Salmon, in a joint dispatch of the 31st of August, say: "The mortality of cattle is frightful, the drought is excessive, and the heat is suffocating. Such hot weather has never been known since the foundation of the colony, and it has now lasted four months without any change. From Christmas to the St. John the waters were very high, so that many levees were broken. The one which is in front of the city gave way, and we were very near abandoning our houses and taking lodgings in boats. Then the drought came, and the river went down fifteen feet—a circumstance which had never been seen before. Hence the mediocrity of our crops, our lands having been under water in the planting season."

While the planters were suffering from drought, after having suffered from inundation, the inhabitants of New Orleans were laboring under a strange kind of infliction. They could hardly venture out of their houses without being bit by mad dogs. These animals had increased to such an extent, that they had become an intolerable nuisance, and to remedy the evil, the royal commissary, Salmon, ordered them to be hunted down on certain days, from five o'clock until six in the morning. He also prohibited negroes and Indians from having dogs, under the penalty for the offender of being sentenced to wear an iron collar.

The colony had always undergone great inconvenience from the want of carpenters, cabinet-makers, tailors, shoemakers, and mechanics of every description. To obviate this difficulty, an ordinance was issued freeing from his military engagement any French or Swiss soldier, if he was a handicraftsman, provided he agreed to remain in the colony, and to exercise his calling.

The troops, which so far had not been supplied with suitable quarters, were, this year, comfortably lodged in barracks, which Bienville and Salmon had ordered, on the 12th of July, 1734, to be constructed on both sides of the public square in the city of New Orleans.

The latter part of 1735, and the beginning of 1736, were marked by great military preparations in the colony. The French government had sent to Bienville a few additional troops, and notwithstanding the doubts he had expressed on the final success of an expedition against the Chickasaws, except it be with such ample means as the government did not seem disposed to grant, had ordered him to undertake one, as soon as possible, against that nation, and to drive it away from the country. In obedience to these instructions, Bienville had sent word to the younger D'Artaguette, the commander of the Illinois district, to collect all the French and Indian forces he could muster, and to meet him on the 31st of March, 1736, at the Chickasaw villages. In the month of January of that year, Bienville drew from Natchez, Natchitoches, and the Balize all the officers and soldiers he could spare without weakening too much the garrisons stationed at those places. He formed a company of volunteers, composed of traders and transient persons then in New Orleans, and another company of unmarried men belonging to the city, and which was called the *company of bachelors*. A depot of ammunition, provisions, and all that was necessary for the intended campaign was established on the Tombekbee, at the distance of two hundred and seventy miles from Mobile, where the several detachments of the army were successively sent through the Lakes, as fast as conveyances could be procured. Several large vessels containing provisions and utensils of every sort were dispatched down the Mississippi to Mobile, and on the 4th of March, Bienville departed from New Orleans, leaving behind him only four companies of regulars under Noyan, which were to follow him as soon as they could be transported. The boats having to struggle against adverse winds, the whole of the French forces did not reach Mobile before the 22d, and it was only on the 28th, that the last of the vessels carrying provisions entered the harbor, when it was discovered that her cargo had been much damaged by the sea. On the 1st of April, the expedition left Mobile, and it was only on the 23d that the army reached the Tombekbee depot, after having had to contend against currents, freshets, storms, and constant rains.

There, while waiting for the arrival of the Choctaws, Bienville reviewed his troops, which were found to consist of five hundred and forty-four white men, excluding the officers, and of forty-five negroes, commanded by free blacks, the balance being composed of Indians. The principal officers were De Léry, D'Hauterive, De Lusser, De Courtillas, Petit, Berthel, De Bombelles, Benac, Le Blanc, De Membrede, De Macarty, De St. Pierre, De Velles, De Bouillé, Des Marets, De Contre

Cœur de St. Protais, Pontalba, Vanderek, Montbrun, and Noyan. At the head of the Swiss companies were Volant and Du Parc; Montmolin was their standard-bearer. The detachments of the militia were commanded by Lesueur and St. Martin.

The Choctaws, to the number of six hundred, having come at last, the army, after innumerable delays and difficulties, resumed its march, and on the 22d of May encamped at about twenty-seven miles from the Chickasaw villages. On the 23d, at daybreak, Bienville had a certain number of trees cut down to make stakes, and ordered the construction of fortifications for the protection of the boats. Leaving in those fortifications the general store-keeper, the captains of the boats, some sick men, and twenty soldiers under the command of Vanderek, on the 24th in the afternoon, and after having ordered the troops to take provisions for twelve days, he marched six miles further, where he encamped for the night, which was very tempestuous. On the 25th, within the space of twelve miles, the army had to cross successively three deep ravines running through a thick cane-brake, and had to wade through water rising up to the waist. The army then emerged on a beautiful and open prairie, on the edge of which they encamped, at the distance of six miles from the villages.

The intention of Bienville was to turn round those villages of the Chickasaws, to march upon the village of the Natchez, which was in the rear, and to attack first those whom he considered as the instigators of the Chickasaw war. But the Choctaws insisted with such pertinacity upon attacking the villages which were nearer, and which, they said, contained more provisions than that of the Natchez; and they represented with such warmth, that, in the needy condition in which they were, it was absolutely necessary they should take possession of these provisions, that Bienville yielded to their importunities. The prairie in which these villages were situated covered a space of about six miles. The villages were small, and built in the shape of a triangle, on a hillock sloping down to a brook which was almost dry; further off was the main body of the Chickasaw villages, and the smaller ones seemed to be a sort of vanguard. The Choctaws having informed Bienville that he would find water nowhere else, he ordered the army to file off close to the wood which enclosed the prairie, in order to reach another hillock that was in sight. There the troops halted to rest and take nourishment. It was past twelve o'clock.

The Indian scouts whom Bienville had sent in every direction to look for tidings of D'Artaguette, whom he had expected to operate his junction with him on this spot, had come back and brought no information. It was evident, therefore, that he could no longer hope for the co-operation on which he had relied, and that he had to trust only to his own resources. It was impossible to wait; and immediate action was insisted upon by the Choctaws and the French officers, who thought that the three small villages which have been described, and which were the nearest to them, were not susceptible of much resistance. Bienville yielded to the solicitations of his allies and of his troops, and at two in the afternoon, ordered his nephew Noyan to begin the attack, and to put himself at the head of a column composed of a company of grenadiers, of detachments of fifteen men taken from each one of the eight companies of French regulars, of sixty-five men of the Swiss troops and forty-five volunteers.

The French had approached within carbine shot of the forts, and at that distance, could plainly distinguish Englishmen, who appeared to be very active in assisting the Chickasaws in preparing their defense, and who had hoisted up their flag on one of the forts. Bienville recommended that they should not be assailed if they thought proper to retire, and to give them time should they feel so disposed, he ordered to confine the attack to the village named Ackia, which was the most remote from the one under the English flag.

The order for the attack being given, the division commanded by Noyan moved briskly on, and under the protection of mantelets carried by the company of negroes, arrived safely at the foot of the hill on which the villages stood. But there, one of the negroes being killed, and another wounded, the rest flung down the mantelets, and took to their heels. The French pushed on, and penetrated into the village, with the company of grenadiers at their head. But being no longer under cover, and much exposed to the fire of the enemy, their losses were very heavy. The noble and brilliant Chevalier de Contre Cœur, a favorite in the army, was killed, and a number of soldiers shared his fate, or were disabled. However, three of the principal fortified cabins were carried by the impetuosity of the French, with several smaller ones which were burned. But as a pretty considerable intervening space remained to be gone over, to assail the chief fort and the other fortified cabins, when it became necessary to complete the success obtained, Noyan, who had headed the column of attack, turning round, saw that he had with him only the officers belonging to the head of the column, some grenadiers, and a dozen of volunteers. The troops had been dismayed by the death of Captain De Lusser, with many of his grenadiers, including a sergeant, who had fallen when they had attempted to cross the space separating the last cabin taken from the next to be taken. Seeking for shelter against the galling fire of the enemy, the French had clustered behind the cabins of which they had already taken possession, and it was impossible for the officers who commanded the tail of the column, to drive them away, either by threats, promises, or words of exhortation, from their secure position. Putting themselves at the head of a few of their best soldiers, in order to encourage the rest, the officers resolved to make a desperate attempt to storm the fortified blockhouse they had in front of them. But in an instant, their commander the Chevalier de Noyan, D'Hauterive, the captain of the grenadiers, Grondel, lieutenant of the Swiss, De Velles, Montbrun, and many other officers, were disabled. Still keeping his ground, De Noyan sent his aid-de-camp, De Juzan, to encourage and bring up to him the wavering soldiers who had slunk behind the cabins. But, in making the effort, this officer was killed, and his death increased the panic of the troops.

Grondel, who had fallen near the walls of the enemy, had been abandoned, and a party of Indians was preparing to sally out to scalp him, when a sergeant of the grenadiers, ashamed of the cowardice which had left an officer in this perilous and defenseless position, took with him four of his men, and rushed to the rescue of Grondel, without being intimidated by bullets as thick as hail. These five intrepid men reached in safety the spot where Grondel lay, and were in the act of lifting him up to carry him away, when a general discharge from the fort prostrated every one of them dead by the side of him they had come to save. But this noble deed was not lost upon the army: the electrical stroke had been given, and was responded to by the flashing out of another bright spark of heroism. A grenadier named Régnisse, rather inflamed than dastardized by the fate of his companions, dashed out of the ranks of his company, ran headlong to the place where Grondel lay weltering in his blood from the five wounds he had received, took him on his athletic shoulders, and carried him away in triumph amid the general acclamations, and the enthusiastic bravos of those who witnessed the feat. To the astonishment of all, he had the good luck to pass unscathed through the fire which was poured upon him by the enemy, but the inanimate body of Grondel which he was transporting received a sixth wound. So generously saved from the Indian tomahawk, this officer slowly recovered, and was subsequently raised to a high rank in the French army.

The spectacle then presented to the sight was truly of an exciting character. The village attacked was enveloped in a thick smoke, through which might be seen to emerge occasionally, a body of soldiers carrying away some of their wounded. Inside of the smoke, concealed behind the heavy logs of which their forts and cabins were made up, the Indians, firing through their loopholes, were uttering such appalling whoops and shouts, such blood-freezing shrieks and fiendish yells, that one would have thought that thousands of demons were rioting in one of their favorite haunts in Pandemonium. To complete the illusion, the six hundred Choctaws, with the other red allies of the French, almost in a state of nakedness, and painted all over in the most frightful colors, as they do, when they go to war, to make themselves more hideously terrific, kept hovering on both wings of the French, at a safe distance from the balls of the enemy, while they fired at random into the vacant air, emulating the Chickasaws in the production only of horrific and unearthly sounds, gesticulating wildly, running and jumping, as if they were delirious, and looking like maniac devils rather than men. One could have imagined that they were the rabble of hell, enraged and thrown into an insurrection, by being excluded from the feast prepared for their betters.

Noyan, seeing at last that he was exposing himself and his bravest companions in vain, and growing faint under the effects of his wound, ordered a retreat from the open field, and taking shelter in one of the cabins, sent word to Bienville, that he had lost about seventy men, of whom many were officers, and that if prompt relief was not afforded, no officer would be left standing on his feet, as they would all have to share the fate of those who had fallen : that himself, although from the nature of his wound in want of immediate assistance, would not venture to retire from the field of action, because he feared it would be the signal of a general scattering away.

On hearing this report, and on seeing the French and Swiss troops beginning to give ground, while demonstrations of an attack on their flank were visible in the direction of the great Indian villages which were further off at the extremity of the prairie, Bienville sent Beauchamp with a reserve of eighty men, to support the troops engaged, and to bring off the wounded and the dead. Beauchamp did not execute his orders without losing several men. One of his officers, by the name of Favrot, was wounded; and when Beauchamp reached the spot where the contest had been the fiercest, and which might, if the expression be allowed, be called the heart of the battle, he found all the officers nobly keeping their ground, and clustered in a solid mass, retaining possession with desperate energy of the foremost cabin they had gained, nearest to the fort of the enemy. Beauchamp gathered together all the men who still remained on that bloody field, and retreated in good order toward the French camp, but he could not prevent some of the dead bodies from falling into the hands of the Indians, who, much to the horror of the French, impaled the naked corpses on their palisades. The Choctaws who, so far, had kept aside and left the French to shift for themselves, seeing them in full retreat, seemed disposed, out of bravado, to show to the white faces, that the red ones could do what the superior race had failed to execute, and marched upon the village as if determined to storm it. But as they approached, a general discharge from the enemy having brought down twenty-two of their men, they did not wait for another, and scampered away like whipped curs, much to the satisfaction and amusement of the French.

This engagement, which had begun at two o'clock in the afternoon, had lasted three hours. It had ceased for more than an hour and a half, when, on looking down on the lovely scene which then presented itself to the eye, one would have been struck with the contrast which it had offered not long before. To the well-known excitement, noise, turmoil, confusion, and incidents of a battle, had succeeded the most complete repose and the most absolute silence. The sun had gone down to rest behind the distant trees of the western horizon, and that portion of the sky through which he had lately trod, had remained gorgeously illuminated by the lingering rays which the eastern monarch had left behind him when he had disappeared. The richly dyed and variegated clouds, which rose up in a pyramid of splendor, looked as if they were the purple mantle and the other vestments which he had carelessly dropped from his shoulders when he had sought his repose. A sweet breeze was sighing and gently sweeping across the prairie as if lulling tired nature to sleep. In the distance, the villages of the Chickasaws produced rather a picturesque effect, and were for the eye an agreeable resting-point in the landscape. Not a sound was to be heard coming from that direction. The Indians seemed to have dropped asleep in the lap of victory, under the protection of the proud banner of England, which floated over their heads. There was but one spot where a hollow murmuring sound might have been noticed. It was in the French camp, situated on the outskirts of the prairie, in the vicinity of the smaller Indian villages which the French had met on entering it, and which seemed to stand sentries for the main body of the larger villages. Encouraged by the silence which had been reigning for two hours, herds of deer were to be seen gracefully stealing away through the prairie, and its feathered tenants, such as partridges, woodcocks, and other birds were heard uttering, in their usual notes, their last farewell to the departing light of day, while seeking their downy nests in the perfumed grass enameled with myriads of wild flowers. The cattle of the Indians, which, frightened by the musketry and the shouts of the combatants, had fled into the neighboring woods, had returned to the prairie, and were seen browsing far and wide over that broad expanse of pasture. Invited by silence and solitude, a troop of horses, headed by a beautiful white mare, which seemed their queen, came leisurely on, to drink at the brook running at the foot of the hill, on which stood the Indian villages. A soft glow hung over the prairie, and it looked like a beautiful picture, of which the dark foliaged woods far off were the appropriate frame.

Not unmindful of the attractions of this truly southern scenery of the North American continent, and reposing under the broad canopy of a gigantic oak which stood a little in front of the French camp, a large group of officers were discussing the events of the day. With them was Simon, a free black, the commander of the company of negroes who had thrown down the mantelets they were carrying to protect the French in their attempt to storm the village of Ackia. Simon, when his men had fled, had stood his ground, and had remained with the French officers at the spot the most exposed, until the retreat was sounded. He was a sort of privileged character, and he was sorely vexed at the cowardice displayed by those of his color. The French officers, who were amused at his chagrin, and at the comical expressions in which it was vented, kept bantering him without mercy on his light-footed companions. Stung to the heart, Simon exclaimed: "A negro is as brave as any body, and I will show it to you." Seizing a rope which was dangling from one of the tents, he rushed headlong toward the horses which were quietly slaking their thirst under the protection of the muskets of the Indian villages. To reach the white mare, to jump on her back with the agility of a tiger, and to twist round her head and mouth the rope with which to control and rein her, was the affair of an instant. But that instant was enough for the apparently sleeping village to show itself wide awake, and that dark mass was seen as if spontaneously girding itself with a zone of fire, so rapid and thick were the flashes from its innumerable loopholes. But away dashed Simon with the rapidity of lightning; frantic with affright, madly reared and plunged the conquered mare under the strong hand of Simon, who forced her to take the direction of the French camp, where he arrived safely amid the cheering acclamations of the troops, and without having received a scratch from the

DESCRIPTION OF THE INDIAN FORTIFICATIONS. 481

balls of the enemy. This noble feat silenced at once the jests of which Simon thought himself the victim.

The modest abnegation of the brave grenadier, Régnisse, who had so heroically saved Grondel, must not be omitted to be recorded also. When the battle was over, Bienville wanted to make him an officer on the spot, but Régnisse obstinately refused, saying that he did not know how to write, and that having no education, he was not worthy of the grade offered to him, and that every one of his brother grenadiers being capable of doing what he had done, he did not deserve and did not wish to be elevated above them; his scruples could not be overcome, but his comrades, joyfully admitting his superiority, insisted upon his name being put at the top of the roll of the company, and upon his taking the lead of them when under arms. On that day, he received from his companions the title of "*the first of the grenadiers.*"

The prairie on which these events took place, was called "*Strawberry Plain,*" on account of the quantity of the fruit of this name with which it was covered, and the battle was called "*the Battle of Ackia,*" from the name of the village attacked.

After the severe repulse which the French had met with, nothing remained for them to do but to retreat. Writing on the causes of the failure of this expedition, and on the reasons which induced him not to renew the attack, Bienville said:—"What remains to add to the previous information given by me with regard to the fortifications which the Indians know how to make is, that after having surrounded their cabins with several rows of thick and large stakes, they dig the ground inside, and bury themselves up to the pit of their arms, which they keep free to fire through loopholes cut almost even with the ground. But they obtain more advantages from the natural situation of their cabins, which are at a distance from one another, and are so located as to cross their fires, than from any thing which English art can teach to make them stronger. The roof of these cabins is a thick covering of mud and wood, which is proof against firebrands or arrows and grenades, so that they could be penetrated through only by bombs. But we had neither cannon nor mortars. After all, when I saw the number of our wounded, I did not doubt but that I was obliged to give up the game, on account of the difficulty which I foresaw of transporting them. In fact, I had no choice, because I feared to be deserted by the Choctaws, who were famished. In that case, we should have been harassed in the woods, and attacked when crossing the ravines; our loss then might have been very great. What justified my fears, is, that I was obliged to divide with the Choctaws our provisions, to induce them to come with us."

On the 27th of May, the day following that of the battle, Bienville had litters made to transport the wounded; and at one in the afternoon, the army forming itself into two columns, which had been the order of marching when coming, began its retrograde movement. The soldiers, who were very much worn out by the fatigues they had undergone, and whose baggage was already a full load, had infinite pains in carrying on the wounded, and it was dark when the army had gone four miles and a half through the woods. It having become necessary to encamp for the night, such slow marching disgusted the Choctaws; and Red Shoe, who nourished an old grudge against the French, with a few others, endeavored to prevail upon their people to abandon their white allies. In order to counteract their intrigues, Bienville sent for the great chief of the

Choctaws, and expostulating with him, begged him to recollect that it was to please the Choctaws that he had attacked the Chickasaws, instead of going round their villages to assail the Natchez, as was his original intention, and that the Choctaws were, therefore, the causes of the defeat of the French, whom they ought to desert much less under such circumstances than under any other. The eloquence of Bienville touched the great chief, who ordered Red Shoe to desist from his designs. A violent altercation arose between them, and the great chief, drawing a pistol from his belt, was in the act of firing at Red Shoe, when his arm was arrested by Bienville. At last, all difficulties were settled, and it was agreed that every Indian chief would have one wounded Frenchman carried by his men. Alibamon Mengo, the chief who had been so useful to the French when they besieged the Natchez, and whose interference had induced the enemy to come to terms, gave the example, and had Bienville's nephew, Noyan, carried by his people. On the 29th, the French reached the place where they had left their boats, after having lost on the way two men, who died of their wounds.

The French found the river falling so fast, that they hastened to embark on that same day, and so low already was the water, that it became hard work in several places to push the boats through. From this circumstance, Bienville had cause to congratulate himself on the resolution he had taken to retreat, it being evident that, a few days later, he would have been obliged to set fire to his boats, and to return by land, which would have been attended with immense difficulties and dangers.

The French arrived at the Tombecbee settlement on the 2d of June, and the wounded were immediately sent forward with all the surgeons. On the 3d, Bienville departed from Tombecbee, where he left Captain De Berthel in command, with a garrison of thirty Frenchmen and twenty Swiss. They were supplied with provisions to last for the balance of the year, and with merchandise to trade with the Indians. Bienville drew the plan of the fortifications which he wished to be made, and instructed Berthel to have them erected as soon as possible on the spot he had designated.

On his return to New Orleans, Bienville wrote to the minister of the colonial department: "Your excellency will have seen by the accounts of this laborious campaign, which I have transmitted to the government, that in its conception and execution, and in the closing retreat, I made the best use I could of the means I had at my disposal, and you will also have remarked that, after having suffered in my preparations from delays which I could not anticipate, much less could I foresee the cowardice of the troops put under my orders. It is true that, considering the pitiful recruits of blackguards which are sent here, one ought never to entertain the flattering hope of making soldiers of them. What is worse, is the obligation under which I am, with such troops, to hazard the reputation of the nation, and to expose our officers to the necessity of meeting death or dishonor. The recruits recently arrived by the Gironde are still inferior to the preceding ones. There are but one or two men among them whose size is above five feet; as to the rest, they are under four feet ten inches. With regard to their moral character, it is sufficient to state that, out of fifty-two who have lately been sent here, more than one half have already been whipped for larceny. In a word, these useless beings are not worth the food bestowed upon them: they are burdens to the colony, and from them no efficient military service is to be expected."

ACCOUNT OF D'ARTAGUETTE'S EXPEDITION. 485

It was only at New Orleans that Bienville learned that D'Artaguette had arrived before him at the Chickasaw villages, and had met with a signal defeat and a tragical death. In conformity with the instructions he had received, D'Artaguette had displayed considerable activity, and had reached, on the 4th of March, a place then called *Ecores à Prudhomme*, on the Mississippi, with thirty soldiers, one hundred volunteers, and almost all the Indians of the Kaskaskia village. There he was joined by De Vincennes with forty Iroquois, and all the Indians of the Wabash tribe. De Montcherval, with the Cahokias and the Mitchigamias, was daily expected. De Grandpré, who commanded at the Arkansas, had dispatched twenty-eight warriors of that tribe to ascertain whether D'Artaguette was at the *Ecores à Prudhomme*, and to come back to him with that information. These Indians, when they reached the spot, finding that D'Artaguette was moving away, followed him, and disregarded the instructions of Grandpré, who in vain waited for their return. D'Artaguette proceeded by short stages, in order to give time to Montcherval and Grandpré to join him. When he arrived on the territory of the Chickasaws, he sent scouts to discover tidings of Bienville's army. These scouts soon returned, and reported that in the neighborhood of the Chickasaw villages, there were no vestiges of the French forces.

On the day following the return of these spies, a courier brought to D'Artaguette a letter, in which he was informed that unexpected delays and obstacles in the preparations to be made, would prevent Bienville from being at the Chickasaws before the end of April, which would be the soonest, wherefore he was requested to take his measures accordingly. On the reception of this letter, D'Artaguette convened a council of war, composed of officers and of Indian chiefs. The Indians were for an immediate attack, representing that they had but few provisions, and therefore would be obliged to abandon the French in a short time; that their spies had reported that, at the extremity of the prairie where the Chickasaw villages were situated, there was an isolated one, (probably the village of the Natchez refugees) which had no more than thirty cabins, of which, no doubt, easy possession could be taken, and that the provisions they would find there would enable the whole army to wait comfortably for the arrival of Bienville, under the protection of fortifications which would soon be erected. Almost all of the French officers were of the same opinion, and the attack was resolved upon. At that moment, the allied forces were composed of one hundred and thirty Frenchmen and of three hundred and sixty-six Indians.

Having taken the determination to attack, the French marched on briskly, and came, without being discovered, as they thought, within the distance of a mile from the isolated village, on Palm Sunday. Leaving all his baggage to the keeping of thirty men commanded by Frontigny, D'Artaguette marched on the village, which he attacked with great vigor. But hardly had the engagement begun, when four or five hundred Indians, who were headed by about thirty Englishmen, and who had kept themselves concealed behind a neighboring hill, fell upon the assailants with such impetuosity, and so unexpectedly, that the Miamis and the Illinois took to flight. Thirty-eight Iroquois, and the twenty-eight Arkansas sent by Grandpré, were the only Indians that stood by the French, who fought with desperate valor against the overwhelming odds they had to contend with. Lieutenant St. Ange was the first to fall, then the Ensigns De Coulanges, De la Gravière, and

De Courtigny, with six of the militia officers. Still the French, hemmed in on every side, did not give way an inch. But soon, Captain Des Essarts, Lieutenant Langlois, and Ensign Levieux, were shot down. Few officers remained on their legs, and the French, having lost forty-five men out of one hundred that they were, thought that it was high time to operate a retreat toward their baggage, where they expected to be supported by the detachment of thirty men they had left there. But they were pursued with such obstinate fury by the Chickasaws, that, at last, they were completely routed in spite of the courage and discipline which they had displayed. D'Artaguette, who had performed prodigies of valor, had fallen covered with wounds, and was taken prisoner, with Father Sénac, a Jesuit, Du Tisné, an officer of regulars, Lalande, a militia captain, and five or six soldiers and militia privates, making nineteen in all. The Chickasaws gave up the pursuit of the fugitives only after having killed fifty of them, and wounded many others. Not one man would have escaped, if a violent storm had not arisen, and checked the pursuers. The Chickasaws took possession of all the provisions and baggage of the French, with four hundred and fifty pounds of powder, twelve thousand bullets, and eleven horses. Their victory was as complete as possible, and the ammunition which fell into their hands was of great use to them, in helping them to resist the subsequent attack of Bienville.

D'Artaguette, Father Sénac, and fifteen others were burned alive, according to the usage of the Indians in festivals for victories obtained, and the remaining two captains were set aside, to be exchanged for a Chickasaw warrior who was in the hands of the French. This exchange effectually took place some time after.

The fugitives, on the second day of their flight, met

Montcherval, who was following D'Artaguette with one hundred and sixty Indians, and fourteen Frenchmen. Montcherval gathered together the broken remnants of D'Artaguette's army, and fell back, after having dispatched a courier to Grandpré. The courier met this officer on Margot River, with all the warriors of the Arkansas tribe. He was waiting for the return of the emissary he had sent to bring him back tidings of D'Artaguette. On hearing of the defeat of the French, he returned to the settlement where he commanded.

The melancholy fate of D'Artaguette and his companions produced on the colony almost as painful an impression as the Natchez massacre; and the bad success of Bienville's expedition was another cause of humiliation, which contributed to increase the gloom hanging over the country. De Beauchamp, who, it will be recollected, had been sent by Bienville to support Noyan when attacking the village of Ackia, and to facilitate his retreat, writing on this expedition, says:—
"To make an end of the Chickasaw war, it is necessary to have a detachment of workmen, of miners and bombardiers, with the implements and instruments necessary to ferret out those savages, who burrow like badgers in their cabins, which are very much like ovens. If fire is set to them, the straw with which they are thatched will be consumed, but the cabin itself, the roof and lateral walls of which are made of mud one foot thick, will not burn. Besides, these cabins which are fortified, are so situated that they defend one another. It is not enough to take three or four of them: all must be taken, or there is no security. The ground being of a nature easy to be worked, miners are necessary to drive those savages out of their cabins; otherwise we should be exposed to lose, in attacking them, a considerable number of men."

The failure of this expedition seems to have been due to a want of concert and foresight. It is probable that if the forces commanded by Bienville, D'Artaguette, Montcherval, and Grandpré, had arrived at the same time, and attacked from different points, the result would have been favorable to the French. As it was, this campaign proved disastrous in the extreme. D'Artaguette's forces had been completely crushed, and Bienville had lost over one hundred and twenty men. The expenses also had been very great, and had turned out to be entirely fruitless. These losses were so many deductions to be made from the scanty resources of the colony.

Lieutenant John Philip Goujon de Grondel, who had been so severely wounded at the attack on the village of Ackia, was three years without being able to resume active service. He was born at Severne, in the French province of Alsatia, on the 27th of November, 1714, and was the son of Lieutenant-colonel Grondel, who served in the Swiss regiment called the Karrer regiment, from the name of its colonel, the Chevalier de Karrer. Grondel the father, and Karrer, were bound by the ties of the most intimate friendship; and Grondel, when his son had hardly attained the age of five years and a half, availing himself of the privilege granted to the sons of gentlemen engaged in the king's service, had him registered as Cadet* on the roll of the regiment of his friend Karrer. In November, 1731, young Grondel embarked for Louisiana with the Karrer regiment, in which he had become an officer, and arrived at last at New Orleans, after a laborious and tempestuous voyage of nearly four months. He was stationed for two years at Pointe Coupée, where he

---

* A Cadet is a person of gentle blood who serves as a volunteer, in expectation of a promised commission.

distinguished himself in several skirmishes against the Indians. In 1734, he was ordered to Mobile, where he made himself conspicuous by his duels, his gayety, the sociability of his manners, his gallantries, and his marauding excursions against the Indians, in which he displayed great daring. In 1736, Bienville was preparing for his expedition against the Chickasaws, and Grondel was at the Tombecbee depot, when it was discovered that a sergeant, by the name of Montfort, had seduced the small garrison of that settlement, and had prevailed upon them to rise upon their officers. It was Grondel who, by his rapidity of action, disconcerted the plan of the rebels, and who arrested Montfort with his own hands. It is already known how bravely he behaved at the siege of the Chickasaw villages. The minister of the colonial department, on being informed of his conduct in that engagement, in which he was so dangerously wounded, sent him a gratuity of six hundred livres, with a promise of the cross of St. Louis.

In 1740, Grondel was the hero of an anecdote which is characteristic of the man who is the subject of this biographical sketch, and of the manners of the time. It was night, one of those glorious nights which are so peculiar to the southern latitude of Louisiana; the sky seemed an ocean of soft liquid light, through which the full moon was serenely floating, when several officers, kept out of their beds by the beauty and purity of the atmosphere, were promenading on the bank of the Mississippi, in front of the public square of the city of New Orleans. They had exhausted all subjects of conversation, and in spite of the buoyancy of their spirits, had become intolerably dull. One of them exclaimed, "What a pity we have no women at hand! We would dance. In the devil's name, what shall we do to amuse ourselves in such fine weather as this?" "In God's name," replied Grondel, "how can you be at a loss? Let us fight. It is the best way to kill time." No sooner said than done. At it they went, each one paired with another, and passes after passes were exchanged in the most jocose and friendly manner imaginable, until one of them received a slight thrust from Grondel, which put an end to this amicable entertainment.

In 1741, a more serious turn of mind seemed to have come upon Grondel, and he married the daughter of Captain Du Tisné, one of the most esteemed and efficient officers in Louisiana, whose son had perished in the ill-fated D'Artaguette expedition. From that time until 1750, when he became a captain of the Swiss grenadiers, he was employed in several military expeditions and diplomatic negotiations with the Indians, in which he acquitted himself with great credit to himself and to the satisfaction of his chiefs. In 1753, he was rewarded for his services by the decoration of the cross of St Louis, which had long been promised to him. Shortly after, happening to be at Dauphine Island when a Spanish vessel was wrecked and went to pieces on that coast, Grondel flung himself into the sea, and being an expert swimmer, saved several of the victims of the storm who were struggling against death. His heroic example was followed with equal success by others, who would have felt ashamed of their inaction. In 1758, Grondel returned to New Orleans from Mobile, and having been enriched by an heritage which befell his wife, became a large planter and the lord of one hundred and fifty negroes. But in 1759, he became embroiled in a quarrel with Governor Kerlerec, who accused him of insubordination and of several other offenses, for which he was thrown into prison, where he remained three years. In the month of August, 1762, he was put by the governor on board of a vessel, in company with the Intendant Rochemore and several other officers, whom the governor charged with being engaged in a scheme of insurrection, and who were sent to France to be finally tried. In the Gulf of Mexico, after having run the risk of being wrecked, they were chased for a while by an English frigate, and escaped with difficulty by the chance favor of a dark night. The next day, at the entrance of the Bahama channel, they met an English privateer, who immediately ran upon them. The French vessel tried in vain to avoid her antagonist, than which she was considerably weaker. The French officers having met in council to deliberate on the propriety of surrendering without an ineffectual struggle, Grondel strenuously opposed any proposition of the kind, and affirmed that he had the presentiment of victory. His ardor was communicative, and his companions unanimously resolved to fight. Grondel having taken the command of the quarter-deck, the engagement soon began, and the English ship became so crippled that she was obliged to drop away and to shrink from the contest. A few days after, Grondel who, by tacit consent, had taken the military command of the French vessel, attacked a large English merchantman, and after a short engagement, in which he disabled several of the crew of his enemy, took possession of the English vessel. He dismissed her after having forced her captain to give to the French all the provisions of which they stood in need, and a draft of forty thousand crowns, which was paid on presentation.

The danger of being taken by the masters of the sea, was not the only one the French had to run. During a voyage of ninety-four days, they were constantly beaten by storms, until at last they were driven into the port of La Coruña in Spain, on the 1st of November, 1762. After having rested three weeks in that city, Grondel departed with seven or eight of his companions, to go by land to Bordeaux. Rochemore, the intendant, with the rest of the passengers, re-embarked in their ship, which had been repaired. Grondel and his followers were all mounted on mules, and slowly pursued their way to the French frontiers. As it was very cold, he was wrapped up in a sort of Canadian morning gown made of very fine wool, and which, having a hood, resembled the gown of a Capuchin. He had appended to it his cross of St. Louis, and as he and his suite had a very respectable appearance, he was taken for a bishop by the peasants, who devoutly kneeled and crossed themselves as he passed. On these occasions, the faithful who courted Grondel's benediction, were blessed by him with a sanctimonious gravity which drew from his companions peals of laughter as soon as they were out of sight of the Spaniards. This was related by them as one of the most amusing incidents of their journey, and was in harmony with the levity of the time. After twenty-four days of painful traveling in an inclement season, Grondel arrived at Bayonne in France, where the Marquis d'Amon, who commanded in that city, and who was a friend of his colonel, received him with warm demonstrations of satisfaction and respect, and gave a public festival in his honor. At Bordeaux, the celebrated Duke of Richelieu, who was governor-general of the province of Guienne, treated him with the most gracious affability, and Grondel, although only a captain, was informed that a seat would be daily reserved for him at the marshal's table. From Bordeaux he went to visit at Rochefort the staff officers of his regiment, which had been recalled to France, and their joy at seeing him showed what a hold he had on their hearts.

On the 17th of January, 1763, Grondel arrived in Paris; the next day he went and presented his respects to the Count of Hallwill, his late colonel, recently promoted to the rank of general, and to whom he complained of the persecution of which he was the object from the governor of Louisiana. General Hallwill took him under his protection, and carried him to Versailles, where he presented him to the minister, the Duke of Choiseul, who promised him promotion, if, on his trial, he was found innocent of the charges preferred against him. Kerlerec, the governor of Louisiana, had also been summoned to France, to make good the very grave accusations he had brought against the intendant Rochemore and so many officers. Kerlerec was a kinsman of Marshal D'Estrées, and on his arrival in France, making use of the influence of this nobleman at court, obtained an order of arrest (lettre de cachet) against Grondel, who, on the 9th of April, 1765, was carried to the Bastile, and whose papers were seized at his domicil, and put under seal. On the tenth day of his incarceration, he was interrogated by M. de Sartines, the minister of police, on whom he produced so favorable an impression, that a few days after he was set at liberty. He immediately left Paris in company with the Duke of Aiguillon, a friend of his father, to visit at Port Louis that gentleman, who was then one hundred years old, and who reached the age of one hundred and seven.

After having remained eighteen days under the parental roof, Grondel returned to Paris to sue for justice in his conflict with the Governor of Louisiana. On the 11th of August, 1769, after long delays, a judgment was rendered in his favor, and soon after he was appointed lieutenant-colonel, with a gratuity of two thousand five hundred livres, and an annual pension of eighteen hundred livres. These favors were rendered more valuable by being accompanied with a letter from the minister of marine, Duke of Praslin, in which the duke informed Grondel that all these rewards had been granted as testimonials of the high sense which the king had of his services. In the mean time, Louisiana having been ceded to Spain, Grondel gave up all thoughts of returning to that colony, and was appointed, on the 30th of December, 1772, to the command of the city of Lorient. According to his instructions, Grondel's wife sold all his property in Louisiana, and joined him in 1776, with all his family, except two daughters, who had married in the colony. In 1788, Grondel had risen to the grade of brigadier-general, which was bestowed on him without any solicitations on his part. The great revolution which was to shatter to pieces the throne of Louis the XVIth, was moving forward with fearful rapidity, and General Grondel who, owing to his advanced age, ceased to be on active service, retired to Nemours to end his days in such peace as was compatible with the storm which shook the very foundations of the state.

In 1792, General Grondel was denounced as an aristocrat and thrown into prison, but after an incarceration of eight days, he was restored to his family and friends. Shortly after, on the 29th of April, he was unanimously elected by the inhabitants of Nemours commanding-general of the national guards of that city, and he discharged the duties of this elevated position until the 1st of September, 1793. While commander of the national guards of Nemours, two corps of troops that were passing through having come to blows, General Grondel had the merit of quelling the riot by throwing himself among the combatants, whom he awed into submission by his firmness and his venerable aspect; and the municipal authorities of Nemours voted him thanks for his noble conduct. In 1796, overwhelmed with grief at the horrors which had swept over France, he left Nemours, and retired to Salins, near Montereau. He was one of those who were most enthusiastic in favor of Bonaparte, when the future despot struck, on the 18*th Brumaire*, his celebrated blow against the legislative assemblies of France. On this occasion, Baudry de Lozieres relates that Grondel rapturously exclaimed: "I have lived long enough; France is saved and her wounds are closed: be it forever recorded, to the eternal glory of the God who has come down from heaven to confer upon us so many benefits! This great restorer is above the human species; for it does not belong to man to execute so many gigantic and immortal things, and to do so in such a short space of time."

So intense was Grondel's admiration for Bonaparte, that, on his being presented to the First Consul, the octogenarian veteran actually sobbed and shed tears on the hand of the youthful general who had become the master of France. The officer who, in 1732, had been fighting in Louisiana to secure that important colony to his country, can not but have felt deeply grateful, in 1802, to the hero who had wrested that rich possession from Spain, and reannexed it to the domains of France. But General Grondel's joy was not of long duration, and he lived to see Louisiana escape from the grasp of France to fall into the motherly lap of the United States of America.

SEVENTH LECTURE.

STATE OF AGRICULTURE IN 1736—EXEMPTION FROM DUTIES ON CERTAIN ARTICLES OF IMPORTATION AND EXPORTATION—WAR BETWEEN THE CHOCTAWS AND CHICKASAWS—SINGULAR JUDICIAL PROCEEDING IN 1738—BIENVILLE'S DISPATCH ON THE SAND-BARS AT THE MOUTH OF THE MISSISSIPPI—DE NOAILLES IS SENT TO LOUISIANA TO COMMAND AN EXPEDITION AGAINST THE CHICKASAWS—BIENVILLE'S JEALOUSY—INTRIGUES OF THE INDIAN, RED SHOE—GENERAL RENDEZVOUS OF THE FRENCH AT THE MOUTH OF RIVER MARGOT—FAILURE OF THAT EXPEDITION—ITS PROBABLE CAUSES—BIENVILLE'S APOLOGY—EFFECTS OF A HURRICANE—SITUATION OF THE COLONY IN 1741—HEROISM OF A FRENCH GIRL IN A BATTLE AGAINST THE INDIANS—BIENVILLE INCURS THE DISPLEASURE OF HIS GOVERNMENT—HE DEMANDS THE ESTABLISHMENT OF A COLLEGE—THAT DEMAND IS REFUSED—BIENVILLE IS RECALLED TO FRANCE—HE DEPARTS NEVER TO RETURN—HE IS SUCCEEDED BY THE MARQUIS OF VAUDREUIL—OTHER FACTS AND EVENTS FROM 1736 TO 1743.

THE bad success of Bienville's campaign against the Chickasaws had, to some degree, checked the progress of the colony, and contributed to increase the disaffection of the inhabitants, who were already very little pleased with their colonial home, and who became still more dispirited by the prospect of protracted warfare with implacable savages. To this feeling of insecurity must be added the stagnation of commerce, and the precarious condition of agriculture, of which Bienville said: "The planters are disgusted with the cultivation of tobacco on account of the uncertainty of the crop, which is alternately affected either by the incessant rains, or by the long droughts so peculiar to this country. We may produce from thirty to thirty-five thousand pounds of indigo, if there be no accident in the way. The inhabitants are turning their attention to this branch of industry. As to silk, very little is made, through ignorance. With regard to cotton, the production is very limited, on account of the difficulty of separating it from its seeds, or rather because the cultivation of indigo is more profitable. As to flax and hemp, hardly any is made. With regard to tar and pitch, the colony produces about six or seven thousand barrels, but it wants an outlet." Such was the state of agriculture in Louisiana in 1736.

On the 4th of February, 1737, the French government issued an ordinance which was to take effect on the 1st of July of that year. The object of it was to exempt from certain duties, during ten years, the productions of Louisiana which should be carried to Martinique, Guadaloupe, Trinity, Dominique, Barbade, St. Lucie, St. Vincent, Grenade, and the other islands of that archipelago, and the productions of these islands when transported directly to Louisiana. This was another measure of sound policy, and it is to be regretted that the whole administration of the colony was not founded on a system equally as praiseworthy.

During the whole of the year 1737, war was kept up, at the instigation of the French, between the Choctaws and the Chickasaws, without producing any result of importance. It consisted of marauding excursions, in which, however, the Choctaws, by their depredations, succeeded in inflicting some partial injuries on the Chickasaws, who were too well provided with means of defense not to set at defiance all the rude and incomplete engines of attack which could be brought to bear against them. In a dispatch of the 28th of February, Bienville had said: "Fortified as they are, with the help and through the instructions of the English, the Chickasaws can not be destroyed, except bombards of a strong caliber and miners are employed against them. It is necessary that we be so provided. The English have sent more than two hundred men to the Chickasaws, to whom they afford every kind of assistance."

Nothing occurred during that year worth being recorded, except it be the phenomenon of the fall at New Orleans, on Palm Sunday, of hailstones as large as the eggs of a common hen, and the foundation of an hospital by a sailor, named Jean Louis, who, in the service of the India Company, had acquired a small capital of ten thousand livres, which, at his death, he consecrated to the relief of suffering humanity. At one of the extremities of the city, a house belonging to one Mme. Kolly was purchased for twelve hundred livres; the repairs went up to two thousand five hundred livres One part of the balance of the sum bequeathed was employed in procuring the necessary apparatus and furniture, and the other part was kept in reserve. In 1849, the Charity Hospital of New Orleans, which is the principal institution of the kind in that city, accommodates in its spacious halls more than one thousand patients, at the annual expense of fifty thousand dollars. What contrasts will spring up from the lapse of a century!

As another exemplification of such contrasts, it may not be indifferent to record that, in 1738, the annals of Louisiana are marked by a singular judicial trial founded on laws, customs, feelings, and ideas which are so foreign to those of our own time, that there seems to be between them a wider chasm of ages than there really is. Thus, an individual named Labarre, having committed suicide, a curator was appointed to the corpse, which was indicted, tried, convicted, and sentenced to be deprived of Christian burial, and to lie rotting and bleaching on the face of the earth among the offals, bones, and refuse of the butcher's stall.

The French government had always felt considerable difficulty in preventing desertion in the troops sent to

Louisiana. In a dispatch of the 18th of March, 1738 Bienville said: "Many of the Swiss desert to Pensacola, where they are protected openly by the monks and secretly by the governor. But as the Spaniards are in want of provisions, I have recommended to Diron d'Artaguette, at Mobile, not to supply them with any until they consent to deliver up our deserters."

In a communication of the 12th of April following, he returned to the same subject: "Three other Swiss," he wrote, "have again deserted to Pensacola, which is in a state of extreme famine. The governor of that place sent to me for some provisions. I refused them on account of the protection he grants to our deserters. Whereupon he sent them back to me. Every day, there come here Spaniards whom hunger drives away from Pensacola. We have already among us more than thirty of them, whose pale and squalid faces are frightful to look at, and testify to the sufferings of these wretches. Such misery is without a parallel."

These dispatches describe a state of things which is almost inexplicable. On one side, we see the Spaniards running away from Pensacola to New Orleans, to escape from starvation, and on the other, the Swiss and French soldiers deserting from the halls of abundance in New Orleans and Mobile, to throw themselves into the arms of famine in Pensacola. The only natural conclusion that one can come to on this subject is, that the French soldiers, blackguards as they are represented to be by Bienville, were disposed to run any risk rather than remain in Louisiana.

Among the official communications of that year to the French government, there is a joint one from Bienville and Salmon, which bears on a subject of much interest to this day. It relates to the sand-bars which obstruct the several mouths of the Mississippi. "There are daily changes," they said, " at the mouth of the river and the Balize bar. It has been remarked that, when the winter is short and the north wind has not prevailed much, these changes become more perceptible and the water is not so deep. This may also proceed from the existence of two other passes, through which water runs with more rapidity than in the one which is called the Balize.*

"Harbor-master Livaudais (capitaine de port) used to find, ten years ago, about sixteen feet water on the Balize bar, but it has since become greatly obstructed. Lately, when piloting the Oroo, Livaudais did not find more than eleven feet and a half on the bar. On account of this diminution of the water, this vessel made her way up with considerable difficulty, the more so, that she draws more water than those ships which preceded her. This shallowness of the water over the bar has frequently been the cause of damages and expenses."

"To obviate this inconvenience, the India Company some twelve years since, had caused to be constructed iron harrows, (herses) which were dragged over the bar, to remove the sand and mud. But this expedient had its disadvantages: it removed the soft mud, and left the sand, which, forming a solid and compact body, would, in time, not only have interfered with the passage of ships, but have prevented it altogether. This caused the harrows to be abandoned. As the ships of the company were large, and could not pass without being lightened, a small vessel (flute) was left stationed on the Balize bar, to receive part of the cargoes, and the spot where this vessel happened to be anchored, deepened gradually to twenty-five feet."

* The Balize is known now under the name of the South-East Pass, and is not used at all, as there is hardly six feet water on the bar

"From this fact the inference has been drawn, that, to deepen entirely the Balize, it would be proper to have a vessel drawing eighteen feet, in the hold of which brick wells should be constructed. By alternately pumping water into and out of these wells, the vessel would rise or sink at will :—and by running her up and down over the bar, it is evident that she would cut a channel through. It is true this would be expensive, but the utility of the measure would be incalculable."

"Livaudais, who is a seaman of thirty years' standing, has long been of great service to the colony, in the piloting of vessels over the bar, and by his prudence, he has frequently preserved them from accidents. After having served some years on the privateers of St. Malo, he came to the colony in the employment of the India Company. He has deserved well of the government, and it would be proper that a commission of ensign be granted to him."

The Balize pass, which, in 1728, had sixteen feet water, in 1738, fourteen feet and a half, and which Bienville represents as filling up rapidly, is known in our days as the South-East pass, and having no more than six feet water, has long been abandoned. The necessity of deepening the mouths of the Mississippi was actually felt by the French government, when the colony was in its infancy, and it is really astonishing, that a work of so national an importance, which can be executed at a cost comparatively insignificant, when taken in connection with the results to be obtained, should not as yet have been accomplished by the government of the United States, with the ample pecuniary and scientific means which it possesses.

But in those remote days, although such an improvement, by the force of its practicability and of its utility, obtruded itself upon the attention of the French government, yet its execution would have far exceeded the expenses which that government was willing and able to bestow upon a colony, of which the existence was so precarious. It was feared, not without reason, that England, favored by the contiguity of her American provinces, would, ere long, make a successful attack upon Louisiana. The fact is, that the English were multiplying their intrigues among the Indian nations, to make them rise upon the French, and had succeeded to a considerable extent. The Illinois, and many other western and northern nations, whose friendship had so far been secured by the French, had become cold and disaffected, if not entirely alienated; and among the Choctaws, Red Shoe, with a considerable party, had again allied himself to the English. With such dangers staring him in the face, Bienville had been more pressing than ever in soliciting additional forces, and was at last successful. The Minister of Marine wrote to him:—"His majesty sends to M. de Bienville, artillery, arms, ammunition, provisions, merchandise, and seven hundred men, the recruits included. His majesty also sends bombardiers, cannoniers, and miners, with M. de Noailles d'Aime, who has long served as lieutenant of a ship of the line, and who is to command the Swiss and the detached marine troops. It is his majesty's wish, that, during the expedition, M. de Noailles should have the command, not only of these troops, but also of the colonial troops and militia which are under the orders of M. de Bienville, to whom his majesty recommends, with regard to the direction and employment of his troops, to act in concert with M. de Noailles, who has the necessary talents and experience to command."

"A second expedition is authorized, if it be thought

of absolute utility to the colony. However, it must not be undertaken without real necessity."

There certainly was no sound policy in this ministerial communication, for it must have been easy to anticipate the feelings which it was calculated to awaken in Bienville's heart. It was telling him in plain terms, that he had not *the necessary talent and experience to command*, and that another who possessed them, was sent to supply his deficiencies. It is clear that the success of the intended expedition, under another chief, would have rendered more glaring Bienville's failure in his past operations against the Chickasaws. He had tasted the bitterness of defeat, and when, after unremitting exertions and importunities, he had obtained the means he wished for, to wipe off the stain which adverse fortune had left on his military reputation, he was not to profit by the boon. In the same field, where he had reaped nothing but disappointment and shame, another was to come and gather a rich harvest of glory. He, Bienville, so at least thought the minister, had not *the necessary talent and experience to command*, and no chance was left him, to prove that the impression was wrong. On the contrary, the success of a rival would be a confirmation of the ministerial judgment. No doubt that Bienville felt, to the very core of his soul, the indignity of his new position, and when it is recollected, that he was the founder of the colony, that he had been forty years connected with it, that he had in it numerous relations, kinsmen, friends, and adherents, who looked up to him with clannish pride, who resented his injuries as their own, and who took the liveliest interest in his reputation and affairs, it does not require a deep insight into human nature, to foresee that the projected expedition was doomed to defeat. It is but seldom that half-way measures do not prove abortive, and do not fall far wide of the mark they were intended for. Bienville had, or had not the qualifications to be trusted with command in war. If he had them, it was cruel and unjust, after the mortifications he had experienced in his struggles against the Chickasaws, through a deficiency of adequate means, as he alledged, not to afford him the opportunity of retrieving his past reverses, and to put all the required implements which he had demanded at the disposal of another. It is evident that Bienville, if he was not qualified to act as the leader of an army, ought to have been superseded at once. But to leave him in his post, with the mocking appearance of command and power, to trample on his pride, his sense of dignity, and his self-love, by putting him under a sort of tutor, was a dangerous experiment to be made. It was gratuitously and imprudently tempting the demon that lurks within the deep and fathomless caves of the human heart. Future events have demonstrated that the French government had not pursued the course of wisdom on that occasion.

The greater part of the year 1739 was devoted to making preparations for that campaign, by which the destruction of the Chickasaws was to be accomplished. In the month of March, Bienville sent his nephew, the Chevalier de Noyan, among the Choctaws, to conciliate them and obtain their support. Noyan succeeded in his mission, and out of the forty-two villages inhabited by the nation of the Choctaws, he gained thirty-two. The remaining ten, who were under the influence of Red Shoe, declared themselves in favor of the English. In some of the thirty-two villages which had pronounced themselves in favor of the French, English traders were plundered, wounded, and put to flight; and parties of warriors were formed, who departed to war against the

Chickasaws. They brought back their usual trophies, which consisted of scalps.

Proud of having prevented the ten villages from joining in the alliance which the majority of them had formed with the French, Red Shoe, at the head of ninety-eight warriors, had gone to the English settlements in Georgia, under the hope of being handsomely rewarded. It appears that he was disappointed, for on his return, he sided with the French, who, no doubt, offered him better terms, and on the 18th of August he plundered three English warehouses, and departed on a war expedition against the Chickasaws. Thus, the whole Choctaw nation had become favorable to the French, and Bienville found himself placed under the most auspicious circumstances to execute his plans of attack against the Chickasaws. He had given up the idea of following the old route through the lakes and up the Tombecbee, although it was the shortest and the easiest, and he took the resolution to ascend the Mississippi up to that part of its bank which was the nearest to the Chickasaw villages. From that spot to the Indian villages, the distance was about one hundred and twenty miles. His reason for taking this other and longer route, was his thinking that it afforded him facilities to procure a more considerable quantity of provisions, and to transport his artillery with less trouble. Since 1737, the engineer Deverges, in compliance with Bienville's instructions, had studied the ground and reported that it offered an easy access to the Indian villages. Acting under this impression, Bienville had fixed for the general rendezvous of his combined forces, the mouth of the river Margot, not far from the present city of Memphis.

Since the arrival of Noailles with seven hundred men, Bienville was abundantly supplied with troops, provisions, ammunition, bombards, and guns, and every thing looked fair at the opening of the campaign. In the month of August, De Noyan, who commanded the vanguard, reached the general rendezvous at the mouth of the river Margot. A short time after, De la Buissonniere, who had succeeded the unfortunate D'Artaguette in the command of the Illinois district, arrived with a detachment of the garrison of Fort Chartres, with a body of the Illinois militia, and about two hundred Indians. A week had hardly elapsed, when Céleron and St. Laurent made their appearance. These intrepid officers were from the far distant Canadian provinces, and had come with a company of Quebec and Montreal cadets, and a considerable number of the northern Indians. This company of cadets was composed of select youths, all of gentle birth, and the sons of officers. After a short apprenticeship, they were entitled to be, in their turn, commissioned as officers. While they were waiting for Bienville, the troops constructed a fort where they were encamped, and called it Fort Assumption, from the circumstance of its having been completed on the day when the Catholic church celebrates the feast of the Assumption.

The rest of the troops, under the command of Bienville, reached the general rendezvous only on the 12th of November. Inexplicable delays had, it seems, prevented the junction of all the forces of the expedition from taking place sooner. In the mean time, that part of the army which had been lingering on the banks of the river Margot since the month of August, had been afflicted with disease, and great mortality had ensued. When the whole army was reviewed on the 12th of November, it was found to be composed of about twelve hundred white men and two thousand four hundred Indians. Bienville had left New Orleans on the

12th of September, and in one of his dispatches boasts of the rapidity with which he ascended the river, considering that he was only two months on the way.

When all the forces of the expedition were brought together, it was discovered that there was a good deal of false reckoning in the quantity of provisions they expected to have, and Bienville informed the French government that more than half of the cattle, horses, and provisions which had been gathered at Fort St. Francis in Arkansas, had been lost in crossing over the marshes and low countries they had to go through on the way to the place of rendezvous at the mouth of the river Margot. Only eighty oxen and thirty-five horses reached the French camp, but in such a condition that they were not fit for any thing. Two hundred and fifty horses, with one hundred head of cattle, which were expected from Natchitoches, had also perished.

The scarcity of provisions had increased the necessity of acting without loss of time. But Bienville did not think proper to take the road discovered since 1737 by the engineer Deverges, because he said it was made impracticable by the overflowing of small rivers. A man by the name of Saucier, who, in the communications of the time, is called *a drawer of plans* (or dessinateur), had also found a road, but it was rejected by Bienville. The engineer Deverges again went to work under the direction of Noyan, and after two months of exploration, discovered, in January, a practicable road on the high lands (sur les hauteurs). Unfortunately, this road came to light precisely at the moment when the provisions began to be exhausted. Even then, Bienville and Noailles appear to have remained in a state of hesitation until the month of February, 1740, when a council of war, composed of Bienville, Noailles, Bellagues,

Du Teillay, De Longueil, De Noyan, De Gauvrit, D'Hauterive, D'Aubigny, and Pepinet, decided that, considering all the untoward circumstances the French had to contend with, it was impossible to march to the Chickasaw villages, *without hazarding the reputation of the king's arms*,* and orders were given to prepare for a retreat. This was the greatest armament which the country had yet seen, and all this bustle, show, and pomp of war had ended in smoke. The mountain had been delivered of a mouse; the French had gathered from the four quarters of the horizon merely to disperse.

What is remarkable is, that Céleron, either authorized by Bienville, or assuming the undertaking on his own responsibility, departed from Fort Assumption, on the 15th of March, after the bulk of the army had moved off down the Mississippi, and marched upon the Chickasaw villages, with his company of cadets, about one hundred Frenchmen and four or five hundred Indians. When Céleron appeared in sight of the villages with his small forces, the Chickasaws, either believing that it was only the head of the French army which was coming behind, or frightened at the vastness of the preparations which had been made against them, and at the unalterable determination which the French seemed to have taken to wage a war of extermination against their nation, presented themselves before the French officer, as suppliants for peace, which they solicited in the humblest terms. Céleron accepted their propositions, and sent some of their chiefs after Bienville, whom they overtook on his way to New Orleans. The French governor made with them a treaty, by which they promised to deliver up the Natchez they had in their possession, and to exterminate the rest of that unfortunate race. However, Bienville declared to them that the

* Sans compromettre les armes du Roi.

treaty of peace did not include the Choctaws, who would continue to make war upon them, and to receive from the French the customary price for every Chickasaw scalp they would raise, until they, the Chickasaws, should grant to the Choctaws the satisfaction which these allies of the French demanded for certain injuries they pretended to have received. In consequence of this treaty, the Chickasaws delivered up to Céleron a few Natchez, whom he put into the hands of the French of Louisiana, and he returned to Canada with his forces, after having razed to the ground Fort Assumption, which had risen like a mushroom growth, and which was thus destined to have but an ephemeral duration.

Céleron is the only officer who gained any reputation in that expedition, which proved so disgraceful to the French, although heralded with so much pomp, and although replete with so ample means of success, Bienville himself felt that the result of that campaign would redound very little to his credit; and in a dispatch of the 10th of May, 1740, he gives for it but a very lame and impotent justification. It is evident that he felt embarrassed and ill at ease under the weight of the circumstances which militated against him. His pen labored for excuses, and it is apparent that they sprung up meager and thin from a barren field. Thus he wrote to the minister of the colonial department:—

"Much to my sorrow, I feel that your excellency will not be satisfied with the result of an enterprise which has cost so many expenses to the king; but, at the same time, I hope that you will be pleased to observe, that I had not failed to take every one of those necessary precautions, which ought to have rendered that campaign as glorious as possible for his majesty. . . . .
. . . .

"At all events, if we did not come out of it with all the success which we had a right to expect, the glory of the king's arms has not been tarnished. All the Indian tribes were struck with the grandeur of our preparations, and have felt the superiority of our forces. They have stood eye-witnesses to the fear with which we impressed our enemies, and which induced them to sue for peace. I think that I can even assert that, considering the tranquillity which the colony now enjoys, our affairs are in a better position than if we had marched to the Chickasaws, from whose own confession we know that they were observing our movements, with the intention of abandoning their villages, as soon as they should have been made aware of our march upon them. . . . .

"After all, those Chickasaws can not, when left to their own resources, be a cause of much uneasiness to the colony. We know from their own mouths that they hardly number three hundred able bodied men, and that their most famous warriors perished in their late wars."

To have mustered, at an enormous expense, an army of three thousand six hundred men, well provided with artillery, bombards, and arms of every sort, and to have come within one hundred and twenty miles of the stronghold of the enemy, without striking a blow; to have lost five hundred men by disease out of the twelve hundred white troops, and after the beginning of a retreat, to have patched up, as it were by accident, a sort of sham and hollow peace, for the observation of which there was no warranty beyond the pledged word of fickle savages, these were circumstances which gave the most positive denial to Bienville's assertion, that, "*if the French did not come out of that campaign with all the success which they had a right to expect, the glory of the king's arms had not been tarnished."* Nor is it possible to agree with Bienville, when he says that the affairs of the colony were in a better condition than if he had marched up to the villages of the enemy, *because in that case the intention of the Indians was to abandon those villages.* But even admitting that supposition to be correct, would not the destruction of such well-fortified strongholds as they were represented to be, have been an immense advantage to the French? And if the conviction that the Indians would have retired before such overwhelming odds be a good reason for not continuing the expedition, it must have been an equally strong one for not undertaking it. Nor is it possible, again, to agree with him when he declares that the Indian nations were struck with the grandeur of his preparations, that they were made aware of the superiority of the French forces, and that they had witnessed *the fear which such a display struck into the bosoms of the Chickasaws,* who were forced to sue for peace. It seems, on the contrary, that the insignificance of the result obtained, when compared with the vast scale on which the expedition against the Chickasaws was conducted, must have been a practical demonstration, particularly in the eyes of the Choctaws, who numbered fifteen thousand warriors, of the utter incapacity of the French to cope with any of the powerful Indian tribes.

A large share, it is true, must be allowed for accidents in the affairs of this world, but those of which Bienville speaks in his dispatches, such as the overflow of rivers, and the loss of cattle and horses, were of a nature to have been foreseen to a certain degree. There certainly was a great want of concert of operations in the movements of the army. How came the head of it to arrive at the mouth of the river Margot in August, and to be obliged to wait until the 12th of November?

Then, from the 12th of November to the month of February, how came twelve hundred white men and two thousand four hundred Indians to remain in a state of torpor? Were the one hundred and twenty miles which separated the French camp from the Chickasaw villages so impracticable? Had not D'Artaguette found these villages of easy access, in 1736, through the same country? If the road discovered in 1737 by the engineer Deverges had become out of the question *on account of the overflowing of small rivers*, as stated by Bienville, what objection was there to Saucier's? And when, in January, a third road was found out on the *high lands*, which road was successfully taken by Céleron, on the 15th of March, how came the whole army to remain motionless through the whole of February? What a series of inexplicable delays from August, 1739, to March, 1740! Bienville had lately been very pressing in demanding additional forces, and had always represented the ferocious Chickasaws as so formidable, that their very existence was incompatible with the tranquillity of the colony. How came he so suddenly to change his tone, and to say, that *those Chickasaws were not, after all, a source of much uneasiness to the colony?* On a calm and dispassionate review of all the circumstances, it is hardly possible not to come to the conclusion, that there was something rotten at the bottom of that expedition.

The solution of the enigma must, I am afraid, be looked for in the impolitic measure taken by the French government to send Noailles to assume the command of the intended expedition against the Chickasaws, and to retain Bienville in a subordinate capacity under him. There were no doubt seeds of much mischief in these words of the French minister to Bienville: " His majesty sends M. de Noailles who has the necessary talents and experience to command." These suppositions, founded on the knowledge of human nature, are fully confirmed by a report of the engineer Deverges, who says, that, although his determination is carefully to abstain from accusing any body, yet he must confess that the failure of the expedition was owing to jealousies, bickerings, and conflicts of power. This was, no doubt, putting the finger on the sore. How could it be otherwise, when the greater the resources granted to a preferred rival, the greater became Bienville's interest that these resources should crumble into dust in the hands of their possessor, in order to justify the sterility of the expedition which he, Bienville, had undertaken with such inferior means? Patriotism and private interest ought seldom to be put in opposite scales, or a hundred to one that patriotism will kick the beam.

It appears from a statement of the 15th of June, 1740, signed by Bienville and commissary Salmon, that from the first of January, 1737, to the 31st of May, 1740, the expenses of the Chickasaw war amounted to 1,088,383 livres, and that for the year 1740, the budget of the ordinary expenses of the colony was put down at 310,000 livres.

On the 11th of September, 1740, there was a dreadful hurricane, which produced very extensive disasters in the colony, of which Beauchamp, the commander of Mobile, gives a description in a dispatch of the 25th of February, 1741.

"This hurricane," says he, "was so violent, that, here, it blew down several houses, and among others, the edifice which M. Bizoton had constructed, not only as a store, but as a house of refuge for sailors. Unfortunately, it contained all the flour and other provisions destined for the subsistence of the garrison. I was obliged to send the garrison a fishing along the coast for the barrels which had been blown into the water, and part of which was staved off. Without this barrel fishing, we should have run the risk of dying of hunger, as our resources were limited to six or eight barrels of flour, which were in the fort.

"The wind was so furious that, if it had continued for forty-eight hours, as all hurricanes generally do, we should have been inundated. Fortunately, it blew only during twelve hours, but with such force, that half of Dauphine Island was carried away, and more than three hundred head of cattle were drowned on the island. We have lost a greater number of them on this coast, and at Pascagoulas. This loss is severely felt by the poor population of this section of the country.

"The effect produced by the force of the wind is almost incredible. There was lying before the guard-house of Dauphine Island, a cannon of four pound caliber. The wind transported it eighteen feet from where it was. This fact is sworn to by all the inhabitants of the island.

"This hurricane, which lasted twelve hours, began in the night of the 11th of September, and ceased on that day at noon. But although its duration was not long, it caused much damage. . . . . .
. . . . . To cap the climax of our misfortunes, there came another hurricane on the 18th of September, which destroyed the rest of our resources. This wind, which blew from N. N. E. and which was accompanied by heavy rains, caused an overflowing of all the rivers, by which were laid waste all the plantations of the Indians from Carolina to this place. The first hurricane was from E. S. E.:—luckily these hurricanes did not pass over New Orleans and the adjacent

country, where the crops have turned out to be pretty abundant. Otherwise, the whole colony would have been in a frightful state from the scarcity of provisions, and it would have been utterly impossible to make presents to the Choctaws, in whose debt, on this score, we have been for two years."

On the 7th of March, Loubois wrote to the French government a communication, which more than confirmed Beauchamp's description of the state of the colony. According to the statement of Loubois, Louisiana was reduced to the lowest degree of misery. Among the other effects which he relates as the result of the hurricane of the 11th, and that of the 18th, he says, that the battery at the Balize was so much damaged that, if attacked, it could be carried by four gun-boats. There was such a scarcity of every thing, that a cask of common wine was sold for 500 livres, of Spanish money, and 800 livres, in the currency of the colony, and the rest in proportion. As to flour, it could be commanded by no price, as there was none to be had. On the 18th of July, the same Loubois wrote: "There are many families reduced to such a state of destitution, that fathers, when they rise in the morning, do not know where they will get the food required by their children." Louisiana, now reposing so luxuriously in the lap of plenty, can hardly, when looking at her plump cheeks in the mirror presented to her by the year 1849, be persuaded to recognize herself in the picture drawn of her in the year 1741.

To increase the somber hue of the horizon which surrounded the colony, the Natchez and Chickasaws had recommenced their depredations, and the Pointe Coupée settlement had been the first to suffer from their excursions. These same Indians, to the number of one hundred and forty, attacked in the Wabash a party of twenty-four French trappers and traders, among whom were a woman and a young girl. Unluckily, the inclemency of the weather had driven the French to take shelter on the banks of a small bayou, and the Indians, who had been following them for some time, took hold of hills which commanded the bayou, and on which they were protected by thick woods. From this vantage-ground, they poured their fire on the French. The battle lasted six hours, during which time the young girl displayed the greatest heroism. She repeatedly exposed her life, by coming out of her place of concealment, to cut the powder horns of those of her companions who dropped dead, and to distribute the much wanted ammunition among the surviving. At last, a bullet put an end to her existence, and the other female was also killed. Of the twenty-four trappers, or traders, sixteen perished. The remaining eight, seeing that they could no longer maintain their ground, made a desperate charge upon their foes, and forced their way through. Three of them were wounded, but they all escaped. Writing on these events, Loubois said, "I am mortified, for the sake of the tranquillity of this unhappy country, to see that I was not mistaken in the judgment which I had passed on our late treaty of peace with the Chickasaws."

Thus, it is seen, that the French officers knew how to reduce to its true value the nugatory peace which Bienville had contracted with the Chickasaws. With regard to the French, it was purely nominal; and the Choctaws, so far, had not obtained the slightest redress for those injuries of which they complained, and for which Bienville had demanded satisfaction of the Chickasaws. These two nations were therefore still in arms against each other, and had several encounters, in which the Choctaws had the advantage. On that occasion,

Bienville informed his government, that he saw with pleasure that the Choctaws were growing more warlike, and that they were no longer afraid of meeting their old enemies in battle.

The establishments at the Balize having been almost destroyed by the hurricanes of the 11th and 18th of September, 1740, it became necessary to renew or restore them. The engineer Deverges estimated the probable cost at 454,974 livres, including only the most important part of the works. Bienville informed the French government, that he had contracted for what it was most urgent to have done, with Dubreuil, who was the only man in the colony sufficiently wealthy, to take charge of such an undertaking, and to whom it had been adjudicated for the sum of 297,382 livres 10 centimes.

On the 31st of October, the council of state, in France, prorogued to ten years the ordinance of the 30th of September, 1732, which exempted from duties the imports into, and the exports from Louisiana. It was a laudable perseverance in the right path.

The budget of the current expenses of Louisiana in 1741, amounted to 319,411 livres. The salary of the governor was 12,000 livres; his secretary, 1200 livres; the royal commissary, 8,000 livres.

The French government, according to Bienville's expectations, had learned with much displeasure the result of the last expedition against the Chickasaws, and the minister of the colonial department addressed Bienville on the subject with some severity. From that time, all the official communications which he received were harsh in their tone, and showed how much ground he had lost at court. In a dispatch of the 19th of January, 1742, the minister, after having expressed his discontent and disapprobation with regard to several acts of Bienville's administration, says:—"Moreover, it has come to my knowledge, that you have permitted two families, established in the colony, to emigrate to St. Domingo, by the ship Triton, and not only have you not laid before me the reasons which may have determined you to grant this permission, but you have not even informed me of their departure. Yet, you must be aware that, independently of the prejudice caused to the colony by the desertion of its inhabitants, such an example can not but be a source of discouragement for those who remain in it. Hence, his majesty forbids you to allow any one to leave the colony, without orders sent to you on this subject. You will be pleased to act in conformity with this instruction. You will also communicate to me the reasons for which you allowed these two families to go to St. Domingo. The suggestion which you have made, that permission be granted to the inhabitants of Martinique to emigrate at will to Louisiana with their goods and negroes, deserves to be examined, and I will see what is to be done in the matter."

From the continuance of the tone in which he was addressed, Bienville saw that he could not weather the disfavor into which he had fallen, and begged to be recalled:—which application was readily acquiesced in.

In the mean time, the Choctaws were continuing to wage war against the Chickasaws with great spirit, activity, and success. The race of the Chickasaws, like that of the Natchez, was threatened with destruction. Their ancient power and renown were ebbing fast away. They had lately lost more than fifty warriors, one hundred and sixty horses, and a large number of their cattle. The few surviving Natchez who had taken refuge with the Chickasaws, finding they were an incumbrance to their generous protectors, who were so sorely pressed, had retired among the Cherokees. So fierce, indeed, had become the struggle between the Choctaws and Chickasaws, that it promised a speedy termination,—the former, who were much more powerful, having sworn that they would drive away the latter from their old hereditary possessions. The Choctaw chief, Red Shoe, acquired great distinction in this war, and became the scourge and terror of the Chickasaws.

The preoccupations, vicissitudes, and dangers of war had much contributed to the neglect of agriculture in the colony. But a fragrant shrub, called the *Anemiche* by the Indians, had attracted the attention of the government. It is the wax-tree, or candle-berry (myrica cerifera), of which the wax is used for making candles. These candles were, at that time, in general use among the inhabitants of Louisiana. The French government thought that they could make of the wax an object of trade, and required information on the subject, which was given in very interesting reports made by Bienville, Salmon, the botanist Alexandre, and others. It resulted from the investigations at that time, that the cultivation of this shrub might be productive, and that, at an average, eight pounds of berries produced one pound of wax.

On the 26th of March, 1742, Bienville wrote to the minister with regard to his recall:—" If success had always corresponded with my application to the affairs of the government, and administration of this colony, and with my zeal for the service of the king, I should have rejoiced in consecrating the rest of my days to such objects; but through a sort of fatality which, for some time past, has obstinately thwarted my best concerted plans, I have frequently lost the fruit of my labors, and perhaps some ground in your excellency's confidence. Therefore have I come to the conclusion, that it is no longer necessary for me to struggle against my adverse fortune. I hope that better luck may attend my successor. During the balance of my stay here, I will give all my attention to smooth the difficulties attached to the office which I shall deliver up to him, and it is to me a subject of self-gratulation that I shall transmit to him the government of the colony, when its affairs are in a better condition than they have ever been." It is impossible not to sympathize with the deep despondency and bitter feeling of disappointment expressed in this dispatch of Bienville, who felt, no doubt, that the ties which for more than forty years had connected him with Louisiana, the joint creation of his family and of himself, were forever to be severed. Who has not met, or will not meet the day when he stood, or will stand up in desolation like Bienville, with what energy he may summon up from his soul, amid the shivered fragments of hereditary affections, long-cherished hopes, and deeply-laid plans of fortune and happiness, which were the very household gods of his heart? Who? But why philosophize? It has become too trite and commonplace.

Although waiting for his successor, and governing the country only ad interim, Bienville was not the less on the lookout for every thing that could be turned to the profit or advantage of Louisiana. On the 15th of June, he wrote to the French government, jointly with Salmon:—"It is long since the inhabitants of Louisiana made representations on the necessity of their having a college for the education of their children. Convinced of the advantages of such an establishment, they invited the Jesuits to undertake its creation and management. But the reverend fathers refused, on the ground that they had no lodgings suited for the purpose, and had not the necessary materials to support such an institution. Yet it is essential that there be one, at least for the study of the classics, of geometry, geography, pilotage, &c. There, the youths of the colony would be taught the knowledge of religion, which is the basis of morality. It is but too evidently demonstrated to parents, how utterly worthless turn out to be those children, who are raised in idleness and luxury, and how ruinously expensive it is for those who send their children to France to be educated. It is even to be feared from this circumstance, that the Creoles, thus educated abroad, will imbibe a dislike to their native country, and will come back to it only to receive and to convert into cash what property may be left to them by their parents. Many persons in Vera Cruz would rejoice at having a college here, and would send to it their children."

This joint application of Bienville and Salmon for a college was set aside on the ground that the colony was *too unimportant* for such an establishment. Strange to say, Louisiana has ever since suffered, through more than a century, from the difficulty of educating her native population within her own limits; and to this day, we may regret with Bienville, that so large a number of Louisianians are yearly sent away to distant colleges, in countries from which they return, perhaps with a distaste for what awaits them under the paternal roof, and often with a much less keen sense of patriotism and of state pride. Nor is it astonishing if, after a long absence, their whole organization requires to be morally and bodily modified to suit the climate of our southern latitude and the atmosphere of our peculiar institutions, ideas, feelings, and manners. Fortunately, the legislature of the state is gradually preparing a remedy for this evil.

The year 1742 was drawing to a close, and the col

ony would have enjoyed perfect tranquillity, if it had not been somewhat disturbed by the war of the Chickasaws and of the Choctaws. However, the Chickasaws had lately suffered so much from the incessant attacks of the Choctaws, that many of them were seeking for an asylum in Carolina, and it was hoped that Louisiana would soon be rid of that turbulent race. But some fears of an attack from a more powerful foe were excited by the circumstance of some Englishmen being found on the Mississippi, in the Illinois district, and of others being arrested about one hundred and twenty miles above Natchez. As it was supposed that Englishmen could not have come to Louisiana with good intentions, those who were made prisoners in the Illinois district were sentenced, some to three, and some to five years' imprisonment; and with regard to those who were caught near Natchez, in small bark canoes, and who were five in number, Bienville wrote that they were spies from Virginia. "They shall be tried," said he, " and I shall endeavor that they be sent to the mines of New Mexico."

The French were then on very good terms with the Spaniards, and Bienville informed the French government that the *Audiencia Real*, or supreme royal tribunal, which, at that time, governed ad interim, the provinces of Mexico, having received intelligence that the English, under Admiral Vernon, meditated an attack against Vera Cruz, had applied to him to obtain six eighteen pounders, and that, in concert with the commissary, Salmon, he had granted them the assistance demanded.

The current expenses of the colony for the year 1742, amounted to 322,629 livres.

The Marquis de Vaudreuil, the successor of Bienville, arrived at New Orleans, on the 10th of May, 1743, and

Bienville departed for France, never to return to the colony, although his life was prolonged twenty-five years. When he left Louisiana, he had reached the age of sixty-five, and he carried away with him the regrets, the esteem, and the affections of all the colonists, who called him the father of the country. With it, as an object of his creation, he was naturally identified, and he loved it with all the fervor of the parental heart. Hence did he, perhaps, think himself possessed of a prescriptive right to its administration, and it is not improbable that he looked with a jealous eye on all that interfered with this right. The fact is, that ill did he seem to brook any authority set over him; and who is he who will fling the first stone and say that, in Bienville's place, he is sure he could have felt and acted differently? Bienville deservedly exercised great influence in the country, which had been settled under his auspices and patronage, and which was full of Canadians like himself, of his numerous friends and dependents, kinsmen and family connections. When in opposition he must have been able to do much, either directly or indirectly. To the fear of this power which he possessed, must be ascribed his recall to France, and his detention there for ten years, when Périer was appointed governor in 1726. Hence, also, the removal from office, at that time, of all his friends, and of all the members of his family. At a later period, to him, or if he remained passive himself, to the ill-will of his creatures, whom he did not exert himself to check, must be attributed the failure of the expedition against the Chickasaws, under De Noailles, in 1739. At least, all appearances and a whole concourse of circumstances combine to impress this belief upon the mind of the historian. Bienville himself, feeling at a loss how to present his justification in a favorable light, and to rebut the presump tions and all the circumstantial evidence which rose in testimony against him, was obliged, as he did in his dispatch of the 26th of March, 1742, to have recourse to *fatality*, and to attribute his misfortunes to this stern and omnipotent cause. With the exception of this single blemish, his career is one of unsullied purity and of continual usefulness. A man of undoubted integrity, a strict observer of his word, punctilious as a knight-errant as to his honor and fair fame, devotedly attached to his country and to his king, true, heart and soul, to his friends, to his kinsmen and family connections, bland and courteous in his manners, humane and generous, possessing a highly gifted personal appearance, having all the distinction inherent to a man of refined and elegant tastes, he retained that air of grandeur so peculiar to the age of Louis XIVth, which had closed when he had already reached manhood, being over thirty years old when the grand monarch died. With all these qualifications, he might have been set up as a faithful representation of the gentlemen of that time. When he left Louisiana forever, although he was under the displeasure of the court, the colonists were loud in expressing their regrets; and whatever faults, inseparable, perhaps, from human nature, he may have committed, his popularity in the province where he had lived to old age, had never been shaken, and he certainly was one of the most honorable and striking characters of the primordial history of Louisiana.

Among the other most conspicuous names in the annals of Louisiana, is that of D'Artaguette, which disappears, however, at the same time when Bienville retires from the colony. The royal commissary of that name, who came to Louisiana in 1708, and who filled in it several high offices until 1742, left behind him a long memory, which made his virtues, his talents, and his deeds, familiar to several succeeding generations; and the melancholy fate of his younger brother, D'Artaguette, the brilliant officer who fell into the hands of the Chickasaws, after a desperate battle, and who was burned by them at the stake, had, it seems, made such a deep impression in the country, that the name of these two men had remained almost a household word in every family. It may be in the recollection of many that, as late as 1815, gangs of negroes, when at work in the fields, sang, among the many songs with which they enlivened their labors, one of which the often repeated burden was, if spelt in French, as pronounced:—

> "Di tems missié d'Artaguette,
> Hé! Ho! Hé!
> C'était, c'était bon tems.
> Yé té ménin monde à la baguette.
> Hé! Ho! Hé!
> Pas nègres, pas rubans
> Pas diamans
> Pour dochans.
> Hé! Ho! Hé!"

which means :—

> "In the days of D'Artaguette,
> Hé! Ho! Hé!
> It was the good old time.
> The world was led straight with a switch,
> Hé! Ho! Hé!
> Then there were no negroes, no ribbons,
> No diamonds
> For the vulgar.
> Hé! Ho! Hé!"

It was also customary to say, when alluding to any thing antiquated, or out of fashion, "This is as old as D'Artaguette," instead of "This is as old as Methusalem." It seems that this name, connected no doubt with the floating recollections of by-gone events, had taken hold of the imagination, even of the most ignorant class of our population.

But with the coming of new generations, the old ditties have ceased, the quaint colonial expressions have fallen into disuse, and the weeds of oblivion are daily creeping over and concealing the vestiges of the past and those traditions which were the impresses of the footsteps of time; while the hand of neglect destroys, or allows to perish, those private and public manuscripts, which, like fossil bones in the hands of the geologist, might have helped the historian in recomposing the frame and physiognomy of Louisiana, when breathing a colonial **life.**

APPENDIX.

APPENDIX.

BLACK CODE.

Art. 1,

Decrees the expulsion of the Jews from the colony.

Art. 2.

Makes it imperative on masters to impart religious instructions to their slaves.

Art. 3,

Permits the exercise of the Roman Catholic creed only. Every other mode of worship is prohibited.

Art. 4.

Negroes placed under the direction or supervision of any other person than a Catholic, are liable to confiscation.

Art. 5.

Sundays and holydays are to be strictly observed. All negroes found at work on these days are to be confiscated.

Art. 6.

We forbid our white subjects, of both sexes, to marry with the blacks, under the penalty of being fined and subjected to some other arbitrary punishment. We forbid all curates, priests, or missionaries of our secular or regular clergy, and even our chaplains in our navy, to sanction such marriages. We also forbid all our white subjects, and even the manumitted or free-born blacks, to live in a state of concubinage with slaves. Should there be any issue from this kind of intercourse, it is our will that the person so offending, and the master of the slave, should pay each a fine of three hundred livres. Should said issue be the result of the concubinage of the master with his slave, said master shall not only pay the fine, but be deprived of the slave and of the children, who shall be adjudged to the hospital of the locality, and said slaves shall be forever incapable of being set free. But should this illicit intercourse have existed between a free black and his slave, when said free black had no legitimate wife, and should said black marry said slave according to the forms prescribed by the church, said slave shall be thereby set free, and the children shall also become free and legitimate; and in such a case, there shall be no application of the penalties mentioned in the present article.

Art. 7.

The ceremonies and forms prescribed by the ordinance of Blois, and by the edict of 1639, for marriages, shall be observed both with regard to free persons and to slaves. But the consent of the father and mother of the slave is not necessary; that of the master shall be the only one required.

Art. 8.

We forbid all curates to proceed to effect marriages between slaves without proof of the consent of their masters; and we also forbid all masters to force their slaves into any marriage against their will.

Art. 9.

Children, issued from the marriage of slaves, shall follow the condition of their parents, and shall belong to the master of the wife and not of the husband, if the husband and wife have different masters.

Art. 10.

If the husband be a slave, and the wife a free woman, it is our will that their children, of whatever sex they may be, shall share the condition of their mother, and be as free as she, notwithstanding the servitude of their father; and if the father be free and the mother a slave, the children shall all be slaves.

Art. 11.

Masters shall have their Christian slaves buried in consecrated ground.

Art. 12.

We forbid slaves to carry offensive weapons or heavy sticks, under the penalty of being whipped, and of having said weapons confiscated for the benefit of the person seizing the same. An exception is made in favor of those slaves who are sent a hunting or a shooting by their masters, and who carry with them a written permission to that effect, or are designated by some known mark or badge.

Art. 13.

We forbid slaves belonging to different masters to gather in crowds either by day or by night, under the pretext of a wedding, or for any other cause, either at the dwelling or on the grounds of one of their masters, or elsewhere, and much less on the highways or in secluded places, under the penalty of corporal punishment, which shall not be less than the whip. In case of frequent offenses of the kind, the offenders shall be branded with the mark of the flower de luce, and should there be aggravating circumstances, capital punishment may be applied, at the discretion of our judges. We command all our subjects, be they officers or not, to seize all such offenders, to arrest and conduct them to prison, although there should be no judgment against them.

Art. 14.

Masters who shall be convicted of having permitted or tolerated such gatherings as aforesaid, composed of other slaves than their own, shall be sentenced, individually, to indemnify their neighbors for the damages occasioned by said gatherings, and to pay, for the first time, a fine of thirty livres, and double that sum on the repetition of the offense.

Art. 15.

We forbid negroes to sell any commodities, provisions, or produce of any kind, without the written permission of their masters, or without wearing their known marks or badges, and any persons purchasing any thing from negroes in violation of this article, shall be sentenced to pay a fine of 1500 livres.

Art. 16, 17, 18, 19,

Provide at length for the clothing of slaves and for their subsistence.

Art. 20.

Slaves who shall not be properly fed, clad, and provided for by their masters, may give information thereof to the attorney-general of the Superior Council, or to all the other officers of justice of an inferior jurisdiction, and may put the written exposition of their wrongs into their hands;

upon which information, and even ex officio, should the information come from another quarter, the attorney-general shall prosecute said masters without charging any costs to the complainants. It is our will that this regulation be observed in all accusations for crimes or barbarous and inhuman treatment brought by slaves against their masters.

Art. 21.

Slaves who are disabled from working, either by old age, disease, or otherwise, be the disease incurable or not, shall be fed and provided for by their masters; and in case they should have been abandoned by said masters, said slaves shall be adjudged to the nearest hospital, to which said masters shall be obliged to pay eight cents a day for the food and maintenance of each one of these slaves; and for the payment of this sum, said hospital shall have a lien on the plantations of the master.

Art. 22.

We declare that slaves can have no right to any kind of property, and that all that they acquire either by their own industry, or by the liberality of others, or by any other means or title whatever, shall be the full property of their masters; and the children of said slaves, their fathers and mothers, their kindred or other relations, either free or slaves, shall have no pretensions or claims thereto, either through testamentary dispositions or donations inter vivos; which dispositions and donations we declare null and void, and also whatever promises they may have made, or whatever obligations they may have subscribed to, as having been entered into by persons incapable of disposing of any thing, and of participating to any contract.

Art. 23.

Masters shall be responsible for what their slaves have done by their command, and also for what transactions they have permitted their slaves to do in their shops, in the particular line of commerce with which they were intrusted; and in case said slaves should have acted without the order or authorization of their masters, said masters shall be responsible only for so much as has turned to their profit; and if said masters have not profited by the doing or transaction of their slaves, the peculium which the masters have permitted the slaves to own, shall be subjected to all claims against said slaves, after deduction made by the masters of what may be due to them; and if said peculium should consist, in whole or in part, of merchandises in which the slaves had permission to traffic, the masters shall only come in for their share in common with the other creditors.

Art. 24.

Slaves shall be incapable of all public functions, and of being constituted agents for any other person than their own masters, with powers to manage or conduct any kind of trade; nor can they serve as arbitrators or experts; nor shall they be called to give their testimony either in civil or in criminal cases, except when it shall be a matter of necessity, and only in default of white people; but in no case shall they be permitted to serve as witnesses either for or against their masters.

Art. 25.

Slaves shall never be parties to civil suits, either as plaintiffs or defendants, nor shall they be allowed to appear as complainants in criminal cases, but their masters shall have the right to act for them in civil matters, and in criminal ones, to demand punishment and reparation for such outrages and excesses as their slaves may have suffered from.

Art. 26.

Slaves may be prosecuted criminally, without their masters being made parties to the trial, except they should be indicted as accomplices; and said slaves shall be tried, at first, by the judges of ordinary jurisdiction, if there be any, and on appeal, by the Superior Council, with the same rules, formalities, and proceedings observed for free persons, save the exceptions mentioned hereafter.

Art. 27.

The slave who, having struck his master, his mistress, or the husband of his mistress, or their children, shall have produced a bruise, or the shedding of blood in the face, shall suffer capital punishment.

Art. 28.

With regard to outrages or acts of violence committed by slaves against free persons, it is our will that they be punished with severity, and even with death, should the case require it.

Art. 29.

Thefts of importance, and even the stealing of horses, mares, mules, oxen, or cows, when executed by slaves or manumitted persons, shall make the offender liable to corporal, and even to capital punishment, according to the circumstances of the case.

Art. 30.

The stealing of sheep, goats, hogs, poultry, grain, fodder, peas, beans, or other vegetables, produce, or provisions, when committed by slaves, shall be punished according to the circumstances of the case; and the judges may sentence them, if necessary, to be whipped by the public executioner, and branded with the mark of the flower de luce.

Art. 31.

In cases of thefts committed or damages done by their slaves, masters, besides the corporal punishment inflicted on their slaves, shall be bound to make amends for the injuries resulting from the acts of said slaves, unless they prefer abandoning them to the sufferer. They shall be bound to make this choice in three days from the time of the conviction of the negroes; if not, this privilege shall be forever forfeited.

Art. 32.

The runaway slave, who shall continue to be so for one month from the day of his being denounced to the officers of justice, shall have his ears cut off, and shall be branded with the flower de luce on the shoulder: and on a second offense of the same nature, persisted in during one month from the day of his being denounced, he shall be hamstrung, and be marked with the flower de luce on the other shoulder. On the third offense, he shall suffer death.

Art. 33.

Slaves who shall have made themselves liable to the penalty of the whip, the flower de luce brand, and ear cutting, shall be tried, in the last resort, by the ordinary judges of the inferior courts, and shall undergo the sentence passed upon them without there being an appeal to the Superior Council, in confirmation or reversal of judgment, notwithstanding the article 26th of the present code, which shall be applicable only to those judgments in which the slave convicted is sentenced to be hamstrung or to suffer death.

Art. 34.

Freed or free-born negroes, who shall have afforded refuge in their houses to fugitive slaves, shall be sentenced to pay to the masters of said slaves, the sum of thirty livres a day for every day during which they shall have concealed said fugitives; and all other free persons, guilty of the same offense, shall pay a fine of ten livres a day as aforesaid; and should the freed or free-born negroes not be able to pay the fine herein specified, they shall be reduced to the condition of slaves, and be sold as such. Should the price of the sale exceed the sum mentioned in the judgment, the surplus shall be delivered to the hospital.

Art. 35.

We permit our subjects in this colony, who may have slaves concealed in any place whatever, to have them sought after by such persons and in such a way as they may deem proper, or to proceed themselves to such researches as they may think best.

Art. 36.

The slave who is sentenced to suffer death on the denunciation of his master, shall, when that master is not an accomplice to his crime, be appraised before his execution by two of the principal inhabitants of the locality, who shall be specially appointed by the judge, and the amount of said appraisement shall be paid to the master. To raise this sum, a proportional tax shall be laid on every slave, and shall be collected by the persons invested with that authority.

Art. 37.

We forbid all the officers of the Superior Council, and all our other officers of justice in this colony, to take any fees or receive any perquisites in criminal suits against slaves, under the penalty, in so doing, of being dealt with as guilty of extortion.

Art. 38.

We also forbid all our subjects in this colony, whatever their condition or rank may be, to apply, on their own private authority, the rack to their slaves, under any pretense whatever, and to mutilate said slaves in any one of their limbs, or in any part of their bodies, under the penalty of the confiscation of said slaves; and said masters, so offending, shall be liable to a criminal prosecution. We only permit masters, when they shall think that the case requires it, to put their slaves in irons, and to have them whipped with rods or ropes.

Art. 39.

We command our officers of justice in this colony to institute criminal process against masters and overseers who shall have killed or mutilated their slaves, when in their power and under their supervision, and to punish said murder according to the atrocity of the circumstances; and in case the offense shall be a pardonable one, we permit them to pardon said masters and overseers without its being necessary to obtain from us letters patent of pardon.

Art. 40.

Slaves shall be held in law as movables, and as such, they shall be part of the community of acquests between husband and wife; they shall not be liable to be seized under any mortgage whatever; and they shall be equally divided among the co-heirs without admitting from any one of said heirs any claim founded on preciput or right of primogeniture, or dowry.

Art. 41, 42.

Are entirely relative to judicial forms and proceedings.

Art. 43.

Husbands and wives shall not be seized and sold separately when belonging to the same master; and their children, when under fourteen years of age, shall not be separated from their parents, and such seizures and sales shall be null and void. The present article shall apply to voluntary sales, and in case such sales should take place in violation of the law, the seller shall be deprived of the slave he has illegally retained, and said slave shall be adjudged to the purchaser without any additional price being required.

Art. 44.

Slaves, fourteen years old, and from this age up to sixty, who are settled on lands and plantations, and are at present working on them, shall not be liable to seizure for debt, except for what may be due out of the purchase money agreed to be paid for them, unless said grounds or plantations should also be distressed, and any seizure and judicial sale of a real estate, without including the slaves of the aforesaid age who are part of said estate, shall be deemed null and void.

Art. 45, 46, 47, 48, 49,

Are relative to certain formalities to be observed in judicial proceedings.

Art. 50.

Masters, when twenty-five years old, shall have the power to manumit their slaves, either by testamentary dispositions, or by acts inter vivos. But, as there may be mercenary masters disposed to set a price on the liberation of their slaves; and whereas slaves, with a view to acquire the necessary means to purchase their freedom, may be tempted to commit theft or deeds of plunder, no person, whatever may be his rank and condition, shall be permitted to set free his slaves, without obtaining from the Superior Council a decree of permission to that effect; which permission shall be granted without costs, when the motives for the setting free of said slaves, as specified in the petition of the master, shall appear legitimate to the tribunal. All future acts for the emancipation of slaves, which may be made without this permission, shall be null; and the slaves so freed shall not be entitled to their freedom; they shall, on the contrary, continue to be held as slaves; but they shall be taken away from their former masters, and confiscated for the benefit of the India Company.

ART. 51.

However, should slaves be appointed by their masters tutors to their children, said slaves shall be held and regarded as being thereby set free to all intents and purposes.

ART. 52.

We declare that the acts for the enfranchisement of slaves, passed according to the forms above described, shall be equivalent to an act of naturalization, when said slaves are not born in our colony of Louisiana, and they shall enjoy all the rights and privileges inherent to our subjects born in our kingdom, or in any land or country under our dominion. We declare, however, that all manumitted slaves, and all free-born negroes, are incapable of receiving donations, either by testamentary dispositions, or by acts inter vivos from the whites. Said donations shall be null and void, and the objects so donated shall be applied to the benefit of the nearest hospital.

ART. 53.

We command all manumitted slaves to show the profoundest respect to their former masters, to their widows and children, and any injury or insult offered by said manumitted slaves to their former masters, their widows or children, shall be punished with more severity than if it had been offered to any other person. We, however, declare them exempt from the discharge of all duties or services, and from the payment of all taxes or fees, or any thing else which their former masters might, in their quality of patrons, claim either in relation to their persons, or to their personal or real estate, either during the life or after the death of said manumitted slaves

Art. 54.

We grant to manumitted slaves the same rights, privileges, and immunities which are enjoyed by free-born persons. It is our pleasure that their merit in having acquired their freedom, shall produce in their favor, not only with regard to their persons, but also to their property, the same effects which our other subjects derive from the happy circumstance of their having been born free.

In the name of the king.

BIENVILLE, DE LA CHAISE.

Fazende, Bruslé, Perry,
March, 1724.

THE END

www.ingramcontent.com/pod-product-compliance
Lightning Source LLC
Chambersburg PA
CBHW030328240426
43661CB00052B/1562